SOCIAL HISTORY
OF
AMERICAN EDUCATION

SOCIAL HISTORY OF

VOLUME II:

AMERICAN EDUCATION

1860 TO THE PRESENT

Edited with commentary by

RENA L. VASSAR

San Fernando Valley State College

RAND MCNALLY & COMPANY • CHICAGO

Rand McNally Education Series
B. Othanel Smith, Advisory Editor

Broudy and Palmer, *Exemplars of Teaching Method*
Broudy, Smith, and Burnett, *Democracy and Excellence in American Secondary Education*
Burns and Lowe, *The Language Arts in Childhood Education*
Childress and Gauerke, eds., *Theory and Practice of School Finance*
Dupuis, *Philosophy of Education in Historical Perspective*
Evans and Walker, *New Trends in the Teaching of English in Secondary Schools*
Farwell and Peters, eds., *Guidance Readings for Counselors*
Foshay, ed., *Rand McNally Handbook of Education*
Haines, *Guiding the Student Teaching Process in Elementary Education*
Kaplan and Steiner, *Musicianship for the Classroom Teacher*
Kimbrough, *Political Power and Educational Decision-Making*
Krumboltz, ed., *Learning and the Educational Process*
Lewenstein, *Teaching Social Studies in Junior and Senior High Schools*
Lieberman and Moskow, *Collective Negotiations for Teachers*
Litwack, Holmes, and O'Hern, *Critical Issues in Student Personnel Work*
Michaelis, ed., *Teaching Units in the Social Sciences*, 3 volumes
Norris, Zeran, and Hatch, *The Information Service in Guidance*, 2nd edition
Parker, ed., *Rand McNally Curriculum Series*
    Ford and Pugno, eds., *The Structure of Knowledge and the Curriculum*
    Parker and Rubin, *Process as Content*
    Wellington and Wellington, *The Underachiever*
Perrodin, ed., *The Student Teacher's Reader*
Peters and Farwell, *Guidance: A Developmental Approach*
Peters, Shertzer, and Van Hoose, *Guidance in Elementary Schools*
Phi Delta Kappa, *Education and the Structure of Knowledge*
Phi Delta Kappa, *Improving Experimental Design and Statistical Analysis*
Rollins and Unruh, *Introduction to Secondary Education*
Shulman and Keislar, eds., *Learning by Discovery*
Smith, ed., *Aesthetics and Criticism in Art Education*
Smith and Ennis, eds., *Language and Concepts in Education*
Taba and Elkins, *Teaching Strategies for the Culturally Disadvantaged*
Trump and Baynham, *Focus on Change: Guide to Better Schools*
Vassar, ed., *Social History of American Education*, 2 volumes
Wolf and Loomer, *The Elementary School: A Perspective*
Zeran and Riccio, *Organization and Administration of Guidance Services*

Also published by Rand McNally
Gage, ed., *Handbook of Research on Teaching*—A Project of the American Educational Research Association

CONTENTS

VOLUME II

PREFACE

The public school system is so much a part of the American ideal of democracy and equality that little attention has been given to the wide differences in educational opportunities that existed in this country for approximately 250 years. Free universal education has become the accepted principle—but only gradually and often over staunch opposition—as during the nineteenth century state after state accepted the responsibility of education for all; first on the elementary level, then secondary; and finally with the state universities and the land grant colleges the keystone was set in the public education arch. By the closing decades of the last century, publicly supported free schooling had become a natural right in theory and in practice, although equal opportunity remains in many areas an unfulfilled ideal.

The purpose of this collection of historical writings is to highlight the divergencies that have long existed in educational opportunities among social and racial groups, and to explain in part how the idea of free universal education came to triumph—in principle by the mid-nineteenth century, and in practice during the present century. In such an approach the complexities of America's educational past become apparent, and, by contrast, the present uniformity and extensiveness of public education seems a startling accomplishment, considering the degree of individual responsibility and the extreme diversity in methods that dominated the colonial and early national eras.

Today, school and education are virtually synonymous, although formal institutions of learning played only a small role in the early years of the American experiment when the family and church were the principal instruments for training and disciplining and for perpetuating the cultural heritage. Individualism in the educational realm explains to a large extent the tremendous variations in educational opportunities and practices during colonial years; the assumption by the separate states of responsibility for schooling is the key to the standardization and uniformity of education in modern America, despite the highly decentralized system. It should not be forgotten that the first Americans were transplanted Englishmen who accepted the idea of education as an individual matter. The transformation of this concept over a period of two centuries into that of public responsibility is one of the major themes of American educational history.

The democratic impulse to provide equality of educational opportunity contributed to unifying the nation and to creating a uniform educational system throughout the nation. This so-called Jacksonian tradition has dominated educational development in both the nineteenth and twentieth centuries. In 1954, the United States Supreme Court reiterated this principle in the famous Brown case. In the last two decades, however, another theme — the Jeffersonian concept of excellence in education — has become a significant issue. In a sense, the present concern with excellence in education has its origin in the overwhelming success of the American nation in achieving equality of educational opportunity.

The extensive bibliography of the history of education attests to the fact that this is not a neglected field of research; but until recent years the traditional approach was a narrow one, concentrating on the institutional developments or the history of a particular school or college rather than on the social and intellectual implications of educational practices, theories, and developments. Thus, the long accepted interpretation was in progressive terms: the emergence of the American public school and the constant movement toward improved and diversified mass education. This is an oversimplified picture of America's educational past: it overlooks the complex interrelationships between education and the forces of change.

The deeper one goes into the rich sources, the more complicated the subject of educational developments becomes; and these selections will undoubtedly raise as many questions as they answer. This would certainly be a measure of the success of such a compilation. The principal problem in organizing a volume of this nature is the matter of selecting from the vast resources those items that are most pertinent and representative. In general, this presentation emphasizes four major themes: education as a reflection of the social and economic order; the evolution of the American idea of free universal education; the role of the school in social change; and the problem of mass education in a complex modern society.

An attempt has been made to reveal the developments of education through a wide sampling of contemporary writings gathered from many different books, newspapers, and periodicals not always readily available to the student of American educational and social history. Necessity — of time and space — determined the exclusion of material pertaining to the important developments of popular and adult education. In putting the final editorial touches on the manuscript, the desire to start anew in reading, selecting, and discarding came over the editor. If patience and perseverance grow with age, then perhaps these other fascinating aspects of America's educational past will be drawn together in a similar collection in the future.

The history is organized into six sections, presenting educational trends and problems from colonial times to the present. The introductory essay for each part offers the continuity; contemporary writings exemplify and reflect the significant developments and ideas of the period. In the essays the numbers in parentheses refer to the selections. The dates in the table of contents and in the headings of each selection indicate when the items first appeared. Editing has been kept to a minimum in an effort to give the reader the full flavor of the age itself.

Rena L. Vassar

Bloomington, Indiana
July, 1964

Part IV:

The Extension of Education

The popular interpretation of the Civil War era as a watershed in American history is equally meaningful when applied to educational developments. The growing importance of the schools as the principal agency for perpetuation of culture and preparation for life; the extension of educational opportunities horizontally and vertically; the entrance of the federal government into the educational realm, and the experimentation with manual training—all exemplify the drastic changes and adjustments that were occurring in America in the late nineteenth century. Despite these innovations in education, the post-war years reflect to a large extent the continuation of the common school idea of the first half of the century. These years brought the fulfillment of the democratic promise of the earlier generation. Free universal education became an established part of the American system. The relationship between education and national progress was widely accepted; and the high ideals of Horace Mann and the other reformers who emphasized education as a force to improve society, to rid it of its ills, to equalize opportunities, and to promote the national welfare remained the guiding principles throughout the closing years of the century.

Among the outstanding developments of the post-war era were the constant extension of educational opportunities for all classes and races and the introduction of new school programs to meet the needs of an industrial and urban society. By the mid-nineteenth century, most northern and western states had accepted the principle of universal free education, but the actual application came slowly, over a period of decades. Only two states, Massachusetts and New York, had compulsory school laws before 1860; by 1918 all states had such regulations, but with great variations in terms of the length of the school year, laws regarding minimum attendance, and the enforcement of these requirements. Standardization would be part of the refinement program.

Another significant accomplishment was the extension upward and downward of free education at public expense. The high school, and to a lesser extent the kindergarten, gradually came to be considered as integral parts of the common school system. William T. Harris and Susan Blow's successful experiments in St. Louis in grafting the Froebel kindergarten on to the American elementary school served as a stimulus to other educational leaders. The public high school first came into existence in Boston in

3

1821, but more than a half century passed before public secondary education was universally accepted by the states. The struggle, unlike that for the common school, was not a political one. It was in the law courts rather than in the legislative assemblies that the principle of universal free secondary education finally triumphed.

The controversy over secondary education at public expense reveals many of the same problems of social stratification and differentiation in education as had the common school battle a half century earlier. The opponents of the public high school movement used familiar arguments: that tax payers were not responsible for such education; that private institutions and religious groups were adequately meeting the needs; that secondary education was largely for those preparing for college, and that such training was not a public matter and thus represented a form of class legislation. However, the reasons for extending public education to the secondary level proved to be convincing, as the Report of the Commissioner of Education for 1877 and its excerpts from the writings of leading educators reveals (32). Every argument from practical to idealistic, from legal to utilitarian is offered: such training would prepare one for life, end inequalities, promote the welfare of mankind, train the masses to be useful and productive members of society, and encourage elementary education.

The leadership viewed high school education as a logical extension of the public school idea. In the famous Kalamazoo Case of 1874 the Michigan court so interpreted the state's educational provisions—that from the beginning the state had sought to furnish rudiments of education and equal opportunity to continue such training. The case became a landmark in the development of public high schools throughout the nation. Other states, through legislation or court decisions, followed the example, and the public high school took its place in the educational ladder of the nation. The problem then revolved about the question of the purpose of such secondary training, and the growing popularity of manual training and industrial education determined to a large extent the nature of secondary education in the United States (See Section V).

In the extension of educational opportunities in the post-war years, one of the most significant innovations in educational policy was the idea of federal aid. Certainly the tremendous expansion of free education and the growing discrepancies and unevenness in the educational achievements of the separate states were important factors, but the more immediate cause for the break with tradition was the overwhelming challenge of educating the newly-freed Negroes and of assisting the struggling and devastated South to reconstruct its social and economic order through the development of a public school system. Strengthening the practical reasons for federal assistance was the more abstract notion that education was directly related to national progress. In the early years of the nation's existence some leaders had envisioned a national system of education, but the plans never materialized. The idea of the federal government's playing a direct role in promoting education through financial assistance remained dormant throughout the first half of the nineteenth century. In 1862, the Morrill Act, which granted lands to states to promote agricultural and mechanical arts colleges, set a precedent of direct national aid, and from that time until the present, federal aid to education has continued to be one of the most controversial issues in America's educational and political developments.

Supporters of federal aid have used either of two arguments: that it is the only solution to the educational inequalities among the states, or that the national government must assume responsibility for the educational welfare of the nation as a whole. As early as 1866, Senator Justin Morrill, who gave his name to the famous act of 1862, proposed that public lands be used to aid the common school as well as the colleges (33). He argued that such assistance would be promoting educational equality, fighting illiteracy, and "leveling upward and not downward." He insisted that education was an inalienable right and that federal aid was constitutionally proper. Above all he emphasized the role of the national government in molding the character of the American people and of guaranteeing through education the promises of the republican experiment. Few of his arguments were new; educational and political leaders had uttered the same ideas in the state-by-state battle to establish universal free elementary education a generation earlier. Americans still viewed free education as a universal panacea, but the idea of the government playing a direct role was new. Only the national government, "superior in it higher nature and wider scope," could assume such responsibility.

Despite their failure to be adopted, Morrill's proposals were important—especially in the context of the existing illiteracy rate, the struggle of states to provide common school education, and the problem of training the newly-freed slaves and introducing public education in the southern states. The precedent of the federal government as the educational benefactor of the nation as a whole existed in the realm of higher education. Federal aid seemed a logical solution then to many in the post-war years. The national government had already stepped in to supervise the reconstruction of the former Confederate states and the rehabilitation of the Negro. These were years of experimentation and of the extension of the powers and privileges of the central government. Morrill's viewpoint is equally pertinent today because of his emphasis on the role of the government in molding the national character and promoting education as a national policy and his insistence on the utilization of the extensive powers and funds of the federal government.

Support for federal assistance was widespread and diverse among the nationalistic Republicans, humanitarians, educational leaders, and even some Southern Democrats. In view of their long-standing states' rights position, it is indeed significant that these Southerners were able to reconcile their political and constitutional principles with necessity and come to favor federal aid. They did accept it as a means of solving the almost insurmountable problem of creating a public school system for both races in the midst of economic disorder and distress. In 1876, for example, Representative Gilbert Walker of Virginia proposed an educational bill which would grant federal funds on the basis of illiteracy (34). His speech to Congress is noteworthy, first for its argument on the constitutionality of the measure, and second, for its advocacy of education as a means of bringing diverse elements of society into the American mainstream. He pleaded the cause of the devastated South and of the illiterate Negro. Yet this could be the speech of a Northern reformer seeking to bring the blessing of free education to the downtrodden classes of the South.

Such were the times that even Southerners could forget states' rights and advocate federal assistance. The climax came with the famous Blair Bill introduced in various forms in the decade of the eighties by Republican Senator Henry W. Blair of New Hampshire. It had support among Republicans of the North and some Democrats in the South. In essence the proposals were to grant federal funds to states in accordance with the illiteracy rate, which meant that the southern states would be the chief beneficiary of such a program. The Senate passed the bill three times, but it never came to a vote in the House, and the Republican leadership abandoned the plan at the end of the decade.

The idea of direct federal aid on a national scale again receded into the background, although it was not abandoned entirely. The government did make generous grants to promote public education: for agricultural experiment stations, for industrial education in the public secondary schools, and for universities and colleges. But not until the middle decades of the twentieth century would the post-Civil War idea of federal assistance as a means of equalizing opportunity and promoting the national welfare again become a national issue.

In fulfilling the promise of universal free education in the last half of the nineteenth century, the achievements in educating the former slave population are among the most outstanding. In general there was widespread acceptance among most social, political, and economic groups both North and South of the necessity of training these people. The middle- and upper-class Southerners, with rare exception, looked upon character and vocational training as absolutely essential in reconstituting the social order and rebuilding the economic structure ruined by the war; thus the freedmen would become reliable, useful, and contributing members of society—not equal, but no longer enslaved. In 1865 the national government created the Freedmen's Bureau to assist in the relocation, rehabilitation, and education of the former slaves and other refugees of the war-torn lands. In establishing the Bureau, the federal government was accepting the Negro problem as a national rather than a sectional one. The educational work of the Bureau continued for only five years. It spent approximately five million dollars to assist missionary societies and other groups in founding and operating schools for the freedmen. The Bureau made its educational contribution mainly in leadership and funds.

In a sense the Bureau was responsible for introducing what came to be known as the dual school system in the South. Several factors explain this development of separate schools for the two

7

races. First, the Freedmen's Bureau cáme into existence primarily as an agency to supervise the newly-freed slaves, thus setting them apart as a special class. Second, the notion of mixed public schools was not widespread in the nation at the time—North or South. Nonetheless, in carrying out Reconstruction there was experimentation with mixed schools in the four states of Mississippi, South Carolina, Florida, and Louisiana where constitutional provisions required a single public school system for both races. In other instances, the constitutions either did not specifically mention separate schools when establishing the public school system, or did permit the establishment of separate schools (35). Thus almost from the beginning of Reconstruction, the majority of southern states did develop a dual public school system, as did many of the other states of the nation. The important fact, however, was that the southern states were for the first time accepting the idea of public support for free universal education for *both* races. In some cases it was the actual introduction of public education for all classes without the stigma of pauperism attached to free schooling.

It should be noted that when Reconstruction ended, the so-called "Redeemers," in rewriting the state constitutions, did not repudiate public school education for the Negro; but the new or revised constitutions provided in every case for separate schools for the two races and prohibited white and Negro children from attending the same institutions. The examples included show early and later constitutional provisions typical of the period. By the end of the century the system of dualism was in existence in every southern state and also in many non-southern areas. Therefore, the decision of *Plessy* v. *Ferguson* in 1896, relating to the matter of transportation facilities, simply gave legal sanction to the "separate but equal" doctrine of education which was already established by custom and law.

In considering developments in Negro education in the South during the late nineteenth and early twentieth centuries, the efforts and ideas of three men—two Negroes and one white—exemplify the prevailing viewpoints and attitudes. Each in his own way played a significant role in promoting education for the race: J. L. M. Curry, General Agent for both the Peabody Fund and the John F. Slater Fund; Booker T. Washington, principal of Tuskegee

Institute and a leading Negro spokesman and American educator; and W. E. B. DuBois, Harvard Ph.D., editor, and militant advocate of Negro rights and equality. Each one represents the mind of the South or the mind of the Negro as they took shape and form in the half century following the chaos and disorder of the war years and Reconstruction.

Curry, as General Agent for the trust funds, held the foremost position of educational leadership in the South in developing the public school system (for so the Peabody Fund was used) and in promoting Negro education through the generous gift of the Connecticut textile manufacturer, John F. Slater. Curry's travels, his administration of the funds, his pronouncements before legislative assemblies and other interested groups played an extremely important part in southern educational developments. Indeed, his remarks, entitled, "Difficulties, Complications, and Limitations Connected with the Education of the Negro," (1895) reveal his dedication to Negro education as well as his conservative social and educational philosophy in regard to the Negro's training and the part he could play in the reconstructed society (36).

Curry and Booker T. Washington, the outstanding Negro leader of his age, were in general in agreement on the idea of practical education and character training as essential for the Negro and suitable for him because of his race and his place in southern society. Underlying Curry's view, as revealed in his essay, was the assumption of the Negro's inferior social and political position. The selection by Washington, "Industrial Education for the Negro," is a statement of his pedagogical views: practical education for the Negro in order to make him a useful and necessary part of the southern social and economic order (37). This was the guiding philosophy of the Tuskegee Institute founded and developed by Washington. Here he preached and practiced the gospel of thrift, industry, and practical learning.

Washington best expressed his ideas on Negro-white relations in his famous Atlanta Exposition Address in 1895 in which he offered a compromise solution to the racial problems and tensions of his times. The speech and its conciliatory suggestions came to be criticized sharply in Washington's own lifetime by DuBois, who labelled it the "Atlanta Compromise." In Souls of Black Folks (1903), DuBois attacked Washington for his policy which encouraged Negroes to accept a subservient position in society and an outdated kind of educational training. DuBois' viewpoint, exemplified in his essay, "The Talented Tenth," was a demand for equal educational opportunities for Negroes, based on talent and on the need for educated leadership (38). He saw such training as a prelude to economic and political as well as social equality. He rejected industrial and practical training — the Tuskegee Idea — as outdated in an industrial age undergoing drastic transformation. DuBois argued that such training would not prepare the Negro and would not contribute to the improvement of his status but rather would solidify his inferior position. Above all, DuBois demanded the opportunity for broad cultural education in order to assimilate the Negro into the mainstream of American culture.

The entire tone of DuBois' writings was in sharp contrast to that of Washington and Curry. Each represented a solution to the Negro problem as it had developed in the years since emancipation. DuBois wanted equal opportunity and equal training for his race, and he interpreted these opportunities in light of the broad economic and political rights the Negro would have to demand and eventually achieve. It was understandable that DuBois would become a leader in the Niagara Movement and the editor of *Crisis,* the journal of the newly organized National Association for the Advancement of Colored People. Curry and Washington, on the other hand, operated on the "philosophy of the possible." This is not to deny Washington's deep interest in Negro rights. He too was concerned about discrimination and inequalities; but his solution lay in gradually preparing the Negro for his economic role within the existing South by making him so vital to the society that he would eventually win and secure social and political rights.

The controversy over the most effective means of solving racial tensions and of improving the Negro's position raged during the lifetime of these three men and continues to this day. Biographers and writers still debate the merits of the two approaches to the Negro problem and the accomplishments of each. Horace Mann Bond, C. Vann Woodward, August Meier, Hugh Hawkins, and Francis L. Broderick are evaluating and reevaluating Washington's and DuBois' contributions to Negro advancement in the age of racial tensions in which they lived and within the context of the tensions of today.

A school system for the freed Negro of the South (with all its shortcomings and inequalities) ranks as one of the major educational accomplishments of the post-war era. And of equal importance is the development of the public school system in the South during these years. Thus the vision of free universal education through public expense was becoming a reality for virtually all social and racial classes by the last decades of the nineteenth century. As noted earlier, the South had lagged behind the North and West in committing itself to the idea of popular education in the antebellum decades. Southern leaders displayed more concern with developing an education fitting southern agrarian society than with providing free education for all classes.

With peace and Reconstruction, there was widespread acceptance of the importance of education and the necessity of inaugurating universal education in the southern states. Each group viewed the purpose of this education in its own terms, but all recognized the early nineteenth century notion of education as a means of progress. To the radical Republicans, education would be the instrument for reforming the southern mind to be sympathetic to the principles of union and liberty and for training Southerners to take their rightful place in the nation. In a sense, the school was the common denominator, the agency for "nationalization" of the sectionally-minded South that had clashed with the Union ideals. This view was in fact a restatement in nationalistic terms of the nineteenth century belief in education as a universal panacea. Some even saw secession as having developed from the widespread illiteracy and social stratification in the South. So education became to the Reconstructionists a means of remaking the South in the Republican image. To the dedicated northern missionaries and humanitarians, who poured into the South, schooling would be the way to bring that section back into the national fold. To most of the Southerners, the public school became a symbol of the future and the means by which a New South would be born.

Through supplying leadership, funds, and teachers, northern religious and humanitarian groups and individuals contributed immeasurably to the development of a public school system in the South. One such individual was the Reverend A. D. Mayo of Massachusetts, trustee of the Peabody Fund. His essay is an emo-

11

tional and somewhat sentimental and sympathetic review of southern accomplishments with high praise for the South's attitude of self-help (39). This is one example of the "healing balm" that northern religious and educational leaders were constantly applying. It exemplifies a new attitude in the closing years of the century that put the North and the South on the road to reunion. This is not a Yankee dictum to the defeated South; rather it is a typical nineteenth century statement with its praise for common education and self-help.

Private benevolence from Northerners was to a large extent the single most important factor in the successful development of the public school idea for both races in the South. The South was not unique in receiving generous grants for education. In the last decades of the century, as the gigantic fortunes were made, Stanford, Rockefeller, Carnegie, Hopkins, and others were turning surplus capital over for educational purposes throughout the nation. In helping to develop the public schools of the South and in promoting Negro education, two New Englanders among others—George Peabody and John F. Slater—played important roles. Here are examples of the successful industrialists' assuming social responsibility as well as displaying a strong strain of early nineteenth century New England humanitarianism.

George Peabody, a transplanted New Englander living in England, exemplifies the old and new concepts of gift-giving. When he made his generous grant to the southern states in 1867, he explained that it was the "duty and privilege of the more favored and wealthy portions of our nation to assist those who are less fortunate" (40). Thus he gave his gift "to the suffering South for the good of the whole country." Peabody was expressing the longstanding hope of Americans who looked upon education as a means of promoting prosperity and progress. In 1890, Curry, the fund's General Agent, restated these nineteenth century views in his report on the accomplishments of the trust: Education was the universal panacea and the means of improving society. Curry also expressed another idea which cast this traditional belief in education into a new mold (41). Education by improving man and his economic lot became a means of securing the established order by guarding against change and disruption. This conservative view of education grew popular in the closing years of the nineteenth century.

12

The Peabody Fund proved to be one of the most influential forces in promoting the common school for both races during the troublesome decades of the late nineteenth century. By encouraging teacher training, by aiding the public schools, by allowing southern states and local agencies to operate the schools, by careful choice — first of the Reverend Barnas Sears of Brown University and then Curry of Alabama as General Agents — the Peabody Fund served the South well. The South accepted the gift in the spirit in which it was given — as stimulus rather than charity. Thus the Fund stands as another milestone in the road to reunion.

Despite the philanthropic aid and the continuation of the Reconstruction's educational programs, the history of education in the South in the last decades of the nineteenth century is not one of growth, expansion, and vitality by any means. In fact, with the drastic retrenchment and repudiation of the economic policies of the reconstructed governments, public education entered into a long phase of lethargy and stagnation. The new governments did not repudiate the idea of popular education, but their "spend nothing unless absolutely necessary" attitude was a serious threat to the newly-established public schools in the South which came to view them as luxuries. Short school terms, miserable physical plants, poorly-trained teachers, a high illiteracy rate, mediocre schools for both Negroes and whites, all reflected the retrenchment program and the growing indifference of the population and leadership.

In the closing years of the century, as a result of economic revival, the growth of the middle class, the emergence of new leadership, and the development of agrarian discontent, the New South began to take shape and form, and an educational revival occurred. Walter Hines Page, a native of North Carolina, sounded the clarion call with his famous "Forgotten Man" address in 1897. He gave the South a by-word and a slogan; but as the essay, "The Rebuilding of Old Commonwealths," reveals, he also offered the South a program and a solution to the backwardness of the area (42). He challenged the South to build a new social order through education. Thus a crusade to educate the public in order to improve public education developed. Again northern philanthropy came to the aid of the South. Through the generosity of Robert Ogden, John D. Rockefeller, Jr., and others, an all-out campaign to sell the idea of public education was launched. The Conference

13

on Southern Education and the General Education Board through organizing conferences, meetings, and rallies carried on an incessant crusade against ignorance. The New South was beginning to emerge, and the success in educàting the populace to the role they were to play in promoting public education was instrumental in the socio-economic regeneration that was taking place. Again, education was viewed as the means of accomplishing the objectives of economic revitalization and social stability. In one respect, the century ended as it had begun — with the belief in education as an agency for reform and progress still deeply entrenched in the American mind.

CHAPTER 13

EXTENDING PUBLIC EDUCATION UPWARDS

Graded and high schools are legitimate, because necessary.

Ezra S. Carr, 1877

32. THE HIGH SCHOOL QUESTION (1877)[1]

The arguments of those who hold that the State has no right to provide education beyond the rudiments may be briefly summarized as follows:

1. The State has the right to educate its children just so far as will enable them to understand their duties and exercise their rights as citizens of a free country governed by the popular voice. A primary education is sufficient for this; therefore the State has the right to furnish a primary education and nothing more.

2. The high school being patronized by but few and the majority deriving no benefit from it, it is unjust to levy a general tax for its support.

3. "Instead of educating the masses of children so as to prepare them for the pursuits and industries upon which they must depend for a living, high schools educate them in such a way as to make them discontented with their condition and unfit to discharge its duties in a manner most beneficial to their own interests."

4. Our common school system has been enlarged and extended beyond the original purpose of its founders. The high school has been ingrafted upon the system contrary to the "original design;" hence it should be cut off.

Others who would not abolish the high schools would still radically change the basis of their organization by compelling those who avail themselves of their privileges to pay a part of the cost of their maintenance. . . .

[ARGUMENTS FOR THE HIGH SCHOOL]

"No system of public education," says Huxley, "is worthy the name unless it creates a great educational ladder with one end in the gutter and the other in the university." "I will thank any per-

---

[1]"The High School Question," *Report of the Commissioner of Education for the Year 1877*. (Washington: U.S. Government Printing Office, 1879), pp. LXXXI–LXXXVII.

16

son," says Everett, "to tell why it is expedient and beneficial in a community to make public provision for teaching the elements of learning and not expedient nor beneficial to make similar provision to aid the learner's progress toward the mastery of the most difficult branches of science and the choicest refinements of literature." "Experience has proved," says Mr. Francis Adams, "that elementary education flourishes most where the provision for higher education is most ample. If the elementary schools of Germany are the best in the world, it is owing in a great measure to the fact that the higher schools are accessible to all classes. In England not only have the aims of the elementary schools been educationally low and narrow, but an impassable gulf has separated the people's schools from the higher schools of the country. In the United States the common schools have always produced the best results where the means of higher education have been the most plentiful."—(Massachusetts State Report, 1877.)

Hon. Ezra S. Carr, State superintendent of public instruction of California, in his report for 1876–'77 says:

"The right of the State and municipal governments to maintain high schools is not legally distinguishable from the right to maintain elementary schools. * * * Schools exist because of a well founded claim, and not because of toleration. The universal recognition of this principle is found in the constitution of every State in the Union."

After quoting from the constitutions of Arkansas, Florida, Kansas, and Massachusetts, Mr. Carr continues:

"Further citations are not required to show that 'the school is created and encouraged as an institution that is purely one of political economy, for increasing the production and accumulation of wealth, and as a means of preventing pauperism and crime, which is still only wealth.' The right to educate is 'one of those inalienable rights which have never been surrendered by the people either to Congress or to legislatures, because of the right of the people to the fruits of intelligence and protection from the folly and crime which result from ignorance.' * * * Education is not a fixed quantity to be measured by one generation for that which succeeds it. The 'common schooling' of the past century, for instance, would not adequately fit the average citizen of to-day for the necessary business of life. The standard of general intelligence is higher. The demand for secondary and high schools is far

17

more general throughout the United States at the present time than was the demand for elementary schools fifty or even twenty-five years ago. 'The school being the creation of the State, and the interests involved being so vital, it would seem to be a legitimate and necessary consequence that all schools should be regarded as to their advancement by the States.' If this be true, graded and high schools are legitimate, because necessary. . . ."

Hon. H. F. Harrington, [Superintendent of the public schools of New York] presents the claims of the high schools to public support as follows:

"1. High schools are important because they give increased efficiency to all the schools below them.

"2. High schools are important because they are the best seminaries from which competent recruits can be obtained for the great army of public school teachers.

"3. More than all, high schools are important as a branch of a public school system, because they constitute the only trustworthy agency to perform the essential service of bringing worthy representatives of the lower classes into the councils of the State and the organism of society. Abolish the high schools, and at once you draw a broad line of separation between the rich and the poor. You limit the higher education to the children of the well to do, for only the well to do would have the means to pay for it, and this would prove a damaging, perhaps a perilous, venture for the state. Mainly the cultured classes are found to be the governing classes, and among its governing classes society needs the representatives of the poor. It needs them, that there may always be strong men coming to the front, with powers so tempered by culture as to make them wise, ❉ ❉ ❉ to represent the humble class from which they sprung, and demand the consideration due to their needs and their rights. These are the men, too, in the social exigencies which sometimes occur, when passion becomes rampant among the masses and the restraints of law are defied, to throw themselves into the track of the storm and allay its violence. Far better this than the alternative if you do not bestow the culture; for those who are born to be the leaders of men will assert their prerogatives whether or no; and the born leaders from among the poor, if they be not tempered by culture, become the ignorant demagogues whose leadership is anarchy. ❉ ❉ ❉ It is the universal confidence in

18

CHAPTER 14

FEDERAL AID TO EDUCATION

*Schools and the means of education
shall forever be encouraged.*

Northwest Ordinance of 1787

elementary education as the right arm of a free state which renders the objection to high schools so strong, for it implies that the state does not need high schools. All the while that protests against the continuance of the high schools are ringing throughout the land, the elementary schools remain as popular as ever. Not a whisper of objection is heard against taxation for their support. They are still lauded as the palladium of liberty; ❋ ❋ ❋ but in a recent address at Baltimore President Eliot used this memorable language: 'There are those who hold that republics can be saved by the general diffusion of primary education, but the most effectively despotic government of Europe is the one in which this education is most diffused. There is, however, a power in the spread of higher education and the sentiment of honor associated with culture.'"

Concerning the objection that "the character of the instruction given in high schools is such as to disqualify their scholars for occupations involving manual labor," Mr. Harrington says:

"This question opens up to view the chief incentives to the present crusade against this class of schools; and no one can do justice to the subject, nor speculate wisely about the future of these schools, without making those incentives an important factor in the solution of the problem.

"'The fact is, the times have changed; the paramount interests and needs of society have changed; the expectations of society in regard to its youth have changed, and the instruction in the high schools has not been conformed to the new order of things. Here we find the kernel of the whole matter. ❋ ❋ ❋ The grand declaratory principle of the fathers, in behalf of education, was, 'a popular government can rest securely only on popular knowledge.' The declaratory principle of the men of to-day is, in the language of Governor Robinson, 'Educate the masses of children, so as to prepare them for the pursuits and industries on which they must depend for a living.' Here is a remarkable change of base; and it is no wonder that those who are swayed by these new ideas should protest against the conservatism which maintains the work of high schools on its ancient basis and clamor for its modification or its extinction. . . .'"

The report of Hon. W. T. Harris, superintendent of the St. Louis public schools for 1876 – '77, contains an elaborate argument in "justification of the public high school" from which the following is extracted:

"The limit to public education is found in the means and the will of the community which affords it. If the community regards education as a disagreeable but necessary charity, the extent of the education will not be great and its results will not have high value. If the community looks upon education as a right, but a right to be allowed only within the narrowest limits, its value as an instrumentality in the solution of social problems will be correspondingly small. If the community proposes to do the best by itself, it will place as large a limit as it may in justice to its other interests, and will debate the quality and fitness of the education and not its amount; it will feel that every dollar spent for education is more than a dollar gained to the one who spends it, both in the decreased need for the expenses for other community interests and in the increased value of every educated citizen. In this country, the probable limit, for local communities at least, is the high school.

⁕ ⁕ ⁕

"The necessity of the work of the high school, briefly stated, is that a high school exerts upon the grammar school a leverage which could not be obtained so economically by any other instrumentality; ⁕ ⁕ ⁕ that the leverage gained by a high school grade is necessary for the load to be lifted and not for the employment of the lever; that the grammar school demands a high school, and not that a high school requires the grammar school; that the grammar schools determine the necessity for a high school, and not that a high school needs the grammar school; that a high school exists for the grammar schools, and not that the grammar schools exist for a high school. ⁕ ⁕ ⁕ As a matter of practical experience, it has been found in communities that the work was improved in quality and that it cost less with a high school course than without it, despite the fact that misconceptions of the true office and relation of a high school have in many cases led to a mismanagement which prevents our seeing the results in their clearest light. ⁕ ⁕ ⁕ Every one knows that unless he goes far enough to secure success, his capital of time, labor, and money is wasted. ⁕ ⁕ ⁕ The sufficiency of education must be determined by the previous considerations of political necessity and reciprocity of duty between the citizen and

the state, modified by the consideration, the ability of the community to obtain what it may desire. ⁕ ⁕ ⁕ The education which fifty years ago would have been generous no longer fits a man for the contest of life. ⁕ ⁕ ⁕ We frequently meet the suggestion that prominent men of the past were provided with but a scanty education preparatory to a useful, influential life, and we do not reflect, as we should, that prominence is merely relative. If these men, so distinguished in our histories as revered in our memories, could be fairly brought into relation with our own times, they would possibly lose much of their preeminence. ⁕ ⁕ ⁕ Therefore we must inquire in regard to the education which we furnish as to its sufficiency for the objects which justify its mere existence. Those who regard education as a right will admit that the right is valueless unless sufficiently extensive to pay for its assertion. ⁕ ⁕ ⁕ Hence, in public schools, regarded as the people's schools, ⁕ ⁕ ⁕ it is reasonable, and indeed imperatively necessary, that a sufficiency of education should be furnished not withstanding the fact that many will, from the necessities of their individual life, be unable to avail themselves of these advantages."

elementary education as the right arm of a free state which renders the objection to high schools so strong, for it implies that the state does not need high schools. All the while that protests against the continuance of the high schools are ringing throughout the land, the elementary schools remain as popular as ever. Not a whisper of objection is heard against taxation for their support. They are still lauded as the palladium of liberty; * * * but in a recent address at Baltimore President Eliot used this memorable language: 'There are those who hold that republics can be saved by the general diffusion of primary education, but the most effectively despotic government of Europe is the one in which this education is most diffused. There is, however, a power in the spread of higher education and the sentiment of honor associated with culture.'"

Concerning the objection that "the character of the instruction given in high schools is such as to disqualify their scholars for occupations involving manual labor," Mr. Harrington says:

"This question opens up to view the chief incentives to the present crusade against this class of schools; and no one can do justice to the subject, nor speculate wisely about the future of these schools, without making those incentives an important factor in the solution of the problem.

"The fact is, the times have changed; the paramount interests and needs of society have changed; the expectations of society in regard to its youth have changed, and the instruction in the high schools has not been conformed to the new order of things. Here we find the kernel of the whole matter. * * * The grand declaratory principle of the fathers, in behalf of education, was, 'a popular government can rest securely only on popular knowledge.' The declaratory principle of the men of to day is, in the language of Governor Robinson, 'Educate the masses of children, so as to prepare them for the pursuits and industries on which they must depend for a living.' Here is a remarkable change of base; and it is no wonder that those who are swayed by these new ideas should protest against the conservatism which maintains the work of high schools on its ancient basis and clamor for its modification or its extinction. . . ."

The report of Hon. W. T. Harris, superintendent of the St. Louis public schools for 1876 – '77, contains an elaborate argument in "justification of the public high school" from which the following is extracted:

"The limit to public education is found in the means and the will of the community which affords it. If the community regards education as a disagreeable but necessary charity, the extent of the education will not be great and its results will not have high value. If the community looks upon education as a right, but a right to be allowed only within the narrowest limits, its value as an instrumentality in the solution of social problems will be correspondingly small. If the community proposes to do the best by itself, it will place as large a limit as it may in justice to its other interests, and will debate the quality and fitness of the education and not its amount; it will feel that every dollar spent for education is more than a dollar gained to the one who spends it, both in the decreased need for the expenses for other community interests and in the increased value of every educated citizen. In this country, the probable limit, for local communities at least, is the high school.

* * *

"The necessity of the work of the high school, briefly stated, is that a high school exerts upon the grammar school a leverage which could not be obtained so economically by any other instrumentality; * * * that the leverage gained by a high school grade is necessary for the load to be lifted and not for the employment of the lever; that the grammar school demands a high school, and not that a high school requires the grammar school; that the grammar schools determine the necessity for a high school, and not that a high school needs the grammar school; that a high school exists for the grammar schools, and not that the grammar schools exist for a high school. * * * As a matter of practical experience, it has been found in communities that the work was improved in quality and that it cost less with a high school course than without it, despite the fact that misconceptions of the true office and relation of a high school have in many cases led to a mismanagement which prevents our seeing the results in their clearest light. * * * Every one knows that unless he goes far enough to secure success, his capital of time, labor, and money is wasted. * * * The sufficiency of education must be determined by the previous considerations of political necessity and reciprocity of duty between the citizen and the state, modified by the consideration, the ability of the community to obtain what it may desire. ❋ ❋ ❋ The education which fifty years ago would have been generous no longer fits a man for the contest of life. ❋ ❋ ❋ We frequently meet the suggestion that prominent men of the past were provided with but a scanty education preparatory to a useful, influential life, and we do not reflect, as we should, that prominence is merely relative. If these men, so distinguished in our histories as revered in our memories, could be fairly brought into relation with our own times, they would possibly lose much of their preeminence. ❋ ❋ ❋ Therefore we must inquire in regard to the education which we furnish as to its sufficiency for the objects which justify its mere existence. Those who regard education as a right will admit that the right is valueless unless sufficiently extensive to pay for its assertion. ❋ ❋ ❋ Hence, in public schools, regarded as the people's schools, ❋ ❋ ❋ it is reasonable, and indeed imperatively necessary, that a sufficiency of education should be furnished not withstanding the fact that many will, from the necessities of their individual life, be unable to avail themselves of these advantages."

CHAPTER 14

FEDERAL AID TO EDUCATION

*Schools and the means of education
shall forever be encouraged.*

Northwest Ordinance of 1787

33. EDUCATION, THE RIGHT OF AMERICANS (1876)[1]

SENATOR JUSTIN MORRILL

Mr. President, the measure I have called up to-day has for its object the aid of common schools and some further assistance to the national colleges. Other propositions are pending, both here and in the other House, in relation to this subject; but with all earnest men, if the leading purposes mentioned can be secured, the details will be of minor importance.

I start with the proposition that all of our public lands, which are hereafter to be sold and are not called for as free homesteads, should be held exclusively for educational purposes — purposes that tower high above and dwarf all others. Should any exception to this rule ever be suggested, let it then be considered on its merits.

SCHOOL LANDS DONATED

We have already given to States, without regard to their population, 140,000,000 acres of land for the support of common schools, and eighteen of the States thus aided have a school fund of $43,866,785. The western or new States, as to common schools, would appear to have been liberally provided for. In the North and East the system of common schools has long held a foremost place in the hearts of the people, and cheerful contributions to their support by self-imposed taxation are made with all the regularity of the seasons. At the South they are far less advanced, and having no accumulated school funds, their people are at present

---

[1]*Congressional Record*, 44th Cong., 1st sess., 4:4 (April 26, 1876), pp. 2761–63.

unequal to the task of establishing and adequately maintaining such schools without some national assistance, not national control, although not unmindful of their utility and fully appreciating their urgent necessity. When even in Spain it is no longer immoral for women to know how to read, and when Sweden and Turkey engage in universal education, no American State will be found to hold back.

All statistics are dry—interesting to few and entertaining to none—and some are by no means pleasant or even tolerable to contemplate; but legislators, like surgeons, must probe the ugliest sores, and courageously examine even such facts as those I am reluctantly about to expose.

SCHOOL POPULATION

Our school population of five years of age to seventeen inclusive is 12,055,443, or nearly one-third of our entire population. A mighty host, led now and controlled by us, but soon to control us and lead the van of civilization in the land of their fathers. Only about one-half of this number, or 6,545,112, attend schools of any sort, and among all of the four or five million of colored population only 180,372 attend school, or hardly enough to furnish a silver lining to a cloud so dark. Five million and a half of our population cannot write and four million and a half cannot read. Of illiterate male adults, twenty years of age and over, we have 1,611,213, of which number 748,470 are whites. There are thus more illiterate voters, among either white or colored, than the usual majority of any party taking part at any national election. They are, therefore, the potent auxiliaries of all parties, the decisive make-weights, and must more or less control the destinies of the country. Can any happy augury of ages to come be drawn from these dismal facts? "Do men gather grapes of thorns?"

The liberty and equality of an immense number of illiterate people, unmarked by intellectual eminence of any sort, empty of all virtuous gratitude springing from the memories of childhood and the schoolroom toward a parental government, is not such a state or condition as freemen toil for, nor such as they can be

24

expected to maintain, love, and cherish. Along with entire liberty and equality before the law we behold among mankind the foremost and the hindermost as well, and there will be distinctions and differences in both the power and the industry of mankind, and both of hand and brain, with no two alike among them all, good or bad. It should be the mission of American legislators to offer sure means for the greatest possible development of this power and industry, and to diminish inequality by leveling upward and not downward. Thus only shall we be able to prove that republican institutions, quick to perceive and to foster the most exalted personal merits and qualifications, will neither dwarf the state nor the people. Thus only shall we show that our boasted equality is not inferiority to everybody else.

The several States are greatly interested in the removal of the deepseated illiteracy to which I have referred, but by no means exclusively, as the interest of the General Government covers the same territory and embraces all and the same voters. The election of President of the United States and of members of Congress cannot be reckoned as less grave and important work than that of State governors and Legislatures. The parts are not greater than the whole.

Through the latest action of the people upon the national Constitution we have bestowed universal suffrage upon our fellow-citizens in all of the States. The nation is primarily responsible for this action, and, while accepting of its advantages, must shield itself as well as the States from the resulting possible perils. The increased magnitude of the burden which has been imposed by the sovereign will of the nation manifestly ought to be borne by the nation. Universal suffrage must be made a blessing and an honor to our country, not a curse to the citizen, nor to the States and the nation. Every one of our citizens has been crowned with equal power in the guidance of national and State affairs; but they have thus far had too little of our aid to fit them even to guide themselves. Many of the States resolutely assume their full share of the great responsibility, and raise by taxation and expend nearly $100,000,000 annually for common schools; and, when so much more is obviously required, shall the General Government look on with total indifference, contributing nothing?

CONSTITUTIONAL POWER

Not only is the General Government proroundly interested in the enlightened and virtuous character of our whole people, but it has the exclusive power touching the disposal of the public lands, the largest and most appropriate educational resource by which that character has been and may be elevated and its deficiencies remedied. The language of the Constitution is:

"The Congress shall have the power to dispose of and make all needful rules and regulations respecting the territory or other property belonging to the United States."

No grant of power could be more ample, none more explicit, and it must be exercised. It should not sleep and it cannot be delegated to other parties. Congress itself must dispose of the lands and make such rules and regulations as it chooses. If it appears needful and proper to dispose of this property for educational purposes, the noblest of all purposes, the power of Congress is supreme, and it can and ought so to ordain. Even if the pathway were less obvious, we have an unerring guide-board in the great ordinance of 1787, reflecting so much honor upon our ancestors, which not only provided the flaming sword to keep the great West free from "slavery and involuntary servitude," but also proclaimed this educational purpose in the strongest and most unequivocal terms, as will be found in one of its prominent articles, namely:

"Art. 3. Religion, morality, and knowledge being necessary to good government and the happiness of mankind, schools and the means of education shall forever be encouraged."

These terms, made and declared at the time of the cession of the lands as "a compact between the original States," are mandatory as to our duty—national duty—in the premises. "Schools and the means of education shall forever be encouraged," not by States alone but by this national fund. The logical concomitants of religion, morality and good government, could not otherwise be secured. We must adhere for all time to this compact, or be justly charged with a plain and palpable breach of a sacred trust.

The Government promised what it would do when it took charge of the land fund, and that promise cannot be avoided by the cranky plea that the Government has nothing to do with education. American citizens are not dependent paupers, and it is no humiliation for them, in spite of all cant phrases, to ask for what is their due. They form a great co-partnership, having, among other privileges, an equal interest in the education and perfection of all its members, and the poorest member is entitled to something better than his unaided resources might otherwise have afforded. If this were not true the association would be a failure, and, after all, the best form of government, controlled by illiterate bunglers, might prove to be the worst. The great crises of our so-called political experiment have passed away. Even the greed of territorial acquisitions and the passion to extend our rule over foreigners, the terrible fanaticism of republics, it is to be hoped has been satiated, and, with ample resources for prosperous trade and commercial independence, it now remains to us as our chiefest concern to establish a more solid basis of hope for our future career through a broader and higher education, adapted to the genius and taste of the American people.

If Congress has a binding duty to perform relative to education—next to religion the highest concern of mankind—it has also a duty scarcely inferior in its scope as to the discharge of an important trust, no less than that of the disposal of the residue of our whole public domain, in such manner as will best promote the present and future welfare, moral and material, of a great, enterprising, and exacting people, and in strict accordance with the terms of our compact.

Is it not a providential conjuncture that, while this moral exigency looms up before us, a national resource of ample dimensions is also waiting as a remedy for this very exigency—a resource unexhausted even by unthrifty husbandry, and which the common voice of the country will agree by acclamation should not be disposed of without a full equivalent, nor for any purpose less than the most sacred? The high duty of ownership, the great trust of the original States, long swaying to and fro, can now be fully, fittingly, and nobly discharged.

The present depleted and unsatisfactory financial condition of many of the Southern States, however substantial the latent elements of their future prosperity may be, needs neither proof nor illustration. None of us can remain unmindful of their wants, and Congress will in any constitutional manner move with alacrity to their relief when it can be done without detriment to the Republic, as here it may be, and done patriotically, with national as well as local advantage. These States need all the aid we can properly grant for both common schools and colleges, and they will still have to rely, in the race with their sister States and the world, largely upon their own efforts and enthusiasm to place themselves on the road to equal rank with those where educational institutions are more deeply rooted and where they have already given promise of good and abundant fruit.

EDUCATION THE RIGHT OF AMERICANS

But while general education must be recognized as the common outfit of all men and the indisputable right of Americans, special and a more comprehensive education has become more than ever necessary to qualify each citizen for his own peculiar duties and position in life. Our latest civilization and the division of labor have opened new destinies and greater fortunes to mankind by wondrously multiplying the more productive and more remunerative occupations in modern society. New educational wants, keeping pace with a century and a half of marked original research, have been rapidly created, and nowhere perhaps more conspicuously than in the United States. The older colleges and universities have served well and, although the relative value of studies is not settled, with the modifications going on, will serve well to continue the eminence accorded to their system of literary education for those who are to obtain subsequent professional or special training; yet, as the sole reliance and last resort of the whole people, they are not only unequally distributed, but they have been hitherto either unable or unwilling to indulge much curiosity for any explorations outside of moss-covered traditions, and have given too little prominence to such scientific studies as might be most useful to the largest numbers, and strangely because of an obsolete theory that such would be accounted as of some use in practical life. A still more serious objection lies in the fact that the usual college course now costs triple the sum required fifty years ago. This objection is a growing one and should be overcome by larger public patronage or be checked by wholesome competition. The ladders by which boys climb from common schools to a college education should not be placed beyond the reach of the common people.

There is, therefore, a boundless field to be occupied by colleges which can and will give to students nowhere else provided for a greater proportion of time to the learning, which is not only disciplinary, but really valuable for its own sake and helpful as some part of the foundation to a chosen sphere in the affairs of a busy world. The tardy process of self-culture, by which men of mark have sometimes made their way, and which to large numbers, postponed until maturity points to other tasks, is the only process available should be aided at the earliest moment by colleges that will enable a larger portion of those who cannot live without earning their living to bring forth and temper all the advantages of genius and talent with which by nature they have been endowed. Uncomputed numbers, with unknown and uncomputed power, ought not to be suffered so largely to run to waste. We are often sad to think of the greater possibilities which even men not destitute of all fame have barely missed through some slight mischance or shortcoming, but we rarely mourn and ponder over the wide possibilities of the unknown multitude fated to live in the shade without culture or sunshine and who fall at last, like crowded trees in the unvisited forest, with all their latent strength and beauty to slumber forever with the moldering past. Among our people there is much of this valuable timber that a Republic promising so grandly as to race, position, and period cannot afford to leave in the background to utter waste. No; each one is—

> A living thing,
> Produced too slowly ever to decay;
> Of form and aspect too mangnificent
> To be destroyed.

DISCONTENT OF LABORING-MEN

Throughout the world, not excepting our own country, there is a deeply-seated feeling of discontent among laboring-men, not that they must labor, for that they are not unwilling, but that so large a share of labor is wholly rude, unlettered, and so rarely loved or respected. Necessity binds them to an unending routine, often transmitted from one unskilled generation to the next, with no training and no guidance up the steep ascent to a higher plane of more congenial toil and to a better intellectual and social life. They feel that much of the existing intellectual superiority with which they have to compete is not entirely natural, but largely artificial, or only the usual and inevitable advantage bestowed by schools and colleges, which, as they believe, ought to embrace a broader field to which they might furnish a much larger proportion of recruits and by which they could make their leisure hours too precious to be spent in idle dissipation. Something of the legitimate distinction conferred by human approbation, now and then a prize among so many blanks, even workingmen, the most industrious and upright, have a laudable ambition to achieve, or to have their children achieve, as they might, if the gate-ways of toil bore not too generally that fearful motto, "All hope abandon, ye who enter here."

Pent-up discontent in worn and weary hearts is not less explosive than pent-up steam. Among the stern wrestlers with the world there are many striving for the mastery of the bottom knowledge and skill — now more than ever necessary — to do more and better work, and thereby to obtain not only somewhat greater pecuniary rewards but such honors as they may fairly earn; not specially political honors, for they know as well as those who have tasted such that they are but ashes in the mouths of even the most voracious. Let them be qualified for any service, but above the need of political employment. A slight difference of earning-power often determines human happiness or human misery. Some opportunity for improvement, for that training which the wisest of men are eager to obtain and find indispensable must be conceded and tendered to this vast human force, which, if not wisely directed, may be mischievously directed, or, if not directed by those to whom it belongs, it will be directed by demagogues to whom it ought not to belong and whose trade ought not to be encouraged. The ever-active toilers, pursuing their vocations with an absenteeism of the heart, are visibly restless under what seems to them the unescapable servitude of their whole class. Each one harbors Shakspeare's mistaken conviction:

> Thence comes it that my name receives a brand,
> And almost thence my nature is subdued
> To what it works in, like the dyer's hand.

30

An opportunity only is wanted by good men to acquire such qualifications as will afford through diligent effort some hope of creditable eminence even while earning their daily bread or some chance to make laborious employments here and there blaze with a few examples of their own shining lights, and possibly to perpetuate the memory of genius, enterprise, and greatness based upon honest industry and worthy manhood. No one here feels that poverty is a disgrace, but the disgrace arises when there is no effort by industry and education to escape from it. Our Government, the United States, provoking so much attention as it does in the history of the world by its unexampled growth, can afford neither cowardice nor indolence, and should awake to its grave responsibilities by being foremost to respond to educational demands so earnest, so reasonable, and so easily satisfied.

NATIONAL CHARACTER

Some learned sophists have claimed that the National Government is not responsible for the national character, that it has no personality, and no duties as to moral elevation or as to education of any kind; and they have also even averred that education can give no guarantee to republican institutions. This is an extreme enunciation of the doctrine of nihilism or of the governmental do-nothing policy, and it follows that the Government should have no conscience, no sense of honor, and be as unmindful of itself as the thistle-blow, when wafted hither and thither by whatever windy currents chance to prevail, with no power of will to choose whether to grow or to perish by the way-side, and if by chance to grow, with no power to propagate anything but thistles. The denial of governmental personality is the disease of atheism, which covets all the sorrows but none of the joys or hopes of life, and is compatible only with a ruling despotism.

But this doctrine is alien to the fundamental idea of our form of government and wide away from the mile-stones which mark its pathway from the start. It was intended that our Government should have special regard to its own character, should exhibit the foresight and statesmanship of the people, and finally, that it should live and not die. It was never intended that its sole functions should be to punish crime, keep the peace, collect taxes, and put down rebellion, and after that to let the world slide. Though we have freedom, wealth, and courage, and have not character, have not virtue and knowledge, we are nothing—less than sounding brass or a tinkling cymbal.

Long ago that sturdy puritanic republican, John Milton, set forth the doctrine, by no means alien to our own era, that "a commonwealth ought to be but as one huge Christian personage, one mighty growth and stature of an honest man." Again he declared, that "to make the people fitted to govern will be to mend our corrupt and faulty education." The formula of John Locke was that "the end of government was the good of mankind." These were some of the principles that guided the robust founders of our own Republic. In the very heart and core of our institutions all the virtues were to find a home. The people here ordained and established a government for the people; their obedience under it was to be obedience to themselves; and they have always felt and always will feel that to it attaches some responsibility for their own national character and that of their posterity. They strove here in the New World to exalt the race of mankind and to build up model institutions. The good of the governed, in the highest political sense of perennial and perfect health, was the chief object, and that could not be secured by constitutional indifference to their virtue and their moral and intellectual elevation. The national character was not to be exalted by faith without works, but by ideas and sentiments springing from a broader education, which inspire manly efforts, and fill and fructify youthful minds.

The States, it is true, have much to do, but the national Government, superior in its higher nature and wider scope, has more important work to do, having given to each State the guarantee of a republican form of government, a guarantee impossible of fulfillment, as our wisest men have never denied, without general and thorough education. Rich universities abroad, if not at home, possibly with a minimum of outspoken partiality to republican institutions and a Ciceronian contempt for labor, may be supported by the voluntary aid of wealth or by the generosity of men flickering in their exit from the world, but such aid rarely steps forth to lift up the masses, whose education has never been supported by spontaneous and continued charity, and can only be firmly supported under the auspices and direct inspiration of government. The national Government, however, is not here called upon to do much, but its flag should march at the head of the great uplifting procession, and cannot afford to hide away a cheap non-committalism when the dignity and character if not the future glory of its citizens are dependent upon its leadership.

To support the character of our national Government and its honor every citizen willingly stands ready to sacrifice not only property but life itself; and shall it be said for this the Government is to do nothing in return? Are there no reciprocal duties? Stripped of personality, character, dignity, virtue, and moral elevation as a basis of Governmental duties, what would there be left to love, or what that patriotism would rush to defend? What that a Christian would pray might be immortal? The character of a nation clearly does not altogether depend upon its geology, climate, soil, oysters, and terrapins, but very much upon its governmental and educational institutions and upon that growth of manhood which is their ripened product. Great living may be very well, but a great life is far better. No nation is more sensitive to the estimate of others than the American people.

Nor is it enough that "the upper ten thousand" of cities have culture and that each rural village has its luminous ring of the educated minister, lawyer, and doctor. The magic circle should be more broadly expanded and include the whole country instead of scattered microscopic patches. Under a free government the nation acquires rank, not by a few daintily-polished individuals, the bell-wethers of a feeble flock, but by the intelligence and majesty of the entire community; not by one stone superbly cut, but by the proportions and grandeur of the completed edifice.

THE COLORED RACE

But it may be objected that this policy includes all, without regard to race or color; and why not? Are we to praise freedom and shirk the duty of making it better than slavery? Having emancipated a whole race, shall it be said there our duty ends, leaving the race as cumberers of the ground, to live or to wilt and perish, as the case may be? They are members of the American family—forever in sight—and their advancement concerns us all. While

33

swiftly forgetting all they ever knew as slaves, shall they have no opportunity to learn anything as freemen? They are to be the sources of great strength or of great weakness, of glory or shame. "It is impossible," says a recent English writer, "that the knowledge which is power in one race can be absolutely impotent in another." This appears to me to be a truth, pertinent to us and our times, which we shall do well to consider. Surely the American Congress will not emulate the courtly cruelty of the Duke of Alva, that minion of Philip II, who promised to some prisoners life, but, when they petitioned for food, replied that "he would grant them life but no meat." Shall we grant liberty and then refuse it all nourishment?

34. ON THE CONSTITUTIONALITY AND EQUALITY OF FEDERAL AID (1876)[1]

REPRESENTATIVE GILBERT WALKER OF VIRGINIA

The provisions of the bill[2] before the House are plain and explicit. The great object to be accomplished is clearly stated and the means for its attainment succinctly set forth. Its object is the consecration of the revenue derived from the public lands to the education of the whole people. At the close of each fiscal year the Secretary of the Interior is directed to certify the net amount of the proceeds of the public lands for that year to the Secretary of the Treasury, who shall within one month thereafter apportion the same among the several States and Territories and the District of Columbia on the basis of population, to be applied by the local authorities of such States, Territories, and District, in accordance with their local laws, to the education of all the inhabitants thereof between the ages of five and sixteen years. For the first five years the whole amount of such net proceeds is to be thus apportioned; for the succeeding five years, one-half the other half, and after ten years the whole amount, to be invested in United States bonds, only the interest on which shall be thus apportioned, and the investments thus made to remain as a perpetual fund for the benefit of free education throughout our entire country. During the first ten years the apportionments are to be made on the basis of illiteracy, but forever afterward on that of the whole population. While the bill leaves it optional with each State to accept or reject its distributive share, yet when once accepted it must be faithfully and honestly applied to the purposes therein indicated under the penalty of forfeiting all right to any other apportionments until full

---

[1]*Congressional Record*, 44th Cong., 1st sess., 4:4 (May 29, 1876), pp. 3368–71.
[2]House Bill No. 748 provided that proceeds from the sale of public lands would be used to promote education.

35

compliance be made with the conditions prescribed. No interference with the existing laws for the disposition of the public lands is contemplated, and the percentages reserved to certain States remain undisturbed. These are substantially the main provisions of the bill under consideration, and I trust they may meet with the cordial approbation of every member of this House. No patent is claimed for them as for an original discovery, for the principal ideas involved have been brought to the attention of Congress and the country at different times and in various forms during almost the entire period of our national existence.

While with consummate wisdom and foresight the fathers laid the foundations of the Republic upon the broad and enduring principles of civil and religious liberty, they also fully comprehended the truth that the perpetuity of the superstructure they reared depended "upon the virtue and intelligence of the people." Amid the throes of the Revolution, and while freedom yet hung tremblingly in the balance, a committee of the Virginia Legislature, composed of Thomas Jefferson, Edmund Pendleton, and George Wythe, reported a bill to establish "a complete public free-school system to be supported by taxation." A few years later, in the justly celebrated ordinance of 1787, the National Government declared that—"Religion, morality, and knowledge being necessary to good government and the happiness of mankind, schools and other means of education shall forever be encouraged."

And two years earlier the Congress, in the ordinance for ascertaining the mode of disposing of the western lands belonging to the Government, expressly provided that—"There shall be reserved the lot No. 16 of every township for the maintenance of public schools within said township."

Thus early, in advance even of the formation of the Constitution, was inaugurated that profound and liberal policy which has been uniformly and unvaryingly pursued in the organization of new States from the public domain. Grants of public lands have also been made to some of the other States, and in 1862 there was apportioned to all the States an amount equal to thirty thousand acres for each of their Senators and Representatives respectively in Congress, for the purpose of establishing agricultural and mechanical colleges. In fact, more than forty-seven different acts of

Congress appropriating nearly eighty millions of acres of the public lands for educational purposes not only attest the wisdom and uniform liberality of the people, as expressed through their governmental agents, but also conclusively and forever silences all question as to the constitutional power of Congress in the premises.

"The Congress shall have power to dispose of and make all needful rules and regulations respecting the territory or other property belonging to the United States," is the language of the Federal Constitution, and it would seem to be sufficiently clear and comprehensive to warrant the action proposed by the bill under consideration, without resort even to contemporaneous and subsequent uniform construction. . . .

Sir, this Government has never owned a foot of soil that she did not hold for the common use and benefit of all her people. And how has this trust been administered? Has equal and exact justice been meted out to all the members of the Union? Has each received its just and equal proportion of this common fund of all or of the benefits flowing therefrom? In fact, until 1862, has one of the original grantors or one of the original thirteen States received one particle of direct benefit from this great trust fund in accordance with the trust, except generally, from the amounts paid into the Federal Treasury? Yet nearly eighty millions of acres have been given to the new States and Territories for educational purposes and 222,469,337 acres to railroads and for other purposes within the same limits. Really the enormous amount of 301,796,139 acres of the public domain, the common treasure of the whole Union, has been disposed of in vioation [sic] of the nation's trust.

But, sir, I am not here to sing jeremiads over the past, nor yet to harshly criticise the action of Congress in making donations of the public lands to the new States and Territories for educational purposes. The grand results which these donations have enabled the new States to achieve in the cause of education, the magnificent systems of public schools which most of them have thus been enabled to establish, palliate at least, if they do not entirely excuse, the wrong done the older States. Congress did right in making these donations, and its only error consisted in its failure to make equally liberal provision for the older States. This injustice, however, has not been suffered to pass unnoticed. Repeated efforts to have this equity of the older States suitably recognized have from time to time been made, and these efforts will continue to be made until justice shall finally triumph. . . .

But not until 1862, amid the terrible agony of internecine war, was this undoubted equity of the older States fully and fairly recognized. While the law of 1862 making an appropriation of public lands for the establishment of agricultural and mechanical colleges enforced the principle for which I am contending, yet it falls far short of the necessities of the times and the unquestioned duty of the Government. It is limited in scope and partial in the benefits conferred. Those only who seek a technical education can derive any substantial aid from it, while in many instances the amount appropriated is too meager to afford the necessary facilities for even this limited instruction. What we need, and what we must have, is the appropriation of the entire proceeds of the public lands to the education of the whole people. Thus only can the Government best discharge its trusteeship of the public lands, and thus only can be conferred "the greatest good upon the greatest number."

To what higher, nobler, or more beneficial purpose could the public domain be devoted than the education, mental and moral elevation of the people? Are not the proceeds of the public lands the common heritage of all the people? Do they not in this respect constitute a peculiar and distinctive fund, differing widely from that received from tariffs and taxation, or any other source, in that they are derived from the common property of all the people instead of from that of the few?

Now, sir, having demonstrated, I trust satisfactorily, not only the constitutionality of this bill, but also that it is grounded upon unquestioned equity, an equity already fully recognized and never in fact denied, I now propose to briefly discuss the necessities which imperatively demand its passage. And, sir, I must confess that I enter upon this discussion with feelings of the profoundest regret. Yes; regret at the existence of terrible and inexorable facts, which have only to be known to fully demonstrate the necessities of our situation.

The census of 1870 disclosed a perfectly appalling amount of illiteracy in this country. About one-fifth of our population or nearly 6,000,000 of our people over ten years of age, could neither read nor write. Of the 8,000,000 of voters who mold our institutions and control our social and political destinies, over 1,600,000 could not even read the ballots they cast. And of the 12,055,443 children of school-age, that is, between the ages of five and eighteen, 5,458,977 or nearly one-half, were growing up in the depths of ignorance, without any school advantages whatever. This is the fearful picture presented by the census of 1870. But a far better and to the ordinary mind a more comprehensive picture was prepared by the Superintendent of the Census, and I trust that every member of this House will take immediate occasion to examine it. It consists of a map of the United States so colored and shaded as to exhibit the relative degree of intelligence of every locality of our country. The higher state of intelligence is naturally illustrated by the lighter color, and this is gradually shaded off into the darkness of ignorance. Sir, there is too much color upon that map, too many intensely dark spots. Promptly pass this bill, however, and our next census will present a more radiant picture, with the darkness gradually but surely receding before the advancing light.

An examination of this map, as well as of the census tables of 1870, discloses the fact that the somber shading of illiteracy obtains at the South in a far greater degree than at the North. While this is readily explainable, and upon grounds which substantially free the South from the charge of neglect or want of appreciation of the inestimable benefits of education, yet the fact exists and cannot be ignored. During the four years of civil war and for several years thereafter, the educational institutions of the South were almost universally closed. While the war prevailed the young men were in the field, and the whole country was too unsettled for the maintenance, to any considerable extent of schools, and after the war poverty, interposed for years insuperable obstacles to educational pusuits. Added to this was the emancipation of the colored race, but few of which had ever enjoyed educational facilities. These people constituted over five-twelfths of the entire population of the eleven southern States in 1870; or, to be more accurate, of a total population of 9,487,386 the colored people numbers 3,939,032. This mass of ignorance was suddenly raised to the dignity and responsibility of citizenship, in the midst of their impoverished and largely bankrupt former owners, with no means of their own and without any provision whatever being made for their education. Of the wisdom, or rather unwisdom of this action, I had occasion some years ago to speak, and I repeat here what I then said as expressive of my present views:

"The war resulted in the emancipation of the negro; but no sooner had the sword been sheathed than the strife was transferred to the forum, and days and months, ay, even years, were spent in efforts to cloth the freedman with rights he could not understand and load him with responsibilities which he was unable to comprehend. Statute after statute was enacted, and the fundamental law of the nation itself repeatedly amended to establish the civil and political rights of the negro; but where in the long catalogue of legislation can be found any provision for his education and elevation even to a partial comprehension of the duties and responsibilities which these rights impose? Why did not the mental and moral necessities of these 'wards of the nation' excite the same paternal solicitude as did their political condition? I shall not pause here, nor is it germane to my present purpose, to answer this very natural inquiry. The facts with which we have alone to deal at the present moment are that, although the negro was emancipated from physical slavery, he was left bound in the more terrible chains of universal ignorance; and that, while the nation invested him with the glorious rights and privileges of American citizenship, it not only failed to make any provision for investing him with a knowledge of the high duties and responsibilities which that citizenship imposes, but left him in the depths of poverty and ignorance, to be educated, if educated at all, by the white people of those States, whom the war had so utterly impoverished that they were unable to educate even themselves.

"That this was unwise, unjust, and impolitic, needs no words from me to demonstrate. In my opinion the Government should not only have provided the means for the education of these new suffragans, but it should have gone further, and aided the people of the South to fulfill this high and holy duty to themselves.

"If it be true that one portion of the body-politic cannot suffer in its mental, moral, or physical condition without injury, more or less, to the whole, and if intelligence and virtue be necessary and desirable in the individual citizen of a republic, then the education of the whole people becomes a matter of public interest and

40

national concern. I am, however, no advocate of a governmental system of education except by the States; but I do advocate the extension to all of the States the policy which has uniformly obtained in the organization of new States. The public lands are the common property of the whole people of the Union, held by it in trust for their benefit and behoof, and if there be reason and sound statesmanship in reserving a portion of this property for educational purposes in the sparsely populated but prosperous new States, do not the same reason and statesmanship in a far higher degree dictate the appropriation of a portion of this property to the education of the larger and poorer populations of the older States of the South?

"But I do not go to the length of urging even this very just and correct view of the subject, based though it may be upon the soundest and most substantial and patriotic reasoning. All I seek and all I demand is equality with all the other States of the Republic in this as in all other respects. I merely advocate the performance of what I believe to be a solemn and imperative duty of the Federal Government to the black race and to the people of the whole country, and that duty consists in appropriating the entire proceeds derived from the sales of the public lands to educational purposes. . . ."

I am aware, sir, that it may be urged that the basis upon which the apportionments are to be made under this bill for the first ten years is an invasion of that very equity the existence of which I have been endeavoring to establish, because of the fact that, there being a greater amount of illiteracy at the South than at the North, the Southern States will receive a larger proportion of the fund than the Northern. But suppose this in a measure to be true, is it not of the highest moment to place this fund where it is most needed and "where it will do the most good?" Can the new States, that have already been so richly endowed in violation of this equity, complain and will the wealthy Northern States of the original thirteen object? I apprehend not. All must admit that ignorance is such a curse, wherever existing in the country, that it becomes the common interest of all to utterly obliterate it. The disease which affects one portion of the body-politic casts its baleful influence over the whole.

The pressing need of the South to-day is for educational aid.

She has not yet recuperated from the terrible devastations and losses of the war, and while most of the States have inaugurated and maintained good systems of free schools, and have largely reduced the sum total of illiteracy in their midst, yet their means are still too limited and the burdens too great for them to maintain their schools for a sufficient period in each year. They need assistance now. Educate the present generation, and those which succeed it will take care of themselves. Once lift the dark pall of ignorance which overshadows the land and the light of universal intelligence will never again be obscured. The history of education in this country shows that it has never turned backward. Its course has been uniformly upward and onward, constantly increasing in strength and expanding in beneficence. The constitution of the human mind itself is such that the acquisition of knowledge begets a thirst for more, and the cultivation and enlargement of its faculties urges it forward to new attainments and new conquests. Has not intelligence ever been the parent of prosperity and the handmaid of virtue? Does not all history teach that a people's productive power and force depends upon its degree of advancement in knowledge, and that crime everywhere recedes as education advances? A modern writer, thoroughly versed in all that appertains to the subject, declares that—

"Ignorance is a source of crime. It operates in various ways: first, to expose men to it and then to prepare them for it. The uncultivated mind is weakened by non-use. For lack of ideas it is often left to the suggestions of the animal appetites, with their debasing and corrupting tendencies. In a land of books and schools ignorance is not consistent with self-respect and manliness. *** Knowing how to read is two-thirds as favorable to honesty as not knowing."

But, sir, I will not detain the House with any further discussion of this branch of the subject, interesting though it be to me; nor is it necessary. The intelligent members of this honorable body stand in need of no arguments to demonstrate the absolute necessity for the education of all the people, who, in a Government like ours, are at once the subjects and the sovereigns, the creators of our institutions as well as the basis upon which they rest. If I shall be able to awaken them to renewed interest in the great cause of free education and to a more full and complete

realization of their duties and responsibilities in this behalf, I shall
have accomplished much that I desire and more perhaps than I had
a right to anticipate. My own convictions upon this subject are so
profound and my desire for success so intense that I trust if my
zeal appear excessive it will be pardoned, though my discretion be
not applauded. . . .

About one hundred years ago the public lands were ceded to
the nation to aid in the preservation of its plighted faith and domestic concord but their mission in this behalf has been accomplished. Our public credit no longer requires their assistance, and
the Union which their cession served to consummate no longer
contains discordant States to be harmonized by their surrender.
Another mission, however, awaits them, and that is to aid in the
elevation of the people to a higher plane of mental and moral
existence. It is our high privilege to inaugurate this exalted mission by the passage of this bill. Rejoicing in the triumphant close
of the first century of the Republic, and standing upon the threshold of the second, with a country united and harmonized, "re-
generated and disenthralled," let us celebrate the outgoing of the
former and the incoming of the latter by a declaration unequaled
in importance save by that which spoke the nation into existence
on July 4, 1776.

Mr. Chairman, in my remarks to-day I have used the words
nation and republic, nationality and people indiscriminately, or as
convertible terms. Although often so used, it is manifestly erroneous. A people are not necessarily a nation, nor a nation a republic, and all three may exist without nationality. By virtue of the
Constitution, the American people constitute a republic, and for
the purposes of administration, as well as in outward form, the
republic is a nation; but nationality springs from other causes. Our
Constitution, with all of its fifteen amendments, never has and
never will make us a nation by the full sense of that term. That
instrument is but the "sovereign law, the States' collected
will. . . ."

Written constitutions, no matter how wisely framed, never yet
made a nation. The real nation lies beyond and beneath these
artificial crusts, and is *the people*. "These constitute the state."
Did England become a nation by virtue of a written constitution?
Has she indeed ever had any? No, sir. Her great fundamental law

is yet unwritten, and, like the nationality of her people, is the outgrowth of centuries of progressive civilization. So will it be with our nationality. As in the physical kingdom, the processes of enduring development are slow and gradual. So in the realm of politics. Nationality is not the product of a day or generation, but rather the slow and steady growth of time and auxiliary causes. A nation without nationality is simply the form without the substance, the skeleton without the flesh and blood. We possess the form, but the development of the substance into completed fulness will be the work of generations of intelligent, educated freemen. Consider, too, that fully one-fourth of our voting population to-day are the offspring of other nationalities, differing widely from our ideal and from each other. The vast and manifold increment to our population, of which they are the index, it is to be hoped will increase in the future. But how is it to be molded and fashioned into and imbued with American nationality? What is the common solvent of all these various elements of our population? Is there any other save that great nursery of freemen, the free public school?

Sir, the fathers, with a wisdom amounting almost to prescience, formed our Government for *perpetuity*. They omitted no principle necessary to its preservation, and they included none which, properly administered, could work its destruction. The absorption of the powers and functions of the States by the Federal Government was as foreign to their design as the nullification or repudiation of the Federal authority by the individual action of the States, for the triumph of either involved the destruction of the Union. To insure the stability of that which they builded so well they early made provision for encouragement to the education of the people. They foresaw that ignorance was one of the gravest dangers that menaced the future of the Republic. They opened wide the doors to the "oppressed of all nations" and bade them welcome to the full enjoyment of American citizenship and the freedom of individual thought and action guaranteed by our laws, fundamental and statutory. How wisely and well they planned is attested by a century of national existence and by a development in wealth, population, and mental activity unexampled in the world's history.

But, sir, if we but fulfill the high duty devolved upon us, our past, however brilliant it may have been, will be excelled by a grander future. I confess to a strong and conscientious belief in what is styled "manifest destiny." It is manifest to my mind that the future destiny of this nation points unerringly to the gradual expansion of its limits until the entire continent shall have been embraced within its boundaries. And I believe that upon this same continent there is to be formed and molded a new, distinctive, well-defined, and grand American nationality. It is true that our country is peopled by all the numerous offshoots of the Caucasian race, differing widely in language, habits, and education; but time and concurring circumstances — above all popular education — will gradually melt together and mold these diverse elements into one united, harmonious, homogeneous people, surpassing all of the great peoples that have preceded them in their mental, moral, and physical development, and in the greatness and grandeur of their achievements. This is our country's manifest destiny. Let us here and now contribute our proportion to its development.

CHAPTER 15

EDUCATING THE FREEDMEN

Education and work are the levers to uplift a people.

W. E. B. DuBois, 1903

35. Constitutional Provisions for Education in the South (1864–1898)[1]

CONSTITUTION OF LOUISIANA, 1864

ARTICLE 141. The legislature shall provide for the education of all children of the State, between the ages of six and eighteen years, by maintenance of free public schools by taxation or otherwise.

CONSTITUTION OF LOUISIANA, 1868

ARTICLE 135. The general assembly shall establish at least one free public school in every parish throughout the State, and shall provide for its support by taxation or otherwise. All children of this State between the years of six and twenty-one shall be admitted to the public schools or other institutions of learning sustained or established by the State in common, without distinction of race, color, or previous condition. There shall be no separate schools or institutions of learning established exclusively for any race by the State of Louisiana.

CONSTITUTION OF LOUISIANA, 1879

ARTICLE 224. There shall be free public schools established by the General Assembly throughout the State for the education of all children of the State between the ages of six and eighteen years; and the General Assembly shall provide for their establishment, maintenence and support by taxation or

---

[1]Francis N. Thorpe, (Ed.), *The Federal and State Constitutions, Colonial Charters, and Other Organic Laws of the States, Territories, and Colonies Now or Heretofore Forming the United States* (Washington: U.S. GPO, 1909). III, 1446, 1465, 1508, 1575–76; V, 2817, 2838; VI, 3300–01, 3338–39, 3469.

otherwise. And all moneys so raised, except the poll tax, shall be distributed to each parish in proportion to the number of children between the ages of six and eighteen years.

CONSTITUTION OF LOUISIANA, 1898

ARTICLE 248. There shall be free public schools for the white and colored races, separately established by the General Assembly, throughout the State, for the education of all the children of the State between the ages of six and eighteen years; provided, that where kindergarten schools exist, children between the ages of four and six may be admitted into said schools. All funds raised by the State for the support of public schools, except the poll tax, shall be distributed to each parish in proportion to the number of children therein between the ages of six and eighteen years. The General Assembly, at its next session shall provide for the enumeration of educable children.

✦ ✦ ✦

CONSTITUTION OF NORTH CAROLINA, 1868

ARTICLE IX, SEC. 1. Religion, morality, and knowledge being necessary to good government and happiness of mankind, schools and the means of education shall forever be encouraged.
SEC. 2. The general assembly, at its first session under this constitution, shall provide, by taxation and otherwise, for a general and uniform system of public schools, wherein tuition shall be free of charge to all the children of the state between the ages of six and twenty-one years.

CONSTITUTION OF NORTH CAROLINA, 1876

ARTICLE IX, SEC. 1. Religion, morality and knowledge being necessary to good government and the happiness of mankind, schools and the means of education shall forever be encouraged.

SEC. 2. The General Assembly, at its first session under this Constitution, shall provide by taxation and otherwise for a general and uniform system of public schools, wherein tuition shall be free of charge to all the children of the State between the ages of six and twenty-one years. And the children of the white race and the children of the colored race shall be taught in separate public schools; but there shall be no discrimination in favor of or to the prejudice of either race.

✧　✧　✧

CONSTITUTION OF SOUTH CAROLINA, 1868

ARTICLE X, SEC. 3. The general assembly shall, as soon as practicable after the adoption of this constitution, provide for a liberal and uniform system of free public schools throughout the State, and shall also make provision for the division of the State into suitable school districts. There shall be kept open, at least six months in each year, one or more schools in each school district.

ARTICLE X, SEC. 10. All the public schools, colleges, and universities of this State, supported in whole or in part by the public funds, shall be free and open to all the children and youths of the State, without regard to race or color.

CONSTITUTION OF SOUTH CAROLINA, 1895

ARTICLE XI, SEC. 5. The General Assembly shall provide for a liberal system of free public schools for all children between the ages of six and twenty-one years, and for the division of the Counties into suitable school districts, as compact in form as practicable, having regard to natural boundaries, and not to exceed forty-nine nor be less than nine square miles in area. . . .

ARTICLE XI, SEC. 7. Separate schools shall be provided for children of the white and colored races, and no child of either race shall ever be permitted to attend a school provided for children of the other race.

✧　✧　✧

CONSTITUTION OF TENNESSEE, 1870

ARTICLE XI, SEC. 12. Education to be cherished; common school fund; poll tax; whites and negroes; colleges, etc., rights of.

Knowledge, learning, and virtue, being essential to the preservation of republican institutions, and the diffusion of the opportunities and advantages of education throughout the different portions of the State, being highly conducive to the promotion of this end, it shall be the duty of the General Assembly, in all future periods of this government, to cherish literature and science. And the fund called the common school fund, and all the lands and proceeds thereof, dividends, stocks, and other property of every description whatever, heretofore by law appropriated, by the General Assembly of this State for the use of common schools, and all such as shall hereafter be appropriated, shall remain a perpetual fund, the principal of which shall never be diminished by legislative appropriations; and the interest thereof shall be inviolably appropriated to the support and encouragement of common schools throughout the State, and for the equal benefit of all the people thereof; and no law shall be made authorizing said fund or any part thereof to be diverted to any other use than the support and encouragement of common schools. The State taxes derived hereafter from polls shall be appropriated to educational purposes, in such manner as the General Assembly shall, from time to time, direct by law. No school established or aided under this section shall allow white and negro children to be received as scholars together in the same school. The above provisions shall not prevent the Legislature from carrying into effect any laws that have been passed in favor of the colleges, universities, or academies, or from authorizing heirs or distributees to receive and enjoy escheated property under such laws as shall be passed from time to time.

36. DIFFICULTIES, COMPLICATIONS, AND LIMITATIONS CONNECTED WITH THE EDUCATION OF THE NEGRO (1895)[1]

J. L. M. CURRY

Civilization certainly, Christianity probably, has encountered no problem which surpasses in magnitude or complexity the Negro problem. For its solution political remedies, very drastic, have been tried, but have failed utterly. Educational agencies have been very beneficial as a stimulus to self-government and are increasingly hopeful and worthy of wider application, but they do not cure social diseases, moral ills. Much has been written of evolution of man, of human society; and history shows marvellous progress in some races, in some countries, in the bettering of habits and institutions, but his progress is not found, in any equal degree, in the negro race in his native land. What has occured in the United States has been from external causes. Usually, human development has come from voluntary energy, from self-evolved organizations of higher and higher efficiency, from conditions which are principally the handiwork of man himself. With the negro, whatever progress has marked his life as a race in this country has come from without. The great ethical and political revolutions of enlightened nations, through the efforts of successive generations, have not been seen in his history.

---

[1]J. L. M. Curry, *Difficulties, Complications, and Limitations Connected with the Education of the Negro* (Baltimore, 1895), pp. 5–23. Curry a member of the southern aristocracy, was elected to Congress by Alabama in 1856, and later served in the Confederate government. Following the war he devoted himself to religious and educational work in the South, serving first as president of a denominational college in Alabama. In 1881 he became the General Agent for the Peabody Fund and, in 1890, for the John Slater Fund. Though an ardent advocate of states' rights, he supported the Blair Bill which provided for federal aid for education because he saw it as a means of solving the educational problems of the South and of improving racial relations.

When on March 4, 1882, our large-hearted and broadminded Founder [Slater] established this Trust, he had a noble end in view. For near thirteen years the Trustees have kept the object steadily before them, with varying results. Expectations have not always been realized. If any want of highest success has attended our efforts, this is not an uncompanioned experience. As was to have been foreseen, in working out a novel and great problem, difficulties have arisen. Some are inherent and pertain to the education of the negro, however and by whomsoever undertaken, and some are peculiar to the Trust. Some are remedial. In this, as in all other experiments, it is better to ascertain and comprehend the difficulties so as to adopt and adjust the proper measures for displacing or overcoming them. A general needs to know the strength and character of the opposing force. A physician cannot prescribe intelligently until he knows the condition of his patient.

The income of the Fund is limited in amount, and the means of accomplishing "the general object" of the Trust are indicated in Mr. Slater's letter and conversations and by the repeatedly declared policy of the Board—as teacher training and industrial training. He specified "the training of teachers from among the people requiring to be taught and the 'encouragement of such institutions as are most effectually useful in promoting this training of teachers.'" No one, in the least degree familiar with the subject, can deny or doubt that the essential need of the race is a higher and better qualified class of teachers. The Fund does not establish nor control schools, nor appoint teachers. It co-operates with schools established by States, by religious denominations and by individuals. Mr. Slater did not purpose "to bestow charity upon the destitute, to encourage a few exceptional individuals, to build churches, school-houses or asylums." Aided schools may accept money to carry out the specific purposes of the Trust, but they often have other and prescribed objects, and hence what the Trustees seek is naturally, perhaps unavoidably, subordinated to what are the predetermined and unchangeable ends of some of these schools.

The most obvious hindrance in the way of the education of the negro has so often been presented and discussed—his origin, history, environments—that it seems superfluous to treat it anew. His political status, sudden and unparalleled, complicated by antecedent condition, excited false hopes and encouraged the notion of reaching *per saltum,* without the use of the agencies of time, labor, industry, discipline, what the dominant race had attained after centuries of toil and trial and sacrifice. Education, property, habits of thrift and self-control, higher achievements of civilization, are not extemporized nor created by magic or legislation. Behind the Caucasian lie centuries of the educating, uplifting influence of civilization, of the institutions of family, society, the Churches, the State, and the salutary effects of heredity. Behind the negro are centuries of ignorance, barbarism, slavery, superstition, idolatry, fetichism, and the transmissible consequences of heredity. . . .

Much of the aid lavished upon the negro has been misapplied charity, and like much other alms-giving hurtful to the recipient. Northern philanthropy, "disastrously kind," has often responded with liberality to appeals worse than worthless. Vagabond mendicants have been pampered; schools which were established without any serious need of them have been helped; public school systems, upon which the great mass of children, white and colored, must rely for their education, have been underrated and injured, and schools, of real merit and doing good work, which deserve confidence and contributions, have had assistance, legitimately their due, diverted into improper channels. Reluctantly and by constraint of conscience, this matter is mentioned and this voice of protest and warning raised. Dr. A. D. Mayo, of Boston, an astute and thoughtful observer, a tried friend of the black man, an eloquent advocate of his elevation, who for fifteen years has traversed the South in the interests of universal education, than whom no one has a better acquaintance with the schools of that section, bears cogent and trustworthy testimony, to which I give my emphatic endorsement:

"It is high time that our heedless, undiscriminating, all-outdoors habit of giving money and supplies to the great invading army of southern solicitors should come to an end. Whatever of good has come from it is of the same nature as the habit of miscellaneous alms giving, which our system of associated charities is everywhere working to break up. It is high time that we understood that the one agency on which the negroes and nine-tenths of the white people in the South must rely for elementary instruction and training is the American common school. The attempt to educate 2,000,000 of colored and 3,000,000 of white American children in the South by passing around the hat in the North; sending driblets of money and barrels of supplies to encourage anybody and everybody to open a little useless private school; to draw on our Protestant Sunday schools in the North to build up among these people the church parochial system of elementary schools, which the clergy of these churches are denouncing; all this, and a great deal more that is still going on among us, with of course the usual exceptions, has had its day and done its work. The only reliable method of directly helping the elementary department of southern education is that our churches and benevolent people put themselves in touch with the common school authorities in all the dark places, urging even their poorer people to do more, as they can do more, than at present. The thousand dollars from Boston that keeps alive a little private or denominational school in a southern neighborhood, if properly applied would give two additional months, better teaching and better housing to all the children, and unite their people as in no other way. Let the great northern schools in the South established for the negroes be reasonably endowed and worked in cooperation with the public school system of the State, with the idea that in due time they will all pass into the hands of the southern people, each dependent on its own constituency for its permanent support. I believe, in many instances, it would be the best policy to endow or aid southern schools that have grown up at home and have established themselves in the confidence of the people. While more money should every year be given in the North for southern education, it should not be scattered abroad, but concentrated on strategic points for the uplifting of both races."

* * *

The negro occupies an incongruous position in our country. Under military necessity slaves were emancipated. . . . Partisanship and an altruistic sentiment led to favoritism, to civic equality, and to bringing the negroes, for the first time in their history, and without any previous preparation, "into the rivalry of life on an equal footing of opportunity." The whole country has suffered in its material development from the hazardous experiment. The South, as a constituent portion of the Union, is a diseased limb on the body, is largely uncultivated, neglected, unproductive. Farming, with the low prices of products, yields little remunerative return on labor or on money invested, and, except in narrow localities and where "trucking" obtains, it is not improving agriculturally, or, if so, too slowly and locally to awaken any hopes of early or great recovery. Crippled, disheartened by the presence of a people, not much inferior in numbers, of equal civil rights, and slowly capable of equal mental development or of taking on the habits of advanced civilization, the white people of the South are deprived of any considerable increase of numbers from immigration and any large demand for small freeholds, and are largely dependent on ignorant, undisciplined, uninventive, inefficient, unambitious labor. Intercourse between the Slavs and the tribes of the Ural-Altaic stock, fusion of ethnic elements, has not resulted in deterioration, but has produced an apparently homogeneous people, possessing a common consciousness. That the two diverse races now in the South can ever perfectly harmonize, while occupying the same territory, no one competent to form an opinion believes. . . . That the presence, in the same country, of two distinctly marked races, having the same rights and privileges, of unequal capacities of development—one long habituated to servitude, deprived of all power of initiative, of all high ideal, without patriotism beyond a mere weak attachment—is a blessing, is too absurd a proposition for serious consideration. Whether the great resources of the South are not destined, under existing conditions, to remain only partially developed, and whether agriculture is not doomed to barrenness of results, are economic and political questions alien to this discussion.

As Trustees of the Slater Fund, we are confined to the duty of educating the lately emancipated race. In *Occasional Papers*, No. 3, the history of education since 1860, as derived from the most authentic sources, was presented with care and fulness. "The great work of educating the negroes is carried on mainly by the public schools of the Southern States, supported by funds raised by public taxation, and managed and controlled by public school officers. The work is too great to be attemptd by any other agency, unless by the National Government; the field is too extensive, the officers too numerous, the cost too burdensome. (*Bureau of Education Report*, 1891–92, p. 867). The American Congress deliberately and repeatedly refused aid for the prevention or removal of illiteracy, and upon the impoverished South the burden and the duty were devolved. Bravely and with heroic self-sacrifice have they sought to fulfil the obligation. . . .

In 1893–94 there were 2,702,410 negro children of school age—from five to eighteen years—of whom 52.72 per cent., or 1,424,710 were enrolled as pupils. Excluding Maryland, Kentucky and Missouri, the receipts from State and local taxation for schools in the South were $14,297,569. It should be borne in mind that there are fewer taxpayers in the South, in proportion to population generally and to school population especially, than in any other part of the United States. In the South Central States there are only 65.9 adult males to 100 children, while in the Western Division there are 156.7. In South Carolina, 37 out of every 100 are of school age; in Montana, only 18 out of 100. Consider, also, that in the South a large proportion of the comparatively few adults are negroes with a minimum of property. Consider, further, that the number of adult males to each 100 children in New Hampshire, Massachusetts and Connecticut is twice as great as in North Carolina, South Carolina, Georgia, Alabama and Mississippi. In view of such and other equally surprising facts, it is a matter of national satisfaction that free education has made such progress in the South.

It is lamentable, after all the provision which has been made, that the schools are kept open for such a short period, that so many teachers are incompetent, and that such a small proportion of persons of school age attend the schools. This does not apply solely to the colored children or to the Southern States. For the whole country the average number of days attended is only 89 for each pupil, when the proper school year should count about 200. While the enrollment and average attendance have increased, "what the people get on an average is about one-half an elementary education, and no State is now giving an education in all its schools that is equal to seven years per inhabitant for the rising generation. Some states are giving less than three years of 200 days each." It is an obligation of patriotism to support and improve these State-managed schools, because they are among the best teachers of the duties of citizenship and the most potent agency for moulding and unifying and binding heterogeneous elements of nationality into compactness, unity and homogeneity. We must keep them efficient if we wish them to retain public confidence. . . .

Whatever may be the discouragements and difficulties, and however insufficient may be the school attendance, it is a cheering fact that the schools for the negroes do not encounter the prejudices which were too common a few years ago. In fact, there may almost be said to be coming a time when soon there will be a sustaining public opinion. The struggle of man to throw off fetters and rise into true manhood and save souls from bondage is a most instructive and thrilling spectacle, awakening sympathetic enthusiasm on the part of all who love what is noble. From a magazine for November, I quote what a teacher says: "We are engaged in a life and death struggle to secure protection of life and property against mob violence and lynch law." An official paper of a strong religious organization charges that "incendiary fires and acts of vandalism were instigated *solely* by prejudice against the education of the negroes. If those who go South to teach are obliged to take their lives in their hands and to live in constant fear of personal violence, it will render work, already difficult, exceedingly trying."

CONCLUSIONS

I.

It follows that in addition to thorough and intelligent training in the discipline of character and virtue, there should be given rigid and continuous attention to domestic and social life, to the refinements and comforts and economies of home.

II.

Taught in the economies of wise consumption, the race should be trained to acquire habits of thrift, of saving earnings, of avoiding waste, of accumulating property, of having a stake in good government, in progressive civilization.

III.

Besides the rudiments of a good and useful education, there is imperative need of manual training, of the proper cultivation of those faculties or mental qualities of observation, of aiming at and reaching a successful end, and of such facility and skill in tools, in practical industries, as will ensure remunerative employment and give the power which comes from intelligent work.

IV.

Clearer a..d juster ideas of education, moral and intellectual, obtained in cleaner home life and through respected and capable teachers in schools and churches. Ultimate and only sure reliance for the education of the race is to be found in the public schools, organized, controlled, and liberally supported by the State.

V.

Between the races occupying the same territory, possessing under the law equal civil rights and privileges, speculative and unattainable standards should be avoided, and questions should be met as they arise, not by Utopian and partial solutions, but by the impartial application of the tests of justice, right, honor, humanity and Christianity.

37. INDUSTRIAL EDUCATION FOR THE NEGRO (1903)[1]

BOOKER T. WASHINGTON

One of the most fundamental and far-reaching deeds that has been accomplished during the last quarter of a century has been that by which the Negro has been helped to find himself and to learn the secrets of civilization—to learn that there are a few simple, cardinal principles upon which a race must start its upward course, unless it would fail, and its last estate be worse than its first.

It has been necessary for the Negro to learn the difference between being worked and working—to learn that being worked meant degradation, while working means civilization; that all forms of labor are honorable, and all forms of idleness disgraceful. It has been necessary for him to learn that all races that have got upon their feet have done so largely by laying an economic foundation, and, in general, by beginning in a proper cultivation and ownership of the soil.

Forty years ago my race emerged from slavery into freedom. If, in too many cases, the Negro race began development at the wrong end, it was largely because neither white nor black properly understood the case. Nor is it any wonder that this was so, for never before in the history of the world had just such a problem been presented as that of the two races at the coming of freedom in this country.

For two hundred and fifty years, I believe the way for the redemption of the Negro was being prepared through industrial development. Through all those years the Southern white man did business with the Negro in a way that no one else has done business with him. In most cases if a Southern white man wanted a

[1]*The Negro Problem* (New York: James Pratt, 1903), pp. 9–29.

house built he consulted a Negro mechanic about the plan and about the actual building of the structure. If he wanted a suit of clothes made he went to a Negro tailor, and for shoes he went to a shoemaker of the same race. In a certain way every slave plantation in the South was an industrial school. On these plantations young colored men and women were constantly being trained not only as farmers but as carpenters, blacksmiths, wheelwrights, brick masons, engineers, cooks, laundresses, sewing women and housekeepers.

I do not mean in any way to apologize for the curse of slavery, which was a curse to both races; but in what I say about industrial training in slavery I am simply stating facts. This training was crude, and was given for selfish purposes. It did not answer the highest ends, because there was an absence of mental training in connection with the training of the hand. To a large degree, though, this business contact with the Southern white man, and the industrial training on the plantations, left the Negro at the close of the war in possession of nearly all the common and skilled labor in the South. The industries that gave the South its power, prominence and wealth prior to the Civil War were mainly the raising of cotton, sugar cane, rice and tobacco. Before the way could be prepared for the proper growing and marketing of these crops forests had to be cleared, houses to be built, public roads and railroads constructed. In all these works the Negro did most of the heavy work. In the planting, cultivating and marketing of the crops not only was the Negro the chief dependence, but in the manufacture of tobacco he became a skilled and proficient workman, and in this, up to the present time, in the South, holds the lead in the large tobacco manufactories.

In most of the industries, though, what happened? For nearly twenty years after the war, except in a few instances, the value of the industrial training given by the plantations was overlooked. Negro men and women were educated in literature, in mathematics and in the sciences, with little thought of what had been taking place during the preceding two hundred and fifty years, except, perhaps, as something to be escaped, to be got as far away from as possible. As a generation began to pass, those who had been trained as mechanics in slavery began to disappear by death, and gradually it began to be realized that there were few to take their places.

There were young men educated in foreign tongues, but few in carpentry or in mechanical or architectural drawing. Many were trained in Latin, but few as engineers and blacksmiths. Too many were taken from the farm and educated, but educated in everything but farming. For this reason they had no interest in farming and did not return to it. And yet eighty-five per cent of the Negro population of the Southern states lives and for a considerable time will continue to live in the country districts. The charge is often brought against the members of my race—and too often justly, I confess —that they are found leaving the country districts and flocking into the great cities where temptations are more frequent and harder to resist, and where the Negro people too often become demoralized. Think, though, how frequently it is the case that from the first day that a pupil begins to go to school his books teach him much about the cities of the world and city life, and almost nothing about the country. How natural it is, then, that when he has the ordering of his life he wants to live it in the city.

Only a short time before his death the late Mr. C. P. Huntington, to whose memory a magnificent library has just been given by his widow to the Hampton Institute for Negroes, in Virginia, said in a public address some words which seem to me so wise that I want to quote them here:

"Our schools teach everybody a little of almost everything, but, in my opinion, they teach very few children just what they ought to know in order to make their way successfully in life. They do not put into their hands the tools they are best fitted to use, and hence so many failures. Many a mother and sister have worked and slaved, living upon scanty food, in order to give a son and brother a 'liberal education,' and in doing this have built up a barrier between the boy and the work he was fitted to do. Let me say to you that all honest work is honorable work. If the labor is manual, and seems common, you will have all the more chance to be thinking of other things, or of work that is higher and brings better pay, and to work out in your minds better and higher duties and responsibilities for yourselves, and for thinking of ways by which you can help others as well as yourselves, and bring them up to your own higher level."

Some years ago, when we decided to make tailoring a part of our training at the Tuskegee Institute, I was amazed to find that it

61

was almost impossible to find in the whole country an educated colored man who could teach the making of clothing. We could find numbers of them who could teach astronomy, theology, Latin or grammar, but almost none who could instruct in the making of clothing, something that has to be used by every one of us every day in the year. How often have I been discouraged as I have gone through the South, and into the homes of the people of my race, and have found women who could converse intelligently upon abstruse subjects, and yet could not tell how to improve the condition of the poorly cooked and still more poorly served bread and meat which they and their families were eating three times a day. It is discouraging to find a girl who can tell you the geographical location of any country on the globe and who does not know where to place the dishes upon a common dinner table. It is discouraging to find a woman who knows much about theoretical chemistry, and who cannot properly wash and iron a shirt.

In what I say here I would not by any means have it understood that I would limit or circumscribe the mental development of the Negro student. No race can be lifted until its mind is awakened and strengthened. By the side of industrial training should always go mental and moral training, but the pushing of mere abstract knowledge into the head means little. We want more than the mere performance of mental gymnastics. Our knowledge must be harnessed to the things of real life. I would encourage the Negro to secure all the mental strength, all the mental culture — whether gleaned from science, mathematics, history, language or literature that his circumstances will allow, but I believe most earnestly that for years to come the education of the people of my race should be so directed that the greatest proportion of the mental strength of the masses will be brought to bear upon the every-day practical things of life, upon something that is needed to be done, and something which they will be permitted to do in the community in which they reside. And just the same with the professional class which the race needs and must have, I would say give the men and women of that class, too, the training which will best fit them to perform in the most successful manner the service which the race demands.

I would not confine the race to industrial life, not even to agriculture, for example, although I believe that by far the greater part of the Negro race is best off in the country districts and must and should continue to live there, but I would teach the race that in industry the foundation must be laid—that the very best service which any one can render to what is called the higher education is to teach the present generation to provide a material or industrial foundation. On such a foundation as this will grow habits of thrift, a love of work, economy, ownership of property, bank accounts. Out of it in the future will grow practical education, professional education, positions of public responsibility. Out of it will grow moral and religious strength. Out of it will grow wealth from which alone can come leisure and the opportunity for the enjoyment of literature and the fine arts.

In the words of the late beloved Frederick Douglass: "Every blow of the sledge hammer wielded by a sable arm is a powerful blow in support of our cause. Every colored mechanic is by virtue of circumstances an elevator of his race. Every house built by a black man is a strong tower against the allied hosts of prejudice. It is impossible for us to attach too much importance to this aspect of the subject. Without industrial development there can be no wealth; without wealth there can be no leisure; without leisure no opportunity for thoughtful reflection and the cultivation of the higher arts."

I would set no limits to the attainments of the Negro in arts, in letters or statesmanship, but I believe the surest way to reach those ends is by laying the foundation in the little things of life that lie immediately about one's door. I plead for industrial education and development for the Negro not because I want to cramp him, but because I want to free him. I want to see him enter the all-powerful business and commercial world.

It was such combined mental, moral and industrial education which the late General Armstrong set out to give at the Hampton Institute when he established that school thirty years ago. The Hampton Institute has continued along the lines laid down by its great founder, and now each year an increasing number of similar schools are being established in the South, for the people of both races.

Early in the history of the Tuskegee Institute we began to combine industrial training with mental and moral culture. Our first efforts were in the direction of agriculture, and we began

63

teaching this with no appliances except one hoe and a blind mule. From this small beginning we have grown until now the Institute owns two thousand acres of land, eight hundred of which are cultivated each year by the young men of the school. We began teaching wheelwrighting and blacksmithing in a small way to the men, and laundry work, cooking and sewing and housekeeping to the young women. The fourteen hundred and over young men and women who attended the school during the last school year received instruction—in addition to academic and religious training—in thirty-three trades and industries, including carpentry, blacksmithing, printing, wheelwrighting, harnessmaking, painting, machinery, founding, shoemaking, brickmasonry and brickmaking, plastering, sawmilling, tinsmithing, tailoring, mechanical and architectural drawing, electrical and steam engineering, canning, sewing, dressmaking, millinery, cooking, laundering, housekeeping, mattress making, basketry, nursing, agriculture, dairying and stock raising, horticulture.

Not only do the students receive instruction in these trades, but they do actual work, by means of which more than half of them pay some part or all of their expenses while remaining at the school. Of the sixty buildings belonging to the school all but four were almost wholly erected by the students as a part of their industrial education. Even the bricks which go into the walls are made by students in the school's brick yard, in which, last year, they manufactured two million bricks.

When we first began this work at Tuskegee, and the idea got spread among the people of my race that the students who came to the Tuskegee school were to be taught industries in connection with their academic studies, were, in other words, to be taught to work, I received a great many verbal messages and letters from parents informing me that they wanted the children taught books, but not how to work. This protest went on for three or four years but I am glad to be able to say now that our people have very generally been educated to a point where they see their own needs and conditions so clearly that it has been several years since we have had a single protest from parents against the teaching of industries, and there is now a positive enthusiasm for it. In fact, public sentiment among the students at Tuskegee is now so strong for industrial training that it would hardly permit a student to remain on the grounds who was unwilling to labor.

It seems to me that too often mere book education leaves the Negro young man or woman in a weak position. For example, I have seen a Negro girl taught by her mother to help her in doing laundry work at home. Later, when this same girl was graduated from the public schools or a high school and returned home she finds herself educated out of sympathy with laundry work, and yet not able to find anything to do which seems in keeping with the cost and character of her education. Under these circumstances we cannot be surprised if she does not fulfill the expectations made for her. What should have been done for her, it seems to me, was to give her along with her academic education thorough training in the latest and best methods of laundry work, so that she could have put so much skill and intelligence into it that the work would have been lifted out from the plane of drudgery. The home which she would then have been able to found by the results of her work would have enabled her to help her children to take a still more responsible position in life.

Almost from the first Tuskegee has kept in mind—and this I think should be the policy of all industrial schools—fitting students for occupations which would be open to them in their home communities. Some years ago we noted the fact that there was beginning to be a demand in the South for men to operate dairies in a skillful, modern manner. We opened a dairy department in connection with the school, where a number of young men could have instruction in the latest and most scientific methods of dairy work. At present we have calls—mainly from Southern white men—for twice as many dairymen as we are able to supply. What is equally satisfactory, the reports which come to us indicate that our young men are giving the highest satisfaction and are fast changing and improving the dairy product in the communities into which they go. I use the dairy here as an example. What I have said of this is equally true of many of the other industries which we teach. Aside from the economic value of this work I cannot but believe, and my observation confirms me in my belief, that as we continue to place Negro men and women of intelligence, religion, modesty, conscience and skill in every community in the South, who will prove by actual results their value to the community, I cannot but believe, I say, that this will constitute a solution to many of the present political and social difficulties.

Many seem to think that industrial education is meant to make the Negro work as he worked in the days of slavery. This is far from my conception of industrial education. If this training is worth anything to the Negro, it consists in teaching him how not to work, but how to make the forces of nature—air, steam, water, horse-power and electricity—work for him. If it has any value it is in lifting labor up out of toil and drudgery into the plane of the dignified and the beautiful. The Negro in the South works and works hard; but too often his ignorance and lack of skill causes him to do his work in the most costly and shiftless manner, and this keeps him near the bottom of the ladder in the economic world.

I have not emphasized particularly in these pages the great need of training the Negro in agriculture, but I believe that this branch of industrial education does need very great emphasis. In this connection I want to quote some words which Mr. Edgar Gardner Murphy, of Montgomery, Alabama, has recently written upon this subject:

"We must incorporate into our public school system a larger recognition of the practical and industrial elements in educational training. Ours is an agricultural population. The school must be brought more closely to the soil. The teaching of history, for example, is all very well, but nobody can really know anything of history unless he has been taught to see things grow—has so seen things not only with the outward eye, but with the eyes of his intelligence and conscience. The actual things of the present are more important, however, then the institutions of the past. Even to young children can be shown the simpler conditions and processes of growth—how corn is put into the ground—how cotton and potatoes should be planted—how to choose the soil best adapted to a particular plant, how to improve that soil, how to care for the plant while it grows, how to get the most value out of it, how to use the elements of waste for the fertilization of other crops; how, through the alternation of crops, the land may be made to increase the annual value of its products—these things, upon their elementary side are absolutely vital to the worth and success of hundreds of thousands of these people of the Negro race, and yet our whole educational system has practically ignored them.

* * *

"Such work will mean not only an education in agriculture, but an education through agriculture and education, through natural symbols and practical forms, which will educate as deeply, as broadly and as truly as any other system which the world has known. Such changes will bring far larger results than the mere improvement of our Negroes. They will give us an agricultural class, a class of tenants or small land owners, trained not away from the soil, but in relation to the soil and in intelligent dependence upon its resources."

I close, then, as I began, by saying that as a slave the Negro was worked, and that as a freeman he must learn to work. There is still doubt in many quarters as to the ability of the Negro unguided, unsupported, to hew his own path and put into visible, tangible, indisputable form, products and signs of civilization. This doubt cannot be much affected by abstract arguments, no matter how delicately and convincingly woven together. Patiently, quietly, doggedly, persistently, through summer and winter, sunshine and shadow, by self-sacrifice, by foresight, by honesty and industry, we must re-enforce argument with results. One farm bought, one house built, one home sweetly and intelligently kept, one man who is the largest tax payer or has the largest bank account, one school or church maintained, one factory running successfully, one truck garden profitably cultivated, one patient cured by a Negro doctor, one sermon well preached, one office well filled, one life cleanly lived — these will tell more in our favor than all the abstract eloquence that can be summoned to plead our cause. Our pathway must be up through the soil, up through swamps, up through forests, up through the streams, the rocks, up through commerce, education and religion!

38. THE TALENTED TENTH (1903)[1]

W. E. B. DuBOIS

The Negro race, like all races, is going to be saved by its exceptional men. The problem of education, then, among Negroes must first of all deal with the Talented Tenth; it is the problem of developing the Best of this race that they may guide the Mass away from the contamination and death of the Worst, in their own and other races. Now the training of men is a difficult and intricate task. Its technique is a matter for educational experts, but its object is for the vision of seers. If we make money the object of man-training, we shall develop money-makers but not necessarily men; if we make technical skill the object of education, we may possess artisans but not, in nature, men. Men we shall have only as we make manhood the object of the work of the schools—intelligence, broad sympathy, knowledge of the world that was and is, and of the relation of men to it—this is the curriculum of that Higher Education which must underlie true life. On this foundation we may build bread winning, skill of hand and quickness of brain, with never a fear lest the child and man mistake the means of living for the object of life. . . .

Can the masses of the Negro people be in any possible way more quickly raised than by the effort and example of this aristocracy of talent and character? Was there ever a nation on God's fair earth civilized from the bottom upward? Never; it is, ever was and ever will be from the top downward that culture filters. The Talented Tenth rises and pulls all that are worth the saving up to their vantage ground. This is the history of human progress; and the two historic mistakes which have hindered that progress were the thinking first that no more could ever rise save the few already risen; or second, that it would better the unrisen to pull the risen down.

---

[1]*The Negro Problem*, pp. 33–34, 45–48, 56–63, 65–75.

How then shall the leaders of a struggling people be trained and the hands of the risen few strengthened? There can be but one answer: The best and most capable of their youth must be schooled in the colleges and universities of the land. We will not quarrel as to just what the university of the Negro should teach or how it should teach it—I willingly admit that each soul and each race-soul needs its own peculiar curriculum. But this is true: A university is a human invention for the transmission of knowledge and culture from generation to generation, through the training of quick minds and pure hearts, and for this work no other human invention will suffice, not even trade and industrial schools.

All men cannot go to college but some men must; every isolated group or nation must have its yeast, must have for the talented few centers of training where men are not so mystified and befuddled by the hard and necessary toil of earning a living, as to have no aims higher than their bellies, and no God greater than Gold. This is true training and thus in the beginning were the favored sons of the freedmen trained. Out of the colleges of the North came, after the blood of war, Ware, Cravath, Chase, Andrews, Bumstead and Spence to build the foundations of knowledge and civilization in the black South. Where ought they to have begun to build? At the bottom, of course, quibbles the mole with his eyes in the earth. Aye! truly at the bottom, at the very bottom; at the bottom of knowledge, down in the very depths of knowledge there where the roots of justice strike into the lowest soil of Truth. And so they did begin; they founded colleges, and up from the colleges shot normal schools, and out from the normal schools went teachers, and around the normal teachers clustered other teachers to teach the public schools; the college trained in Greek and Latin and Mathematics, 2,000 men; and these men trained full 50,000 others in morals and manners, and they in turn taught thrift and the alphabet to nine millions of men, who to-day hold $300,000,000 of property. It was a miracle—the most wonderful peace-battle of the 19th century, and yet to-day men smile at it, and in fine superiority tell us that it was all a strange mistake; that a proper way to found a system of education is first to gather the children and buy them spelling books and hoes; afterward men may look about for teachers, if haply they may find them; or again they would teach men Work, but as for Life—why, what has Work to do with Life, they ask vacantly. . . .

69

The problem of training the Negro is to-day immensely complicated by the fact that the whole question of the efficiency and appropriateness of our present systems of education, for any kind of child, is a matter of active debate, in which final settlement seems still afar off. Consequently it often happens that persons arguing for or against certain systems of education for Negroes, have these controversies in mind and miss the real question at issue. The main question, so far as the Southern Negro is concerned, is: What under the present circumstance, must a system of education do in order to raise the Negro as quickly as possible in the scale of civilization? The answer to this question seems to me clear: It must strengthen the Negro's character, increase his knowledge and teach him to earn a living. Now it goes without saying, that it is hard to do all these things simultaneously or suddenly, and that at the same time it will not do to give all the attention to one and neglect the others; we could give black boys trades, but that alone will not civilize a race of ex-slaves; we might simply increase their knowledge of the world, but this would not necessarily make them wish to use this knowledge honestly; we might seek to strengthen character and purpose, but to what end if this people have nothing to eat or to wear? A system of education. is not one thing, nor does it have a single definite object, nor is it a mere matter of schools. Education is that whole system of human training within and without the school house walls, which molds and develops men. If then we start out to train an ignorant and unskilled people with a heritage of bad habits, our system of training must set before itself two great aims—the one dealing with knowledge and character, the other part seeking to give the child the technical knowledge necessary for him to earn a living under the present circumstances. These objects are accomplished in part by the opening of the common schools on the one, and of the industrial schools on the other. But only in part, for there must also be trained those who are to teach these schools—men and women of knowledge and culture and technical skill who understand modern civilization, and have the training and aptitude to impart it to the children under them. There must be teachers, and teachers of teachers, and to attempt to establish any sort of a system of common and industrial school training, without *first* (and I say *first* advisedly) without *first* providing for the higher training of the very best teachers, is simply throwing your money to the winds. School houses do not teach themselves—piles of brick and mortar and machinery do not send out *men*. It is the trained, living human soul, cultivated and strengthened by long study and thought, that breathes the real breath of life into boys and girls and makes them human, whether they be black or white, Greek, Russian or American. Nothing, in these latter days, has so dampened the faith of thinking Negroes in recent educational movements, as the fact that such movements have been accompanied by ridicule and denouncement and decrying of those very institutions of higher training which made the Negro public school possible, and make Negro industrial schools thinkable. It was Fisk, Atlanta, Howard and Straight, those colleges born of the faith and sacrifice of the abolitionists, that placed in the black schools of the South the 30,000 teachers and more, which some, who depreciate the work of these higher schools, are using to teach their own new experiments. If Hampton, Tuskegee and the hundred other industrial schools prove in the future to be as successful as they deserve to be, then their success in training black artisans for the South, will be due primarily to the white colleges of the North and the black colleges of the South, which trained the teachers who to-day conduct these institutions. There was a time when the American people believed pretty devoutly that a log of wood with a boy at one end and Mark Hopkins at the other, represented the highest ideal of human training. But in these eager days it would seem that we have changed all that and think it necessary to add a couple of saw-mills and a hammer to this outfit, and, at a pinch, to dispense with the services of Mark Hopkins.

I would not deny, or for a moment seem to deny, the paramount necessity of teaching the Negro to work, and to work steadily and skillfully; or seem to depreciate in the slightest degree the important part industrial schools must play in the accomplishment of these ends, but I *do* say, and insist upon it, that it is industrialism drunk with its vision of success, to imagine that its own work can be accomplished without providing for the training of broadly cultured men and women to teach its own teachers, and to teach the teachers of the public schools.

But I have already said that human education is not simply a matter of schools, it is much more a matter of family and group

71

life—the training of one's home, of one's daily companions, of one's social class. Now the black boy of the South moves in a black world—a world with its own leaders, its own thoughts, its own ideals. In this world he gets by far the larger part of his life training, and through the eyes of this dark world he peers into the veiled world beyond. Who guides and determines the education which he receives in his world? His teachers here are the group-leaders of the Negro people—the physicians and clergymen, the trained fathers and mothers, the influential and forceful men about him of all kinds; here it is, if at all, that the culture of the surrounding world trickles through and is handed on by the graduates of the higher schools. Can such culture training of group leaders be neglected? Can we afford to ignore it? Do you think that if the leaders of thought among Negroes are not trained and educated thinkers, that they will have no leaders? On the contrary a hundred half-trained demagogues will still hold the places they so largely occupy now, and hundreds of vociferous busy-bodies will multiply. You have no choice; either you must help furnish this race from within its own ranks with thoughtful men of trained leadership, or you must suffer the evil consequences of a headless misguided rabble.

I am an earnest advocate of manual training and trade teaching for black boys, and for white boys, too. I believe that next to the founding of Negro colleges the most valuable addition to Negro education since the war, has been industrial training for black boys. Nevertheless, I insist that the object of all true education is not to make men carpenters, it is to make carpenters men; there are two means of making the carpenter a man, each equally important: the first is to give the group and community in which he works, liberally trained teachers and leaders to teach him and his family what life means; the second is to give him sufficient intelligence and technical skill to make him an efficient workman; the first object demands the Negro college and college-bred men, but enough to leaven the lump, to inspire the masses, to raise the Talented Tenth to leadership; the second object demands a good system of common schools, well-taught, conveniently located and properly equipped. . . .

What is the chief need for the building up of the Negro public school in the South? The Negro race in the South needs teachers

today above all else. This is the concurrent testimony of all who
know the situation. For the supply of this great demand two things
are needed—institutions of higher education and money for school
houses and salaries. It is usually assumed that a hundred or more
institutions for Negro training are today turning out so many
teachers and college-bred men that the race is threatened with an
over-supply. This is sheer nonsense. There are today less than
3,000 living Negro college graduates in the United States, and less
than 1,000 Negroes in college. Moreover, in the 164 schools for
Negroes, 95 per cent of their students are doing elementary and
secondary work, work which should be done in the public schools.
Over half the remaining 2,157 students are taking high school
studies. The mass of so-called "normal" schools for the Negro, are
simply doing elementary common school work, or, at most, high
school work, with a little instruction in methods. The Negro colleges and the post-graduate courses at other institutions are the
only agencies for the broader and more careful training of teachers. The work of these institutions is hampered for lack of funds. It
is getting increasingly difficult to get funds for training teachers in
the best modern methods, and yet all over the South, from State
Superintendents, county officials, city boards and school principals
comes the wail, "We need TEACHERS!" and teachers must be
trained. As the fairest minded of all white Southerners, Atticus G.
Haygood, once said: "The defects of colored teachers are so great
as to create an urgent necessity for training better ones. Their
excellencies and their successes are sufficient to justify the best
hopes of success in the effort, and to vindicate the judgment of
those who make large investments of money and service, to give to
colored students opportunity for thoroughly preparing themselves
for the work of teaching children of their people."

The truth of this has been strikingly shown in the marked
improvement of white teachers in the South. Twenty years ago the
rank and file of white public school teachers were not as good as
the Negro teachers. But they, by scholarships and good salaries,
have been encouraged to thorough normal and collegiate preparation, while the Negro teachers have been discouraged by starva-
tion wages and the idea that any training will do for a black teacher. If carpenters are needed it is well and good to train men as
carpenters. But to train men as carpenters, and then set them to

teaching is wasteful and criminal; and to train men as teachers and then refuse them living wages, unless they become carpenters, is rank nonsense.

The United States Commissioner of Education says in his report for 1900: "For comparison between the white and colored enrollment in secondary and higher education, I have added together the enrollment in high schools and secondary schools, with the attendance in colleges and universities, not being sure of the actual grade of work done in the colleges and universities. The work done in the secondary schools is reported in such detail in this office, that there can be no doubt of its grade."

He then makes the following comparisons of persons in every million enrolled in secondary and higher education:

	Whole Country.	Negroes.
1880	4,362	1,289
1900	10,743	2,061

And he concludes: "While the number in colored high schools and colleges had increased somewhat faster than the population, it had not kept pace with the average of the whole country, for it had fallen from 30 per cent to 24 per cent of the average quota. Of all colored pupils, one (1) in one hundred was engaged in secondary and higher work, and that ratio has continued substantially for the past twenty years. If the ratio of colored population in secondary and higher education is to be equal to the average for the whole country, it must be increased to five times its present average." And if this be true of the secondary and higher education, it is safe to say that the Negro has not one-tenth his quota in college studies. How baseless, therefore, is the charge of too much training! We need Negro teachers for the Negro common schools, and we need first-class normal schools and colleges to train them. This is the work of higher Negro education and it must be done.

Further than this, after being provided with group leaders of civilization, and a foundation of intelligence in the public schools, the carpenter, in order to be a man, needs technical skill. This calls for trade schools. Now trade schools are not nearly such simple things as people once thought. The original idea was that the "Industrial" school was to furnish education, practically free, to those willing to work for it; it was to "do" things—i.e. become a center of productive industry, it was to be partially, if not wholly, self-supporting, and it was to teach trades. Admirable as were some of the ideas underlying this scheme, the whole thing simply would not work in practice; it was found that if you were to use time and material to teach trades thoroughly, you could not at the same time keep the industries on a commercial basis and make them pay. Many schools started out to do this on a large scale and went into virtual bankruptcy. Moreover, it was found also that it was possible to teach a boy a trade mechanically, without giving him the full educative benefit of the process, and, vice versa, that there was a distinctive educative value in teaching a boy to use his hands and eyes in carrying out certain physical processes, even though he did not actually learn a trade. It has happened, therefore, in the last decade, that a noticeable change has come over the industrial schools. In the first place the idea of commercially remunerative industry in a school is being pushed rapidly to the background. There are still schools with shops and farms that bring an income, and schools that use student labor partially for the erection of their buildings and the furnishing of equipment. It is coming to be seen, however, in the education of the Negro, as clearly as it has been seen in the education of the youths the world over, that it is the *boy* and not the material product, that is the true object of education. Consequently the object of the industrial school came to be the thorough training of boys regardless of the cost of the training, so long as it was thoroughly well done.

Even at this point, however, the difficulties were not surmounted. In the first place modern industry has taken great strides since the war, and the teaching of trades is no longer a simple matter. Machinery and long processes of work have greatly changed the work of the carpenter, the ironworker and the shoemaker. A really efficient workman must be today an intelligent man who has had good technical training in addition to thorough common school, and perhaps even higher training. To meet this situation the industrial schools began a further development; they established distinct Trade Schools for the thorough training of better class artisans, and at the same time they sought to preserve for the purposes of general education, such of the simpler processes of elementary trade learning as were best suited therefor. In this differentiation of the Trade School and manual training,

75

the best of the industrial schools simply followed the plain trend of the present educational epoch. A prominent educator tells us that, in Sweden, "In the beginning the economic conception was generally adopted, and everywhere manual training was looked upon as a means of preparing the children of the common people to earn their living. But gradually it came to be recognized that manual training has a more elevated purpose, and one, indeed, more useful in the deeper meaning of the term. It came to be considered as an educative process for the complete moral, physical and intellectual development of the child."

Thus, again, in the manning of trade schools and manual training schools we are thrown back upon the higher training as its source and chief support. There was a time when any aged and wornout carpenter could teach in a trade school. But not so today. Indeed the demand for college-bred men by a school like Tuskegee, ought to make Mr. Booker T. Washington the firmest friend of higher training. Here he has as helpers the son of a Negro senator, trained in Greek and the humanities, and graduated at Harvard; the son of a Negro congressman and lawyer, trained in Latin and mathematics, and graduated at Oberlin; he has as his wife, a woman who read Virgil and Homer in the same class room with me; he has as college chaplain, a classical graduate of Atlanta University; as teacher of science, a graduate of Fisk; as teacher of history, a graduate of Smith,—indeed some thirty of his chief teachers are college graduates, and instead of studying French grammars in the midst of weeds, or buying pianos for dirty cabins, they are at Mr. Washington's right hand helping him in a noble work. And yet one of the effects of Mr. Washington's propaganda has been to throw doubt upon the expediency of such training for Negroes, as these persons have had.

        ✿ ✿ ✿

Men of America, the problem is plain before you. Here is a race transplanted through the criminal foolishness of your fathers. Whether you like it or not the millions are here, and here they will remain. If you do not lift them up, they will pull you down. Education and work are the levers to uplift a people. Work alone will not do it unless inspired by the right ideals and guided by intelligence. Education must not simply teach work—it must teach Life.

The Talented Tenth of the Negro race must be made leaders of thought and missionaries of culture among their people. No others can do this work and Negro colleges must train men for it. The Negro race, like all other races, is going to be saved by its exceptional men.

CHAPTER 16

THE NEW SOUTH

The building of a new social order.

Walter Hines Page, 1902

39. LAST WORDS FROM THE SOUTH (1884)[1]

THE REV. A. D. MAYO

. . . I am not here to speak for the sixteen Southern States of this Union; they are here to speak for themselves. I only propose to tell you of a few things I have seen in a four years' ministry of education through fourteen of these States—a ministry conducted with open eyes, and I hope, with open mind and heart, to find out what these, our brothers and sisters of the southern portion of our country, are doing in behalf of the children and youth, and in the building up of the new American civilization that is coming to pass in all these United States.

I shall not burden your patience by any account of my personal adventures in this deeply interesting ministry of education. But this I may say, that in all my wanderings through the vast regions of these Southern States, I have always kept in mind the golden law of judgment set up by Coleridge, greatest of British critics, when he said, *"No man is competent to speak of the defects of a book or work of art till he knows its merits."* I accept that golden rule of judgment in my estimation of men, states, and peoples. In my journeyings to and fro, I have come across enough to furnish material for a political lower-story investigation of Southern society through indefinite presidential campaigns. But, leaving this work, however important it may be, in abler hands, I have given myself a good deal to the more hopeful task of upper-story investigation in the regions where the moving powers of society are located, out of which must finally issue the destiny of the Southern people. So I am not here to speak to you of a thousand things our

[1]National Education Association, *Proceedings and Addresses* (1884), pp. 117–124. The Rev. A. D. Mayo, a Unitarian minister, played an active role in education in the last decades of the nineteenth century. From 1880–85, he served as an associate editor of the *Journal of Education*. Then as a private citizen, he devoted his energies and time to the development of education in the South.

neighbors are not, but to remind you of a few profoundly significant things which these people are doing and becoming. And so
powerful has been the impression on my own mind of this upper-
story investigation, that I am ready to assert that, if we, in the
North, will stand by what I may call the Educational Public of the
South, man and woman fashion, for a generation to come, all good
things for which all good men and women now hope and pray will
surely come to pass down there and all through our beloved land.

The first note of hope and cheer that I strike is this: that the
most influential people of the South, of all classes and both races,
are learning the true American way of education, by learning to
help themselves. Every American state, city or little border hamlet must finally be educated by itself, in league with the educating
Providence, as revealed to that locality. I always lose interest in
our most eminent teachers of foreign birth, as soon as they entrench on the "genuine method," from over the sea. Of course, we
need all that Europe, the rest of the world, ancient and modern,
can give us. But we need all this, first and foremost, plus the
Almighty God, here and now, to help us train American citizens
with the flavor of this new age and its mighty revelations in human
affairs.

I am glad that the North and the nation have given $50,000,000
to our brothers of the South within the past twenty-five years, as a
friendly lift in the beginning of the great work of the education of
the whole people. I pray that Congress, after the presidential
agony is over, and men are again free to stand up in their places
and say they believe in God and man and the Ten Commandments, may confirm the grant of $70,000,000 voted by the Senate
to reinforce the whole country in its death struggle against our
national illiteracy; that illiteracy being only the fine dictionary
name for the new American barbarism which is the home devil of
New York and New Orleans alike. But all this is only the friendly
encouragement of that radical work of training the younger third of
the Southern people for our new civilization, which they must and
will do of themselves within the coming fifty years, and I go to
these people and ask you all to go out to them with the power of
your noblest sympathies and most practical aid, because they are
waking up to this great obligation and because your sympathy will
be the most potent encouragement to its speedy performance.

Even the Southern colored citizen, the least educated of all Americans, is gradually waking up to this American idea of self-help; is coming to understand that he is nobody's man, but God's man and his own. The seven million Southern colored people cannot be gathered in as an attachment to any great ecclesiastical party, North or South, or even garnered up as an humble Anglo-Saxon annex. Everywhere I find him making commendable efforts to get himself in hand and place himself in line with the great American family, into whose house of freedom of many mansions he is the latest comer, and in which he is to be not the least favored occupant in the long ages to come. The Southern colored man does not specially need our pity or our patronage, and takes no stock in any man's despair. Coming up the Mississippi in its annual overflow, last April, our little steamer was weighted almost to the water's edge by the poor people we picked up along shore, drowned out by the wide waste of weltering waters that changed the valley to a muddy ocean a hundred miles wide. Down in the bow huddled a crowd of disconsolate-looking white laborers and tramps, the very image of despondency. At one landing we took in a group of colored women with their flock of babies and the poor household wrecks saved from the flood; the most complete human "object lesson" in "reduction to its lowest terms" I had ever seen. At first, these poor creatures dropped where they were, on a level with their demoralized white brothers. But, by and by, a big, jolly sister stood up, six feet in her muddy shoes and stockings, surveyed the field, and with a grand toss of her head and a superb sweep of her hand spoke up: "Ladies, this is no place for us, come up here on deck!" I am glad to report that in all my wanderings among the Southern people I have come across no considerable class of any color who propose to be saved by anybody but God Almighty and themselves. The poorest of them, as soon as they hear the cry of despair from school-man, politician, or priest, rise up and say: "Brothers and sisters, this is no place for us, come up here on deck!" Believe me, friends, the key to the present situation down South, is the glorious American gospel of self-help. It is our duty and privilege to do all we may, for years to come, in the opening era of training our Southern youth for the glorious future that is coming to them like morning over the kindling eastern hills. But all this is as nothing to the demand that will test the uttermost invention, enterprise, and consecration of the Southern people; to educate the myriads of children that God is sending down that way, innumerable as the leaves on the trees and the waves of the sea. And the best of all we can offer is the love that sweetens every gift and lifts giver and receiver to the plane where both are henceforth one.

So let the little group of Southern senators who seem to be worried lest a moderate National Aid for education should demoralize their people, possess their perturbed souls in peace. Big Texas and little Delaware will take and ought to take all of Uncle Sam's money they can honestly get for the children. The whole South will and ought to take all it can honorably get from all sources for the training of the children and youth. For when all is given that can be had, these millions will hardly be enough to fill its big pocket with change to buy educational "goodies" for the little ones. Whatever we do, the final work of educating the generations must be done by the "old folks at home." So the first note of hope and cheer I strike is, that the Southern people are learning the great American way of educating the coming generation by learning to help themselves. God bless them! Let us take hold and do all we can to help them and then look on, with patriotic joy and pride, to see them do it.

The second note of hope and cheer, like all that follow, is only a variation of the grand theme of American self-help: is the great awakening of the Southern people, of the better sort, to this work of the Education of all the children. I am afraid our busy people, north of the Potomac and the Ohio, do not know much of this; and some of them are unwilling to believe when told of it. I, too, as long as my own knowledge of the Southern people was from the press, supposed that the leading people of these States were largely occupied in watching on the border for a change of political administration at Washington that would restore them to their old place in national affairs; that the white men did the voting and the colored brethren did the work; and that their young men were held in leash for a political outbreak that was sure to come unless certain great civic fathers continued to sit up in the places of power. When I went among them I did find a good many politicians, probably as many and as unreliable as in Massachusetts or New York. I also learned what I was not obliged to go South to

learn; that there are always, in this country, ten men yearning for
an offical chair when there will be one chair vacant in ten years.
But, after pushing through this outer fringe of partisan politicians,
I learned that the "solid South" has set its heart on two things:
First, to keep the wolf from the door; and second, to put the chil-
dren at school.

No people, in modern times, has been so overwhelmed and
impoverished by the wreck of civil war as the superior class of the
South. And where one of these men is now crying aloud for an
office, ninety-nine are hard at work, building up their new interests and enterprises and laying the foundations of their new era of
free labor by the faithful performance of the homely duties of
common life. Old Dr. Johnson used to say, "Whatever the parsons
may preach, men are seldom so usefully and morally employed as
in honestly making money." The Southern people must and ought
to be greatly engrossed, for a generation to come, in the development of their magnificent country, a wonder land, from which the
veil of centuries is being slowly lifted to the amazement of the
civilized world.

Next to this revival of industrial life, along with it, goes the
great awakening of the better sort of people, of both races, for that
Education which is the great American chance for every American
child. I have never been in any locality so obscure that I didn't
find this spirit abroad, like fire running under ground, ready to
burst into an open flame. And nowhere, in any city, have I found
such electric popular attention as in many of these communities,
where a whole neighborhood rises up, and, forgetting past and
present discouragements, laying aside local contentions, rising
above the natural jealousy of outside interference, has welcomed
the Minister of Education, though a stranger, with a spirit as fresh
and a confidence as sacred as the first love of confiding youth.

No estimate of Southern affairs is reliable that does not take
into account this widespread and irresistible movement of the
Southern people for that Education which is the great American
chance for every American child. Of course, there are thousands of
people who are not reached by it; many who do not know of it and
some who will not hear of it. But this I have noticed; that, when a
public man mounts a pile of antiquated political rubbish for an
old-fashioned harangue against modern times, unless the political

sense is clean leaked out of him, he straightway feels the ground shaking beneath him and a mighty stir in the air warns of a coming cyclone of the people's wrath. I noticed that a week after the beginning of the great debate, last winter, in the Senate, on National Aid, almost every Southern statesman of first-class reputation came to the front in its support; solemnity was in order; and "fools who came to scoff remained to pray." Every Southern senator who opposed that bill will have abundant opportunities to "rise and explain" to constituents within the coming six months. The school question is coming to the front, below tariff and currency; below sectional and partisan issues; perhaps the most powerful educator of the class of intelligent younger men of affairs who will lead the people in the years to come.

I wish I could reproduce in you the feeling that comes upon every generous mind at the sight of this wonderful uplifting of the spirit of whole communities and peoples through these great commonwealths. It reminds me of a voyage down the Mississippi, on the first big steamer that carried the electric light. The news of the coming glory ran ahead and, at every landing where the light was let on, we saw crowds of wondering people, worshipping the midnight sunrise; while every city and hamlet was revealed, as by an awful judgment-day radiance, from its topmost spire to its lowest slum. Let any man who has lost faith in the people go with me, and from the platform where I face the gathering multitudes, look upon the flush of pride on the cheek of maidens and youth; the waking up of the irrepressible crowd of small boys on the front benches; the coming out of sweet and noble looks in faded old faces, with new and grander visions, through springing tears, in dimmed and waiting eyes; as the glorious gospel of the New Education is proclaimed; and he will know the divine meaning of the old words — "The people that sat in darkness have seen a great light, and to them that dwelt in the region and shadow of death light is sprung up."

The third note of hope and cheer is: that this awakening is not a sentiment or a temporary excitement, but is gradually "materializing" into the establishment of the American system of Education in all the Southern States. I know what the experts can say about a good deal of the school life already on the ground. I understand all that the lower-story critic can offer concerning the terrible illiteracy and lack of opportunity in the most favored of these commonwealths. But here are a few stubborn facts. During the most dreary twenty years that ever clouded the upward struggle of any modern people, the better class of the South has restored their old system of collegiate, academical, and professional schools for whites, on broader foundations and with better methods than before the flood, with but little aid from abroad. They have also, in the last fifteen years, domesticated the American system of common schools, for all classes and both races, in every State; in almost every State made this a little better every year; and never was the outlook for popular education so favorable in these sixteen States as it is now. This year, the South will pay $15,000,000 for common schools alone; beside all the money expended on the higher academical, professional, and artistic education; a sum, considering their pecuniary condition, equivalent to ten times $15,000,000 in our powerful, wealthy, and prosperous North.

Even the Freedman, from a condition of absolute ignorance and poverty, in twenty years has made good progress in building up that aristocracy of intelligence, character, and industry, on which, like every race, he must rely, as the chief elevator to the American order of citizenship. In the same time there has been developed a body of several thousand creditable teachers of common schools, some of them eminent instructors in the higher grades of education. The Freedman has not died out; he is very much alive; increasing and multiplying faster than any of us; has already laid up $100,000,000 in one short generation, and wherever I go I find his children crowding the school-house door, like little Oliver in the story, "asking for more."

Everywhere I find the evidence of this work for the children. I have visited a score of towns whose eminent respectabilities assured me were dead and buried in educational indifference. But almost invariably, if I went back to one of these places in two years, I was welcomed by crowds of children, with their teachers in the graded school, and the unrespectable thing turned out to be want of faith in the people. And one good thing in this building up is the home flavor that is coming into the best of these schools. These best graded schools are no more an imitation of similar institutions in the North than a South Carolina cotton-field is like an Ohio corn-field; a Texas prairie in April like a village common in

Vermont, or a Florida orange-grove like a California wheat-farm. The old professor of dust and ashes is already becoming an antiquity, and the bright young men and women who are called to superintend the New Education are making it, as it should be, American in substance, but instinct with the best spirit and flavor of the home life. It is a new revelation of our national type of Education; with the *elan* and electric enthusiasm of these people in the very atmosphere; in its own way doing for the children in the South what Iowa and Wisconsin are doing in the great Northwest. Even our faithful Northern graduates who have gone to be Professors and Presidents in the new universities and colleges for the colored folk have builded better than anybody knew, because compelled to turn their back on the past and forget themselves in the effort to shape the university of the future for God's last people introduced to civilization. Harvard and Yale and Columbia and Princeton may smile at the big names put on by these superior schools for colored youth. But, tried by the most eminent educators of ancient and modern times, Hampton and Fisk and Atlanta, and the whole group of superior schools for colored youth are nearer the type of the true university than many a notable college in the cultivated Northeast. The leading teachers of the South are better informed of the disabilities and perils of their educational life than their most eloquent advisers from the North or abroad. Neither they nor the educational public they represent have "attained." But they are laying the foundations of that Southern American system of universal education which, in due time, Providence permitting, and all good men helping, will bring out the Southern youth abreast of his companions in the North, in the republic of the years to come.

The final note of hope and cheer I strike is this: that, in the South, as in the North, the most vital department of education is passing into the hands of woman. The most radical element in the new American education is the woman power;—already so potent in the elementary and coming into such prominence in the secondary and higher school. No people in Christendom has called its young womanhood to such a responsibility as the American people has laid on the head and heart of the army of heroic girls that "hold the fort" in the little children's school. It is not because the people are stingy; although the woman teachers are too often

poorly paid. It is not that they are indifferent to the best in education; as they are not indifferent to the best elsewhere in American
life. But it is because our people has made up its mind to trust her
whom God calls to the maternity of the child with the most vital
training of the child during the years of infancy and early
youth; — also to invite her to a full copartnership with man in the
work of the secondary and higher school. So far, despite all drawbacks, the girl-teachers have not disappointed the people. No class
of persons, to-day, is doing more to meet the high demand of the
country than the leading class of woman-teachers, in every grade
of the American school.

The South is showing itself American in this: that it is calling
its choicest young womanhood to serve in the schoolroom. And, as
if to give Providential endorsement to this tendency, I find multitudes of the daughters of the better sort of families compelled by
their condition to look to the schoolroom, not only for the most
convenient means of pecuniary support, but as the best opportunity for honorable station in life. The most affecting and pathetic
scenes in my wanderings among the Southern people are the
efforts of so many of these noble young women to gain this furnishing for service in the upper regions of Southern society. The
greatest opportunity of a people sometimes comes from what
appears the most appalling calamity. The two most apparent perils
and drawbacks of Southern life, — the widespread poverty, and the
terrible ignorance of its lower grades of society, — are already
waking up the Christian womanhood of that section to toils and
sacrifices which always bring down the consecration of the Holy
Spirit upon any earnest soul. It will be years before the finest
young men of the South, in any large numbers, can be directed
from the activities and the ambitions that are now so absorbing in
the direction of industrial enterprise. It will only be gradually that
our new industries will be developed in these States, out of which
so many women are gaining an honorable support in the great
centres of labor in the North. But, meanwhile, the young womanhood of all these States will be assigned to the charge of the whole
upper-story of Southern life; and through her the school, the
church, society, and the higher public opinion will be wonderfully
reinforced in all things true and beautiful and good. I meet this
spirit everywhere and work with it like a man under a spell; and if

I speak of it in this way it is not from a sentimental illusion, but from a sober estimate of the power of such an agency in our American affairs.

The conclusion of the whole matter is: that the foremost people of the Southern States, of all classes and both races, are awake and at work to bring their commonwealths up to their primal duty as members of a true union of States. And so believing, I declare it our noblest privilege and most imperative duty to aid them as friends in all practical ways that God has put into our power. If it were only for a wise comprehension of national self-protection, I would say: Help the Southern people educate their children for a generation to come; for national Illiteracy is the nation's peril, and the least State is big enough to let in a raging deluge of barbarism that may swamp us all. But I rise above the common level of secular self-interest and invoke, not only your "material aid," but friendly co-operation, philanthropic interest, personal love for our brothers and sisters of the Southland. Do not believe anybody who tells you these people are not worth all we can do for or give to them; or that they need us more than we need them. We gave the lives of a quarter of a million of our dear boys in blue and the earnings of a generation to keep them from going away from us twenty years ago; not a man too many or a dollar too much for the mighty hope that demanded and the glorious consummation that crowned the nation's sacrifice. They are not our enemies and it will be our sin and shame if their children are not our children's lovers, and their country's friends. They are waiting for our last word of hope and cheer, and we shall never be at peace with ourselves or with Heaven till we give it them and all around the Republic peace and good will shall ebb and flow like the swelling and sinking of ocean tides that enfold us all. And I rejoice, with joy unspeakable, that whatever men and women elsewhere, or whatever we in other relations may not be doing; we, the men and women of the East and West, and North and South, here assembled to take counsel for the cause of God and the human race, can work together, with no cloud above our heads and no pitfall beneath our feet, to think and talk and pray for those who shall come after us in the mighty upbuilding of the new Republic which, Heaven willing, and all good men helping, in God's own time, will surely come.

40. The George Peabody Trust Fund (1867)[1]

To Hon. Robert C. Winthrop, of Massachusetts; Hon. Hamilton Fish, of New York; Right Rev. Charles P. McIlvaine, of Ohio; General U. S. Grant, of the United States Army; Hon. William C. Rives, of Virginia; Hon. John H. Clifford, of Massachusetts; Hon. William Aiken, of South Carolina; William M. Evarts, Esq., of New York; Hon. William A. Graham, of North Carolina; Charles Macalester, Esq., of Pennsylvania; George W. Riggs, Esq., of Washington; Samuel Wetmore, Esq., of New York; Edward A. Bradford, Esq., of Louisiana; George N. Eaton, Esq., of Maryland; and George Peabody Russell, Esq., of Massachusetts.

Gentlemen: I beg to address you on a subject which occupied my mind long before I left England; and in regard to which one at least of you (the Hon. Mr. Winthrop, the distinguished and valued friend to whom I am so much indebted for cordial sympathy, careful consideration, and wise counsel in this matter) will remember that I consulted him immediately upon my arrival in May last.

I refer to the educational needs of those portions of our beloved and common country which have suffered from the destructive ravages, and the not less disastrous consequences, of civil war.

With my advancing years, my attachment to my native land has but become more devoted. My hope and faith in its successful and glorious future have grown brighter and stronger; and now, looking forward beyond my stay on earth, as may be permitted to one who has passed the limit of threescore and ten years, I see our country, united and prosperous, emerging from the clouds which still surround her, taking a higher rank among the nations, and becoming richer and more powerful than ever before.

---

[1] From J. L. M. Curry, *A Brief Sketch of George Peabody, and a History of the Peabody Education Fund* . . . (Cambridge: Harvard University Press, 1898), pp. 19–22.

But to make her prosperity more than superficial, her moral and intellectual development should keep pace with her material growth, and, in those portions of our nation to which I have referred, the urgent and pressing physical needs of an almost impoverished people must for some years preclude them from making, by unaided effort, such advances in education, and such progress in the diffusion of knowledge, among all classes, as every lover of his country must earnestly desire.

I feel most deeply, therefore, that it is the duty and privilege of the more favored and wealthy portions of our nation to assist those who are less fortunate; and, with the wish to discharge so far as I may be able my own responsibility in this matter, as well as to gratify my desire to aid those to whom I am bound by so many ties of attachment and regard, I give to you, gentlemen, most of whom have been my personal and especial friends, the sum of one million of dollars, to be by you and your successors held in trust, and the income thereof used and applied in your discretion for the promotion and encouragement of intellectual, moral, or industrial education among the young of the more destitute portions of the Southern and Southwestern States of our Union; my purpose being that the benefits intended shall be distributed among the entire population, without other distinction than their needs and the opportunities of usefulness to them.

Besides the income thus derived, I give to you permission to use from the principal sum, within the next two years, an amount not exceeding forty per cent.

In addition to this gift, I place in your hands bonds of the State of Mississippi, issued to the Planters' Bank, and commonly known as Planters' Bank bonds, amounting, with interest, to about eleven hundred thousand dollars, the amount realized by you from which is to be added to and used for the purposes of this Trust.

These bonds were originally issued in payment for stock in that Bank held by the State, and amounted in all to only two millions of dollars. For many years, the State received large dividends from that Bank over and above the interest on these bonds. The State paid the interest without interruption till 1840, since which no interest has been paid, except a payment of about one hundred thousand dollars, which was found in the treasury applicable to the payment of the coupons, and paid by a mandamus of the Supreme Court. The validity of these bonds has never been questioned, and they must not be confounded with another issue of bonds made by the State to the Union Bank, the recognition of which has been a subject of controversy with a portion of the population of Mississippi.

Various acts of the Legislature—viz., of February 28, 1842; February 23, 1844; February 16, 1846; February 28, 1846; March 4, 1848—and the highest judicial tribunal of the State have confirmed their validity; and I have no doubt that at an early day such legislation will be had as to make these bonds available in increasing the usefulness of the present Trust.

Mississippi, though now depressed, is rich in agricultural resources, and cannot long disregard the moral obligation resting upon her to make provision for their payment. In confirmation of what I have said, in regard to the legislative and judicial action concerning the State bonds issued to the Planters' Bank, I herewith place in your hands the documents marked A.

The details and organization of the Trust I leave with you, only requesting that Mr. Winthrop may be chairman, and Governor Fish and Bishop McIlvaine Vice-Chairmen, of your body: and I give to you power to make all necessary by-laws and regulations; to obtain an Act of Incorporation, if any shall be found expedient; to provide for the expenses of the Trustees and of any agents appointed by them; and, generally, to do all such acts as may be necessary for carrying out the provisions of this Trust.

All vacancies occurring in your number by death, resignation, or otherwise, shall be filled by your election as soon as conveniently may be, and having in view an equality of representation so far as regards the Northern and Southern States.

I furthermore give to you the power, in case two-thirds the Trustees shall at any time, after the lapse of thirty years, deem it expedient, to close this Trust, and, of the funds which at that time shall be in the hands of yourselves and your successors, to distribute not less than two-thirds among such educational or literary institutions, or for such educational purposes, as they may determine, in the States for whose benefit the income is now appointed to be used. The remainder may be distributed by the Trustees for educational or literary purposes, wherever they may deem it expedient.

In making this gift, I am aware that the fund derived from it can but aid the States which I wish to benefit in their own exertions to diffuse the blessings of education and morality. But if this endowment shall encourage those now anxious for the light of knowledge, and stimulate to new efforts the many good and noble men who cherish the high purpose of placing our great country foremost, not only in power, but in the intelligence and virtue of her citizens, it will have accomplished all that I can hope.

With reverent recognition of the need of the blessing of Almighty God upon this gift, and with the fervent prayer that under His guidance your counsels may be directed for the highest good of present and future generations in our beloved country, I am, gentlemen, with great respect,

Your humble servant,

George Peabody.

Washington, Feb. 7, 1867.

41. ANNUAL REPORT TO THE TRUSTEES OF THE PEABODY FUND (1890)[1]

J. L. M. CURRY

. . . My next privilege is to congratulate you, as I heartily do, on the signal success of our work during the past year,—as it will be abundantly unfolded to you in the Annual Report of our devoted and untiring General Agent. You will rejoice with me to find ample evidence in that Report that an increased, I might almost say an intensified, interest in the cause of education has been evinced in many of the States within the provisions of the Peabody Trust, if I may not say absolutely in all of them.

The field is, indeed, a vast one, and requires, as we must all be deeply conscious, far greater aid than we, or our valued fellow-workers in the same cause, are able to bring to it. The illiteracy in some parts of our land betrayed by the last census was appalling, and we can have little hope that the new census, now approaching its completion, will exhibit less deplorable returns. We almost shrink from learning its details. But the public mind both at the South and at the North seems to be at length throughly re-awakened to the old truths which were so well understood by those who have gone before us,—that the welfare of our whole country is at stake on the education of its children; that Free Common Schools are essential to any worthy or rightful citizenship of our Republic; that illiteracy degrades the dignity of the Elective Franchise; and exposes it to unjust manipulation and suppression; that universal suffrage is a farce, and may prove a tragedy, without universal instruction; that ignorance anywhere is danger everywhere; and that the safety of our institutions demands impera-

---

[1]*Annual Report of the General Agent. Proceedings of the Peabody Education Fund* (Cambridge: Harvard University Press, 1890), pp. 4–5, 16–17, 71–84.

tively that every man who has a vote should be able to read it and write it and understand it. Let these great truths be marked, learned, and inwardly digested anew, as they are in the way of being at this moment more than ever before, and we may look forward with confidence to the census of 1900 to tell us better things of the state of education in our country than we can honestly boast of at the present hour.

During the ten years which will have elapsed before the census of 1900 is taken, our Peabody Trust may have come to an end, and not a few of us who are here to-day will have followed so many of our lamented associates to the grave; but the Trust itself, and its munificent founder, will still be gratefully remembered, not only as having extended the earliest sympathy and succor to our brethren who were suffering from the disastrous consequences of Civil War, but as having given the first impulse and the most effective aid to the Southern States in that great cause of universal elementary education which is so inseparably identified with the secure enjoyment, if not with the continued maintenance, of Free Institutions. . . .

The Peabody Fund, if faithful to the wishes of its founder, must keep prominently in view the value and the obligations of American citizenship. Trained intelligence and personal integrity are of the very essence of patriotism. One of our chiefest social dangers is ignorance,—not ignorance merely of reading and writing, but ignorance of the origin, character, and ends of our free representative governments, and of the enlarged duties of American citizens. Reckless agitators, conspirators against the peace and property of society, venal and corrupt demagogues, misguided philanthropists and religionists, find greedy listerners and ready instruments in the uneducated masses. Suggestions of social reform are now as openly and freely discussed as political questions. Property, labor, wages, association, industrial and economic questions, extension and control of franchise, institutional environments, are all inseparably related to the character and the diffusion of education. Frequent quotation has almost solidified into a proverb the statement that a free government, with its delicate and complicated mechanism, demands unusual intelligence, honesty, and patriotism. . . .

THE EXTENSION OF EDUCATION

ADDRESS DELIVERED MAY 20, 1890
BEFORE THE GENERAL ASSEMBLY OF LOUISIANA

Senators and Representatives: —

I. The compliment of the invitation to address the lawmakers of Louisiana, in joint session here assembled, is properly appreciated. I am not so vain as to ascribe it to anything personal to myself, notwithstanding the words of eulogy with which I have just been introduced by Senator Goldthwaite. The honor, growing out of this suspension of public business and the meeting of both Senate and House in this hall, is due to George Peabody, the South's greatest benefactor. He came with benevolent intent and munificent hand in the time of our desolation, bankruptcy, and despair, and his sagacious prevision saw that material growth should be accompanied by "moral and intellectual development," and his generous bounty was directed to the stimulation of "good and noble men" to the placing of "our great country foremost, not only in power, but in the intelligence and virtue of her citizens." It is fortunate that, day by day, stronger convictions of the importance of universal education are taking possession of the public mind. We may learn profitable lessons from foreign states which have made more progress than we can show in extinguishing illiteracy and in developing a complete and well-thought-out system of public schools. To the legislator free schools are of paramount importance. Other questions are local, temporary, and debatable. In free schools, every individual, family, and neighborhood has a vital concern. They may become the most effective of the forces to be set in motion by the law-maker. More than any agency ever yet devised, they are applicable to every child and community in the commonwealth.

Germany is said to sacrifice the development of the individual man to the perfection of the administration of the social whole. A critic responds that America sacrifices the welfare of the social whole in order to give an unreasonable margin for individual whims and preferences. The essence of democracy, of Christianity, is the exaltation of the individual, his evocation from the undistinguishable, irresponsible mass into the clear light and separateness of personal freedom and personal duty. Instead of arbitrary division into classes with graduated privileges, instead of conceding to particular families exclusive privileges in civil and ecclesiastical affairs, our free representative institutions recognize the man in man, do what is just and possible for developing potentialities and securing for society all the capabilities of the individual soul. Character of the aggregate is determined by the units, and the endowments that belong to all are what society needs.

II. Mind differentiates man from the lower animal kingdom, and yet is given less perfectly. The child begins on a lower plane, and needs training, discipline, development. What it is to be, depends on that. A child uneducated becomes a savage. Whether the fittest will survive, or should survive, depends first on definition of fitness, and secondly on environments. In the struggle for mere existence, fitness implies cunning or physical strength; but true fitness includes moral and intellectual qualities as well as toughness, etc. Our moral and intellectual faculties have been developed from *nil* to their present wonderful perfection, but every child begins with undeveloped powers. Development is the result of a thousand agencies which we call education.

Take a bee, performing a geometrical wonder, solving somehow a beautiful geometrical problem, using wax with absolute mathematical economy. The insect started with this architectural tendency, and the skill has belonged in perfection to the insect from the beginning. Only one line in its unvarying history; no growth, no progress.

A child is a lump of inert possibilities. No knowledge, no skill, no trend in earliest days, no prophecy. No evolution into a good citizen, a legislator, inventor, artist, by a predetermined transformation, as from tadpole to frog, caterpillar to butterfly. Wonderfully interesting to see the unfoldings. A vast, unexplored continent of psychology, inviting the Stanleys, Maurys, Agassizs, Darwins. After unfolding begins, even under adverse circumstances, what illimitable progress! Defeats, obstacles, limitations occur, yet what attainments in Bacon, Shakspeare, Napoleon, Bismarck, Gladstone, Morse, Edison, Webster, Calhoun! Yet these are not transmissible, they are personal, not hereditary, and are to be acquired anew, each one for himself.

No legislation more involves the public weal, the best interests of the state, than the education of the people, beginning with the primary and culminating in the university. The school enlightens and disciplines the mind, but it also trains the will into habits of industry and temperance, in the virtues of punctuality, order, and good behavior. Education is the condition to material development, the chief means of prosperity, the best assurance of strength, honor, and peace, the best security against internal disorders and broils. Adapting education to subtle needs of the human mind is no easy task. There is ample room for practical sagacity and soundest philosophy of best thinkers, of wisest statesmen. The subject has enlisted the best thought, and still there is much sciolism, dogmatism, quackery.

The expenditure by individuals, communities, denominations, and States for buildings, furniture, apparatus, teachers, books, etc., has been immense. During ten years ending 1887 the public-school expenditure increased from $79,000,000 to $112,000,000 and eighty-nine per cent of all the money now expended for schools comes from self imposed local and State taxation. Louisiana recognizes the duty and benefit and has imbedded in her organic law this mandatory provision: "There shall be free public schools established by the General Assembly throughout the State for the education of all the children of the State between the ages of six and eighteen years, and the General Assembly shall provide for their establishment, maintenance, and support by taxation or otherwise."

The right of every being to completest education a state can give, is necessary to his enjoyment of himself. Deprived of education, he has no opportunity to ascertain natural aptitudes or to cultivate them. A failure to ascertain, in some systematic way, and develop and utilize natural aptitudes for industries or special avocations, begets waste, unhappiness, poverty. Neither poverty nor social prejudices should hamper in choice or prosecution of life-work. The more efficiency education gives to labor, the more the time lost in acquiring the education is made up. Let every citizen be put in the way of maintaining an honest independence, earning bread by honest toil. The education of a human being is necessary for the enjoyment of his society. The refined and intellectual can better dispense with aids to culture than those less fortunate in natural endowments and artificial advantages. Life is not worth living if we are to be surrounded by and are incapable of rising above boorish, coarse, vulgar men and women. No single thing is more important than intelligent and moral companionship. Man does not live by bread alone.

It is the right of the unborn to be granted an intelligent and refined parentage. A consumptive, scrofulous, epileptic person should be forbidden to marry; so also a depraved criminal. Children should have secured a parentage physically, morally, and intellectually healthy.

III. Lord Bacon, speaking of the looseness or negligence that hath taken no due regard to the choice of schoolmasters, says that the ancient wisdom of the best times did always make a just complaint that states were too busy with their laws and too negligent in point of education.

Education must come from without,—primarily from family; but to be a father does not confer nor import ability or willingness to educate. The greater the need, often the less capacity to bestow.

1. With state aid, universal education is difficult and slow; without, unattainable, impossible. Government exercises extraordinary functions to protect against yellow fever and flood. Why not against ignorance? Levees are constructed against overflow of the rivers, which is not an unmixed evil, for a sediment is left which enriches the soil. The overflow is local and occasional. The overflow of ignorance is constant, general, permanent; covers the present and the future; leaves no fertilizing deposit.

Government schools are the only agency for securing the education of all. That is the unexceptional experience of all times and countries.

2. They are the cheapest. The expense of educating ten thousand youth is not ten nor five times that of educating one thousand. Statistics from Pennsylvania, Ohio, Indiana, Virginia, and other States show an average cost per pupil of from $7 to $12. In private schools the tuition per capita is three or ten times as much. It is our duty to break down the enormous barriers of expense which make highest education the privilege of the wealthy only. If the amount annually expended in "female institutes," boarding-schools, academies, etc., could be aggregated into one sum, we should be startled at the prodigality of means in comparison with the poverty of results. The same sum judiciously expended should

supply every neighborhood with a competent teacher. The true policy is to have rich and poor equally provided with rudimentary instruction. Here are so many minds to be unfolded and so many energies to be directed, and this is the problem you are to meet.

3. They are the best. The State should keep a sharp lookout, with adequate supervision, for weak points in the system both as to cost and efficiency. Education is a connected work, and its parts should be so arranged that while each is a whole in itself, it should, at the same time, be a part of a still greater whole.

The underlying principles of a state system are—

a. The State, as a matter of right and duty, enjoins the maintenance in every town and school district of a sufficient number of schools for the education of every child in the rudimentary branches, by a proper rate of taxation upon persons and property.

b. These schools should be properly graded.

c. They should, as to tuition, be absolutely free.

d. The State should make an authoritative provision for a proper and careful supervision of the schools.

e. The whole educational system should be divorced from party politics.

f. By means of Normal Schools and Teachers' Institutes, or such like agencies, teachers should be trained for their work.

The State provides school-houses and furniture; qualified teachers, subjected to careful examinations by competent persons, with limited license to teach; systematized courses of instruction; just and equal discipline; frequent visits and inspections.

Private schools are generally classified very imperfectly, are often controlled by wealthy or imperious patrons, by personal or family influence, are established for money-making, and where they will yield the largest income, and are terribly expensive. A private teacher will not, cannot, establish his school among the ignorant and poor. He is self-appointed. No one is responsible for his fitness or good conduct. Of him there is no supervision. It is not easy for a teacher to be firm or impartial in discipline. Public schools are established in all localities, and are conducted with reference to the best and least expensive methods of education.

Private schools perish; the State does not die. Through all its mutations, revolutions, upheavals in peace and in war, Louisiana has lived. School-systems should be put above the haphazards of popular elections and the uncertain whims and caprices of a community.

IV. General education is a debt due from property to citizens. Government can do much for the betterment of economic, moral, and social conditions, without attacking the rights of property or becoming dangerously paternal. Property has its duties as well as rights. Limiting the government strictly to the administration of civil and criminal justice is pushed to dangerous extremes when it permits parents to choose illiteracy for their children. The "maximum of education gives minimum of government and maximum of liberty." De Tocqueville said "the greatest despotism is an untaught public sentiment." The Talmud says the world is saved by the breath of school-children.

General education is essential to prosperity; it is a condition to industrial progress; it has the highest economical value; it is the grand means for developing or increasing natural resources; it is the producer of wealth. Africa is the Dark Continent, with its infinite capabilities, because of the gross ignorance of her children. Agriculture, manufacturing, mechanic arts, all internal improvements, are the creations of intelligence. Contributions to human welfare have come from knowledge. Brute force is wasteful, unproductive. Cultivated mind subsidizes the forces of nature, changes crude materials into useful fabrics, creates those arts which sustain and comfort and embellish human life.

Ignorant, unskilled labor is limited to a few products, prevents diversification of industries. In the simplest operations the mental element is present to a controlling extent. Over the most menial, unproductive employments predominates the directing influence of the mind. Will, motive, judgment, need to be put in exercise. Slavery, from an economic standpoint, is wholly indefensible. It cursed us with ignorant, thriftless labor; it put a premium on bad cultivation, on deterioration of soil. Slaves made no inventions. Beyond ploughing and hoeing and rude tillage of tobacco, cotton, rice, sugar, corn, they knew nothing.

An efficient system of common schools is the best possible investment for Louisiana. Beneficent nature has been lavish towards the State in fertile soil and navigable rivers. In area it exceeds Massachusetts, with her granite and ice, six-fold; but what a difference! Why? Common schools give the answer.

100

Civil society establishes rights of property and makes things become property by confirming ownership. Highest kinds of property, vested rights, franchises, patents, banks, insurance, etc., imply high intelligence in communities. So do corporations. In an enlightened community property has a high potency of value; in a barbarous community it is not worth the risks incident to possession. Property, being dependent on education, can afford to pay to make education universal.

V. Every human being has an absolute, indefeasible right to an education; and there is the correlative duty of government to see that the means of education are provided for all. Government protects childhood, but childhood has more than physical wants. Infanticide is prohibited, but life is not worth living unless instruction supervenes. Otherwise, no true life, no real manhood. It is a travesty on manhood to make a brutal prize-fighter its representative. Education is due from government to children. The school is supplementary to family, to churches, in the province of education. Society rests upon education, in its comprehensive meaning. Man must be educated out of, lifted above, animal impulses,—a state of nature,—and made to respect social forms, the rights and duties of persons and of property. Education is to prepare the individual for life in social institutions. Crime and igno rance and non-productiveness are antagonistic to society. A child cannot choose his parents, his environments; and the state of which he is to be a member should give him an education, "to awaken to the consciousness of the higher self that exists within him." The first necessity of civilization is a system of universal education.

VI. Education is the only security for our free institutions; an essential condition of personal and civil liberty, of equality before the law. The political requirements of the complex, correlated governments under which we live, make education in public free schools a necessity. With universal, and largely ignorant and often corrupt suffrage, representation is a farce. We have manhood suffrage. Wyoming has woman suffrage, and the Governor of Massachusetts recommends it for that State. Only a wise people can govern itself; an ignorant people must be governed. We must accept the influence of the lowest stratum of population on politics. What we permit our neighbor to be, that we set up as the arbiter of our political well-being. Ignorance of the voter is an abridgment of the liberty of others. His ballot determines more or less our government. An enlightened and moral people is the best constitution of a state, the best preventive against anarchy and misgovernment. Monarchical governments are careful to have the heir to the throne well educated. History and common-sense teach that a government by the people requires more education, more self-restraint, than any other, and that the despotism and cruelty of an untutored mob may be more odious and oppressive than the despotism of any one man. The school should go before the ballot; otherwise an uninstructed democracy will become the facile tool of the demagogue and the villain. Macaulay said for every pound you save in education, you will spend five in prosecutions, in prisons, in penal settlements. Public education is one of the functions of government, and goes along with the right to exist. The life or death of the state means the intelligence or ignorance of the citizen.

VII. It is an easy transition to the commonest objection and the most formidable difficulty, — the ever-recurring, many-sided negro problem. I shall not underrate it; it cannot be magnified. Shutting our eyes, doing nothing, doing wrongly and unjustly, will not remove the danger. An old proverb says, "Cheating never thrives." Injustice has in it, always and everywhere, the seeds of retributive mischief and harm. Whatever a State sows, that also will it reap. The negro is ignorant, superstitious, non-tax-paying, with centuries of barbarism and slavery behind him. What limitations, race, heredity, environments, have put upon his intellect, I do not know. I do know that he is a free citizen and a voter, and that he is capable of progress and of moral accountability. I know also that he is a hapless creature of party expediency, a blind tool, a transferable cipher, and that by double organic law and the supremacy of those remote from and not in sympathy with you, you are tethered to him by indissoluble bonds, and that if you do not lift him up he will drag you down.

Emancipation was a great and needed revolution, marred in its benefits by giving suffrage to men who, according to those who imposed the boon, were brutalized by slavery. Right or wrong, wise or unwise, the act is irrevocable. Morally, socially, politically, its influence upon the white people, upon both races, has been

102

deplorable, incalculably vicious. We must save ourselves. Passion, prejudice, blind adherence to the past, a Micawber spirit, will avail no good. Until near the end of the eighteenth century it was the common belief that the ancient industrial system was to last indefinitely. In a brief interval a marvellous transformation occurred. One of the proofs of Caucasian superiority is the readiness with which men accustom themselves to social and legal changes, and conquer their surroundings. Let us not be impatient or over-hopeful. It sometimes requires generations, or centuries, to breed high qualities of body, mind, or heart.

At the risk of repeating what I have for years been saying, I must not omit to emphasize that a most important factor in the solution of the "negro problem" is industrial education. The negro needs to be taught, by line upon line, precept upon precept, thrift, economy, looking beyond to-day, self-support, accumulation of property, and the application of some skill—the rudimentary principles of science—to daily occupations and pursuits. The industrial arts, or their basal universal rules, can be taught in schools, and must be, if we would enlarge the productive capacity of the "laboring classes." Wedded largely to the soil, the negro can learn something of improved tillage and husbandry, and of mechanical appliances. Those who become mechanics in towns or cities can have some manual training. Wherever the negro works he should learn to work to better advantage and to save. Whatever else he does, whatever his conduct on farm, or in shop, or at the polls, it is of imperative need to expel ignorance and indecency from the *home* life, and to ally inseparably religion and morals.

The statesman, the legislator, who busies himself exclusively about capital and labor, or takes a microscopic view of merely material agencies, and leaves out of view a widespread mental development, is a blind leader and guilty of egregious folly. Louisiana needs the activities of every human brain. She needs a high state of general intelligence to make science and skill preside over labor and God's profuse and beneficent endowments, to create and diversify industries, to diffuse wealth, to build up a prosperous and advanced civilization, with all the elements of comfort and refinement; and free schools are the most effective and economical measure for accomplishing these ends. The first duty of government is self-preservation; and the noblest function of statehood is to develop and use to the maximum degree the brain-power of the country. In the use or non-use of this intellectual power lies the difference betwixt nations and epochs. The proportion of well-taught children to the population is the measure of the civilization of that people. Ours is a government of the people. Our rights are not dependent on birth, race, color, social condition, or any mere accidents. Our institutions open the prizes of life to the competition of all, and true republican equality is the equal opportunity of every citizen to promote his own self-elevation without any drawback imposed upon him by the government, or without any special benefit or privilege conferred on him to the detriment of others. Conditions of life may vary greatly, but no one should be permitted to say that the commonwealth and the laws treated him unfairly, or placed him at a disadvantage. Education should, therefore, be given to all; and to let a child grow up in ignorance is treason to the state, to humanity, to God. The conduct and character of no one man can be said to be a matter of indifference to others. Man is a voter, witness, juryman; he may be a public officer. He has duties and relationships beyond his trade or his civil functions. The last census shows, out of a population of less than a million in Louisiana, 318,380 persons, nearly one third of the population, over ten years of age, who cannot read. A majority nearly of the legal voters cannot read their ballots and are non-tax-payers. Gladstone, in 1878, said: "I have never heard of an attempt, as yet, to register those who sleep under the dry arches of Waterloo Bridge." Modern American statesmanship has given him the knowledge of the absurd and the inconceivable. Any man whose opinion is worth having knows that a majority of illiterate voters will, in the long run, ruin any country. It is political suicide not to make an honest, energetic, persistent effort to remove this mass of illiteracy and unproductiveness.

Universal education is an imperative duty. Judge Breaux, in his late excellent Report, says with emphasis: "Louisiana cannot afford to be parsimonious in so far as relates to her schools. Every consideration demands that school advantages be offered to the youths of this State. Without these advantages, the fertility of the soil and other natural resources will be as nought. . . . The schools are an absolute necessity. Therefore they should be established on a certain foundation, and the authority of the State should be strongly felt in their maintenance."

VIII. There are two postulates which I commend to you as the basis of legislative action. *First*, that the benefits of free-school education shall be brought within the reach of every child in the State; and *secondly*, that the property of the State shall support a system of schools adequate to confer this universal education. . . .

The State, in assuming the responsibility of education, has taken upon herself the consequent duty of providing competent teachers. Practically, the people are compelled to educate in the public schools, and they should be satisfied with none but the best. That is secured only by good teaching. That wanting, all is wanting. The superintendent wisely says: "The State and the community at once feel the good character of its schools. This is obtained and determined only by the quality of its teachers; the superintendent should, therefore, bring to bear a searching scrutiny into the intellectual, moral, and professional worthiness of teachers." The most approved means are by Normal Schools and Teachers' Institutes. The Normal School at Natchitoches, which I have just visited, is doing good work. It has been a pleasure heretofore to aid it, and the Trustees will continue the help. There is need of a president's house, of larger accommodations for teachers and pupils, and of more complete devotion to the Normal idea. I beg to commend the school to your liberality. In this connection it may be well to remark that while the Peabody Education Fund has heretofore appropriated to Louisiana over $100,000, and will cheerfully continue its gifts, yet the greater portion of the aid will hereafter be for teachers' training. Teaching seems to be the only profession or work in the world in which experience and professional preparation are not considered of indispensable importance. Those poorly equipped in knowledge or in teaching skill should not be content without professional training. If one has ceased to learn he is unfit to teach. Imparting information is not education. Hearing a lesson is not inspiring a thirst for knowledge. "Sins of teachers are teachers of sins." The mind's powers are to be educed and trained rationally, judiciously, methodically. An untrained teacher teaches words and formulas of books. A trained teacher teaches things, principles, thoughts; proceeds from concrete to abstract, from special to general, from rule to principle, from names to powers. Fantastical and absurd ideas of things are often found in minds of pupils. One of them recently defined the Passover to be the pouring of cologne on the head. As is the teacher, so is the school. Among the agencies which shape our lives, the personal factor is predominant. Truth comes with power when backed by a great personality.

In the opening chapter of his "Meditations," Marcus Aurelius enumerates the sources from which he had derived the precepts and principles which had entered as constructive forces into his character. It is noticeable that the entire list consists of persons. No mention is made of literature or philosophy, though the famous Stoic was a devotee of both. By his own testimony his character had been moulded by the influence of persons. It is always so. The most potent forces that enter our life are the forces which spring from personal example and contact. Such forces are vital and formative. They spring from life, and they continue with life. They represent the contact and interaction of spirit upon spirit.

"Ideas," says George Eliot, "are often poor ghosts; our sun-filled eyes cannot discern them. They pass athwart us in their vapor, and cannot make themselves felt. But sometimes they are made flesh; they breathe upon us with warm breath; they touch us with soft, responsive hands; they look at us with sad, sincere eyes, and speak to us in appealing tones. They are clothed in a living, human soul, with all its conflicts, its faith, its love. Then their presence is a power. Then they shake us like a passion, and we are drawn after them with a gentle compulsion, as flame is drawn to flame."

New Orleans is the centre of a vast area of territory and of millions of people,—the entrepôt of sixteen thousand miles of navigable waters bordering twenty-two States and Territories and conveying a vast internal commerce. Mexico and Central America and South America and the West Indies are her neighbors. Canals and railroads are to cross the isthmus. The great Northwest and Southwest are demanding a Gulf outlet and a capacious harbor. The soil of Louisiana is equal to the Delta of the Nile. The possibilities of the future are committed, in some degree, to your hands. The responsibilities of legislators are proportionate to their opportunities. What is to come of such boundless resources is to be determined, not by stolid ignorance, but by enlightenment and virtue.

At the battle of Tel-el-Kebir, in Egypt, the English army had a terrible night-march over the sterile desert. In the pitchy darkness, without natural or artificial objects by which to direct the course, rigorous silence being enforced, Lieutenant Rawson, chosen as the directing guide, was instructed to keep his eye fixed on a certain star, and regulate by that the forward movement of the column. At the break of dawn the fierce charge was made, under a shower of bullets and across the deep trenches, with the steady tread which has immortalized British valor. After the victory, among the dead and disabled piled in ghastly confusion, was found Lieutenant Rawson, mortally wounded When Sir Archibald Alison, who commanded the advance, was told of the sad fate of the gallant lieutenant, he went at once to see him. "Didn't I lead them straight, sir?" were the last faint words of the dying man, faithful to duty even unto the end. I trust that when your account shall be rendered to constituents and to the fast-coming future, which may enter upon the fruition of developed capabilities, you will be able to look back upon institutions of learning and well-endowed appliances for universal education, and proudly say: "Didn't I, in that time of uncertainty and peril, lead the people straight and nobly?"

42. The Rebuilding of Old Commonwealths (1902)[1]

WALTER HINES PAGE

These old commonwealths were arrested in their development by slavery and by war and by the double burden of a sparse population and of an ignorant alien race. When the weight of these burdens is considered, the progress made these thirty years in the development of the innate democratic tendency is without parallel in our history. The present backwardness of Southern life in rural communities and in old academic or social circles is but a picturesque reminder of the distance we have travelled. Descriptions of these may entertain us, as the charm of the obsolete appeals to all cultivated minds, but they give no hint except by contrast of the real forces of the period in which we live.

The process that has been going on in the upland South in particular is a process of conscious and natural State-building, constructive at every important step. Reactionary influences have been respectable, but they are spent impulses. There are two great constructive forces. The first is Industry, which has already given the essential power over to a class of men that bring mobility to social life and opportunity to them that can take it. This industrial development would finally work out the inherent democratic tendency of the people if no other force were brought into play. But no man who knows the gentleness and the dignity and the leisure of the old Southern life would like to see these qualities blunted by too rude a growth of sheer industrialism.

The other great force that frankly recognizes the arrested de-

---

[1]Walter Hines Page, *The Rebuilding of Old Commonwealths* (New York: Doubleday and Page, 1902), pp. 139–53. A native of North Carolina, Page was a prominent journalist and publisher before he assumed the role of educational statesman in the cause of the South. From 1913 to 1918 he served as the ambassador to Great Britain.

velopment of the people and is taking hold of the problem of their natural growth is the new impulse in public education. This is native, and it is nothing different from Jefferson's creed and plan. So strong is it that its recent manifestation may fairly be called a new chapter in our national history. In the presence of this revolutionary force, fear of reaction and doubt about the democratic "essence" of Southern civilization falls away. Beside this all other forces except the force of industrial life count for nothing.

Formal education has been going on in the South these thirty years with increasing efficiency in the cities and the large towns and at the colleges. There are communities in which the whole attitude towards modern life has been changed by the influence of the schools. But it is not of town life, nor of higher education, that I now write. I write rather of that new impulse for the right training of the neglected masses that is a larger matter than school-room work or academic or professional training—of the subject as it affects the direction of the whole people's development. From this point of view a dozen or two colleges count for little, however excellent they may be; and life in the cities is, in a sense, of secondary importance, because the cities are few and the wide stretches of rural life are almost immeasurable.

The situation is discouraging enough, Heaven knows. In the ten cis-Mississippian Southern States the proportion of illiterate white voters is as large as it was in 1850; and the public schools in these States now give "five cents' worth of education per child per day for only eighty-seven days a year." This is to say that the total expenditure on the public schools is five cents a school-day per pupil and they are kept open an average of only eighty-seven days a year. But it is precisely because the situation is so bad that it is becoming so hopeful. Schools of this sort are little better than none. The people do not care for them. The stolidity of ignorance can not be overcome by any such perfunctory attack as this. The leaders of the best Southern opinion have come to recognize this truth, and they have begun work in a new way. They have discovered that the schools must do something more than teach the three R's, for a people without diversified occupations and without training do not care for the three R's, nor do the three R's profit them greatly. An idle and unproductive man is no less useless because he can read and write.

109

It was this fundamental fact that General Armstrong saw when he worked out the system of training towards occupations at Hampton Institute for the Negroes; and it is this fundamental fact that the present leaders of popular education in the Southern States understand. They are training hand and mind together. The experience in every rural community where a school of this kind has been established, is that the people who cared nothing for what they called "education" are so eager for this training that they will make any sacrifice to obtain it. Herein is the beginning of a complete change in neglected village and rural life. Here, too, is proof that the people are not "in the essence of their civilization" different from the people of the other parts of the country. The "way out" has been found. The problem that the South now presents has at last become so plain that thoughtful men no longer differ about it. It is no longer obscured by race differences, nor by political differences. It is simply the training of the untrained masses. As slavery and war and an isolated life arrested their development and held them in a fixed social condition, so the proper training of them to helpful occupations will release them to usefulness in a democracy.

The new movement is revolutionary for another reason. The old notion of education was that it meant the training of a few. It is now understood that none can be well educated unless all are trained. The failure to educate the masses has sometimes brought tragic results to the educated. There was a man, for instance, in an old Southern town who became a famous scholar in the law; and I suppose that he was a man of very unusual learning. He became a judge, and he was regarded as the foremost jurist in his State. But his income hardly kept his library replenished. He lived in respectable want and died without making provison for his family. His son also was trained to the law; and, since the family felt it a sort of sacred duty that he should remain where he was born, his practice, too, was so small that he became discouraged and his life was a failure. The daughter sold the family mansion to pay the family debts. "But," as one of her neighbours said, "she is the first happy and independent member of that family." She teaches wood-work in the public school, and is training her nephews to scientific agriculture.

The men and women of both races who are leading this great

popular movement work with an inspiration that puts conventional teachers to shame. For example: A young agricultural chemist several years ago began with enthusiasm a campaign of education among the farmers. He put much faith in bulletins and leaflets, which were sent broadcast. "I soon found out," said he, "that sending out literature did little good as long as many farmers could not read, and many more would not." He left his laboratory and became an educational statesman, and there are few men in America whose influence in building up the people is greater than his. Out of a comparatively small acquaintance, I know many similar experiences. A well-trained preacher, for example, who has had much to do with the administration of the churches of his sect in rural regions, lately gave up his work and became a superintendent of public schools. "Till the country people are educated," said he, "church work will not stick."

Anyone who knows the work that such men are doing could fill these pages with a bare catalogue of heroic deeds — deeds like these for example: The principal of a school for training white teachers proposed to the faculty that they give a part of their salaries, which were meagre to the edge of poverty, to erect a new building for the school. Not one demurred. The building was put up, but there is yet not room enough for the self-supporting students that apply for admission; and twleve teachers have only four recitation rooms. They are occupied almost every hour of the day. Yet no sooner had their winter vacation come than the principal hurried to Hampton Institute to study its method of teaching handicrafts; and half the faculty went to New York to hear lectures at the Teachers' College. A vacation does not suggest rest to them but opportunity to equip selves better. One of them went, as soon as his vacation began, to organize a model school in a village of two hundred people. They had collected $1,000. He secured $500 from some other source. The building was opened and every white parent in the neighbourhood went to the dedication of it; and the school, with its garden, its kitchen and its workshop as well as its books, provokes such enthusiasm as the community never would have felt for a mere book-school.

Educational work in these States is, therefore, something more than the teaching of youth; it is the building of a new social order. The far-reaching quality of the work that the energetic educators

111

in the South are doing lifts them out of the ranks of mere school-masters and puts them on the level of constructive statesmen. They are the servants of democracy in a sense that no other public servants now are; for they are the re-builders of these old com-monwealths.

Any man who has the privilege to contribute even so small a thing as applause to this great movement feels the thrill of this State-building work so strongly that he is not likely to take a keen interest in such tame exercise as historical speculation. Yet it would be interesting to speculate on the effects of Jefferson's plan for public education if it had been carried out. Would the public schools not have prevented the growth of slavery? True, public schools and slavery, as well as most other human institutions, are the results of economic forces; but, if the masses of the Southern population had been educated, or trained to work, (and such training is education) a stronger economic impetus might have been given to diversified pursuits than cotton-culture gave to slavery, and the whole course of our history might have been changed. But, whatever may have been the results of Jefferson's educational policy if it had been worked out in Virginia, the de-velopment of Southern life in the next hundred years will be determined by the success with which it shall now be worked out. The nature of the problem is clear. The work will be slow and the recovery from these last effects of slavery may require as long a time as it required to abolish slavery; but of the ultimate result no man who can distinguish dominant from incidental forces can have a doubt.

The Southern people were deflected from their natural devel-opment. They are the purest American stock we have. They are naturally as capable as any part of our population. They are now slowly but surely working out their own destiny; and that destiny is a democratic order of society which will be an important contri-bution to the Republic that their ancestors took so large a part in establishing. Rich undeveloped resources of American life lie in these great rural stretches that are yet almost unknown. The fore-most patriotic duty of our time is to hasten their development.

Part V:

EDUCATION IN AN
INDUSTRIAL-URBAN SOCIETY

One of the greatest challenges to education in America came as a result of the transformation of America into an industrial and urban nation in the last decades of the nineteenth century. The value of education in creating a happy, democratic society remained a basic and fundamental tenet, and the education leadership still expressed and sought these high ideals and objectives. But more and more they concerned themselves with the immediate problem of determining the kind of education necessary to cater to the needs and demands of modern America.

The America of the late nineteenth century with its complex social, economic, and cultural structure required drastic changes in the traditional educational patterns. The breakdown of the family unit as a basic educational agency placed a far greater burden on the schools than earlier. The tremendous growth of cities far outdistanced the educational facilities available; and the rural segment of society consistently voiced its criticism of the inadequate and sometimes meaningless education available for the sons and daughters of the farming class. Immigrants were pouring into the urban centers creating slums and ghettoes which posed not only social and economic problems but educational ones as well. The new industrial order undermined almost completely the old apprenticeship system of vocational training. Corruption in administration, inferiority or inadequacy in training, and outdated techniques and subject matter were characteristic of the educational situation throughout the nation.

The modern America that was rapidly emerging was teeming with friction and unrest on the one hand and opportunities and achievements on the other. It was a dynamic age, frought with tension and change and with the promise of national gains and progress. Farmers were agitating for a fair return from their labors; workingmen through the newly organized labor unions were demanding rights and protection; industrialists were applying their know-how and farsightedness in the never-ending process of exploitation and expansion of the nation's potentialities. On the positive side was the cultural richness of the ever-growing cities which served as a center of intellectual exchange and a beacon light for the discontented elements of society. Not to be overlooked is the fact that the industrial magnates with their giant fortunes did share with the people, for one reason or another, some of their great wealth by founding institutions of learning and promoting the arts and culture.

In the vast literature pertaining to education in this era, sharp criticism of the failure and shortcomings of the traditional practices in education is expressed by such diverse groups as farmers, labor organizations, and social reformers, but the general tone is a constructive one of seeking to redirect American education in order to meet the needs of an industrial society. Few questioned the old faith in the American democratic experiment, but the role that education would play in adjusting and preparing the nation for the new economic conditions did receive considerable attention. The social purpose of education is the principal theme of these writers and innovators. Some of the more conservative forces saw the school as an agency to preserve the social order and assure its stability through emphasizing in the educational process disciplining of the mind and training of character.

Others, such as Lester Ward, pioneer sociologist, restated the case for universal education through the state rather than private means (43). His arguments sound like those of the proponents of free schools of an earlier generation, but his emphasis is on the social purpose of education. He succinctly expressed his belief in the efficacy of education: "The object of education is social improvement." "The distribution of knowledge underlies all social reform." In reply to the reformers, utopians, and critics of the existing economic and social system, he insisted that only through the spread of knowledge would inequalities be eliminated. Here is the continuation of the democratic and liberal strain in American educational thought which views education as a dynamic force capable of changing the social environment and improving society. It is an acceptance of the traditional view of education and the democratic ideal, but it is cast into the context of a social system with an inequitable distribution of wealth and power.

Ellwood P. Cubberley, educator and innovator, in his writings dealt specifically with the problem of how pedagogical methods and theories could best adjust to the changing conditions (44). He too looked upon education as an agency to promote democratic institutions and as a social institution that had to assume a new role in preparing man for the industrial order. How the school was to answer the needs of modern society became one of the most perplexing and controversial issues in the educational arena at the turn of the century. The crux of the problem centered on the question of industrial education, or as it was first called, manual training. This became the great debate among the pedagogical leaders as well as among labor, farmer, and business groups.

Officially the debate began with the Philadelphia Centennial Exposition of 1876 where a display of tools, drawings, and models from the Moscow Imperial Technical School attracted the attention of some of the foremost educators of the nation. Not that the tools and equipment were so unusual, but they represented a pedagogical innovation in solving the problem of technical education so important in an industrial age. To President John D. Runkle of the Massachusetts Institute of Technology the use of instruction shops for teaching techniques in the crafts was the "philosophical key to all industrial training"—an idea he introduced in his institution.

The manual training idea, which sought to balance mental and manual education, steadily gained in popularity in the United States. The supporters of the program stressed the fact that they were not advocating purely vocational education, that is, training in a particular craft or skill principally for productivity and sale. This was not the philosophical foundation of the manual training concept. Rather the purpose was to break the monopoly of mental training and of book learning with its emphasis on preparation for college work through a study of the classics. Advocates of the new scheme argued that traditional secondary education separated the schools from their goal of training individuals for the existing social order and taught youths to think without teaching them to work.

The first successful experiment in manual training was at Washington University in St. Louis, where a three-year secondary program came into being in 1879. With a combination of mental and manual training, the purpose was to provide a broad liberal and cultural education which would prepare one to take his place in an industrial society. With the success and spread of the experiment, a heated debate ensued in the meetings of educational societies and in the professional journals. For about a quarter of a century the manual training idea held the center of the stage as far as secondary training is concerned. Mental versus manual, book

117

learning versus industrial education were argued, while schools —both private and public—experimented with industrial education in the curriculum. The supporters of the idea used practical as well as theoretical arguments. The democratic basis of education was a principal one: the nation was committed to universal education, and it must meet all kinds of objectives and train all men. For example, Eugene Davenport, an advocate of industrial education, explained that the high school was the institution through which "the people are fitted for life" and thus it must "uplift and sustain and develop all men" (46).

The opponents rallied around the view that such training, instructing in skills, was basically vocational education—practical and narrow—and not rightly a part of the high school idea which emphasized the acquisition of knowledge and the development of the mental faculties. However, Nicholas Murray Butler, one of the leading educators of his age, answered the critics by presenting the case for manual training as a part of a general and liberal education and not simply vocational in purpose (45). His argument is a convincing one with its emphasis on training the receptive faculties and developing the power of expression.

The industrial training movement steadily gained in popularity. The interesting and significant fact is that it was supported by every important economic group—the business world, organized labor, and agrarian societies—each for its own reasons. Each viewed industrial education as beneficial to its own social and economic class. The industrialists were early supporters of the idea of the public schools providing industrial education, not so much for idealistic and democratic reasons as for the practical ones: their shops and factories could be manned by those trained in the mechanical arts at public expense. Furthermore, this would free their workers from the apprenticeship system controlled by organized labor. Thus to the business men industrial education was a weapon against labor and a means to promote their own well being. The National Association of Manufacturers was a staunch advocate of the manual training idea.

Organized labor in the form of the American Federation of Labor was ambivalent about the movement. Its main concern in these years was survival and recognition, and apprenticeship education was one of its few established controls over the quality and rights of the labor force. Yet labor leaders recognized the inadequacy and ineffectiveness of the old apprenticeship system and came to accept the idea of industrial education as a common right for all. In the selection presented, Samuel Gompers, the President of the AFL, traces the organization's position and reveals a somewhat mixed attitude on the question (47). As expected, his chief concern was for the welfare of the workingmen of the nation and the ways in which organized labor could in turn promote the well being of the community. It was always the interest of labor unions to dignify and elevate the status of their class. They accepted the idea of industrial education as a solution, and they found the justification for it.

When, by the first decade of the twentieth century, organized labor had accepted the principle of the public schools' assuming responsibility for industrial training and with the business world strongly supporting it, the two urban forces—usually opposed to each other—found themselves united. The industrial education movement succeeded in winning many other adherents, but the problem that loomed large was the matter of financing such an elaborate program, which required not only specially trained teachers but vast expenditures in equipment, tools, and machinery. The obvious solution was to seek federal assistance. Here the success of the agricultural groups in receiving national funds for educational purposes set the precedent, and the agrarian organizations joined the movement for industrial education as well.

This was a rare occasion in which the three major economic and social classes—business, labor, and farm groups—all accepted the importance of revising and changing traditional secondary education with its emphasis on classical and intellectual training. To the farmers, who were experimenting with organization as a means of political agitation as well as an educational device, the schools seemed completely out of step with the needs of agriculture. Whereas rural opposition had been strenuous in the common school movement, the farm organizations of the late nineteenth century and early twentieth had come to accept education as a practical panacea of their ills. Education was a way of revitalizing rural life and economy; but education had to be more practical. Agricultural and domestic sciences were necessary to prepare youth for farming and to elevate the entire class.

119

In 1906 the National Society for the Promotion of Industrial Education came into being. Once organized labor joined the ranks of supporters, it was only a matter of time and effort before the Society would succeed in winning over the national government to the principle of federal aid for vocational education. The success of the agricultural experiment stations and the home demonstration programs won over the agrarian elements — staunch individualists — to the idea. And in 1917 the Smith-Hughes Act passed Congress, a victory for the National Society. Certainly the preparedness campaign of 1916–17 played a part in the victory as did the fact that business, labor, and agriculture were solidly behind the plan. Secondary public schools were to receive federal aid for vocational training. In many ways, this was a drastic shift in educational policy; yet it was in line with the precedent set in 1862 when federal grants were made to promote agricultural and mechanical training in colleges and universities.

The Smith-Hughes Act symbolized for education the triumph of the industrial order and the modification of traditional secondary education to meet the needs of the new social-economic system. In idealistic terms this seemed to be the case. The modern comprehensive high school of the twentieth century was far removed from the traditional "Latin Grammar" institution and "academy" of the eighteenth and nineteenth centuries. The introduction of industrial subjects and domestic science attested to the changes that had occurred and represented the educational adjustment to an industrial age. Yet at the very time that the Smith-Hughes Act meant the extension of vocational training, the underlying principles and pedagogical methods were already outdated or on the brink of being useless for the new industrialism of the 1920s. Equipment, techniques, and instruction in the schools reflected the industrial and mechanical developments of the late nineteenth century rather than the innovations of the twentieth. And it soon became apparent that the manual training idea of broad, general education was principally becoming vocational training for those entering the employment field. The more practical objectives of the business and labor world replaced the high ideals of Butler, Davenport, and the other advocates of the liberal and cultural aspects of industrial training.

As early as 1916, John Dewey, already America's foremost

educational spokesman and critic, expressed his concern about the tendency of education to reduce itself to a mechanical kind of training (48). Yet he was completely dedicated to the need for industrial education for an industrial society. He insisted, however, that such training must develop mental capacities and imagination, must broaden and liberate the mind, and must promote the aesthetic and intellectual sensitivity of the individual to prevent the domination of man by the machine. Dewey's reservations were to a degree those of the earlier critics of industrial education, but he was committed to the idea of a new order in which democracy would be reborn in each generation, with "education as its midwife." He rejected traditional general education which did not train men for their role in an industrial age. Dewey called for new subjects, new methods, and a new general education; he insisted that the schools move with the times.

Business men played an important role in promoting industrial education, but their influence went far beyond this and proved to be a dominant force in the cultural life of the nation. With their enormous fortunes, the new breed of men could collect art masterpieces and rare books, build magnificent mansions and museums, contribute handsomely to the founding and support of orchestras, opera companies, libraries, galleries, and establish and help maintain schools, colleges, and universities. The America of the twentieth century bears the imprint of these men of wealth: the public libraries across the nation with "Carnegie" chiseled in the cornerstones; the great art and rare book collections; colleges and universities—Johns Hopkins, Leland Stanford, Jr., Vanderbilt, Cornell—to name a few. Finally the great wealth of the corporations, which were spawned by the accelerated industrialization, produced a new kind of institution which plays a most significant role in promoting and molding education—the great foundations: Carnegie, Guggenheim, Rockefeller, Ford, etc.

Philanthropy in education was not new in nineteenth-century America. It had come with the colonists centuries before. What was new was the vastness of the riches poured into education and cultural life. Furthermore a new theory or philosophy of gift-giving evolved that reflected the age and the means by which the fortunes had been made. In a sense it became a rationale or defense for the accumulation of great wealth.

Two men who contributed enormously to America's educational and cultural life were Peter Cooper and Andrew Carnegie— each representative of the philanthropic impulse of the century and of the changes that were taking place. Both are excellent examples of the well-entrenched American dream of success as the reward of hard work. Both lives reinforce the rags to riches legend. Neither was a member of the old aristocracy who had respectable though not spectacular fortunes and held supreme positions in political, social, and intellectual affairs. Peter Cooper, born in 1791, into a humble New York family, is more representative of the old idea of philanthropy that emphasized giving funds to promote the welfare of society, to train youth in thrift and industry, and to provide educational opportunities for the common man than the new philanthropists of the late nineteenth century. His fortune was modest, but there is another aspect of the Cooper gift, which created Cooper Union in New York City, that reflects the changing economic and social conditions of American life (49). The grant of $300,000 in 1852 was for the promotion of *free* education for *urban* dwellers, youths and adults; and such training was to be of a *scientific* nature in order to serve a *useful* purpose. It was the recognition of the need for technical training that makes Cooper a transitional figure in the area of philanthropy. In some respects he was the forerunner of the advocates of manual training. He too was primarily concerned with education that would fit one for life, but he did not advocate trade education but rather training that would advance both the sciences and the arts. His gift and the generous support of Andrew Carnegie and others made Cooper Union a reality in 1858. In the selection presented, Cooper tells in his own words why he founded the Union, and its director in 1902, Abram S. Hewitt, presents an excellent summary of the purpose and accomplishments of the "Union for the Advancement of Science and Arts" (50).

Among the later philanthropists who sought to promote learning and knowledge, Andrew Carnegie is perhaps the most important figure—not only because of the tremendous size of the gifts, but also because he represents a new kind of philanthropist. It was Carnegie who evolved a new philosophy for the men of wealth that came to be known as the "gospel of wealth" (51). In the *North American Review* of 1889, Carnegie reviewed the complex problem of administering wealth and came up with the solution of gift-giving as an "antidote for the temporary unequal distribution of wealth, [and] the reconciliation of the rich and the poor." The existing system of free enterprise and the *laissez faire* doctrine had brought great fortunes to a few, and also the recognition of social responsibility. Through proper gifts for public purposes, the new philanthropists would socialize their profits by converting the surplus wealth of the few to the property of the many and thus contribute to the elevation of mankind. The underlying philosophy was an acceptance of the right of the few to make their wealth as a result of their own excellence plus the application of knowledge as well as the cumulative contributions of society. This principle was a recognition of society's part in the acquisition of the fortune but also a safeguard against violent or radical changes and a justification of the free enterprise system and the existing social order. Here, too, is the concept of self-help applied by Peabody and the other philanthropists of the late nineteenth century. One of the most significant aspects of the generosity of the industrial philanthropists is that it focused on promoting education and culture.

The extension—both horizontally and vertically—of educational opportunities was the great achievement of the American people in the second half of the century. The public school, the state university, the Chautauqua movement, municipal libraries and museums, public lectures and institutes, and the settlement house were all part of the popularization of education. On the surface it seemed a fulfillment of the Jeffersonian principle of an enlightened people achieving the democratic ideal. But a strong conservative philosophical orientation is apparent by the early twentieth century. One of the best examples of the conservative strain—the desire to preserve the existing order—is particularly evident in the changing attitude toward the immigrant and his ability to be assimilated into the modern American social structure.

Long before the Nativist movement of the mid- and late nineteenth century, there was evidence of concern about the assimilation of immigrants because of their cultural, political, and religious differences. New England had a long history of suspicion of Catholics; Benjamin Franklin was distressed by the growing influence of the German people and their culture in Pennsylvania; and in the early national period factions showed their distrust and distaste for certain foreign elements whom they feared politically.

In regard to the question of Americanizing the immigrant and educating him to his new national status, not until the second half of the nineteenth century was there any deliberate and planned educational program introduced. The ideal of equality for the foreign-born was an integral part of the American tradition, and the long-established method of educating and assimilating the immigrant was considered a natural process. Living in America, experiencing American ways, was all that was required. When the common school came to be incorporated into the American educational scheme, this too became a part of the natural democratizing force, molding the immigrants' children into an ethnic and cultural unity. Pluralism was an accepted axiom of social diversity. As one nineteenth century educator optimistically expressed his faith in education, "Education will solve every problem of our national life, even that of assimilating our foreign element."

President Woodrow Wilson, in 1916, reaffirmed this old faith and optimism in the educative process and in the experience of living in a free nation as the most effective Americanization methods (52). This reaffirmation of the American ideal and the American vision seemed contradictory in 1916 when the immigrants were blamed for the social and economic ills of society and the idea of restriction was steadily gaining popularity. In fact, in the same speech Wilson tempered his idealism in regard to the American experiment by his pleas for loyalty to the American principles. This tone seemed more in keeping with the existing attitude toward immigration in the early twentieth century than did his expression of belief in the efficacy of education and community life in assimilating the immigrant.

The new immigration to modern America, the growth of slums, the formation of the American Protective Association, the immigration restriction movement, the fear of Americans toward the so-called "hyphenates" as a result of the European war all contributed to the formation of a new viewpoint on Americanization. The old belief in natural assimilation could not flourish in such an environment; the common school no longer seemed an adequate institution. Thus developed the idea of a formal Americanization program, sponsored by the state, patriotic societies, industrialists and humanitarian groups. That the Bureau of Education created a Division of Immigration Education in 1915 is indicative of the new trend. Here was an example of the abandonment of the American dream of the nineteenth century which viewed the educational experience as a process of inculcating love of country. Now in the twentieth century a new era had dawned; the newcomer was expected to conform to the standards deemed American by the dominant forces in the nation.

Two concluding and contrasting selections, both appearing in 1916, by Randolph Bourne and George Creel reveal what was occurring in American life and the place of the new immigrant in the new industrial-urban society. Bourne—editor, writer, critic—recognized the failure of the so-called melting pot idea and expressed fear of the growing demand for conformity to Anglo-Saxon traditions and the insistence that Americanization be in that image (53). The selection by Creel, who became Wilson's Executive Head of the Committee on Public Information during the war, expressed the more popular view of the immigrant—that he must be educated to the fundamental principles of American citizenship (54). This was one indication of the use of education as a means of protecting and preserving the status quo—a new strain in American educational and social thought as compared to the nineteenth century liberal and progressive doctrine.

CHAPTER 17

UNIVERSAL EDUCATION AND DEMOCRACY

The object of education is social improvement.

Lester Ward, 1883

43. EDUCATION AND THE STATE (1883)[1]

LESTER WARD

. . . we may proceed to enumerate a few of the special reasons why all educational work should be intrusted to the state.

Education can not be successfully conducted on the competitive system. It is an enterprise so wholly dissimilar from those of ordinary business life that an entirely different set of principles must be applied to it throughout. In the first place, it is not prosecuted in order to supply any of the demands of the physical being. No true social force can be named as its original motive. It is from first to last the result of cold calculation based on observation and experience. There exists no natural desire for education. Even admitting the natural craving of the youthful mind for knowledge, this would never be sought in any of the ways in which education requires it to be conferred.

Again, the recipients of education are not the same individuals as those who really desire that education be given. Where this desire is more specialized than in society itself, it inheres in parents or guardians, viz., the desire that their children or wards receive it. This is obviously a wholly anomalous form of enterprise, and finds no analogue within the whole domain of social undertakings. This radical difference of nature, therefore, clearly requires a radically different form of treatment, and the principles and formulas that apply to other enterprises are wholly inapplicable to this one. Adam Smith excepted education from the law of supply and demand, and similarly it must be excepted from every other established law of politico-economics.

---

[1]Lester Ward, *Dynamic Sociology* (New York: D. Appleton, 1883), II, 584–602, 607–14. Though best known as a pioneer sociologist, Ward was also a geologist and natural scientist. He became involved in the controversy between theology and science and developed an evolutionary interpretation which reflected his democratic and humanitarian views.

Every thing that is done by intelligent beings must of course have a motive, and, since all motives are merely desires, every act must proceed from some desire. Thus far, but no further, education conforms to all other human undertakings. The fundamental characteristic which distinguishes it from all others is that here the individuals who receive the direct benefit are not the same as those who desire the end. To those who desire the end the benefit is indirect. Those directly benefited usually have no desire but rather an aversion for the end.

There are three possible sources from which the motives to education may proceed, viz.:

1. The actual recipient.
2. Parents or guardians.
3. Society in its collective capacity.

Examples of the first class are rare, and are exclusively confined to recipients who have already reached the age at which education should be nearly complete. Such cases are rendered possible only by defective systems which neglect some until they come to the age of reflection and perceive the great need of education. A proper system would render all such cases impossible, and thereby eliminate the first class entirely. For in no proper sense can children be said to desire education. Very few crave knowledge even after they have been given the opportunity of tasting its sweets, with sufficient force to overcome their love of play and freedom. Until first taught somewhat, no child ever desires any such knowledge as education confers. The desire for education on the part of the actual recipients, therefore, can not be regarded as in the smallest degree constituting a *demand* for it, such as tends to induce a supply in the commercial sense. To them education is exclusively a matter of blind obedience to some authority. Every system of education, however free from state interference, must possess this character. It is nothing more than applies to all the acts of parents in the rearing of children. It is compulsory in the sense that it is required as a matter of obedience to authority, and it is immaterial in this respect whether such obedience be yielded through fear or through love. So far then as the recipients of education are concerned, a system conducted by the state is no more compulsory than one conducted at the homes of the pupils. State and private education are in this respect identical.

128

In education the economic laws which control other forms of enterprise are not only inapplicable, but in many cases they are directly reversed. This is the case with respect to the motives and the requirements. In general, those who most need education desire it least, or rather, manifest the strongest aversion to it. Youth is the period when the mind is most plastic and impressible. It is therefore the proper time to impart such knowledge as is within the capacity of the mind. Yet the love of knowledge increases in children with their age and with the amount supplied. Those who have most need least, and those who have least need most; but those who have most want most, and those who have least want least. If, therefore, education has any value at all, it is clearly nonsense to talk of leaving it to regulate itself, which is equivalent to leaving it wholly unsupplied.

The second class in whom the motives to education may reside, viz., parents and guardians, is a more legitimate one, since many such do desire it for their children and wards. Here the demand, consisting of many such desires, may and does secure a normal supply. This supply will correspond to the demand, *i.e.*, no more education will be supplied than is demanded, those who do not desire it will not have it, those who desire it least will have least, and each one will have about the amount he is willing to pay for. This is the character of all private education. It is the approximately exact supply of a greatly varying demand. The variations in this demand are not only quantitative, but qualitative. Not only will each one obtain about the same amount of education for his children that he desires them to have, but he will also secure for them something like the same kind. Individuals differ as much in their ideas of what constitutes an education, both in amount and in kind, as they do in all other characteristics. Hence all degrees and all kinds of education will necessarily be secured.

There exists one practical consideration which tends somewhat to lessen the degree of variation and heterogeneity of private education. This is the fact that it is economical to combine a number of these varying desires under one general direction, the children of many parents under one teacher. For the sake of economy each is willing to yield somewhat of his own peculiar preferences and allow at least an apparent uniformity. This is education as a business. The teacher, like the tailor, is obliged to suit his customers. He lives by his trade, and he must retain the patronage of those he serves. The differences existing in the desires of parents, and which are nominally ignored by co-operative instruction, are really recognized and respected by corresponding variety in the treatment of the pupils. A few parents have a sincere and intelligent desire to have their children acquire knowledge. The wishes of this class are complied with, as nearly as may be. Many conceive education to consist in attending school a certain length of time, passing through certain books, and receiving certain certificates. These, too, are gratified to the best of the teacher's ability. Others have ideas of their own about what their children ought to learn and are to become, and require them to be placed on special diet. Of course, the actual capacity of a pupil can have nothing to do with his rate of progress. In private education there is truly "no such word as fail." For a pupil to fail at an examination would be for the teacher to lose a patron and a part of his income. The great laws of business economics will regulate such matters as that. This is the self-regulating system. If a parent requires his son to complete his studies within a prescribed period, the teacher, on pain of having him removed to another school, will readily find means of proving his superior capacity and bringing him through with honors. Children of wealthy parents must of course receive special favors, and those whose parents regard them as precocious must be so marked as to sustain that opinion. The variety of textbooks will correspond to the variety of notions which parents hold about them, those which each used "when he went to school," however antiquated, being usually the only ones allowed. Such is, in brief, the general character of private education, proceeding upon the economic principles of supply and demand, the latter consisting in the desires of parents and guardians.

But here, as in the preceding case, it must be pointed out that in reality this law is reversed. The desire of the parents, so far from indicating the true need of education, is in inverse proportion to such need. Those whose children stand in greatest need of it are those who do not desire them to have it at all, and whose children, therefore, never receive it. From these the gradations to such as intensely desire their children to be truly educated correspond rigidly to the gradations in the necessity for education, the case last mentioned being the least necessitous, since, were there no school, the intelligence of the parents would insure a fair education of their children.

The system of private education, all things considered, is not only a very bad one, but, properly viewed, it is absolutely worse than none, since it tends still further to increase the inequality in the existing intelligence, which is a worse evil than a generally lower state of intelligence would be. The redeeming feature, therefore, is that under its operation very little real knowledge can be conferred. The less society has of it the better, and therefore its very inefficiency must be set down as a blessing.

The third and last source capable of moving a system of education is the will of society itself. As in all other cases, this will can only be expressed through the organized authority of society, or the state.

The peculiar aptitude of the state for carrying on educational work has already been mentioned. Its *rationale* consists in the fact that what society desires is what is really needed. The object of education is social improvement. Education is really needed for the purpose of making better citizens. This is practically the same thing as the higher end, social progress, which we saw to be the condition to increased human happiness. If education can not accomplish this end, it is worth nothing. Neither the recipients of education nor their parents regard it in any such light. With the former no desire exists. With the latter it is some personal caprice, some parental pride or social emulation—an empty motive leading to a fruitless result.

Again, society desires most the education of those most needing to be educated. From an economical point of view, an uneducated class is an expensive class. It is from it that most criminals, drones, and paupers come. From it—and this is still more important—no progressive actions ever flow. Therefore, society is most anxious that this class, which would never educate itself, should be educated. The universality of education, which is the logical sequence of its enforcement by the state, will be more specially considered presently.

The secret of the superiority of state over private education lies in the fact that in the former the teacher is responsible solely to society. As in private, so also in public education, the calling of the teacher is a profession, and his personal success must depend upon his success in accomplishing the result which his employers desire accomplished. But the result desired by the state is a wholly different one from that desired by parents, guardians, and pupils. Of the latter he is happily independent. This independence renders him practically free. His own ideas of method naturally harmonize more or less completely with those of the state. Systematic organization is what he constantly feels to be needed. Uniformity not only vastly facilitates the labor of teaching, but it enormously increases the product of educational effort. The teacher also naturally prefers to see his pupils improve and acquire sound knowledge. The tricks of diplomacy at the expense of educational progress, to which he must resort in order to please the fancies and gratify the caprices of the heterogeneously-minded patrons of his "select school," are irksome in the extreme. Freed from the necessity of planning to meet such cases, he finds time to plan true educational work.

Once more, state education is far better for the pupil. It is distinguished fundamentally from private education in dealing with all in a strictly impartial manner. The lowest *gamin* of the streets here meets the most pampered son of opulence on a footing of strict equality. Nothing counts but merit itself. Pupils take their places according to what they are, not what they are called. Public education operates as a gauge of the capacities of the mind. Each mind is, as it were, measured and its capacity recorded. A thorough trial of it would doubtless be of the highest value, merely as a means of eradicating popular errors respecting the fancied superiority of birth, rank, and station. But this is not its aim. Its aim is to diffuse intelligence. The fact that, under its undiscriminating rule, each mind must find its natural level, wholly regardless of conventional circumstances, is simply an incident to its operation. The child comes to look upon it as he looks upon other processes of nature, as something over which he has no control. He feels that in coping with it, as in coping with other natural forces, his success will be determined by his power. It is not something which can be accommodated to his whims. His tasks can not be shirked, or imposed upon other more willing ones. Violations of its requirements, like violations of the laws of health, bring their own certain penalties, and he learns to regard it, as he regards the other natural forces to which his life is subject, as both inexorable and irresponsible. This kind of discipline is the most valuable that could be administered, and does more to square up the character than any amount of moral teaching.

Lastly, public education is immeasurably better for society. It is so because it really accomplishes the object of education, which private education does not. What society most needs is the distribution of the knowledge in its possession. This is a work which can not be trusted to individuals. It can neither be left to the discretion of children, of parents, nor of teachers. It is not for any of these to say what knowledge is most useful to society. No tribunal short of that which society in its own sovereign capacity shall appoint is competent to decide this question. To the teacher duly trained for his work may be left certain questions of method, especially of detail; but even the method must be in its main features unified with a view to the greatest economy in its application. This must necessarily also be the duty of the supreme authority.

If society ever collectively realizes what the ultimate end of its being is, and comprehends the true relations of the hierarchy of means to that end, it will necessarily regard the distribution of knowledge as the one great function, outside of its regulative functions, which it is specially constituted to perform. It will concentrate its entire dynamic energy upon it, to the neglect of all those ends which, as we have seen, must follow from this one initial motive power.

The state education implied in the foregoing remarks is, of course, ideal state education. That no very near approach to it has ever yet been made is apparent. Society has not yet recognized in any well-defined form the first principle upon which its title to perform this function rests. It does not realize the nature of the disease with which society is afflicted, much less that of the remedy to be applied.

There does, however, exist a vague conception of the superiority of state education. It has been perceived that, where education is left to private efforts, it is limited to a comparatively small proportion of the members of society. It has also been realized that in some way education is a social benefit. These two conceptions have already become so definitely formed in the public mind that in most civilized countries systems, more or less efficient, of pub-

133

lic instruction have been adopted. That of Germany is supposed to be the most complete, but it consists of the education of culture and the education of research, paying very little attention to the diffusion of knowledge. In France public instruction is of later origin, and, though of late it has been greatly improved, a large proportion of the educational work is still intrusted to private enterprise and to religious societies. In England, *laissez faire* principles so far prevail that no system of public education can be said to exist. As a consequence, while there are many intellects of the very highest capacity, the masses are in a state of abject ignorance.

The systems of state education in the United States have been devised by the several States of the Union, and are exceedingly heterogeneous and defective. In certain States scarcely any thing worthy of the name of education exists, while in others the systems have attained a high degree of perfection. Defective as these are, however, they have certainly exerted an immense influence upon the people, and done much to render them capable of self-government.

While in all existing systems of state education, discipline, culture, and origination occupy much more prominent places than information or distribution, still in all there is doubtless much real knowledge conferred and great benefit derived by society. In all, however, there exists one fundamental defect, which goes far to neutralize their advantages, and stamps them all as unworthy to be regarded as the work of enlightened society, conscious of its interest and its needs. This defect and its remedy we are next to consider.

UNIVERSAL EDUCATION

[Another] principle which inheres in our definition of education is that it must be *universal*. The knowledge which society requires to be extended to one it must require to be extended to all. Otherwise the true end in view is not attained.

We have seen that in matters of education the ordinary laws of economics do not apply, that in many particulars they are reversed. In addition to the anomalies pointed out a few pages back, we have now to recognize the important fact that the value of education increases in an accelerated ratio as the number of uneducated diminishes. Just as the shepherd rejoices more over the one sheep that was lost and is found, than over the ninety-nine that went not astray, so society, when it fairly realizes its interests, will care more for the education of a mere handful hitherto neglected than for the mass already provided for.

It is to knowledge that civilization is due, and the true object of education is to confer knowledge. Civilization, as much as religious belief or moral character, is a personal matter. It is as false to call all the inhabitants of the so-called civilized world civilized, as to call all the people in Christendom Christians. Both these errors are prevalent. A civilized man must be a civil man, a gentleman. He must be assimilated to the conditions of civilization around him. The mark of a barbarian is not the language he speaks nor the deity he worships. It is his rude intellectual development, his narrow range of views, his rough treatment of others. Every thing that distinguishes a savage from a civilized man can be directly or indirectly traced to the differences of education. From the native Guinean to Toussaint L'Ouverture, from the prehistoric cavedweller to the *savant* who studies his ancient abode, only differences of civilization are perceptible. Doubtless there are differences of brain-development, but education, when long periods are considered, is the most potent agency in developing brain.

But civilization must reach its object in order to effect it. Left to chance, there are a thousand ways in which its influence is escaped. In sweeping down through the ages, it has only skimmed the surface of society. The great, the exceptionally talented, the influential, the fortunately circumstanced, the heirs of plenty and of leisure, such alone have reaped its advantages. The mass has scarcely felt its breath. In more recent times great reorganizing and redistributing agencies have upturned the ancient systems, and civilization has been more generally diffused. But, in this, chance has still ruled supreme. Modern civilization is wholly unsystematic. Those to whose lot it has chanced to fall have received it in proportion to their opportunities. A thousand angles and eddies have been missed entirely. A large proportion of the inhabitants of the civilized world are still uncivilized. In every large city there exist throngs of true barbarians—nay, savages.

135

Throughout the regions of the globe where civilization prevails, there are multitudes who are not in the least assimilated to it. They are, by their culture and conduct, far better adapted to Zulu-land or the Fiji Islands. They make the great bulk of the pauper, beggar, and criminal classes of every country. The total cost of supporting, punishing, and guarding against them constitutes half the charge of all legitimate government.

Yet this so-called "heathen population" have normal faculties and developed brains. Their bodies form the only attainable "subjects" for anatomical study, and it is upon their study that our ideas of the human system almost wholly depend. Of course, this is a disgrace, since anatomy should be studied from the most perfect specimens of the race, both physically and intellectually; but it shows that educationalists do not believe the immense gulf which separates these savages from civilized men to be due to any perceptible deficiencies in their physical constitutions.

Just as poverty in the midst of wealth aggravates its evils, so ignorance in the midst of intelligence is intensified by the contrast. A generally low state of intelligence is comparatively harmless, since there is a normal degree of correspondence among all the parts of the social fabric. But a stolid and vicious class in the midst of science, learning, and culture, like a "bull in a china-shop," presents such a complete state of inharmony and unfitness that the effect is out of proportion to the cause. Civilization, like all organized progress, has only been achieved at vast expense to the social energies. Its constitution is necessarily delicate in proportion as it is refined. Its differentiation has gone so far, and its integration is on so extensive and exact a scale, that it will not stand to be rent in pieces by internal discords. Every assault of savagery upon so complicated and expensive an organization costs society an immense sacrifice, and is felt in all parts of the social system. It can not afford thus to nurse a viper daily threatenting its life.

There is even a worse consequence. So long as society has this burden on its shoulders it can not progress in refinement. It must cling to a large part of its old crudeness, as a protection against its unassimilated membership. It must be perpetually hampered by a heavy coat of mail in consequence of the perpetual dangers that beset it. This tends powerfully to neutralize the progressive agencies within and to equilibrate the rhythm of its motion. In a word, while the state of civilization around them has no tendency to raise the uncivilized classes up toward its level, but rather aggravates the contrast, the presence of these classes in the midst of civilization tends powerfully to lower the condition of the latter and clog its advance. The need of ridding itself of these classes, therefore, becomes twofold, and, since they can not be annihilated, and will not civilize themselves, the importance of undertaking their artificial civilization is doubly great.

It is evident, therefore, that any system of education which falls short, even in the least particular, of absolute universality, can not proceed from any true conception of what education is for, or of what it is capable of accomplishing. Civilization is essentially artificial at best, and is in no way changed in this respect by being artificially and teleologically extended to all the members of society. The only effect is to hasten its progress and lessen its cost.

While the equal distribution of knowledge will thus prove an immense gain to society in preventing the encroachments of the ignorant upon the intelligent, it will prove of equally great value in preventing the encroachments of the intelligent upon the ignorant. Indeed, it is difficult to decide which of these weighty arguments for universal education is the more convincing. Either is alone sufficient; both taken together, conflicting at no point, but harmonizing throughout, are overwhelming.

Looking at the subject from the point of view of social welfare alone, it is obviously less important that a great amount of intelligence shall exist than that the data of intelligence shall be in possession of all alike. The end of life is enjoyment, not intelligence. The latter is only a means to the end, and to be worth any thing it must exist in such a form as really to constitute such a means. It is demonstrable that intelligence may, and often does, exist in forms which render it a positive evil in society. The knowledge which enables man to manufacture intoxicating beverages is unquestionably an immense damage to society, and strikes directly at human happiness. The knowledge which enables one class of men to enslave another class brings misery to thousands and enjoyment to but few. The greater part of the evils of society, which are usually and correctly ascribed to ignorance, might with almost equal propriety be ascribed to intelligence. The ignorance which causes them is only *relative* ignorance. The power that enacts them is the power of relatively greater intelligence.

Some thoughtful and well-balanced minds will doubtless say of the proposed scheme of education that it is only one of the many panaceas that are constantly being recommended by those who see all things from one single point of view. Others will wonder why so little is said in this work of the great social economic problems; why the distribution of wealth, rather than of education, is not insisted upon, since happiness depends greatly upon the possession of the objects of desire; why the contrast between civilization and barbarism, intelligence and ignorance, has been so strongly drawn, while that between wealth and indigence, "progress and poverty," has been neglected. The answer to all such criticisms must be that the sole object of this treatise is to arrive at the *initial means*, and that even did space permit, as it clearly does not, all other means to the common end of all reformatory writers, would be purposely neglected. And it is high time for socialists to perceive that, as a rule, they are working at the roof instead of at the foundation of the structure which they desire to erect. Not that much of the material which they are now elaborating will not "come in play" when society is ready to use it, but that their time would be better spent in working out the basal principles which will render social reform possible. Present attempts in this direction consist essentially in seeking to attain progress or even happiness *directly*, as ends, without employing the necessary means. Their failure is therefore as certain as their efforts are premature. The fact is, that these ends will take care of themselves whenever the proper means are adopted. Not that they will come without action, but the adoption of the proper means will necessarily dispose to action, and action must result, and of the kind and amount necessary to secure the end.

The distribution of knowledge underlies all social reform. So long as capital and labor are the respective symbols of intelligence and ignorance, the present inequity in the distribution of wealth must continue. It may be urged that, since there exists so great inequality in the natural capacity of the human mind, there must still ever exist, even after knowledge shall have been equally distributed, a corresponding inequality of intelligence, and that therefore the proposed change will only substitute one species of inequality for another. The answer is twofold:

First, the differences in native capacity, though admittedly great, are small compared to the differences of information. The supposed intellectual inequality is greatly exaggerated. The large fund of good sense which is always found among the lower uneducated classes is an obtrusive fact to every observing mind. The ability with which ignorant people employ their small fund of knowledge has surprised many learned men. While there may doubtless be found all grades of intellect, from the highest philosophic to the lowest idiotic, the number who fall below a certain average standard is insignificant, and so, too, is the number who rise above it. The great bulk of humanity are fully witted, and amply capable of taking care of themselves if afforded an opportunity. In fact, it is out of this class that the majority of the great names of history have been taken. It is a mistake to suppose that the sole element of excellence is superior intellectual power. It is usually an average intellect joined to an indomitable will, a tenacious perseverance, or an unquenchable ambition. It is *emotional* force, not intellectual, that brings out exceptional results. This is unfortunately often too apparent in the labors of so called "self-made men," whose real intellectual mediocrity, though overlooked when accompanied with so great energy, renders the results achieved comparatively worthless and short-lived. On the contrary, the really best minds are not the ones that accomplish most. They usually lack aspiration, they are too critical, too sensitive to the least defect. Great causal penetration and all-sidedness are antagonistic to energetic, independent effort under difficulties. Contrary to the common belief, the most permanently useful and solid work that has ever been done has come from such minds when so circumstanced as to find themselves in the very current of their labors. Had they not been so placed, they would probably never have made the effort necessary to place themselves there. The best minds require to have opportunity brought to them. Those who seek opportunities and create circumstances do so by virtue of emotional forces which usually accompany only average talents.

It is a prevalent belief that so-called self-made men attain their distinction in consequence of the adverse circumstances against which they are compelled to contend. The phenomenon so frequent in modern times of men working up from obscurity to eminence is supposed to support this view. Looked at more closely, however, this argument is found to involve a fatal fallacy. It must first of all be remembered that "obscurity" embraces all but a minute fraction of the human race. The proportion to their class of those who thus rise out of it is next to infinitesimal. On the other hand, the class having means and leisure is numerically very small. One case of distinction from this class would be relatively equal to all that can be named from the other. Yet no one can deny that there are many great names belonging exclusively to the latter class. It is sufficient to mention Lord Bacon, Sir Isaac Newton, Alexander von Humboldt, Sir Charles Lyell, or Charles Darwin, in order to show that leisure is not, as is claimed, a detriment to aspiration. It shows, on the contrary, that the want of it is the great barrier to intellectual excellence; that poverty and monotonous toil crush out millions of potential luminaries in society. Yet the phenomenon of self-made men is not without its lessons. It teaches the average native capacity of all men, without regard to rank or circumstances, a truth which is also generally ignored or denied, and whose denial is often made an argument against universal education, as is the fallacy just pointed out. The other fact of the relatively frequent rise of men of leisure to eminence, and the great achievements of such men, also teaches a useful truth, viz., that if the true merits of mankind are to be all brought out, it must be done by equalizing the opportunities of all. And it should be remembered that, while the work of the so-called self-made men has generally possessed only a temporary and fleeting value, that of men of leisure has usually possessed a permanent and lasting value. This is partly because all truly useful work requires *preparation*, and this the mushroom growth of the self-made man can not provide.

Thus some of the most specious arguments against education in general, and universal education in particular, are seen to rest upon facts which, rightly interpreted, really argue powerfully in their favor.

Mediocrity is the normal state of the human intellect; brilliancy of genius and weight of talent are exceptional. To read the current literature of the age, one would think the reverse to be the case. All calculations are based on the possibilities of the highest; the low and the average are wholly ignored. Too much stress is laid on the exceptions, and no importance is attached to the normal cases which constitute the great mass. This mass can not be expected to reach the excessive standards of excellence which society sets up. The real need is to devise the means necessary to render mediocrity, such as it is, more comfortable.

The fact that most of the important contributions to science and literature emanate from men holding chairs in universities or high official posts with abundant opportunities, and which bring them into direct relation with their subject, makes it evident that almost any one else under the same circumstances would have done equally well; or at least if some would have done less well others would have done better, the chances either way being about equal. These and a thousand other facts tend to show that the distinctions now so apparent between men are for the most part differences of position, of education, of opportunity—artificial differences—and that the real, or intellectual, differences are comparatively slight.

Secondly, admitting, as we must, that such differences exist, and are, when regarded absolutely, very considerable, we must still insist that the inequality of intelligence resulting from them alone is, as regards its effects upon society, comparatively harmless. Whatever may be the inequality of advantages thus produced, they must be due to inequality of *merit*, and not of accident or chance. To this none would reasonably object. It is a return to the natural and normal state of things such as prevails in the animal world. Each individual would hold his natural position in society. In this case, at least, the natural is superior to the artificial condition, but the natural condition can only be secured through the use of highly artificial means.

In this condition must also be found the true solution of all those troublesome questions about which the prophets of a millennium have so needlessly and prematurely worried. While with advancing intelligence higher views of the dignity of labor will prevail, still the varied kinds of labor will, as now, differ in the degree of talent required to perform them. But the natural differences of intellectual capacity will be great enough to furnish each vocation with laborers who are capable of performing its duties, but not capable of performing those of higher grades. The adaptation must necessarily be more complete than now, when sages do menial service and fools rule empires. The fitness of things will then reach its highest stage of completeness, and servants as well as poets will be "born, not made."

The present enormous chasm between the ignorant and the intelligent, caused by the unequal distribution of knowledge, is the worst evil under which society labors. This is because it places it in the power of a small number, having no greater natural capacity, and no natural right or title, to seek their happiness at the expense of a large number. The large number, deprived of the *means* of intelligence, though born with the capacity for it, are really compelled by the small number, through the exercise of a superior intelligence, to serve them without compensation. This is the result of the ultimate analysis of the problem of the present unequal distribution of wealth. For it is not the idler, but the toiler, the real producer of wealth, who has none; while the man who has wealth is usually a man of leisure — at least he has rarely or never acquired it through labor in creating it. The former occupies his position solely in consequence of his *relative* ignorance, the latter occupies his solely in consequence of his relative intelligence. Knowledge is power, and power has ever been wielded for self-aggrandizement, and must ever be so wielded. To prevent inequality of advantages there must be equality of power, *i.e.*, equality of knowledge. . . .

COMPULSORY EDUCATION

The objection that universal education implies compulsory education may be conveniently anticipated here. Since all do not desire education, the fact must be broadly admitted. But, when once squarely met, much of its repulsiveness disappears upon closer acquaintance. For what does compulsory education mean? As we have already seen, so far as the actual recipients of education are concerned, all education is compulsory. It is not this that is commonly understood by compulsory education. It is the supposed hardship of requiring parent to send their children to the public schools. It is thought that this is an unwarrantable abridgment of the liberty of adult citizens.

It has already been pointed out that government usually seeks to attain its ends by negative, or prohibitory, rather than by affirmative, or mandatory, enactments. It was also seen that this was because all direct efforts to attain ends are so difficult. A negative effort is the first step toward an indirect proceeding on the intellectual plan, and, as such, is in so far more successful than a positive direct effort. The odium of all mandatory laws is a good illustration of this truth. Yet such laws are by no means rare. They are constantly being enacted, and are more or less successfully enforced. The objection to them is often irrational, and is the cause of heavy losses to society. The case referred to above, of the groundless opposition to direct taxation, is also in point here. In fact, the collection of taxes by a state generally involves affirmative legislation, and its universality and success furnish a sufficient reply to the general charge against such legislation. It happens, however, to be an unusually appropriate example in the present connection, since the same ones who imagine it to be a hardship to be compelled to patronize the public schools usually have to pay taxes, not only for defraying the general expenses of the government, but also for defraying the expenses of these same schools. These they pay, with only the customary opposition.

It is the word *compulsory* rather than the meaning it really conveys which is so objectionable. All action in society is constrained action. Every thing any one does is simply a choice among many things he might do. Not alone by the national code, but also by the moral and conventional codes, we are all required to make constant sacrifices and sustain many important losses. If this were always upon the whole to our advantage, there would be less cause to complain. But all these powers which so absolutely control our conduct are perpetually compelling us to do useless things, and forbidding us to do harmless ones that we desire to do. We all submit almost without remonstrance. Those who are unwilling to allow the state to educate their children submit with the rest. Why, then, should they deem it a hardship to be required to perform the most important duty which a citizen can render to his country? But it is not as though this opposition were deep-seated and wide-spread. It is only a few even now who, without compulsion, are absolutely unwilling to patronize the public schools, such as they are. Those who believe in education at all—and most men have some idea of its value, though they may at first object, as they would to any change—soon come to see the personal advantage which it secures to themselves. Aside from the feeling that they ought to derive some benefit from the taxes they have to pay, they soon perceive that they are exempted from the payment of private tuition. Thus the dictates of pecuniary interest, the most powerful of all influences, tend to diminish the original aversion to public instruction. The few who object on the ground of conscientious religious scruples, considering the entirely secular character of state education, are not sufficiently numerous to command respect. The only remaining class is the poor and ignorant, who know nothing of education or its value. This class is large, it is true, but it is for their more especial benefit that state education should be established. To allow these to have a voice in the matter would be suicidal to the whole scheme. They are the true game of education. From this point of view, paradoxical though it may be, every such citizen is of vastly greater value to society than an enlightened citizen. He has a negative value. While each such citizen must now be counted as a negative term in the equation of civilization, education converts him into a positive term. His value, therefore, when reached, is twofold. The great superiority of state over private education, from this point of view, is that it can compel this class to become educated. Unless it does this, it can scarcely be said to have established its right to exist. To argue hardship here is to give undue dignity to an unworthy and unprofitable element. Such respect would not be appreciated any more than a fine point of honor is appreciated by a savage.

But there is another point of view from which this question may be regarded. It is due to this class that the state stretch forth its arm in their behalf and elevate them to full citizenship. It is really not their fault that they are what and where they are. They are simply the victims of the existing social system. They have been crowded further and further down by the force of unorganized circumstances. The state has stood by and calmly witnessed the process by which this has been effected. It has seen the social forces work out this result, and has not interfered. It has winked at the inequality of intelligence due to the inequality in the means of acquiring knowledge, and now it is paying for its neglect by being compelled to support paupers and prosecute criminals. Aside from its duty to itself, it owes a duty to this merely unfortunate class, and it can not plead the lack of willingness on their part as an excuse for longer neglecting this duty. They can not be expected to be competent to reason out what constitutes their true interests. Society *does* know and should take immediate steps to secure them, especially since in so doing it will secure its own.

While the scope of what can really be called compulsory education is thus narrowed down to a few fanatics and the irresponsible dregs of society over which the state should exercise absolute control, there are ways in which it might doubtless be still further narrowed. As nearly all social action is already constrained action, and much of it consists in a choice between two evils, human ingenuity is capable of making much of this latter a choice between two advantages. In other words, much of the action which is now unpleasant may be rendered agreeable, and much that is now done because it is required may be done because it is desired. Instead of being compelled to patronize the public schools, parents and guardians should be *induced* to do so. Even the lowest classes are capable of being thus *attracted*, and nothing should be left undone to secure this consummation.

The many practical questions which rise upon the consideration of an absolutely universal education, while they are not ignored, can not be here treated with that completeness which it is admitted their importance demands. They are questions of detail, of method, of administration, and would require a separate volume for their thorough consideration. All that can be said is that no practical objection can be sufficient to detract from the importance and necessity of the end itself, which is nothing less than the completion, by teleological direction and intelligent foresight, of the work of civilization which nature has begun but is unable to finish.

While the word *universal* ought to convey to the minds of all a sufficiently definite idea of its meaning in this connection, a few remarks upon its scope may not be wholly without use. Recognizing the fact that there exist all grades of native capacity for receiving education, it must be admitted that there exists a minimum limit to the degree of intellectual power which would repay the attempt to impart information. Below this lies the class which, while still differing from one another, must, for all practical purposes, be regarded as idiots. But, while these gradations are to be found when searched for, it must not be supposed that there is any corresponding *numerical* gradation. These cases of undeveloped intellect are the mere exceptions, and must be regarded as in a certain sense abnormities, or monstrosities. The fact that this class does not admit of education does not affect the other fact that the great mass of mankind does admit of it. It can not be concluded, because many human beings are so sunk in ignorance as to appear almost idiotic, that such are incapable of receiving information. On the contrary, there is no knowing what powers may be made to spring forth from such repulsive sources. There is such a thing as *latent intellect*.

Throughout society there are limits between which the sum of intellectual vigor in all its manifestations (faculties) in any one mind simply oscillates. In some minds, this co-efficient is equally distributed among all the faculties (well-balanced minds). In some, it is more or less concentrated in some one set of faculties at the expense of the rest (great specialists and geniuses). In a few, it is almost totally absorbed in one single faculty, leaving the rest of the mind next to idiotic (prodigies). In a great many, the particular faculty in which the mind might have displayed its power never finds an opportunity to manifest itself, the proper circumstances never presenting themselves for its development. It is in such cases that it may be said to be latent. This class embraces the greater part of those who are reputed dull, stolid, or generally uninteresting. They have never found their element, and, like a sloth on the ground, their mental activities seem awkward and sluggish.

When we reflect how few opportunities exist for the development of certain aptitudes, and yet how often these few openings are filled by men who seem to have been born expressly for them, dismissing the supernatural view which may be said to prevail, that such cases are providential coincidences, the thoughtful observer is led to reflect upon the probability that there exist throughout society minds fully capable of matching the most brilliant examples which the race has produced, but which, for want of opportunity, never shed a single ray of light from the fire that smolders within them. Putting this with many other facts and deductions which society as it exists affords, the error of supposing that it is of no use to educate any class because it is now low, or any individual because he is dull, becomes obvious, and another powerful argument for universal education is furnished.

The adage "No excellence without labor" would be equally true, though a truth too obscure to have ever become an adage, had it been "No excellence without opportunity." Where opportunities are rare and talents equally rare, since these must join to produce any results, such results are doubly rare. But talent can not be created artificially, while opportunities to a great extent can be so created. Unless the circumstances are favorable, success is impossible. The circumstances which conspire to create opportunities are of many kinds and degrees. Many of them are too special to admit of being generally produced and brought within the reach of all. But there are many that admit of this in varying degrees. Universal education could not fail to extend many such fundamental advantages to all mankind equally.

There is one such fundamental circumstance which may, from this point of view, be regarded as the mother of circumstances. This consists in an initial acquaintance with the given field of labor—knowledge that such a field exists. There has been no discoverer so great in this world as to owe nothing to this circumstance, none who might not have lived and died in the profoundest obscurity had not some external force first lifted him to that height, however humble, from which he was able, more or less clearly, to overlook the field of his future labors; none, who, had he chanced to live in another land or a prior age, could have achieved the results which he was enabled to achieve under the actual circumstances. The number of Newtons who may really be said never to have had an opportunity to watch an apple fall to the ground, may be great; for to the sons of toil and want and circumscribed existence, reflection even is forbidden. It is just this initial circumstance, this vision of the promised land, that education is specially adapted to furnish to those naturally bright minds whom fortune has restricted to dark and narrow regions.

There will come the objection from the value of time. Many parents commence to derive assistance from their children at an early age, and others apprentice them long before they can have received the amount of education which society should require of all. None of these considerations, however, should be allowed to have any weight except in dictating a policy which shall bring the minimum discomfort from these causes without in the least prejudicing the end in view. Should the case be so severe as to threaten parents with pauperism, it is far better that they be placed on the dependent list and supported by society than that their children should grow up in ignorance only to follow in their footsteps. The making of a few paupers is a less evil that the failure to prevent many from becoming such. It is still more for the good of the children thus educated. For not only is the prevailing child-labor a crying evil in society, but labor at large has as its only hope the intelligence, *i.e.*, the education, of the laborer.

Much the same general argument applies to those homeless and houseless urchins of the streets who live by selling newspapers, or perhaps by trivial thefts and sharp practices, or by begging. Independently of education, this class are proper subjects for state guardianship. They are to some extent a dangerous element, and their mode of life tends to render them more so when they become men and women. Add to this that they are usually endowed with very acute intellectual perceptions, and are fully capable of coping with the rest of mankind. They are therefore in a peculiar sense the fit subjects of public education.

44. Changing Conceptions of Education (1909)[1]

ELWOOD P. CUBBERLEY

From 1897 to 1907, our country experienced an unprecedented period of industrial development and national prosperity. It was a period marked by the concentration of capital and business enterprises in all fields; undertakings on a scale heretofore unattempted were begun; capital changed from a national to an international basis; "trusts," combinations, and associations were formed in all lines of business; the specialization of labor and the introduction of labor-saving machinery took place to an extent before unknown; new inventions destroyed old trades and threw hundreds out of employment; the immigration of people racially further removed from our own stock reached a maximum; city conditions everywhere became even more complex and potentially more dangerous; villages became more urban, and a more cosmopolitan attitude began to pervade our whole life; the frontier practically disappeared; the national feeling was deepened and intensified, and the national government was called upon to do many things for the benefit of the people which it had become clearly evident that the states could not do.

Such periods of rapid development subject educational systems to increased strain. National progress outruns the possibility of education to keep pace with it. Many readjustments are called for, and readjustments are not easy to make, and cannot be made at once. The need of broad, general, and diversified training, adapted to the needs of the future rather than to the needs of the present or the past, becomes even more evident. The educational system is subjected to new and increased criticism. We hear this on all sides

---

[1]Ellwood P. Cubberley, *Changing Conceptions of Education* (New York: Houghton-Mifflin, 1909), pp. 50–58, 61–68. Cubberley was Professor of Education at Stanford University.

149

to-day. The practical man would make the school over; the conservative schoolmaster clings tenaciously to the past. Criticism and skepticism alike prevail. At last the tension becomes so great that something has to give way, and progress, often rapid progress, ensues. A new view-point is attained, a new inspiration directs our work, new means and methods are introduced, and often a new philosophy actuates the work of the school.

There are many reasons for thinking that our school system has entered on another such period of change and development now, and that we are standing on the threshold of a new era in educational progress. The period since 1900 has certainly been a remarkable one. The number of new educational societies and associations which have been formed, and the number of congresses which have been held to promote some one phase or another of educational work, is so large that one can scarcely remember their names. The great educational awakening which has taken place in the Southern states is only paralleled by that started by Horace Mann in Massachusetts seventy years ago. The large endowments for higher education, and the deep interest taken in popular education by many laymen, are certainly significant. The many state educational commissions which have been created within the past five years indicate a general dissatisfaction with existing conditions and a desire for change and improvement. The new interest in school hygiene and the physical welfare of the child indicates a new and a commendable desire to care for the bodies as well as the heads of our children. The great educational lessons to be learned from a study of the educational, political, and industrial progress of the German Empire during the past forty years are at last beginning to take root with us. Above all, the new and extensive interest in industrial and vocational training is especially significant of the changing conception of the function of the school and the classes in society which the school is in future expected to serve.

A right-about-face movement, too, is taking place in our educational theory. When the school first became conscious and critical of itself it turned to methods and class-room procedure for lines of improvement, and psychology became its fundamental science. Its gaze was turned inward upon itself. Many reforms and improvements in methods and in the teaching process were made, but the

150

advances in organization and in the enrichment of the curriculum have nearly all been forced upon the school by practical men from without. The school now shows signs of becoming conscious of itself in a new and a truer direction; it gaze is now outward instead of inward, and the relation of the school to the world outside has now become a question of the first importance in educational procedure. The school is essentially a time and labor saving device, created—with us—by democracy to serve democracy's needs. To convey to the next generation the knowledge and the accumulated experience of the past is not its only function. It must equally prepare the future citizen for the to-morrow of our complex life. The school must grasp the significance of its social connections and relations, and must come to realize that its real worth and its hope of adequate reward lies in its social efficiency. There are many reasons for believing that this change is taking place rapidly at present, and that an educational sociology, needed as much by teachers today as an educational psychology, is now in the process of being formulated for our use.

Child life is everywhere experiencing to-day a new lengthening of the period of dependence and training. In proportion as our social life becomes broader and more complex, a longer period of guidance becomes necessary to prepare the individual for active participation in it. As our industrial life becomes narrower and its processes more concealed, new and more extended training is called for to prepare the future worker for his task, to reveal to him something of the intricacy and interdependence of our modern, social, and industrial life, and to point out to him the necessity of each man's part. With the ever increasing subdivision and specialization of labor, the danger from class subdivision is constantly increasing, and the task is thrown more and more upon the school of instilling into all a social and a political consciousness that will lead to unity amid diversity, and to united action for the preservation and betterment of our democratic institutions. The great numbers of aliens who yearly come to our shores and at once become a part of our industrial classes, many of whom are illiterate and few of whom have any real conception of the meaning of democratic life, add new emphasis to this point of view. Five or six months of common school education each year for a few years are no longer enough, and on all sides the school year is being lengthened and the educational requirements increased. So marked has been the change in this direction within recent years, that sixteen years of age bids fair to be the earliest time at which we will, ultimately, permit children to entirely cease attendance at some form of the public school.

Our school curriculum bids fair, too, to experience many modifications during the next one or two decades, and chiefly along a line that will lead toward preparation for increased social efficiency. Much antiquated material, adapted largely to the needs of a society that has preceded us, will doubtless be eliminated. New subjects and new points of emphasis in old subjects, better adapting the school to our changed and changing social and industrial life, will probably be added. Our city schools will soon be forced to give up the exceedingly democratic idea that all are equal, and that our society is devoid of classes, as a few cities have already in large part done, and to begin a specialization of educational effort along many new lines in an attempt better to adapt the school to the needs of these many classes in the city life. City, town, and country schools alike have, in the past, directed most of their training to satisfying the needs of the children of the well-to-do classes, and those headed for business life or the professions. More recently, most of the larger cities have provided some form of work leading to preparation for the executive positions in technical pursuits. The common wage earners, those who enter the industries as workmen, and the country boy and girl have been forced to take what was provided for the others, or to do without.

The situation has been somewhat analogous to that of the old colleges, with their Latin, Greek, and Mathematics curriculum and their small student body and limited support. With the introduction of many new lines of work and the democratization of all instruction, the colleges have experienced a great increase in students and in popular favor and support. Our public schools are at present experiencing some such change, and it is one that is likely to increase rather than to diminish with time. Vocational schools and special type schools of many kinds are likely soon to find a place in our more important school systems. There is some reason to hope, too, that the aim and direction of the country school and the small town school will also change, and that in the future these will seriously turn their attention to the needs of rural life. Ever since the establishment of rural schools they have been giving instruction of a kind which has led to the city rather than to the farm. The introduction of manual training, domestic science, and agriculture would do much toward making the country school and the small town school a more useful social institution.

* * *

A people who express themselves as completely as we do in free political institutions, and whose whole life is experiencing such rapid changes and advances as our own, is increasingly dependent on education for guidance and progress. As a nation we have been slow to realize this. We have cared for higher or university education relatively well, and our secondary schools are in many places well provided for, but our elementary, supplementary, continuation, and vocational schools have been as yet but imperfectly developed. The recent German commission sent to this country to investigate our educational conditions mentioned this as one of our most vulnerable points.

The new period of advance which we now seem to be entering also bids fair to be very paternalistic, perhaps even socialistic, in the matter of education. The old principle, fought for so vigorously fifty or sixty years ago, that the wealth of the state must educate the children of the state, bids fair to be even further extended with a view to a greater equalization of both the burdens and the advantages of education. Poor and overburdened towns and districts will be supplied with sufficient means to enable them to provide a good school for their children, and the present great difference in tax rates, to provide practically the same educational advantages, will be in large part equalized by the state. There is, as yet, a small but a very significant tendency for the school to free itself from the financial control of the town board or city council, and to erect itself as an independent and a coördinate branch of the town or city government, responsible only to the people for its work and its expense. There are many signs of an increasing centralization of management which will ultimately lead to greater efficiency. Many options which communities have to-day will in time be changed into obligations. The state oversight of private and parochial education is likely to increase slowly, especially along the lines of uniformity in statistics and records, sanitary inspection, common standards of work, and the enforcement of the attendance laws. In particular, the attitude toward the control of the child is likely to change. Each year the child is coming to belong more and more to the state, and less and less to the parent. In all that relates to proper care, kindness, education, and advantages, the child belongs to the parent; but when neglect, abuse, and the deprivation of the child of any natural right takes place, the child belongs to the state. The right to reasonably good treatment, proper care, an education, protection from vice, and protection from labor beyond his strength and years, the state will soon guarantee. The plea in defense that "the child is my child" will not be accepted much longer by society. Our future welfare is too thoroughly in the keeping of the child to permit of such a policy.

The movement for general education for all of the people has been essentially a democratic movement. Everywhere west of the Alleghany Mountains the girl has shared equally with the boy in all of the advantages provided. The masses, who have been the voting strength of the movement, have seen in it a chance for their children to rise, and educators and statesmen have seen in it the safety of the republic. School systems with us are thoroughly democratic. An educational ladder for all who can afford it and have the mental capacity to use it extends from the kindergarten or primary school to and through the state university. Only in the states of the North Atlantic group, Maine alone excepted, has there been a failure to carry the system to its logical conclusion at the top.

The evils and shortcomings of democracy are many and call loudly for remedies and improvement. Whether we shall have remedies and improvement or not depends very largely on how the next generation is trained. The ideas taught in the school to-day become the actuating principles of democracy to-morrow. Because the school is so thoroughly a democratic institution and responds so quickly to democratic sentiment, the school has for long hesitated to touch, except in a very cautious manner, many of the evils and shortcomings of democracy. The greatest obstacle to intelligent educational and social progress is the lack of intelligence and grasp of democracy itself. It takes time and patience to educate and move the mass, yet in some way the school must touch these sores. Our state governments are weak and inefficient, we say; the school must then teach, and teach in some effective manner, the

154

principles of strong and effective government. Our city governments are corrupt, we hear; fundamental moral and economic principles must then be taught to the masses, so that they may realize the importance of civic righteousness, and understand as well who ultimately pays the bills for all mismanagement. Our people waste their money and their leisure in idle and profligate ways, we say; a knowledge of values and of how to utilize leisure time must then be taught. The list might be prolonged over pages, with similar conclusions. Through all the complicated machinery of the school, some way must be found to awaken a social consciousness as opposed to class consciousness, to bring out the important social and civic lessons, to point out our social and civic needs, and to teach our young people how to live better and to make better use of their leisure time. Reading, Writing, Arithmetic, Grammar, Geography, and History, the staples of the elementary curriculum, are really of little value except as they are closely related with the needs and problems of our social, civic, and industrial life.

This new conception shifts the emphasis in education from methods to men, and this new conception has underlain many of the better courses of study issued for our schools during recent years. It also underlies much of the discussion of the present time. Teachers as a body, though, are not thoroughly conscious of such a purpose or need, and courses of study alone cannot produce results. If our schools are to become more effective social institutions, our teachers must become more effective social workers. What teachers need, as much as anything else, is a knowledge of democracy's needs and problems, and of conditions to be met. Our teaching force is composed largely of women, and women are seldom interested by nature in this point of view. Their training for generations has been along different lines. Those teachers who enter the work wholly by examination have little opportunity ever to acquire this point of view, and the examination door should be closed as soon as financial conditions will permit. The time to impart ideals is during the training period, and an introduction to the social point of view and the social and industrial problems before us as a nation ought to be an essential part of the training of every normal school. A normal school which is essentially an apprentice school will inevitably turn out teachers with limited vision and little power of growth, while the call to-day for far-sighted teachers of large adaptability is greater than ever before in our history.

The work of public education is destined in the near future to be one of the most important lines of work which our republic has to do. Its importance in a government such as ours can scarcely be overestimated. Each man with us is the captain of his own fate and the carver of his own destiny. It is within his power to do great good or to do great harm. To decide righteously and to act wisely he must know. Knowledge and training, if of the right type, can hardly be provided too extensively. The over educated man is scarcely possible if an education adapted to his needs and station in life is given him. The work of public education is with us, too, to a large degree, a piece of religious work. To engage in it is to enlist in the nation's service. Its call is for those who would dedicate themselves in a noble way. Those who would serve must be of the world, with red blood in their veins; they must know the world, its needs, and its problems; they must have largeness of vision, and the courage to do and to dare; and they must train the youth with whom they come in contact for useful and efficient action.

CHAPTER 18

THE GREAT DEBATE ON INDUSTRIAL EDUCATION

Education to teach us how to live.

Dr. Munger, quoted by
Nicholas Murray Butler, 1888

45. THE ARGUMENT FOR MANUAL TRAINING (1888)[1]

NICHOLAS MURRAY BUTLER

No phase of the history of civilization is more interesting than that which deals with the theory and practice of education. In the educational theory of an age we find the summation of its philosophy; in the educational practice, an epitome of its activities. The school is a microcosm, and properly studied it will furnish us the clue to the proper estimation of the status of every problem that vexed a particular generation. It will not solve those problems, but it will tell us how its contemporaries tried to solve them. The reason for this is that the school is the point of contact between each generation and its successor. It is the only point at which one generation meets its successor systematically and with a definite purpose in view. And to the attainment of this purpose—the preparation of the rising generation to take its place in life—it brings all its best energies and all its ripest experience.

There is much confusion in the popular mind between the end and the means of education, and this confusion effectually prevents any proper estimation of the meaning and the lessons of educational history. Unless this confusion is removed it will be impossible to understand the latest development of pedagogic thought, the one which we are to consider briefly in this paper.

The immediate end in all formal education is the development of the mind's powers and capacities. This end is always the same and is never absent. The means of education, on the other hand, are continually changing and depend upon two varying factors— our knowledge of the child's mind and the character of its envi-

---

[1]Nicholas Murray Butler, *The Argument for Manual Training* (New York and Chicago: E. L. Kellog, 1888), pp. 373–95. Butler was a prominent figure in education in America until his death in 1947. He served as Professor of Philiosphy at Columbia University, President of Barnard College and of Teachers College, and from 1901–45 as President of Columbia University.

ronment. These two factors vary with the progress of knowledge, and are not quite the same in two consecutive decades, probably wholly different in two consecutive centuries. The psychology of Descartes is not that of Aristotle, nor is the psychology of Locke that of Descartes: and neither Aristotle, Descartes, nor Locke approximated the knowledge of the working of the human mind that we possess today. The changed conditions of practical life and the altered characteristics of civilization are even more marked than the advances in mental science. It is far easier to contrast than to compare the civilization of Greece at the time of Socrates, of England at the time of the Stuarts, and that of the New World today. The magnitude of the changes and their rapidity do not admit of appropriate expression and defy the power of statistics to portray. It is plain, then, that the means of education, — what is sometimes called its content as distinguished from its form, — should and must vary to keep pace with our widening knowledge and our broadening and deepening civilization. Some difficulty is found in making this argument plain, especially to teachers. They are quite unwilling, very often, to believe that the curriculum in which they themselves were trained and on which they are now actively at work, is not the best — or at all events good enough for an indefinite length of time. Many of them would doubtless be considerably surprised could they see clearly what changes are wrought almost annually. The course of study in the common school today is not just what it was ten years ago, and any comparison between our school programmes and those of Horace Mann would exhibit a striking diversity. This diversity is even more marked in the manner of imparting the instruction than in the material imparted. The truth is that progress in this, as in other matters, goes on without our knowing it, and it is only after the lapse of considerable time that the visible effects of this progress engage our attention.

It would be a gross error for those who attach themselves to a new educational movement, to denounce preceding systems and conditions as misleading, worthless, bad. The most beautiful flower depends for its existence upon a clumsy and unattractive root. The flower loses its beauty and attractiveness if torn from the source of its life and strength. So it is with educational systems. The last makes the next possible; and the newest has quite enough to do without undertaking the profitless task of pointing out how all earlier systems would have failed had they been called upon to do something which in the nature of the case it was not possible for them to be called upon to do. Growth is continuous. Each stage is necessary; and it is worse than useless to attempt to exalt any one at the expense of that which laid the basis for it. Each system and each theory of education may have been the best for its own time. It can not be fairly judged by the standards of a later period. All of these points must be borne in mind in coming to the consideration of the question, shall manual training be given a place in the school curriculum?—for that is the concrete form in which the latest development of educational thought presents itself to us.

The two phrases, "manual training" and "industrial education,"—the latter term being intended to signify an education which recognizes and includes manual training,—are ambiguous and subject to serious misconstruction. It is a misfortune that no acceptable substitute for them has yet been found. Industrial education is an education in which the training of the pupil's powers of expression goes on side by side with the training of his receptive faculties, and in which the training of both is based on a knowledge of things and not of words merely. Industrial education is not technical education, though many persons confound the two. Technical education is a training in some particular trade, industry, or set of trades or industries, with a view to fitting the pupil to pursue it or them as the means of gaining his livelihood. It is a special education, like that of the lawyer or the physician. It takes for granted a general education and builds upon it as a foundation. Industrial education, on the other hand, is the foundation itself. It is the general and common training which underlies all instruction in particular techniques. It relies for its justification upon the nature of the human mind, its powers, and capacities. It may fairly be asked, then, why if this is the case, is the word "industrial" used; why is not this general and fundamental training denominated simply education? Though the question is natural, the answer is plain. We cannot give the word education the signification intended, because at present another and narrower signification attaches to the word. Education shifts its meaning continually to accord with the ideals of the age. . . . We might

160

trace the history of educational theories to the present time, and we should find it a continual illustration of the fact that education means something different at each stage of the world's progress. If, then, the argument for manual training is as sound as I believe it to be, what we mean by industrial education today will be included in the concept of education as understood by the next generation. For the present, however, the prefixing of some adjective is necessary to mark the divergence. For this purpose the word "industrial" was unfortunately selected.

The manual training movement, as we know it, is new. It was put upon a strictly scientific basis a very short time ago indeed. But it has been "in the air," as the saying is, for a long time. Over two hundred and fifty years ago Comenius prescribed manual training as part of the true curriculum. The *Didactica Magna* contains specific directions concerning it. Locke, Rousseau, and Fichte all emphasized manual training, though for different reasons. Locke agreed with Comenius, and regarded it chiefly from the standpoint of its value for practical life. Rousseau and Fichte, however, saw that its influence on the growth of the pupil, mental as well as physical, was to be desired. Froebel in his Kindergarten reduced theory to practice, and in the Kindergarten all manual training, as well as all rational and systematic education, has its basis. But Froebel's work did not include the development of a scheme of manual training for older pupils. This was furnished many years later and from an unexpected quarter. M. Victor Della-Vos, director of the Imperial Technical School of Moscow, took the initiatory step. His report, made at the Expositions in Philadelphia in 1876 and Paris in 1878, contains this passage: "In 1868 the school council considered it indispensable, in order to secure the systematic teaching of elementary practical work, to separate entirely the school workshops from the mechanical works in which the orders for private individuals are executed. By the separation alone of the school workshops from the mechanical works the principal aim was, however, far from being attained. It was found necessary to work out such a method of teaching the elementary principles of mechanical art as, first, should demand the least possible length of time for their acquirement; secondly, should increase the facility of the supervision of the graded employment of pupils; thirdly, should impart to the study of practical work the character of a sound, systematic acquirement of knowledge; and fourthly, should facilitate the demonstration of the progress of every pupil at stated times."

This Russian experiment was made known to the people of the United States in 1876 by Prof. John D. Runkle, then president of the Massachusetts Institute of Technology. In his annual report for 1876 Prof. Runkle gave an elaborate account of the Russian system and pointed out its application to the work of the institution over which he presided. In consequence a school of Mechanic Arts was added to the equipment of the Institute. In 1879 the St. Louis Manual Training School was organized, and the subject of manual training was formally put before American educators for investigation and criticism. Both the Boston and the St. Louis experiments, however, only suggested the real question at issue — they did little or nothing to solve it. They made it plain that for boys of high-school age manual instruction could be devised that would be practical yet disciplinary, educational not technical.

The next step was to recognize the unity of principle which underlay the Kindergarten at one end of the educational scheme and the manual training school at the other. It was observed that both recognized the activities and the expressive powers as well as the receptivities and assimilative powers. It was seen that the Kindergarten and the manual training school were evidences of one and the same educational movement, though appearing at different points on the line. The observation of investigators was then directed to schools of the grades commonly known as primary and grammar, in order to determine whether or not their curricula were organized in accordance with the principle in question. It was soon found that they were not, and it then remained to be decided whether the application of the principle extended to them, or whether for some peculiar reason it could not be applied there. When this stage was reached the very essence of the manual training movement was involved. If it was based on a pedagogic principle and if that principle was sound, then manual training must be placed in schools of every grade. This question has now been fully answered. The manual training movement is based on a sound pedagogic principle and manual training must be introduced into schools of every grade. To the statement and brief elucidation of that principle we may now turn.

162

In the first place, let me remind you of the distinction already made between the end and the means of education; that the one, the development of the mental faculties, is always the same, but that the second varies according to our knowledge of the child's mind and the changing character of its environment. The manual training which is to be introduced into the school must accord with the end of education and also be abreast of the present requirements of the means of education.

It is objected as to the first that manual training is not mental training, but simply the development of skill in the use of certain implements. This is bad common sense and worse psychology. Manual training is mental training through the hand and eye, just as the study of history is mental training through the memory and other powers. There is something incongruous and almost paradoxical in the fact that while education is professedly based upon psychology, and psychology has ever since Locke been emphasizing the importance of the senses in the development of mental activity, nevertheless sense-training is accorded but a narrow corner in the school-room and even that grudgingly. Industrial education is a protest against this mental oligarchy, the rule of a few faculties. It is a demand for mental democracy, in which each power of mind, even the humblest, shall be permitted to occupy the place that is its due. It is truly and strictly psychological. In view of the prevalent misconception on this point, too much stress cannot be laid upon the fact that manual training, as we use the term, is mental training. What does it matter that the muscles of the arm and hand be well-nourished and perfectly developed, that the nerves be intact and healthy, if the mind that directs, controls, and uses them be wanting? What is it that models the graceful form and strikes the true blow, the muscles or the mind? Do the retina and optic nerves see, or does the mind? It is the mind that feels and fashions, and the mind that sees; the hand and the eye are the instruments which it uses. The argument for manual training returns to this point again, and again, not only because it is essential to a comprehension of what is meant by manual training, but because it furnishes the ground for the contention that manual training should be introduced into the public schools. No one with any appreciation of what our public school system is and why it exists, would for a moment suggest that it be used to train appren-

163

tices for any trade or for all trades. It is not the business of the public school to turn out draughtsmen, or carpenters, or metal-workers, or cooks, or seamstresses, or modellers. Its aim is to send out boys and girls that are well and harmoniously trained to take their part in life. It is because manual training contributes to this end, that it is advocated. We will all admit, indeed I will distinctly claim, that the boy who has passed through the curriculum which includes manual training will make a better carpenter, a better draughtsman, or a better metalworker than he who has not had the benefit of that training. But it is also true that he will make a better lawyer, a better physician, a better clergyman, a better teacher, a better merchant—should he elect to follow any one of those honorable callings—and all for the same reason; namely, that he is a better equipped and more thoroughly educated man than his fellow in whose preparation manual training is not included. Therefore manual training is in accord with the aim of education.

We may accept such psychological postulates as we will, yet for educational purposes we may agree that the mental powers are roughly divisible into two classes, the receptive and the expressive or active. . . . It is essential in training both the powers of reception and the powers of expression that the child deal with things and objects, and not alone with what some one has said or written about things. . . .

Because of this psychological and practical soundness of manual training, the argument in its favor calls for the remodelling of the present curriculum. Manual training cannot be added as an appendix to any other study; it must enter on a plane with the rest. It does not ask admittance as a favor; it demands it as a right. It is suggested that much time now wasted could be saved by better methods of teaching, that logical puzzles over which so much time is now spent be eliminated from arithmetic, that spelling be taught in conjunction with writing, and history with reading. The time thus saved is to be appropriated in about equal parts to drawing and constructive work, both together to occupy from one-quarter to one-third of the pupil's time. Drawing lies at the basis of all manual training, and is to be taught in every grade as a means of expression of thought, only incidentally as an art. The constructive work is to be in material adapted to the child's age and powers. It is at first in paper and pasteboard, then in clay, then in wood, and

164

finally, in the academic grades, in metal. These means are, so far as our present experience goes, the best ones for the training desired. But wider experience and deeper insight may alter or improve them at any time, just as our readers, our spellers, and our arithmetics have been improved.

The curriculum which includes manual training, in addition to meeting the demands of our present knowledge of the pupil's mind and its proper training, is better suited to prepare the child for life than that curriculum which does not include it. The school is to lay the foundation for intelligent citizenship, and as the conditions of intelligent citizenship change with the advance of civilization, the course of study must change in order to adapt itself to these new conditions. No one who can read the lessons of history will assert that the ideally educated man is always the same. Greek education sought beauty, mental and physical; monastic education sought asceticism and a soul dead to the world; Renaissance education sought classical culture and minute acquaintance with the literatures of Greece and Rome; modern education has broadened this conception of culture until it embraces the modern literatures and natural science; common school education in the United States in these closing years of the nineteenth century has broadened its ideal yet further, and is now demanding that the pupil be so trained that the great, busy life of which he is so soon to form a part be not altogether strange to him when he enters it. It demands practicality. It demands reality. It demands that the observation, the judgment, and the executive faculty be trained at school as well as the memory and the reason. Despite the fact that the three former are the most important faculties that the human mind possesses, it is astounding how completely they are overlooked in the ordinary course of study. . . .

At certain stages of civilization and national development there is a natural training of the expressive or active powers which though desultory, is by no means ineffective. I refer to the training which is the result of an active, out-of-door life, especially in rural districts. The country boy receives this training in the hundred and one small occupations about the farm, and the old-time mechanic's son obtained it in his father's shop. The conditions which once made this natural training available for a large proportion of the rising generation are now altered, and the alteration goes on

165

year by year, with increasing rapidity. We must bear in mind the growth of large cities and our unprecedented commercial and industrial development. The specialization of labor has destroyed one of the above-mentioned possibilities, and the growth of great cities is rapidly removing the other. When our first national census was taken in 1790 only 1/30 of our population lived in cities having more than 8000 inhabitants, and there were only six such cities in the country. At the present time we have over 320 such cities, and their inhabitants number almost 30 per cent of our total population. This fact has a most important bearing on practical life and thus on the public school. We must remember also that between 1850 and 1880 our manufactured product increased in value 550 per cent; and the number of those employed in factories increased 325 per cent. This, when interpreted, means that indefinitely more people than ever before have to employ their observation, their judgment and their executive faculty, and employ them accurately, in the performance of their daily duties. For them, and through them, for all of us, the conditions of practical life have changed and are changing. Has the school responded to the new burdens thus laid upon it? The argument for manual training says no, it has not. A more comprehensive, a broader, a more practical training is necessary.

There is a further argument for manual training, but I have not touched upon it because I desire to discuss the subject from a strictly educational standpoint and according to the requirements of a rigorous pedagogic method. If we permit other than educational considerations to enter into the discussion of questions purely educational, we may be setting a bad precedent. Having premised this, it will not be amiss to refer briefly to the social and economic arguments in favor of manual training.

It is unquestionable that many of our social troubles originate in misunderstandings about labor and in false judgments as to what labor really is. They originate, I take it, from the same misunderstanding that causes the average young man to think it more honorable to add columns of figures for $3.00 a week than to lay bricks for $3.00 a day. Some of us affect to despise manual labor. It must be because we do not understand it. It must be apparent that if manual training is accorded its proper place in education, if we come to see that manual work has in it a valuable disciplinary and educational element, our eyes will be opened as to its real dignity and men will cease to regard it as beneath them and their children. This is what I would call the social argument for manual training. The economic argument is similar. It points out that the vast majority of our public school children must earn their living with their hands, and therefore if the school can aid them in using their hands it is putting just so much bread and butter into their mouths. Now I have no sympathy with the purely utilitarian conception of the school, with what we may call the dollars and cents idea of education. On the contrary I cordially indorse the pungent aphorism of Dr. Munger: "Education is to teach us how to live, not how to make a living." But while standing firmly on the platform, I do say that if the best and most complete education happens to aid a boy in earning his living that is no reason why it should be supplanted by something less thorough and less complete. . . .

A movement at once so philosophic and so far-reaching as that in favor of manual training, has not come into educational thought since Comenius burst the bonds of mediaevalism two and a half centuries ago. It is the educational question of the time. Other matters are important as affecting administration, organization, methods of teaching, and other details—all having to do with applications of principle, but the manual training movement is a principle itself. As might have been predicted, it meets with no little opposition and considerable misrepresentation. The forces of conservatism are arrayed against it as something new; and it is doubtless well that it is so, for education is altogether too important a matter to be swayed by any and every crude theory. Any new movement to establish itself in education must run a gauntlet of opposition and criticism, the safe passage of which is a guarantee of excellence. This gauntlet the manual training movement has successfully run, and it is today the newest phase of educational thought. In the first place it is a deduction from our increasingly complete and exact knowledge of mind, and in the second place it meets the demands for a more practical education made by the conditions of contemporary life. It so happens, and happily, that the education which our increased scientific knowledge points us to as the best, is more practical, in the best sense of that much-abused word, than that which it supersedes.

46. A Phase of the Problem of Universal Education (1909)[1]

EUGENE DAVENPORT

Rightly or wrongly, for good or for ill, we are committed to a policy of universal education, a policy whose wisdom, I believe, has passed the stage of discussion among thinking people.

Now, no system of education, however good in itself, can claim to be or hope to become universal if it does not touch and benefit all classes of men, and all legitimate branches of their activity, both industrial and non-industrial, vocational and non-vocational. Indeed, universal education means exactly what it says — the education of all sorts of men for all sorts of purposes and in all sorts of subjects that can contribute to the efficiency of the individual in a professional way or awake and develop the best that was born into him as a man and a human being.

Looked at in this broad way, industrial education does not differ logically from any other form of professional training that requires a large body of highly specialized knowledge. Nor do industrial people, as such, necessarily constitute a class by themselves, but are men like other men, who love and hate, who earn and spend, who read and think, and act and vote, and do any and all other acts which may be performed by any other citizens. Now all of this leads me to maintain the thesis that industrial education is not a thing apart but is only a phase, albeit an important phase, of our general system of universal education, a thesis that is the more plausible when we remember that all men need two educations — one that is vocational and one that is not; one that will fit them to work and one that will fit them to live. When we remember that there is less difference between industry and occupation

[1]NEA *Proceedings* (1909), pp. 277–88. Eugene Davenport was primarily interested in agricultural education.

than we once assumed; when we remember that 90 per cent. of the people follow industrial pursuits and will continue to do so; when we remember that all major industries like other essential activities most go on in the future as in the past, even tho every man in the community were a college graduate, and when we remember that it is for the public good that these major industries be developed and occupied by educated men, surely this position is not unreasonable.

All parties are agreed these days that in order to secure a fair degree of efficiency in some way some sort of specialized instruction should be given in industrial pursuits. The old apprentice system has passed away and the work of instruction for industrial efficiency seems to be thrown upon the schools. It is a new problem and they appear not to know quite what to do with it. It is perfectly clear that industrial education calls for new and different courses of instruction from those designed to fit for non-industrial pursuits, and the question is whether these constitute a part of our public-schools duty or whether the peculiar educational needs of industry and of industrial people may be left to take care of themselves. In discussing industrial education, as with all other forms of education, it must always be remembered that we are dealing with the man as well as with the craftsman, and I use the term craftsman in its broadest sense to cover the work of the lawyer as well as that of the farmer. . . .

But no scheme of education is truly universal or can hope to become so until it not only touches and uplifts all classes of men but also touches and uplifts their industries as well; for it is not expedient that men should desert industry as soon as they are educated, but rather that they should remain and apply their education to the development of the industries, that the people may be better served and the economic balance of things be not disturbed by the evolution of an educational system aiming to become universal. . . .

But as yet we have no system of *secondary* education that can be called universal and until the matter is settled, and settled right at this point, our system is weak at its most important level, because it is our secondary education that touches our people during their formative period and that really reaches the masses in such a way as to be truly universal in extent.

I say that our secondary education is not yet universal. True, the high schools are open to all who have finished the grades, but they do not offer to most classes of people that instruction which is a preparation for life and which the needs of the times and the impulse of the people demand.

The high schools took their cue originally from the old-time academies which were training-schools for classical colleges. Since then primary education has become universal because it involved nothing but opening the schools to all the people free of tuition. The education of the colleges has become, or is rapidly becoming, universal because the people demand that the benefits of higher education shall not be limited to a few favored occupations and those who follow them—all upon the ground that such a course would be pernicious because against the public welfare.

The same influences are beginning to work in our high schools, which are moving in the wake of the colleges, it seems to me, in a way that is wholly commendable, and that needs only to be accelerated and not retarded.

The high schools are schools of the people and in response to their demand they have added to the old-time classical courses those in modern science, in manual training, in household science and, indeed, many are now adding agriculture, stenography, telegraphy, book-keeping, type setting, and a list of vocational courses almost too long to be mentioned, all without prejudice to, but vastly to the enrichment of, the old-time courses of study.

So the high schools are rapidly following in the lead of the colleges and if matters go on as they are now drifting in some of our best schools, it will not be long until, in response to public demand and common-sense, we will have a complete system of universal education in the largest sense of the term and of all grades from the elementary schools upward, in which men and women of all kinds and preferences will be able to get that education which will not only fit them for life but fit them to live. In the name of progress let this good work go on. . . .

If present tendencies can go on unhampered, it will not be long until every community can have its high school which will reflect with a fair degree of accuracy its major industries and do it, too, in the light of the world's knowledge and of the world's ideals. Such schools will turn out men and women ready to do the world's work and think the world's thoughts as well as to dream the world's dreams and share in its ambitions. If we combine our energies we can have such schools in America wherein every young man and every young woman can secure an education that is at once both useful and cultural, and that, too, within driving distance of the father's door. If we unite our educational energies we can do this but we cannot do it in separate schools.

We can combine the vocational and the non-vocational in our high schools if we will and each be the better for the other. . . .

So, all things considered, I most earnestly advocate the taking over of our industrial education in all its forms into the existing system of secondary schools, seeing to it that one-fourth the time of every pupil is devoted to something vocational, something industrial, if you please, and no industry is too common for this purpose. It is the common things of life that are fundamental and it is thru them that we teach life itself. . . .

Thinking men now know that, education or no education, culture or no culture, whatever the grade of civilization we may evolve, certain fundamental industries must still go on. Moreover, they know that if these fundamental industries are to be well conducted and our natural resources developed, then these activities must be in the hands of capable men; yes, of educated men, for industry, like every other activity of man, is capable of development by means of orderly knowledge and trained minds.

They know, too, these thinking people, that men of capacity cannot be found to develop these fundamentals except they may also themselves partake of the blessings of life and the full fruits of our civilization. They know that the days of the hewers of wood and the drawers of water, as such — condemned to a life of drudgery — are over on this earth wherever civilization exists, and that education, like religion, must somewhat rapidly readjust itself to new conditions and prepare to help the common average man to lead a life that is both useful to the community and a satisfaction to himself.

The aristocracy of education, like the aristocracy of religion, whereby a few were saved at the expense of the many, is over, and education, like religion, must help the common man to meet and solve the common issues of life better than they have ever been met and solved before—hence industrial education; hence vocational education; hence universal education.

These good people who shy at the term industrial education are remnants of a past condition when educators and others entertained that old-time and curious conception of industry, whereby industrial people were assumed to be uneducated and were by common consent assigned a social position of natural inferiority, as if a farmer or mechanic, for example, acquired by his daily life a kind of toxic poison that not only destroyed his better faculties but was likely to exude and soil or injure others.

Let me call the attention of these good people to the fact that whatever their social status the industrial people hold the balance of power politically and socially, for they constitute 90 per cent. of the population, and that for all practical purposes and in the last. analysis they are the people, and their education, whatever it is to be, will really constitute our system.

The colleges learned long ago that to meet modern needs they must afford every man two educations: one intensely technical to meet his business needs and make him an efficient member of society but which would tend to narrow him as a man; the other non-vocational, which has no money-making power, but whose effect is to liberalize and broaden the man by attracting his interests and widening his knowledge outside the field wherein he gains his livelihood.

Now the high schools must learn the same lesson and the sooner they do so the better for all interests. Therefore these high schools that are introducing the industrial are developing in the right lines. The high schools are not preparatory schools for college. They are pre-eminently the schools wherein the people are fitted for life. Where one man is educated in college, twenty will get all their preparation in high schools. The high school, therefore, is the place wherein the boy shall find himself to the end that if he goes to college he will have, upon matriculation, exceedingly clear ideas about what he intends to do, and if he does not he can go out from the high school at once and take some useful part in the world's work. The large number of high-school men, even graduates, who have no plans and, more than all, no fitness, preparation or inclination for any sort of useful activity, is a pathetic and a dangerous fact — pathetic because so much good material has been wasted; dangerous because the high schools must either change their ideals and introduce the industrial freely, or the industrial masses will find other schools of their own that will meet their needs as they have been met on college levels but as they have not yet been met in secondary grades where the masses go.

Now the colleges have learned that it is not necessary to absorb all the time of a student in order to turn out an efficient man vocationally. Much less is it necessary in secondary schools. On college levels, from one-half to two-thirds of the student's time suffices for the vocational, and when we learn better how to teach, results can doubtless be attained with still less, leaving a generous amount of time for the pursuit of the non-vocational and therefore of liberalizing courses, for the effect of a course of study, whether narrowing or broadening, depends less upon the subject matter than upon the attitude of the student and the purpose for which he takes the course. Chemistry is a professional study to the prospective farmer, while to the journalist or the lawyer it is non-professional and liberal.

If we will honestly take into our high schools, as we have taken into our universities, all the major activities, splitting no hairs as between the industrial and the professional, for no man can define the difference, so imperceptibly do they shade the one into the other — if we will take them all into the high school as we have already taken them into the universities, and carry them along together, the vocational and the non-vocational side by side, day after day, from first to last, so the boy is never free from either, then will all our educational necessities be met and we will have met a goodly number of substantial achievements. . . .

I am perfectly well aware that all this will be held by some as a lowering of standards and a degrading of education by commercializing it. Against this conclusion I protest most emphatically. Does it degrade a thing to use it? Does it degrade religion to uplift the fallen or to sustain the masses of men from falling? Is education a luxury to be restricted to a few favored fortunates or is it a power to uplift and sustain and develop all men?

Are you afraid to educate the ditch-digger? Is the education of the gentleman too good for him? Are the facts of history too profound or the satisfaction of knowledge too precious to be common property of man? Does it make my satisfaction less when it makes his more, or are you afraid that he will climb out of the ditch if he is enlightened? There is no danger of that. I have dug ditch and laid tile every month of the year and that since I was a college graduate, and I am ready to do it again. I am ready to do my share of the world's work: yes, of the world's dirty work. It was Colonel Waring who cleaned up New York City. It was the educated engineer who made a sanitary Cuba. The educated man does anything that needs to be done to get results. It is the uneducated or the badly educated who fails to comprehend the eternal balance of things.

I desire to call attention to one more phase of our problem, to what may be called our leisure asset. There are two leisure classes, one few and unimportant, the other large and important. The first consists of the idle rich who by accident were born after their fathers, and who intend to live a parasitic existence, paying for their needs with other people's money. They are altogether useless. It matters little how they are educated and the sooner they die off the better for the world. They do not think: they do not act: they only vegetate and glitter. The wealthy who do not belong to this class are too busy for leisure.

The other leisure class is the great industrial mass, who, after all, own and control about all the useful leisure in the world. The minister has no leisure. The teacher has no leisure. The lawyer, the leader everywhere, has no leisure. What he does he does under pressure and because he must.

But the farmer, the craftsman, the industrialist generally, labors only in the daylight hours and for a portion of his time. What he does with the balance of his waking energies is of the utmost concern. Here is the racial asset, both social and psychical; both economic and political.

If this great mass of men, constituting all but the degenerates, can be properly educated, the racial asset of their leisure moments will in the end be tremendous. It is this mass, and what it thinks and does in its leisure hours either blindly or intelligently, that will ultimately fix the trend of our development and the limits of our achievements. It is better that they be educated and educated broadly.

174

Moreover, it is out of this mass that leaders arise, and if their education be sound, then will our leaders be wise and safe. You cannot maintain any more an educated aristocracy. There will be but one aristocracy and that will be the aristocracy of personal achievement, and if we do not want the world entirely commercialized we must so merge our industrial education into our general system as to have in the end not a mass of separate schools with distracting aims and purposes, but a single system of education catering to all classes and all interests. It is the only influence that will preserve a homogeneous people.

In thus amalgamating the vocational and the non-vocational, I would like to say a word for what might be called the parallel system as distinct from the stratified. That is, I would have a boy from his first day in the high school to his last have to do with both the vocational and the non-vocational. I would have him every day take stock of things vocational in terms of world values. I would have him devote a full fourth of his time to what will bring him earning power, to be used for that purpose if he needs it, and to give him an independent spirit if he does not need it. Every man is a better man if he feels the power to earn his way, whether he needs to do it or not.

Do you say that this will so cut into his time as to prevent his getting an all-round education? Then I will say that he will never get an all-round education any way: that the most he knows at forty will be learned out of school and that the business of the school is to give him a good start.

I beg, too, for a reform in the idea that a course is framed mainly for the one who graduates. If the vocational and the non-vocational are properly paralleled the course is good from whatever point it is left, and whenever abandoned it has taught the student the proper balance between industry and life: between the means and the ends of life.

All this will take time because it means to some extent the readjustment of ideals, the addition of new courses of study and of new materials and methods of instruction. It means the making of a new class of teachers who must largely train themselves by a generation of experience. It means the making of a more complicated system of instruction than has ever been undertaken — a system as complicated as American democratic life.

But it is worth the while for nothing better is possible. It is easier, of course, to short-circuit the matter by assenting to the separation of industry and education, but no race need hope for supremacy nor for the evolution of its best till it combines industry and education, which belong together in the schools as they do now and always must in life.

So I say to the high schools — Do not wait for approved courses of study, nor for the production of skilled teachers. Go ahead and do the best you can. An honest effort is half the battle, and it is worth more now than it ever will be again. Do not hesitate till methods are marked out. If you do that, you and the cause are lost, for the separate industrial school will surely come. We know the ideal — an educated American in all the activities of life. Let us go ahead and produce him and mend our methods later on.

Education is no longer a luxury. It has become a necessity for the doing of the world's work. It is no longer for the edification of the few; it is for the satisfaction of the many. And whether we regard it as industrial or non-industrial; as contributing to the efficiency of men or to their elevation in civilized society; however this or any other educational problem is regarded they are all but phases of our general and stupendous problem of universal education, in the working-out of which there are as yet no models for the American secondary school.

47. INDUSTRIAL EDUCATION
AND THE AMERICAN FEDERATION OF LABOR (1915)[1]

SAMUEL GOMPERS

An argument, I take it, is not required of me in support of industrial education, nor any exposition of the purposes or ideals of industrial education. You know what industrial education is and what are its purposes and ideals. The question in your minds is perhaps with reference to myself as a representative of organized labor. Do I know what industrial education is, and what are its purposes and ideals? But as my personal knowledge is of very little consequence to anyone, except as a sort of reflex of the knowledge of the millions of workers, the question is, in fact, does organized labor understand what industrial education is, and what are its purposes and ideals? Finally, if it does understand these purposes and ideals, does it approve of them? And will it cooperate sincerely in the development of tried and proven rational schemes of industrial education?

A great part of my life and energy has been devoted to combating wrong-headed notions about the attitude of organized labor with reference to every sort of social and economic question. These questions have increased in number and in variety with the development of industrial civilization. The need for efficient industrial education for our boys and girls is now more urgent than ever before. Nor is the need of educational training for greater efficiency confined to the factory or the shops; it is manifest in the home life, and in demands for instruction in domestic economy. The factory system and modern industrial organization have resulted in such high specialization that only what have been re-

---

[1]Emily Robinson (Comp.), *Vocational Education* (New York, H. W. Wilson, 1921), pp. 159–66. Gompers served as President of the AFL from its founding in 1886 to his death in 1924 with the exception of one year.

ferred to tonight as the tag-ends of industry have been left to women in the homes, and in modern industrial establishments the subdivision of labor has gone on to such a degree that workers perform the same set task a thousand, or ten thousand, or a hundred thousand times a day. The same task is automatically repeated again and again without knowledge of its relation to the rest of the industry for the sole purpose of gaining time and speed. I repeat that if ever industrial education was essential it is essential today. We cannot turn back the wheels of industry, but we can make the knowledge and the effectiveness of the workers such that they will have some comprehension of the entire article produced and of every branch of the production.

In the work I have sometimes felt that the presumption is always against labor—that it is always assumed as a matter of course that labor is by a sort of "natural depravity" and strange blindness, opposed to everything, including everything that is for its own interest. Sometimes it is assumed that this opposition is due to pernicious temperament on the part of labor leaders, and sometimes that it is due to simple ignorance and incapacity to understand complex social conditions. The workers are essentially honest and sincere, and let me assure you, the degree of their ignorance is not so great as the presumptuous and supercilious often assume it to be.

It may be difficult to cram into twenty minutes' time all that may be necessary to say with reference to the attitude of organized labor toward industrial education, but I shall endeavor to comply with the limit set.

You should know that organized labor does not oppose the development of industrial education in the public schools. Indeed, that would not at all fairly indicate the attitude of organized labor. I say to you that the organizations constituting the American Federation of Labor have been for years engaged in the work of systematically providing industrial education to their members. This instruction has been given thru the medium of the trade union journal and schools established and maintained by them. Organized labor, I repeat, is not opposed to industrial education. It is eager to cooperate actively in instituting industrial education in our public schools. The workingman has too little time, and can therefore take but little interest in any other sort of education.

178

You will agree with me that there is absolutely no reason why labor, organized or unorganized, should oppose the sort of industrial education proposed here in Richmond, and I can assure you that labor does not oppose anything without good reason. When it has good reason to oppose so many things why should it oppose anything without reason?

Organized labor has opposed and will continue to oppose some enterprises which have been undertaken in the name of industrial education. It has opposed and will continue to oppose the exploitation of the laborer even when the exploitation is done under the name of industrial education. It may continue to regard with indifference, if not with suspicion, some private schemes of industrial education. With regard to such enterprises where they are instituted by employers, organized labor is from Missouri—it will have to be shown that the given enterprise is not a means of exploiting labor—a means of depressing wages by creating an over supply of labor in certain narrow fields of employment.

Organized labor cannot favor any scheme of industrial education which is lop-sided—any scheme, that is to say, which will bring trained men into any given trade without regard to the demand for labor in that trade. Industrial education must maintain a fair and proper apportionment of the supply of labor power to the demand for labor power in every line of work. Otherwise its advantages will be entirely neutralised. If, for example, the result of industrial education is to produce in any community a greater number of trained machinists than are needed in the community, those machinists which have been trained cannot derive any benefit from their training, since they will not be able to find employment except at economic disadvantages. Under these conditions industrial education is of no advantage to those who have received it, and it is a distinct injury to the journeymen working at the trade who are subjected to a keen competition artificially produced. Industrial education must reach the needs of the worker as well as the requirements of the employer.

I can see that in some respects the most difficult task before industrial education is that of maintaining an equilibrium of supply and demand of efficient artisans, and equilibrium as nearly perfect as is physically possible. How shall this most difficult problem be solved? How shall such an equilibrium of labor supply and demand be maintained and industrial education be entirely freed from any suspicion of working injury to labor by causing a maladjustment of supply to demand?

The answer to these questions seems obvious. There is in my opinion only one way to avoid the difficulty, only one way in which to avoid the danger of working serious injury to labor — working injury in spite of the very best intentions to benefit labor. The only way to avoid working an injury to labor under the name of industrial education is to find out what is the demand for labor in a community. In a word, it seems to me the only safe basis for understanding industrial education in any community is the basis which, as I understand, has been established here in Richmond. Industrial education should be in every instance based upon a survey of the industries of the community — upon an accumulation of facts regarding the employments in the community. Upon such a basis the public schools may properly proceed to provide for the particular industrial needs of the community, and with such an accumulation of data in hand there can be no excuse if industrial education does not prove to be of undoubted benefit to labor and to the community.

Industrial education comes close to the life and happiness of labor. It involves the means of livelihood for the workingman. The test of efficiency of industrial education is wage-earning power — not simply increase in efficiency of labor to produce. It is perfectly possible for industrial education, even when provided by the public schools, if it is not organized with regard to the industrial needs of the community, to increase the productivity and efficiency of certain groups of labor and at the same time to reduce the wage-earning power of the laborer in those groups. There is nothing mysterious in this. It would result from the working of a universal economic law. To the extent that industrial education is not precisely adapted to the needs of the community, it will tend to have exactly this result, namely, it will increase the productive efficiency of certain groups of labor and by bringing into these groups an oversupply of labor will tend to economic deterioration.

I can assure you that no disposition will be found anywhere among workingmen to oppose this effort to make our schools more democratic in serving the real bread-and-butter needs of the community.

180

Let me tell you further that labor—organized labor—has been active for years to secure this end, active in its efforts to make the public schools do precisely that which some misinformed people even think labor opposes. In 1903 the American Federation of Labor at its annual convention appointed a committee on education. What sort of education interested the delegates of that convention? It was not that education which deals with the syntax of dead languages; it was not even the education which deals with the development of the fine arts, or with the systematic teaching of the science. These are all of them legitimate ends of education and the American Federation of Labor approves of these educational ends, but the sort of education which the American Federation of Labor was particularly interested in, and the sort of education which was under consideration when this committee on education was appointed in 1903, was industrial education. This was more than a decade ago and during the entire period which has elapsed since the appointment of the committee the American Federation of Labor has been active in fostering and furthering every legitimate enterprise for the industrial education of workers. . . .

We have been working for industrial education for more than a decade. This committee appointed in 1903 was to consider what the trade unions themselves could do to make up for the deficiency. of the public schools. The trade unions whose members paid taxes to support the public schools were not getting from those schools the sort of education which they needed to enable them to become skilled, efficient, and better paid workingmen.

They were getting, in so far as they got anything at all, a sort of education which had for them very little value, and they therefore took under consideration the possibility of organizing a scheme of education which would be of value to them.

Now when the public schools come forward with a proposition to provide the sort of education needed by the workingmen, do you think that they are going to oppose that undertaking? I do not think so. In fact I know that they will welcome any such development.

In 1904 another committee on education was appointed, and again in 1905 another committee, and again in 1906. In 1907 the A. F. of L. at its annual convention resolved that "we do endorse any policy or any society (this I may state included and had special reference to the National Society for the Promotion of Industrial Education) or association, having for its object the raising the standard of industrial education and the teaching of the higher technic of our various industries."

The committee to which this resolution was referred reported it "decided to record itself in favor of the best opportunities for the most complete and best industrial and technical training obtainable," and it recommended an investigation of industrial school systems.

In 1906 the committee on education tested "with satisfaction the splendid progress accomplished by the Executive Council along the lines of industrial education," and submitted to the convention a set of resolutions in which it stated that "industrial education is necessary and inevitable for the progress of an industrial people."

Industrial education was before the convention of 1909, at which time I myself stated in my report that the A. F. of L. favored public industrial education, and opposed only narrowly specialized training under the control of private interests. Organized labor has always opposed and will continue to oppose sham industrial education, whether at public or private expense. It has opposed and will continue to oppose that superficial training which confers no substantial benefit upon the worker, which does not make him a craftsman, but only an interloper, who may be available in times of crisis, perhaps, as a strike breaker, but not as a trained artisan for industrial service at other times. Industrial education must train men for work not for private and sinister corporation purposes.

I refer to this by way of explaining what it is that has at times in the past aroused labor's opposition to what has been unfairly called industrial education. It will be found that wherever labor has opposed what has been put forth as industrial education, the enterprise called industrial education has been something entirely different from that which Richmond is instituting in its public schools today.

To the 1909 convention of the American Federation of Labor I took pleasure in submitting this: "That since technical education of the workers in trade and industry is a public necessity it should not be a private, but a public function, conducted by the public and the expense involved at public cost." You people in Richmond are doing today precisely what the committee of the A. F. of L. recommended five years ago should be done.

In 1911 the A. F. of L. came forward in support of a bill in Congress providing for national aid in establishing vocational education in the public schools of the country. Since that date up to the present time the A. F. of L. has consistently, persistently, and unremittingly advocated the establishment of industrial education in the public schools.

The sort of industrial education which Richmond is instituting is the one and the only sort of industrial education which can enlist the sincere cooperation of trade unionists and should receive the cooperation of employers as well. It is equally to the interest of the employers as of labor, that workingmen shall be trained for real efficiency. The efficient worker produces more and by virtue of his efficiency makes for a higher economic, industrial, commercial, and social development. I believe that the welfare of labor depends to a very large extent upon the development of industrial education, and that in this case at least, the welfare of the employer, and of the community is equally involved with that of the workingman. In the matter of industrial education there is absolutely no controversy between labor and the employers of labor—provided always that the industrial education is what it purports to be—industrial education, organized by the public schools for the benefit of the youth of the community. Organized labor represents the fathers and mothers of the youths, and the fathers and mothers are not going to oppose the best interests of their own children.

Those who wish documentary proof that organized labor has for years been actively agitating for the institution of industrial education in the public schools, I shall be very glad to provide with such proofs. They are spread through the annual reports of every convention held by the A. F. of L. beginning with that of 1903 and including that of 1914. In 1910 the Federation published a preliminary Report on Industrial Education, and in 1912 a full report of its Committee on Industrial Education, approved in conformity with a resolution of the convention held in Denver in 1908. . . .

48. NEED OF AN INDUSTRIAL EDUCATION IN AN INDUSTRIAL DEMOCRACY (1916)[1]

JOHN DEWEY

The need for industrial education may be approached from many standpoints. Industrial education may be treated as an indispensable factor in material prosperity, or as a factor in promoting the ability of a nation in the competitive race for commercial supremacy among nations—a point of view from which the example of Germany is urged. Or it may be regarded from the standpoint of its effect upon the contentment of the workers, or as a means of providing a more stable and efficient set of employes, and reducing the waste now found in most manufacturing enterprises. All of these things have their importance. But they all look at education as an instrument for external ends, and they pass lightly over that part of the subject represented in our title by the words, "education in an industrial democracy." The standpoint from which we are to approach the matter is, in short, that of the demands laid upon education by the need of fostering democracy in a country largely industrial, and where the need of making the spirit of democracy permeate industry is recognized.

Hence, a few words about democracy itself seem to be called for. Democracy has its political aspect. Probably this is the first aspect to present itself to view. Politically, democracy means a form of government which does not esteem the well-being of one individual or class above that of another; a system of laws and administrations which ranks the happiness and interests of all as upon the same plane, and before whose law and administration all individuals are alike, or equal. But experience has shown that such a state of affairs is not realizable save where all interests have an opportunity to be heard, to make themselves felt, to take a hand

---

[1]Reprinted by arrangement with the John Dewey Foundation.

184

in shaping policies. Consequently, universal suffrage, direct participation in choice of rulers, is an essential part of political democracy.

But political democracy is not the whole of democracy. On the contrary, experience has proved that it cannot stand in isolation. It can be effectively maintained only where democracy is social — where, if you please, it is moral. A social democracy signifies, most obviously, a state of social life where there is wide and varied distribution of opportunities; where there is much social mobility or scope for change of position and station; where there is free circulation of experiences and ideas, making possible a wide recognition of common interests and purposes, and where there is such an obvious utility of the social and political organization to its members as to enlist their warm and steady support in its behalf. Without ease in change, society gets stratified into classes, and these classes prevent anything like fair and even distribution of opportunity for all. The stratified classes become fossilized, and a fedual [sic] society comes into existence. Accident, rather than capacity and training, determine career, reward, and repute. Since democracies forbid, by their very nature, highly centralized governments working by coercion, they depend upon shared interests and experiences for their unity and upon personal appreciation of the value of institutions for stability and defense.

Such qualities as these, such qualities as insistence upon widespread opportunity, free exchange of ideas and experiences, extensive realization of the purposes which hold men together, are intellectual and emotional. The importance of such qualities is the reason why we ventured to call a social democracy a moral democracy. And they are traits which do not grow spontaneously on bushes. They have to be planted and nurtured. They are dependent upon education. It is no accident that all democracies have put a high estimate upon education; that schooling has been their first care and enduring charge. Only through education can equality of opportunity be anything more than a phrase. Accidental inequalities of birth, wealth, and learning are always tending to restrict the opportunities of some as compared with those of others. Only free and continued education can counteract those forces which are always at work to restore, in however changed a form, feudal oligarchy. Democracy has to be born anew every generation, and

185

education is its midwife. Moreover, it is only education which can guarantee widespread community of interest and aim. In a complex society, ability to understand and sympathize with the operations and lot of others is a condition of common purpose which only education can procure. The external differences of pursuit and experience are so very great, in our complicated industrial education, that men will not see across and thru the walls which separate them, unless they have been trained to do so. And without this lively and ardent sense of common life, it is hopeless to secure in individuals that loyalty to the organized group which needs to be an animating motive of conduct.

To recall these generalities, these commonplaces, would be idle were it not that there is a tendency to drop them from view when the topic of industrial education is under consideration. Its purpose is often thot to be so much narrower, more practical and technical, than the object of other established modes of education, that these features may be—nay, must be—left out of account. But the contrary is the case. Just because of the part played by industry in modern life, an education which has to do with preparation for it, must bear these considerations in mind more than other forms, if democracy is to remain an actuality. Just these things provide the controlling considerations for deciding the curriculums, methods, and administration of a system of industrial education.

There are many phases of industry, as at present carried on, which are unfavorable to a genuine democracy, just as, on the other hand, the development of modern industrial and commercial methods has been a chief factor in calling political democracy into existence and then endowing it with social aspirations. There are extreme divisions of work between the skilled and unskilled, and also between the most skilled workers on the technical side, whether inventors or doers, and the managers on the fiscal and marketing side. These tend to segregate men and women into exclusive classes. The difference on the side of consumption between those who can barely maintain a low standard of living and those who are relieved by circumstances from any responsible thot for expenditure, and who give themselves up to display and idleness, has never been as large or as overtly conspicuous as it is

186

today. Older divisions of master and subject class tend to reinstate themselves in a subtle form.

Machine industry, moreover, tends to reduce great masses of men to a level where their own work becomes mechanical and servile. Work loses its intellectual and esthetic cast and becomes a mere necessity to procure the pay which buys daily support. The machine operator engaged in manipulation of a machine becomes identified with the monotonous movements of the monster he tends. As long as he has to do new things, he learns. The moment he has mastered his unchanging work it masters him; its habits absorb and swallow his. Employers whose methods have bred lack of initiative, and have practically forbidden workers to think, complain because men can not be found for places of greater responsibility. But the evils are far from being confined to the laboring class. When social responsibilities have at most to do with the expenditure of wealth, not with earning it, when business is pursued not as an exercise in social cooperation but as a means of power, the mind is so hardened and restricted that democracy becomes a mere name.

To recall such danger is to recognize some of the offices thrust upon industrial education in a democracy. To counteract the soulless monotony of machine industry, a premium must be put upon initiative, intellectual independence, and inventiveness. Hence schooling must not model itself upon the automatic repetitiousness of machines, whether in the name of the false gods of practical skill or discipline. Personal control of power, strong discontent with whatever subordinates mental capacity to merely external regulation, must be made primary. The imagination must be so stored that in the inevitable monotonous stretches of work, it may have worthy material of art and literature and science upon which to feed, instead of being frittered away upon undisciplined dreamings and sensual fancies. New inventions and applications of science are actively remaking technical and technological methods of industry. Hence the desire for immediate results and immediate efficiency must be held in check by the need of securing powers which will enable individuals to adapt themselves to inevitable change. Otherwise they will become helpless burdens on society as the methods in which they have been trained pass

187

away. Moreover, since the worker is to be an integral part of a self-managing society, pains must be taken at every turn to see that instead of being prepared for a special, exclusive, practical service, as a hide might be prepared for a shoemaker, he is educated into ability to recognize and apply his own abilities, is given self-command, intellectual as well as moral.

Let it not be thot that this is a plea for the continuation of the older so-called "general education," on the ground that it also made its defense that it trained general capacity and brot the individual to a consciousness of himself and his surroundings. The material of his traditional general education is not adapted to the needs and activities of an industrial society. It was developed (as were its methods) in times when our present industrial society was not. The simple fact is, that no attempt has ever been made to discover the factors of scientific and social importance in present-day industry and in a common democratic life, and then to utilize them for education purposes; as was done by our spiritual progenitors in the work of selecting the factors of value in a non-industrial and feudal society so as to make them count for education. The work which has to be done by a system of industrial education in an industrial democracy is to study the most important processes of today in farming, manufacturing, and transportation to find out what are the fundamental and general elements which compose them, and thereby develop a new kind of general education on top of which the more special and technical training for distinctive vocations may be undertaken.

As a new subject-matter is needed, so are new methods. Our inherited instruction knows, in the main, two kinds of methods. One is that of habituation in various specialized modes of skill, methods of repetition, and drill, with a view to getting automatic skill. This is the method which is most likely to be resorted to in an unintelligent industrial training. It is adapted to securing mechanical proficiency in a narrow trade, but is no more adapted to the specific needs of industrial democracy than is the other inherited method—the theoretical and scholastic method of acquiring, expounding, and interpreting *literary* materials. What is needed is a recognition of the *intellectual* value of labor—the same kind of recognition of intellectual results in facts, ideas, and methods to be got from ordinary industrial materials and processes that the laboratory (significant name) has accomplished for a limited range of materials and processes. Or, put the other way about, what is needed is a development of laboratory methods which will connect them with the ordinary industrial activities of men. In that case, there will be no danger that the necessary personal insight and initiative will not be secured.

The value of the older humanistic methods was that they had a vital relation to human affairs and interests. But that is a reason for attempting to discover the humanism contained in our existing social life, not for the reverse policy of despising the present and taking flight to the past. I do not underestimate the difficulties in the way of taking a spiritual survey of our present industrial society and applying its results to education. Strong class interests stand in its way, for it would be sure to utilize education as a means for bringing to more general recognition the evils and defects of present industrial aims and methods, and in making more wide-spread a knowledge of the means by which these evils are to be eliminated. An effective study of child labor, of the sanitary conditions under which multitudes of men and women now labor, of the methods employed in a struggle for economic supremacy, of the connections between industrial and political control, and of the methods by which such evils may best be remedied, is a need of any education which is to be a factor in bringing industrial democracy out of industrial feudalism. But to propose this is to invite the attack of those who most profit by the perpetuation of existing conditions. Yet since this knowledge is an obvious concern of the masses, and we have already a political machinery adapted for securing control of the masses, this spirit is bound in the future to animate our educational system. In the universities, in spite of their seeming closer connection with existing economic forces, this scientific spirit has already come into education. As the merely propagandist and merely philanthropic spirits give way to a scientific spirit, it will find its way also into lower education, and finally become a part of the working mental disposition of the masses.

It hardly needs to be said, in closing, that it is a need of industrial education in an industrial democracy that its administration be kept unified with that of ordinary public education. To make it a separate system, administered by different officers having different aims and methods from those of the established public school system, is to invite the promotion of a narrow trade system which shall in effect make the pecuniary, rather than the social and democratic, factors in industry supreme. The natural counterpart to free and universal public education is a system of universal industry in which there are no idlers or shirkers or parasites, and where the ruling motive is interest in good workmanship for public ends, not exploitation of others for private ends. This is the reason why industrial democracy and industrial education should fit each other like hand and glove.

CHAPTER 19

THE BUSINESSMAN AND EDUCATION

Wealth . . . for the elevation of our race.

Andrew Carnegie, 1887

49. PETER COOPER'S STATEMENT (1864)[1]

It happened more than thirty years ago that I was elected a member of the Common Council of this city. At that time I became acquainted with a gentleman who had then lately returned from France. That gentleman informed me that while he was in Paris he had attended the free Polytechnic school provided by the government. He spoke in glowing terms of the great advantage he had received from the consummate ability of the teachers and the perfect appliances used for illustration. What interested me most deeply was the fact that hundreds of young men were there from all parts of France, living on a bare crust of bread a day to get the benefit of those lectures. Feeling then, as I always have, my own want of education, and more especially my want of scientific knowledge as applicable to the various callings in which I had been engaged, it was this want of my own, which I felt so keenly, that led me, in deep sympathy for those whom I knew would be subject to the same wants and inconvenience that I had encountered,—it was this feeling which led me to provide an institution where a course of instruction would be open and free to all who felt a want of scientific knowledge, as applicable to any of the useful purposes of life. Having started in life with naked hands and an honest purpose, I persevered through long years of trial and effort to obtain the means to erect this building, which is now entirely devoted, with all its rents and revenue of every name and nature, to the advancement of science and art.

---

[1]*Old South Leaflets*, VI (Boston, n.d.) No. 147, p. 488.

50. Speech at the Annual Commencement of the Cooper Union, May 31, 1902[1]

ABRAM S. HEWITT

For forty-three blessed years it has been my privilege to present, on behalf of the Trustees, the report of the operations of the Cooper Union. I have never had the report read, but usually talked to the audience here assembled in a confidential sort of way, pointing out various matters which I thought might interest us as members of one family, all devoted to one great object, — the diffusion of knowledge through the Cooper Union. Usually I have had no difficulty in selecting the topic upon which I desired to talk. It was generally a statement that the income of the Institution was entirely inadequate to meet the demands made by the public for its privileges; that we wanted more money; that we wanted more room; that we wanted to get rid of the tenants; that we wanted more funds to pay more teachers, and to let in more of the public until every foot of space, from this floor where we are assembled tonight, right up to the roof, should be entirely devoted to the purpose for which Mr. Cooper designed it; namely, the free education of the masses of the people of the city of New York, who desired not only to be self-supporting, but to aid others in the course of time in getting an honest livelihood. . . .

I really do not want to take up your time, but this is such an extraordinary event, and the results of it are so far-reaching, that I think I will have to ask your indulgence while I go into a little history of the Cooper Union. Mr. Cooper was a poor boy, born of good Revolutionary stock, but, like most of the patriots of that time, had had a good deal more patriotism than money. He began life as an apprentice. There were no schools in New York in those days, — no night schools. He was very anxious to get on, but there was no place where he could obtain an education. He had no money with which to pay a teacher. So he had to get what knowl-

---

[1] *Old South Leaflets,* VI, No. 145, pp. 480–87.

193

edge he could get by himself, and, as I have often heard him say, by the light of the single tallow candle which his means made him able to get; and that every night he passed his time trying to acquire some knowledge which would be of use to him in the battle of life. This made a great impression on him, and he determined that the reproach of New York, of its lack of means for free education, should be removed.

This occurred about the beginning of the last century, in 1804 or 1805, and he set himself to work, alone, without friends, without suggestions from any quarter, to get money enough together to open what he called a night school, for at that time there was not a single free night school in New York City. This was the purpose of his life. He never lost sight of it; and I will tell you this—I tell these young men and women here this story particularly in order that they may see how a noble purpose formed by even the most friendless boy may result in course of time in great benefits to society. And so he pursued his course. He was, of course, a man of great natural ability and great strength of character. I have often heard him say that the first thing a young man should do was to save a little money; that no man could succeed in life who did not begin by saving; and that when a man had saved a little money and had acquired some property he was pretty sure then to make a good citizen. So, in the institution which he proposed to found, he never lost sight of the fact that he wanted to inculcate thrift; he wanted to teach industry; he wanted the lesson of saving to be learned; and he left the rest to the conscience of the good citizens he knew would be produced by such lessons. And, as he provided for the kind of education which these young gentlemen have had, he said that of all the things to be taught in the Cooper Union the pre-eminent one must be the art—the science, as he called it—of good government. He did not mean by this merely the teachings of political economy or political science, but an inculcation of the principle that men "shall do unto each other as they would have others do unto them."

The time came when he had accumulated money enough to begin to build a building. His original idea of a night school was of a rather moderate character, but it very soon enlarged itself until at last, having selected this site, on which he had carried on business for some years, he was able to buy the whole block, and he proceeded to erect this building. He knew, when he undertook this task, that his means would not suffice for more than the erection of the building, and he was determined not to incur any debts. When he called the Trustees together to receive the property at his hands, he said to them: "Here is this building. I want it appropriated as soon as possible to the education of the young men and young women of New York City, and appropriated to free education. There must be no fee paid in the Cooper Union, for education ought to be as free as air and water." He said: "I have given practically all the property that I can control to build this building, and here is thirty thousand dollars more which I have left over, with which you can furnish the apparatus required, and for carrying on the work of instruction. I have called this building the Union for the Advancement of Science and Art. Against my wishes and against my will the legislature have, unfortunately, attached to it the name of Cooper. I did not want my name attached to the Union. I wanted this to be a union of all well-disposed people in New York who are willing to contribute to carry out the work of free education in the building I have created. But," he said, "the use of this name will inevitably, to some extent, interfere with my views for that purpose, and hence you will have to rent as much as is necessary of this building in order to maintain the classes and the reading-room."

Under those circumstances, forty-three years ago, the Trustees entered upon their task. From the very outset the demands upon the institution for admission to it were far greater than the income which they could possibly derive from the rented portions of the building. Hence the great object of these Trustees was to secure an endowment fund; and Mr. Cooper before his death was able to provide two hundred thousand dollars, the income from which he thought would be able to pay the running expenses of the building and keep it in order, but would not, of course, pay the expenses of instruction. He said to the Trustees, "I hope, before you die, the day will come when some one will give money enough to free this institution from the encumbrance of tenants, and devote it entirely to the work of free education."

Up to the time of his death very little money had been contributed; but soon after his death the family of his younger brother, Mr. William Cooper, who had obtained a fortune in connection with Mr. Cooper, gave in successive gifts, owing to the death of successive members of the family, the sum of three hundred and forty thousand dollars. Those of you who have been in the institution for any length of time will remember that this happened about five years ago, and was immediately followed by the enlargement of the classes in the rooms in the two floors above this. That was the first considerable sum of money the Trustees had received, and it did not come until thirty years after the building had been established. In giving an account of this transaction in the report of that year, it was mentioned that this sum would enable the extension of the work, but it was also stated that it was entirely inadequate to gain the great object which we all had in view, of ridding the building of tenants, and an appeal was made to the public to gain money, but none came.

But this appeal came to the notice of Mr. Carnegie, who was a great admirer of Mr. Cooper, and he has never tired of saying that Mr. Cooper's example had been of great help to him, and had given him great inspiration in the use of his money in advancing public education. He wrote to me that he wanted in some way to manifest his admiration for Mr. Cooper and his sympathy for our efforts in enlarging the institution. The amount he offered to give us was one hundred thousand dollars. In reply to this offer I mentioned to Mr. Carnegie that we were very glad to get it, and that it would be the beginning of a fund that would be sufficient in the course of time to keep the whole institution. He said in reply: "I did not understand the case. Let me give three hundred thousand dollars."

"Yes," I replied, "three hundred thousand dollars, with three hundred thousand dollars more added to it, will enable us to begin to take possession of the greater part of the building,—of all the building except the stores,—and to widen the scope of the scheme of education."

Later Mr. Carnegie offered to give three hundred thousand dollars more. And this reminds me of President Lincoln during the war times, when he was always asking for three hundred thousand more. It had previously been arranged by Mr. Peter Cooper's descendants that a trust fund of three hundred and fifty thousand dollars created by him for the benefit of his grandchildren, and the residuary interest of his children of two hundred and fifty thousand dollars in the property subject to the trust, should come to the institution on the deaths of the members of the family as they occurred. It was now arranged that the whole property should be transferred to the institution at once to meet Mr. Carnegie's gifts, so that in the month of January last between this six hundred thousand dollars and Mr. Carnegie's two gifts of three hundred thousand dollars each there was an increase in the amount of the endowment fund of twelve hundred thousand dollars over what it was before Mr. Carnegie gave his first three hundred thousand.

On the strength of this gift I thought I saw the way clear to notify the tenants to quit the stores, and most of them have moved out, all but two, who have leases which will not be terminated until next year. We shall then have possession of the floor above, and practically the whole floor will be made into a great physical laboratory.

But this would not be sufficient. The scale on which the operation of the institution was to be carried on would require another sum of money, and I was speculating in my own mind where the next three hundred thousand dollars would come from. You can imagine my astonishment at what followed. A gentleman whom I have long known—a gentleman who had never manifested any special interest in the Cooper Union—called at my house, and after chatting pleasantly on various subjects, and after having had a little cup of tea with me, as he was just going away, he said, "By the way, I have got something for you, a little gift for Cooper Union"; and to my intense astonishment he handed me two hundred and fifty thousand dollars. I confess that I have not recovered. I cannot realize it, that for forty odd years we have been struggling with this problem, with a sort of vague hope that in some way or other the answer would come from some quarter or other,—I cannot realize that it has been answered. There was an arrangement which Mr. Edward Cooper and I had made with our respective families by which we knew that ultimately six hundred thousand dollars would come to the institution, so as to at least replace the rents which would be lost. But we had gone on for forty years considering this matter, and every trustee doing what he could to make the position more tolerable. Let me say that three of us of the original trustees, Mr. Cooper, Mr. Parsons, and myself, are still living. There were originally five trustees, and three of them are still alive. To them he gave this charge, that they should see to it, if they could that this institution should be made free from every occupation except that of the distribution of knowledge. Mr. Parsons is not here tonight. For forty odd years he has gratuitously attended to all the legal business of this institution, and that in itself is no small undertaking. And besides this he has contributed to the endowment fund, he has given twenty thousand dollars to the endowment fund in order to manifest his interest in the institution.

And here we are, with an income of not less than ninety thousand dollars, possibly it may amount to a hundred thousand dollars, sufficient to pay the expenses of this institution according to the original plans of Mr. Cooper, made nearly a hundred years ago; yes, quite a hundred years ago, when he was a poor boy, working as an apprentice, and followed during his long lifetime of ninety-three years; followed by his children since his death, and prior to his death for forty years, and before his immediate family has passed away this great undertaking had been accomplished.

Now, young gentlemen, I want you to see and to learn that a noble resolution, once formed and resolutely adhered to from generation to generation, will ultimately work out its destiny and secure its triumph. That is the great moral lesson which this institution has taught, and, while I do not underestimate the value of the technical and scientific instruction which has been given by this institution, let me say that the moral lesson afforded by the Cooper Union in the story as I have told it to you,—the moral lesson is one of the greatest I have ever known, or ever expect to know, in the history of man. . . .

Now a word or two more. I may be saying so much on account of your applause. I have not always had so much applause given me in the course of my lifetime. They say, "Old men dream dreams." Well, Dr. Slicer says that it is the young men who dream. And the dream that I dreamed forty years or more ago has to-night come true. "Old men see visions." I think I am right, but it may be that I have reversed the Scriptures. I am an old man, and I see a vision of the future. The Cooper Union is now complete. It is a finished institution, although, as a matter of course, we can spend a great deal more money when it is sent to us. But it can run from this day forward on the resources which it has acquired. But I should be sorry to see that the Cooper Union was going to stop with this building or the work it is doing here. The work which we have undertaken to do is to teach the scientific principles which underlie the arts of the country. We never undertook to teach the trades. We never intend to teach what are known as the constructive trades. But there are established in Germany, England, and, to some extent, in France, industries which are not extensively carried on in the United States, although we have the richest country in the world. These trades are what are known as the handicrafts. They deal with the application of the arts to the finer classes of constructive work and materials, the textiles, gold, silver, and the metals, the manufacture of instruments of precision, and a high order of mechanical work. Work of this class we chiefly import, as a rule, for not many Americans are art workers of that kind. To carry out this work, we require a good deal of money and a good deal of space. That is the second chapter in the history of the Cooper Union. The present Trustees have no hope of being able to execute this object in their lifetime. They but look forward to these handicrafts. In Paris at the present time there are ninety schools which are giving instruction in art industry.

Now we have located in this neighborhood the armory of the Sixty-ninth Regiment, which is soon to be vacated. This armory belongs to the city, and if the city would turn it over to us after it is vacated, for the establishment of these classes of handicraft work, I am very sure, from what I now know, that I can secure an endowment sufficient to carry on the work. This would cost the city nothing, and there would be no burden on the city for keeping it up. The city would merely appropriate the armory for the work in the same way that they have appropriated land and buildings for the establishment of the Museum of Art and the Museum of Natural History.

By the time our new laboratory is done, the Astor Library will be vacant. The building in itself is of no value except as a library, and we need it for a library. It is admirably designed for this purpose, and is admirably located for the extension of the work of this institution, and in proximity to this building, where the work of administration would have to be carried on. The most economical use to which it could be put would be to turn it over to Cooper Union, as otherwise it would be of no value except for the value of the land. Now I hope it will enter into the heart of some one, after I am dead and gone,—though I do not object if they do it while I am alive,—to add to the Cooper Union one or both of these great buildings for the extension of the work we are carrying on here. We could then remove our reading-room and library to the Astor Library, and that space could be devoted to the Art Museum, which I think is getting to be one of the most instructive additions to the education of New York.

If Dr. Slicer had not told me it is the old men who have visions, I should think that I was a young man. Perhaps it was after all not a mistake, but a twist of the tongue. I am in my eightieth year. I am seeing visions because I am so much younger than some of less years than are mine, because I am still young and fresh. If so, I shall be quite glad to live to see any extensions to the Cooper Union which may be possible. In conclusion let me again quote the Scriptures, and say, for the Trustees, that we have "fought the good fight. We have finished our course with joy." And for myself, since I have got in the quotation line, I think I am quite prepared to say, "Lord, now lettest thou thy servant depart in peace, for mine eyes have seen thy salvation."

51. THE GOSPEL OF WEALTH (1887)[1]

ANDREW CARNEGIE

The problem of our age is the proper administration of wealth, that the ties of brotherhood may still bind together the rich and poor in harmonious relationship. The conditions of human life have not only been changed, but revolutionized, within the past few hundred years. In former days there was little difference between the dwelling, dress, food, and environment of the chief and those of his retainers. The Indians are to-day where civilized man then was. When visiting the Sioux, I was led to the wigwam of the chief. It was like the others in external appearance, and even within the difference was trifling between it and those of the poorest of his braves. The contrast between the palace of the millionaire and the cottage of the laborer with us to-day measures the change which has come with civilization. This change, however, is not to be deplored, but welcomed as highly beneficial. It is well, nay, essential, for the progress of the race that the houses of some should be homes for all that is highest and best in literature and the arts, and for all the refinements of civilization, rather than that none should be so. Much better this great irregularity than universal squalor. Without wealth there can be no Maecenas. The "good old times" were not good old times. Neither master nor servant was as well situated then as to-day. A relapse to old conditions would be disastrous to both—not the least so to him who serves—and would sweep away civilization with it. But whether the change be for good or ill, it is upon us, beyond our power to alter, and, therefore, to be accepted and made the best of. It is a waste of time to criticize the inevitable.

It is easy to see how the change has come. One illustration will serve for almost every phase of the cause. In the manufacture of

---

[1]Andrew Carnegie, *The Gospel of Wealth, and other Timely Essays* (New York: The Century Co., 1900). The original essay, entitled "Wealth," appeared in the *North American Review*, CXLVIII (June 1889). There are minor changes of wording in the 1900 version.

products we have the whole story. It applies to all combinations of human industry, as stimulated and enlarged by the inventions of this scientific age. Formerly, articles were manufactured at the domestic hearth, or in small shops which formed part of the household. The master and his apprentices worked side by side, the latter living with the master, and therefore subject to the same conditions. When these apprentices rose to be masters, there was little or no change in their mode of life, and they, in turn, educated succeeding apprentices in the same routine. There was, substantially, social equality, and even political equality, for those engaged in industrial pursuits had then little or no voice in the State.

The inevitable result of such a mode of manufacture was crude articles at high prices. To-day the world obtains commodities of excellent quality at prices which even the preceding generation would have deemed incredible. In the commercial world similar causes have produced similar results, and the race is benefited thereby. The poor enjoy what the rich could not before afford. What were the luxuries have become the necessaries of life. The laborer has now more comforts than the farmer had a few generations ago. The farmer has more luxuries than the landlord had, and is more richly clad and better housed. The landlord has books and pictures rarer and appointments more artistic than the king could then obtain.

The price we pay for this salutary change is, no doubt, great. We assemble thousands of operatives in the factory, and in the mine, of whom the employer can know little or nothing, and to whom he is little better than a myth. All intercourse between them is at an end. Rigid castes are formed, and, as usual, mutual ignorance breeds mutual distrust. Each caste is without sympathy with the other, and ready to credit anything disparaging in regard to it. Under the law of competition, the employer of thousands is forced into the strictest economies, among which the rates paid to labor figure prominently, and often there is friction between the employer and the employed, between capital and labor, between rich and poor. Human society loses homogeneity.

The price which society pays for the law of competition, like the price it pays for cheap comforts and luxuries, is also great; but the advantages of this law are also greater still than its cost—for it is to this law that we owe our wonderful material development, which brings improved conditions in its train. But, whether the law be benign or not, we must say of it, as we say of the change in the conditions of men to which we have referred: It is here; we cannot evade it; no substitutes for it have been found; and while the law may be sometimes hard for the individual, it is best for the race, because it insures the survival of the fittest in every department. We accept and welcome, therefore, as conditions to which we must accommodate ourselves, great inequality of environment; the concentration of business, industrial and commercial, in the hands of a few; and the law of competition between these, as being not only beneficial, but essential to the future progress of the race. Having accepted these, it follows that there must be great scope for the exercise of special ability in the merchant and in the manufacturer who has to conduct affairs upon a great scale. That this talent for organization and management is rare among men is proved by the fact that it invariably secures enormous rewards for its possessor, no matter where or under what laws or conditions. The experienced in affairs always rate the MAN whose services can be obtained as a partner as not only the first consideration, but such as render the question of his capital scarcely worth considering: for able men soon create capital; in the hands of those without the special talent required, capital soon takes wings. Such men become interested in firms or corporations using millions; and, estimating only simple interest to be made upon the capital invested, it is inevitable that their income must exceed their expenditure and that they must, therefore, accumulate wealth. Nor is there any middle ground which such men can occupy, because the great manufacturing or commercial concern which does not earn at least interest upon its capital soon becomes bankrupt. It must either go forward or fall behind; to stand still is impossible. It is a condition essential to its successful operation that it should be thus far profitable, and even that, in addition to interest on capital, it should make profit. It is a law, as certain as any of the others named, that men possessed of this peculiar talent for affairs, under the free play of economic forces must, of necessity, soon be in receipt of more revenue than can be judiciously expended upon themselves; and this law is as beneficial for the race as the others.

Objections to the foundations upon which society is based are not in order, because the condition of the race is better with these than it has been with any other which has been tried. Of the effect of any new substitutes proposed we cannot be sure. The Socialist or Anarchist who seeks to overturn present conditions is to be regarded as attacking the foundation upon which civilization itself rests, for civilization took its start from the day when the capable, industrious workman said to his incompetent and lazy fellow, "If thou dost not sow, thou shalt not reap," and thus ended primitive Communism by separating the drones from the bees. One who studies this subject will soon be brought face to face with the conclusion that upon the sacredness of property civilization itself depends—the right of the laborer to his hundred dollars in the savings-bank, and equally the legal right of the millionaire to his millions. Every man must be allowed "to sit under his own vine and fig-tree, with none to make afraid," if human society is to advance, or even to remain so far advanced as it is. To those who propose to substitute Communism for this intense Individualism, the answer therefore is: The race has tried that. All progress from that barbarous day to the present time has resulted from its dis-placement. Not evil, but good, has come to the race from the accumulation of wealth by those who have had the ability and energy to produce it. But even if we admit for a moment that it might be better for the race to discard its present foundation, Individualism,—that it is a nobler ideal that man should labor, not for himself alone, but in and for a brotherhood of his fellows, and share with them all in common, realizing Swedenborg's idea of heaven, where, as he says, the angels derive their happiness, not from laboring for self, but for each other,—even admit all this, and a sufficient answer is, This is not evolution, but revolution. It necessitates the changing of human nature itself—a work of eons, even if it were good to change it, which we cannot know.

It is not practicable in our day or in our age. Even if desirable theoretically, it belongs to another and long-succeeding sociologi-cal stratum. Our duty is with what is practicable now—with the next step possible in our day and generation. It is criminal to waste our energies in endeavoring to uproot, when all we can profitably accomplish is to bend the universal tree of humanity a little in the direction most favorable to the production of good fruit under existing circumstances. We might as well urge the destruc-tion of the highest existing type of man because he failed to reach our ideal as to favor the destruction of Individualism, Private Property, the Law of Accumulation of Wealth, and the Law of Competition; for these are the highest results of human experience, the soil in which society, so far, has produced the best fruit. Une-qually or unjustly, perhaps, as these laws sometimes operate, and imperfect as they appear to the Idealist, they are, nevertheless, like the highest type of man, the best and most valuable of all that humanity has yet accomplished.

We start, then, with a condition of affairs under which the best interests of the race are promoted, but which inevitably gives wealth to the few. Thus far, accepting conditions as they exist, the situation can be surveyed and pronounced good. The question then arises, — and if the foregoing be correct, it is the only question with which we have to deal, — What is the proper mode of administering wealth after the laws upon which civilization is founded have thrown it into the hands of the few? And it is of this great question that I believe I offer the true solution. It will be understood that fortunes are here spoken of, not moderate sums saved by many years of effort, the returns from which are required for the comfortable maintenance and education of families. This is not wealth, but only competence, which it should be the aim of all to acquire, and which it is for the best interests of society should be acquired.

There are but three modes in which surplus wealth can be disposed of. It can be left to the families of the decedents; or it can be bequeathed for public purposes; or, finally, it can be administered by its possessors during their lives. Under the first and second modes most of the wealth of the world that has reached the few has hitherto been applied. Let us in turn consider each of these modes. The first is the most injudicious. In monarchical countries, the estates and the greatest portion of the wealth are left to the first son, that the vanity of the parent may be gratified by the thought that his name and title are to descend unimpaired to succeeding generations. The condition of this class in Europe to-day teaches the failure of such hopes or ambitions. The successors have become impoverished through their follies, or from the fall in the value of land. Even in Great Britain the strict law of entail has been found inadequate to maintain an hereditary class. Its soil is rapidly passing into the hands of the stranger. Under republican institutions the division of property among the children is much fairer; but the question which forces itself upon thoughtful men in all lands is, Why should men leave great fortunes to their children? If this is done from affection, is it not misguided affection? Observation teaches that, generally speaking, it is not well for the children that they should be so burdened. Neither is it well for the State. Beyond providing for the wife and

daughters moderate sources of income, and very moderate allowances indeed, if any, for the sons, men may well hesitate; for it is
no longer questionable that great sums bequeathed often work
more for the injury than for the good of the recipients. Wise men
will soon conclude that, for the best interests of the members of
their families, and of the State, such bequests are an improper use
of their means.

It is not suggested that men who have failed to educate their
sons to earn a livelihood shall cast them adrift in poverty. If any
man has seen fit to rear his sons with a view to their living idle
lives, or, what is highly commendable, has instilled in them the
sentiment that they are in a position to labor for public ends without reference to pecuniary considerations, then, of course, the
duty of the parent is to see that such are provided for in modera-
tion. There are instances of millionaires' sons unspoiled by
wealth, who, being rich, still perform great services to the community. Such are the very salt of the earth, as valuable as, unfortunately, they are rare. It is not the exception, however, but the rule,
that men must regard; and, looking at the usual result of enormous
sums conferred upon legatees, the thoughtful man must shortly
say, "I would as soon leave to my son a curse as the almighty
dollar," and admit to himself that it is not the welfare of the children, but family pride, which inspires these legacies.

As to the second mode, that of leaving wealth at death for public
uses, it may be said that this is only a means for the disposal of
wealth, provided a man is content to wait until he is dead before
he becomes of much good in the world. Knowledge of the results
of legacies bequeathed is not calculated to inspire the brightest
hopes of much posthumous good being accomplished by them.
The cases are not few in which the real object sought by the testa-
tor is not attained, nor are they few in which his real wishes are
thwarted. In many cases the bequests are so used as to become
only monuments of his folly. It is well to remember that it requires
the exercise of not less ability than that which acquires it, to use
wealth so as to be really beneficial to the community. Besides this,
it may fairly be said that no man is to be extolled for doing what he
cannot help doing, nor is he to be thanked by the community to
which he only leaves wealth at death. Men who leave vast sums in
this way may fairly be thought men who would not have left it at
all had they been able to take it with them. The memories of such
cannot be held in grateful remembrance, for there is no grace in

their gifts. It is not to be wondered at that such bequests seem so generally to lack the blessing.

The growing disposition to tax more and more heavily large estates left at death is a cheering indication of the growth of a salutary change in public opinion. The State of Pennsylvania now takes — subject to some exceptions — one tenth of the property left by its citizens. The budget presented in the British Parliament the other day proposes to increase the death duties; and, most significant of all, the new tax is to be a graduated one. Of all forms of taxation this seems the wisest. Men who continue hoarding great sums all their lives, the proper use of which for public ends would work good to the community from which it chiefly came, should be made to feel that the community, in the form of the State, cannot thus be deprived of its proper share. By taxing estates heavily at death the State marks its condemnation of the selfish millionaire's unworthy life.

It is desirable that nations should go much further in this direction. Indeed, it is difficult to set bounds to the share of a rich man's estate which should go at his death to the public through the agency of the State, and by all means such taxes should be graduated, beginning at nothing upon moderate sums to dependents, and increasing rapidly as the amounts swell, until of the millionaire's hoard, as of Shylock's, at least

> The other half
> Comes to the privy coffer of the State.

This policy would work powerfully to induce the rich man to attend to the administration of wealth during his life, which is the end that society should always have in view, as being by far the most fruitful for the people. Nor need it be feared that this policy would sap the root of enterprise and render men less anxious to accumulate, for, to the class whose ambition it is to leave great fortunes and to be talked about after their death, it will attract even more attention, and, indeed, be a somewhat nobler ambition, to have enormous sums paid over the the State from their fortunes.

There remains, then, only one mode of using great fortunes; but in this we have the true antidote for the temporary unequal distribution of wealth, the reconciliation of the rich and the poor — a reign of harmony, another ideal, differing, indeed, from that of the Communist in requiring only the further evolution of existing conditions, not the total overthrow of our civilization. It is founded upon the present most intense Individualism, and the race is prepared to put it in practice by degrees whenever it pleases. Under its sway we shall have an ideal State, in which the surplus wealth of the few will become, in the best sense, the property of the many, because administered for the common good; and this wealth, passing through the hands of the few, can be made a much more potent force for the elevation of our race than if distributed in small sums to the people themselves. Even the poorest can be made to see this, and to agree that great sums gathered by some of their fellow-citizens and spent for public purposes, from which the masses reap the principal benefit, are more valuable to them than if scattered among themselves in trifling amounts through the course of many years.

If we consider the results which flow from the Cooper Institute, for instance, to the best portion of the race in New York not possessed of means, and compare these with those which would have ensued for the good of the masses from an equal sum distributed by Mr. Cooper in his lifetime in the form of wages, which is the highest form of distribution, being for work done and not for charity, we can form some estimate of the possibilities for the improvement of the race which lie embedded in the present law of the accumulation of wealth. Much of this sum, if distributed in small quantities among the people, would have been wasted in the indulgence of appetite, some of it in excess, and it may be doubted whether even the part put to the best use, that of adding to the comforts of the home, would have yielded results for the race, as a race, at all comparable to those which are flowing and are to flow from the Cooper Institute from generation to generation. Let the advocate of violent or radical change ponder well this thought.

We might even go so far as to take another instance—that of Mr. Tilden's bequest of five millions of dollars for a free library in the city of New York; but in referring to this one cannot help saying involuntarily: How much better if Mr. Tilden had devoted the last years of his own life to the proper administration of this immense sum; in which case neither legal contest nor any other cause of delay could have interfered with his aims. But let us assume that Mr. Tilden's millions finally become the means of giving to this city a noble public library, where the treasures of the world contained in books will be open to all forever, without money and without price. Considering the good of that part of the race which congregates in and around Manhattan Island, would its permanent benefit have been better promoted had these millions been allowed to circulate in small sums through the hands of the masses? Even the most strenuous advocate of Communism must entertain a doubt upon this subject. Most of those who think will probably entertain no doubt whatever.

Poor and restricted are our opportunities in this life, narrow our horizon, our best work most imperfect; but rich men should be thankful for one inestimable boon. They have it in their power during their lives to busy themselves in organizing benefactions from which the masses of their fellows will derive lasting advantage, and thus dignify their own lives. The highest life is probably to be reached, not by such imitation of the life of Christ as Count Tolstoi gives us, but, while animated by Christ's spirit, by recognizing the changed conditions of this age, and adopting modes of expressing this spirit suitable to the changed conditions under which we live, still laboring for the good of our fellows, which was the essence of his life and teaching, but laboring in a different manner.

This, then, is held to be the duty of the man of wealth: To set an example of modest, unostentatious living, shunning display or extravagance; to provide moderately for the legitimate wants of those dependent upon him; and, after doing so, to consider all surplus revenues which come to him simply as trust funds, which he is called upon to administer, and strictly bound as a matter of duty to administer in the manner which, in his judgment, is best calculated to produce the most beneficial results for the community—the man of wealth thus becoming the mere trustee and agent for his poorer brethren, bringing to their service his superior wisdom, experience, and ability to administer, doing for them better than they would or could do for themselves.

We are met here with the difficulty of determining what are moderate sums to leave to members of the family; what is modest, unostentatious living; what is the test of extravagance. There must be different standards for different conditions. The answer is that it is as impossible to name exact amounts or actions as it is to define good manners, good taste, or the rules of propriety; but, nevertheless, these are verities, well known, although indefinable. Public sentiment is quick to know and to feel what offends these. So in the case of wealth. The rule in regard to good taste in dress of men or women applies here. Whatever makes one conspicuous offends the canon. If any family be chiefly known for display, for extravagance in home, table, or equipage, for enormous sums ostentatiously spent in any form upon itself—if these be its chief distinctions, we have no difficulty in estimating its nature or culture. So likewise in regard to the use or abuse of its surplus wealth, or to generous, free-handed coöperation in good public uses, or to unabated efforts to accumulate and hoard to the last, or whether they administer or bequeath. The verdict rests with the best and most enlightened public sentiment. The community will surely judge, and its judgments will not often be wrong.

The best uses to which surplus wealth can be put have already been indicated. Those who would administer wisely must, indeed, be wise; for one of the serious obstacles to the improvement of our race is indiscriminate charity. It were better for mankind that the millions of the rich were thrown into the sea than so spent as to encourage the slothful, the drunken, the unworthy. Of every thousand dollars spent in so-called charity to-day, it is probable that nine hundred and fifty dollars is unwisely spent—so spent, indeed, as to produce the very evils which it hopes to mitigate or cure. A well-known writer of philosophic books admitted the other day that he had given a quarter of a dollar to a man who approached him as he was coming to visit the house of his friend. He knew nothing of the habits of this beggar, knew not the use that would be made of this money, although he had every reason to suspect that it would be spent improperly. This man professed to be a disciple of Herbert Spencer; yet the quarter-dollar given that night will probably work more injury than all the money will do good which its thoughtless donor will ever be able to give in true charity. He only gratified his own feelings, saved himself from annoyance—and this was probably one of the most selfish and very worst actions of his life, for in all respects he is most worthy.

In bestowing charity, the main consideration should be to help those who will help themselves; to provide part of the means by which those who desire to improve may do so; to give those who desire to rise the aids by which they may rise; to assist, but rarely or never to do all. Neither the individual nor the race is improved by almsgiving. Those worthy of assistance, except in rare cases, seldom require assistance. The really valuable men of the race never do, except in case of accident or sudden change. Every one has, of course, cases of individuals brought to his own knowledge where temporary assistance can do genuine good, and these he will not overlook. But the amount which can be wisely given by the individual for individuals is necessarily limited by his lack of knowledge of the circumstances connected with each. He is the only true reformer who is as careful and as anxious not to aid the unworthy as he is to aid the worthy, and, perhaps, even more so, for in almsgiving more injury is probably done by rewarding vice than by relieving virtue.

The rich man is thus almost restricted to following the examples of Peter Cooper, Enoch Pratt of Baltimore, Mr. Pratt of Brooklyn, Senator Stanford, and others, who know that the best means of benefiting the community is to place within its reach the ladders upon which the aspiring can rise — free libraries, parks, and means of recreation, by which men are helped in body and mind; works of art, certain to give pleasure and improve the public taste; and public institutions of various kinds, which will improve the general condition of the people; in this manner returning their surplus wealth to the mass of their fellows in the forms best calculated to do them lasting good.

Thus is the problem of rich and poor to be solved. The laws of accumulation will be left free, the laws of distribution free. Individualism will continue, but the millionaire will be but a trustee for the poor, intrusted for a season with a great part of the increased wealth of the community, but administering it for the community far better than it could or would have done for itself. The best minds will thus have reached a stage in the development of the race in which it is clearly seen that there is no mode of disposing of surplus wealth creditable to thoughtful and earnest men into whose hands it flows, save by using it year by year for the general good. This day already dawns. Men may die without incurring the pity of their fellows, still sharers in great business enterprises from which their capital cannot be or has not been withdrawn, and which is left chiefly at death for public uses; yet the day is not far distant when the man who dies leaving behind him millions of available wealth, which was free to him to administer during life, will pass away "unwept, unhonored, and unsung," no matter to what uses he leaves the dross which he cannot take with him. Of such as these the public verdict will then be: "The man who dies thus rich dies disgraced."

Such, in my opinion is the true gospel concerning wealth, obedience to which is destined some day to solve the problem of the rich and the poor, and to bring "Peace on earth, among men good will."

CHAPTER 20

IMMIGRATION AND AMERICANIZATION

The failure of the 'melting pot.'

Randolph Bourne, 1916

52. ADDRESS TO THE CITIZENSHIP CONVENTION (1916)[1]

WOODROW WILSON

It is not fair to the great multitudes of hopeful men and women who press into this country from other countries that we should leave them without that friendly and intimate instruction which will enable them very soon after they come to find out what America is like at heart and what America is intended for among the nations of the world.

I believe that the chief school that these people must attend after they get here is the school which all of us attend, which is furnished by the life of the communities in which we live and the nation to which we belong. It has been a very touching thought to me sometimes to think of the hopes which have drawn these people to America. I have no doubt that many a simple soul has been thrilled by that great statue standing in the harbor of New York and seeming to lift the light of liberty for the guidance of the feet of men; and I can imagine that they have expected here something ideal in the treatment that they will receive, something ideal in the laws which they would have to live under, and it has caused me many a time to turn upon myself the eye of examination to see whether there burned in me the true light of the American spirit which they expected to find here. It is easy, my fellow-citizens, to communicate physical lessons, but it is very difficult to communicate spiritual lessons. America was intended to be a spirit among the nations of the world, and it is the purpose of conferences like this to find out the best way to introduce the newcomers to this spirit, and by that very interest in them to enhance and purify in ourselves the thing that ought to make America great and not only ought to make her great, but ought to make her exhibit a spirit unlike any other nation in the world.

[1]Winthrop Talbot (Comp.), *Americanization* (New York: H. W. Wilson, 1920), pp. 28–31. The address was delivered on July 17, 1916.

213

I have never been among those who felt comfortable in boasting of the superiority of America over other countries. The way to cure yourself of that is to travel in other countries and find out how much of nobility and character and fine enterprise there is everywhere in the world. The most that America can hope to do is to show, it may be, the finest example, not the only example, of the things that ought to benefit and promote the progress of the world.

So my interest in this movement is as much an interest in ourselves as in those whom we are trying to Americanize, because if we are genuine Americans they cannot avoid the infection; whereas, if we are not genuine Americans, there will be nothing to infect them with, and no amount of teaching, no amount of exposition of the Constitution,—which I find very few persons understand,—no amount of dwelling upon the idea of liberty and of justice will accomplish the object we have in view, unless we ourselves illustrate the idea of justice and of liberty. My interest in this movement is, therefore, a two-fold interest. I believe it will assist us to become self-conscious in respect of the fundamental ideas of American life. When you ask a man to be loyal to a government, if he comes from some foreign countries, his idea is that he is expected to be loyal to a certain set of persons like a ruler or a body set in authority over him, but that is not the American idea. Our idea is that he is to be loyal to certain objects in life, and that the only reason he has a President and a Congress and a Governor and a State Legislature and courts is that the community shall have instrumentalities by which to promote those objects. It is a cooperative organization expressing itself in this Constitution, expressing itself in these laws, intending to express itself in the exposition of those laws by the courts; and the idea of America is not so much that men are to be restrained and punished by the law as instructed and guided by the law. That is the reason so many hopeful reforms come to grief. A law cannot work until it expresses the spirit of the community for which it is enacted, and if you try to enact into law what expresses only the spirit of a small coterie or of a small minority, you know, or at any rate you ought to know, beforehand that it is not going to work. The object of the law is that there, written upon these pages, the citizen should read the record of the experience of this state and nation; what they have concluded it is necessary for them to do because of the life they have lived and the things that they have discovered to be elements in that life. So that we ought to be careful to maintain a government at which the immigrant can look with the closest scrutiny and to which he should be at liberty to address this question: "You declare this to be a land of liberty and of equality and of justice; have you made it so by your law?" We ought to be able in our schools, in our night schools and in every other method of instructing these people, to show them that that has been our endeavor. We cannot conceal from them long the fact that we are just as human as any other nation, that we are just as selfish, that there are just as many mean people amongst us as anywhere else, that there are just as many people here who want to take advantage of other people as you can find in other countries, just as many cruel people, just as many people heartless when it comes to maintaining and promoting their own interest; but you can show that our object is to get these people in harness and see to it that they do not do any damage and are not allowed to indulge the passions which would bring injustice and calamity at last upon a nation whose object is spiritual and not material.

America has built up a great body of wealth. America has become, from the physical point of view, one of the most powerful nations in the world, a nation which if it took the pains to do so, could build that power up into one of the most formidable instruments in the world, one of the most formidable instruments of force, but which has no other idea than to use its force for ideal objects and not for self-aggrandizement.

We have been disturbed recently, my fellow-citizens, by certain symptoms which have showed themselves in our body politic. Certain men—I have never believed a great number—born in other lands, have in recent months thought more of those lands than they have of the honor and interest of the government under which they are now living. They have even gone so far as to draw apart in spirit and in organization from the rest of us to accomplish some special object of their own. I am not here going to utter any criticism of these people, but I want to say this, that such a thing as that is absolutely incompatible with the fundamental idea of loyalty, and that loyalty is not a self-pleasing virtue. I am not bound to be loyal to the United States to please myself. I am bound to be loyal to the United States because I live under its laws and am its citizen, and whether it hurts me or whether it benefits me, I am obliged to be loyal. Loyalty means nothing unless it has at its heart the absolute principle of self-sacrifice. Loyalty means that you ought to be ready to sacrifice every interest that you have, and your life itself, if your country calls upon you to do so, and that is the sort of loyalty which ought to be inculcated into these newcomers, that they are not to be loyal only so long as they are pleased, but that, having once entered into this sacred relationship, they are bound to be loyal whether they are pleased or not; and that loyalty which is merely self-pleasing is only self-indulgence and selfishness. No man has ever risen to the real stature of spiritual manhood until he has found that it is finer to serve somebody else than it is to serve himself.

These are the conceptions which we ought to teach the newcomers into our midst, and we ought to realize that the life of every one of us is part of the schooling, and that we cannot preach loyalty unless we set the example, that we cannot profess things with any influence upon others unless we practice them also. This process of Americanization is going to be a process of self-examination, a process of purification, a process of rededication to the things which America represents and is proud to represent. And it takes a great deal more courage and steadfastness, my fellow citizens, to represent ideal things than to represent anything else. It is easy to lose your temper, and hard to keep it. It is easy to strike and sometimes very difficult to refrain from striking, and I think you will agree with me that we are most justified in being proud of doing the things that are hard to do and not the things that are easy. You do not settle things quickly by taking what seems to be the quickest way to settle them. You may make the complication just that much the more profound and inextricable, and, therefore, what I believe America should exalt above everything else is the sovereignty of thoughtfulness and sympathy and vision as against the grosser impulses of mankind. No nation can live without vision, and no vision will exalt a nation except the vision of real liberty and real justice and purity of conduct.

53. TRANS-NATIONAL AMERICA (1916)[1]

RANDOLPH S. BOURNE

No reverberatory effect of the great war has caused American public opinion more solicitude than the failure of the "melting-pot." The discovery of diverse nationalistic feelings among our great alien population has come to most people as an intense shock. It has brought out the unpleasant inconsistencies of our traditional beliefs. We have had to watch hard-hearted old Brahmins virtuously indignant at the spectacle of the immigrant refusing to be melted, while they jeer at patriots like Mary Antin who write about "our forefathers." We have had to listen to publicists who express themselves as stunned by the evidence of vigorous nationalistic and cultural movements in this country among Germans, Scandinavians, Bohemians, and Poles, while in the same breath they insist that the alien shall be forcibly assimilated to that Anglo-Saxon tradition which they unquestioningly label "American."

As the unpleasant truth has come upon us that assimilation in this country was proceeding on lines very different from those we had marked out for it, we found ourselves inclined to blame those who were thwarting our prophecies. The truth became culpable. We blamed the war, we blamed the Germans. And then we discovered with a moral shock that these movements had been making great headway before the war even began. We found that the tendency, reprehensible and paradoxical as it might be, has been for the national clusters of immigrants, as they became more and more firmly established and more and more prosperous, to cultivate more and more assiduously the literatures and cultural traditions of their homelands. Assimilation, in other words, instead of washing out the memories of Europe, made them more and more intensely real. Just as these clusters became more and more objectively American, did they become more and more German or Scandinavian or Bohemian or Polish.

---

[1]*Atlantic Monthly*, CXVIII (July 1916), 86–87.

To face the fact that our aliens are already strong enough to take a share in the direction of their own destiny, and that the strong cultural movements represented by the foreign press, schools, and colonies are a challenge to our facile attempts, is not, however, to admit the failure of Americanization. It is not to fear the failure of democracy. It is rather to urge us to an investigation of what Americanism may rightly mean. It is to ask ourselves whether our ideal has been broad or narrow—whether perhaps the time has not come to assert a higher ideal than the "melting-pot." Surely we cannot be certain of our spiritual democracy when, claiming to melt the nations within us to a comprehension of our free and democratic institutions, we fly into panic at the first sign of their own will and tendency. We act as if we wanted Americanization to take place only on our own terms, and not by the consent of the governed. All our elaborate machinery of settlement and school and union, of social and political naturalization, however, will move with friction just in so far as it neglects to take into account this strong and virile insistence that America shall be what the immigrant will have a hand in making it, and not what a ruling class, descendant of those British stocks which were the first permanent immigrants, decide that America shall be made. This is the condition which confronts us, and which demands a clear and general readjustment of our attitude and our ideal.

54. The Hopes of the Hyphenated (1916)[1]

GEORGE CREEL

The question for the United States to decide is whether the same old policy of neglect, stupidity, and oppression shall be pursued, or whether a new and sincere approach shall be made to the task of assimilation. In this connection, let it be borne in mind that while the immigrant seems to suffer and die in seeming helplessness, he works his revenge upon society in a thousand ways. Out of his ignorance and despair he drags down the wage-scale, acts as a strike-breaker, lowers the American standard of living, and adds the note of actual ferocity to the competitive struggle. Out of the slums where aliens fester in dirt and disease come the defectives and delinquents that fill our jails and asylums, and their ignorance and lack of civic interest make them easy prey for the unclean political influences that prosper by municipal maladministration.

Ludlow, Calumet, Lawrence, Paterson, Cabin Creek, and other revolts of oppressed aliens have cost millions in actual loss and scarred whole States with hatred. Even if justice to the alien contains no appeal, there is the instinct of self-preservation to compel drastic changes.

Certain steps [are] already being taken in the direction of reform. Mr. Caminetti, Commissioner-General of Immigration, has vitalized the division of information so that it is truly aiding the immigrant in making the choice of a home, and is doing a splendid work in connection with the employment problem. Also, by an arrangement with Mr. Claxon, Commissioner of Education, the names of all immigrant children of school age are sent immediately from the various ports of arrival to the school authorities at the point of destination.

Several cities, notably Cleveland, have established immigration bureaus that guard that immigrant from the time of his arrival,

[1]*The Century Magazine*, n.s. LXIX (Jan. 1916, 354–63.

watching his education, protecting his rights, promoting his interests, and helping him in the advance to naturalization. Of the States, California has moved to the front with a statute providing teachers to work in the homes of immigrants, instructing children and adults in education laws, labor laws, sanitation, and the fundamental principles of American citizenship.

The North American Civic League for Immigrants is a powerful volunteer body that attempts the promotion of helpful legislation, the positive work required to protect the immigrant, and the teaching of the English language. Through the medium of the Baron de Hirsch Trust, the Jewish immigrant receives far larger consideration than that accorded to any other nationality. The Trust maintains distributing agencies at all points of entry, and not only is the alien placed in the business or job for which he has been trained, but in event of his poverty he is loaned the money necessary for transportation and equipment.

These activities are praiseworthy indeed, but they do not by any means contain the solution of the immigrant problem. The work that is to be done cannot wait upon private generosity or individual initiative, nor will the true answer ever be given by cities or states acting by themselves. The task of assimilation is national. It is the Federal Government that lets in these millions from other shores, and it is the Federal Government that must accept the responsibility for their protection, development, and Americanization. The one policy that carries with it any certainty of success is a policy that will regard every alien as a ward of the nation, to be guarded, aided, and protected from the very day of arrival to the day of naturalization. Until they have mastered the language, become acquainted with their rights as well as their duties, and gained a sense of belonging, these strangers within our gates are as children, and must be so treated.

Such a policy, taking account of the muddles and maladjustments of the past, will invent machinery of distribution that will end the disastrous stupidity of farmers huddled in industrial centers, tradesmen and professional men herded in mills and factories, and skilled labor wasting itself in unskilled drudgeries—a machinery that will place every immigrant to his own advantage as well as to the advantage of the state.

In the growth of the unemployment problem, and the increase in involuntary poverty, may be seen the evil results of the theory that has insisted upon government as a sovereign power rather than as a working partnership with the people. In the formulation of a sane immigration policy there is the chance for the Government of the United States to put off its purple robes of aloofness and put on the overalls of empire-building.

Government lands and state lands lie idle while the business of pioneering is turned over to promoters who are concerned only with their profits, caring nothing for the human element that figures in their close bargains. Where is there larger promise of happiness and prosperity than in the transportation of immigrant agriculturists, in community groups, to this public land, together with such equipment as will enable them to make a flying start in their conquest of the soil? It is not a new idea, or radical, for other countries are using the twenty-year-loan system to put people upon the land.

In those isolated cases where immigrant groups have succeeded in getting into agriculture, the result has been industry, thrift, sobriety, education, and Americanization. Italians are growing cotton on the Mississippi delta, fruit in the Ozarks and Louisiana, and raising garden-truck in the Atlantic Coast States and New England, either rendering worthless land productive by their toil or else developing supposedly waste tracts.

The Poles are lovers of the land, ninety per cent of them that come to the United States being eager to engage in agriculture, and the small number able to achieve their ambition have only stories of success to tell. The Polish farmers of Wisconsin, Illinois, Texas, and Kansas are not behind the native-born in their contributions to the general good, and the Bohemians are others who have done well wherever their feet have touched the soil.

The investigations of the Immigration Commission proved that all of those thus brought into contact with opportunity were grasping it, taking out naturalization papers, Americanizing in every way, and playing their proper part in municipal, state, and national affairs.

A second necessary step is the creation of a federal system of public employment bureaus which may minister to the needs of the native-born as well as of the alien. Individual states have failed abjectly in this respect, for even the nineteen commonwealths that have created free employment bureaus have done little more than to pile up records of inadequacy. Federal control would cover the whole country, supplementing and assisting the work of existing organizations, regulating private agencies, and bringing together definitely the jobless man and the manless job. Here again it is a matter of imitation rather than innovation, for Great Britain and Germany have for years been operating national labor exchanges successfully.

The United States must follow the example of European countries, which meet the difficulties of poverty by the advancement of transportation costs, and also guard against class control of the machinery by providing that both workers and employers shall have representation on a governing committee.

Justice must be made swift and inexpensive, and this cannot be done until the simple and innumerable disputes of the industrial world are removed from the wearisome processes of traditional jurisprudence. As long ago as 1806, France created industrial courts, and the example has been followed by Germany, Switzerland, Italy, and Belgium. A president, who represents the public, and an equal number of workers and employers sit as a jury rather than as a court. Lawyers are barred; the parties to the dispute take turns relating grievance and defense, and in consequence of this simplicity, ninety per cent of the cases are adjusted without formal hearings. In event of threatened strikes or lockouts, the courts have the power to sit as boards of arbitration, and it is only in rare cases that satisfactory agreements are not reached.

Compare the simplicity of this procedure with the American method of frequent trials, frequent appeals, reversed decisions, remanded cases, court costs, lawyers' fees, and months of delay, a gauntlet that no poor man dares to run. The dollar out of which an alien is cheated may mean to him the difference between a bed or a park bench, and certainly his sense of injustice will not inspire him with respect for democratic institutions.

The processes of education must be quickened, and greater emphasis should be put upon the preparation of human beings for the business of life. Immigrant adults, as well as immigrant youth, should have the privilege of instruction in the English language, national, state, and municipal government, industrial laws, customs, and ways of American life, hygiene, sanitation, and all other allied subjects that will fit them to be intelligent, useful American citizens.

Germany, through a compulsory system of continuation schools, has control over a youth until his eighteenth year; and although the system has been in force since 1891, it is only now that the United States is taking timid, tentative steps in the same direction.

Federal standards of education must be raised, and the established principle of federal aid to the poorer states should be carried through to the point where illiteracy will vanish, whether the illiterate be a native-born child or an adult alien. Not the least vital task of the public school system is to serve the immigrant during his struggle for prosperity and citizenship.

Health is no less important than education, and authoritative investigation has shown that adult delinquency and dependency are largely due to neglect in connection with the physical defects and deficiencies of the growing youth. Not alone is it necessary to have medical inspection and dental clinics for every child that passes through the public schools of the United States, but particularly in the case of the immigrant and the poverty-stricken native-born there is need of infant dispensaries, model kitchens, milk stations, visiting nurses, and a program of preventive medicine.

While new machinery in large measure may be necessary for the doing of all these things, the plant for its housing is already at hand. The school buildings of the United States offer themselves for the purpose in full perfection of convenience, economy, and effectiveness. As it is today, the schools, which represent the largest single investment of the people's money, are in use a scant seven hours a day for an average of one hundred and forty four days a year.

The neighborhood is the group unit next in importance to the family itself, and the school building is the center of the neighborhood. What reaches every child in the United States can reach every parent, and not only does the wider use of the school plant hold out its rich promise to the alien, but to the native born as well.

In every building serving its neighborhood group may be placed the official representative of the federal system of immigrant distribution, the branch office of the federal employment exchange, the industrial court, the medical inspection bureau, the dental clinic, the milk station, the visiting nurses, the infant dispensary, the free-legal-aid bureau, the health office, and the juvenile court. Here is the natural and suitable place for the instruction of the adult alien in English and citizenship, for the art gallery, for the branch library, for the model kitchen, and for the development of the play instinct.

Night use of the school buildings strikes at the very heart of the leisure-time problem. In cities thousands of little children play in the streets, menaced alike by evil environment and the police court, and in the country life is admittedly dull and stagnant. Growing girls are forced into the dance hall, men into the saloon, and women either gossip across stoops and fire escapes or become fungous growths in kitchens. In competition with the reckless greeds of commercialized amusement, the social center offers amateur theatricals, debates, dancing parties, moving picture shows, receptions, gymnasium games, all in a clean, inspiring environment, subjected to the wholesome restraints of the family group and neighborly friendship.

The immigrants can be tapped for their rich store of folk songs, games, and traditional customs, so that not only will the native born be enriched and broadened, but the alien given that absolutely essential sense of belonging. To watch an interracial pageant in a New York school building, shared in by twenty nationalities, happy, laughing, proud, and friendly, is [a] complete answer to the question of assimilation.

The school building should be the polling-place, and through the medium of the social center it is possible to effect the self-organization of voters into a deliberative body that will always be in session, the school house its headquarters. Would not this be more inspiring to the alien than the location of voting booths in livery stables, barber shops, and sheds, or the gathering of voters in some saloon-connected room or in a hall paid for by interested parties out of mysterious funds?

With specific reference to the alien, the school-principal employed by the educational authorities to look after the children of immigrants may also be employed by the immigration authorities to care for the adults as well. His should be the position of neighborhood guardian of these wards of the nation, looking after their inclusion in the proper classes, acquainting them with the services rendered by employment bureau, health office, free legal aid bureau, and visiting nurses, and drawing them into the night play of the social center. In thickly settled communities, where a principal would not have the necessary time, an assistant or assistants might be appointed.

A beginning has been made. Wisconsin, Indiana, Massachusetts, Kansas, New York, Washington, New Jersey, and the District of Columbia are in possession of a law that permits the people to use school buildings, aside from school hours, for the purpose of meeting and discussion "any and all subjects and questions which in their judgment may appertain to the educational, political, economic, artistic, and moral interest of the citizens." Out of it has grown the new profession of social secretary.

All that is necessary is the adoption of a federal policy that will give unity, purpose, and dynamic direction to what is now isolated and sporadic, and the task of immigrant assimilation is a sound base for such a policy. Fortunately enough, the money for the work is at hand, and what is more, it is money provided by the immigrant himself. To-day, in the United States Treasury, there is a balance of $10,000,000 in the head-tax fund contributed to by every new arrival. There is no question that this income was primarily intended as a sacred trust fund, for the law of 1882, levying a tax of fifty cents on every immigrant, provided that the "money thus collected . . . shall constitute a fund to be called the immigrant fund, and shall be used . . . to defray the expenses of regulating immigration under this act and for the care of immigrants arriving in the United States, for the relief of such as are in distress, and for the general purposes and expenses of carrying this act into effect."

In 1894 the head-tax was raised to one dollar, in 1903 to two dollars, and in 1907 to four dollars. In 1909 the immigrant fund was abolished, and the head-tax receipts were dumped into the Treasury, the regulation of immigration being forced to depend upon such annual allowances as Congress saw fit to make. The $10,000,000 balance belongs to the immigrants, and even if their need were less bitter, it would still be unfair and dishonest to divert a trust fund from its avowed object to purposes that were never intended.

The dreadful European conflict will not have been without its service if the United States, alarmed by the persistence of the hyphen in American life, adopts an immigration policy that in its essence will be a policy of hope, justice, aspiration, and progress for all the oppressed and unhappy, whether they be native born or strangers within the gates.

PART VI:

EDUCATION IN MODERN
AMERICA

The complexities and intricacies of educational developments during the present century plus the lack of historical perspective in analyzing them, add to the difficulty of surveying the period and presenting representative selections. Any one development—the Progressive Movement, the influence of John Dewey, the impact of the new science and scientific techniques on education, the re-evaluation of educational ideals and objectives, the role of education in national policy especially in the face of the Communist threat, the extension of educational opportunities, or the matter of federal aid—all deserves extensive discussion, and many other aspects of recent trends could be included. Perhaps the greatest difficulty in analyzing the major developments is the fact that the present century has produced an abundance of self-analysis and criticism of the traditional system of education and its purpose. This is a century pulsating with tensions and friction, and its educational practices, theories, and experiments are one index of the changing pattern of American thought and institutions.

Not since the common school movement has there been so much concern about the purpose of education and its relationship to democracy. The leadership of the late nineteenth century had dedicated itself largely to extending opportunities to those classes who had earlier been denied them and to discovering the means of adjusting and modifying institutions and objectives to fit the needs of an industrial society. In the twentieth century, the theme of democracy and education is repeatedly expressed. Progressive and democratic ideals have been restated and reaffirmed, but the existing order has been severely indicted for failure to meet the demands of a democratic people. More and more there is concern with the inevitable problem resulting from the success of the nineteenth century educational ideal of equal opportunity: that of mass education versus quality. There has been a growing demand for the school to help build a new social order. This century has reverberated with criticism and rejection, with questioning and evaluating, but has generally accepted the principles of the nineteenth century educational reformers.

Despite the attacks and counter-attacks on American educational practices and ideas, the common school and popular education remain the foremost means of promoting the democratic aims of society. Social improvement and progress are the two key educational objectives of this century as they were in the preceding one. Whether expressed in the abstract realm of American thought, or

229

through the reform notions of the educational theorists, or by the methods and concepts of progressivism—faith in democracy and in education as a means of improving social institutions is still a dominant theme. The main difference between the views of the twentieth century leadership and that of the past is in the recognition of the complexities and peculiar problems and conditions of an industrial-urban society. The result is a variety of innovations and reforms and a sharp break with the traditional educational patterns of the nineteenth century.

The ideas of Herbert Croly, leader of the intellectuals committed to Progressivism, are an excellent example of the continuity of American educational thought. In *The Promise of American Life* (1909), he expressed faith in American education as a means of uplift (55). Yet he rejected the traditional Jeffersonian views which emphasized individualism. Croly envisioned an intellectual awakening in which education would cross the gulf between American ideals and American practices.

John Dewey offers another example of the dedicated democrat and educational critic. In *Schools of Tomorrow* (1915), Dewey, the apostle of Progressivism, sought to evolve a methodology and a philosophy which would fit the democratic experiment (56). His emphasis was on reform through education—a traditional nineteenth century view; but he attacked the established methods, theories, and practices as inadequate and useless in an industrial age. His principal concern was with the separation between intellectual training for the upper classes and practical education for the working class. Dewey called for an end to the separation between liberal and mechanical training. As for the school, its aim should be to liberate and enlarge the mind rather than to discipline. Dewey viewed the public school as "the only fundamental agency for good." Through his writings and teachings and his experiments in the laboratory school, he sought to provide a model for a school that would have a beneficial influence on the course of social progress and would become an agency of democracy.

Recasting the school to reflect the democratic principles and the scientific innovations and to serve an industrial and urban society became the chief project of the reformers of the twentieth century; and out of this impulse evolved the progressive movement in education. As Boyd Bode, one of its chief spokesmen explained it: "If democracy is to have a deep and inclusive human meaning, it must have also a distinctive educational system" (57). The concept and application of Progressivism began as an answer to the problems of an industrial-and-urban civilization and as a means of furthering the democratic promise. It originated in the intellectual changes of the past century and was nurtured by the social changes, the scientific innovations, and the reform impulse active since the turn of the century. From the closing decades of the nineteenth century, Progressivism permeated every aspect of American life; it dominated the educational scene until the 1950s.

The impact of Progressivism on the schools and education was enormous and continued as a vital force long after its political and social aspects had receded. As Lawrence Cremin describes it in *The Transformation of the School* (1961), Progressivism changed the nineteenth century schools and ideas of education into the institutions and practices of the present century. It indeed transformed the schools: Method, philosophy, objectives, teacher training, curriculum, even the physical plants all were changed, influenced, and affected by Progressivism. Progressivism in education is difficult to define exactly, because the movement became so fragmented; and also because through the years critics have belittled, ridiculed, condemned, and even distorted it.

Yet Progressivism stands out as the most significant force in educational developments in the twentieth century. Its true influence and meaning can be understood only if placed within its complex and pluralistic framework. Progressivism in education was many movements and ideas, involving a wide range of individuals. Its unifying force was the acceptance of the idea of reform and change in order to improve society through the schools, through education. Francis W. Parker's experimentation and achievements in the Quincy, Massachusetts, schools and in the Cook County Normal School of Illinois; in Chicago, John Dewey's Laboratory School as a "cooperative community", the progressive schools of Gary, Indiana, under the superintendency of William Wirt—are all representative of the gamut of progressive ideas and practices which permeated the educational scene. Gary's system became the model of Progressivism as the "most complete and admirable application" of Dewey's principles, "a synthesis of the best aspects of the progressive 'schools of tomorrow,'" according to Randolph Bourne, who made the system nationally known through his articles in the *New Republic* and later through a book,

The Gary Schools. Despite criticism of the Gary Plan, Progressivism spread. By 1929 over 200 cities in forty-one states had adopted in whole or part the "progressive idea" of education.

In 1919, what began as criticism of the old order and individual suggestions for changes and reform evolved into a formal organization, the Association for the Advancement of Progressive Education (PEA), under the leadership of Stanwood Cobb. Its guiding principle was, "the freest and fullest development of the individual, based upon the scientific study of his mental, physical, spiritual, and social characteristics and needs"; its aim was the reformation of the school system. Thus the Progressive Movement in education became formalized. From a small membership composed largely of interested laymen and parents, it grew steadily in number, influence, and professionalism. Foundation support, committee reports, meetings, recommendations, a journal all became part of the progressive movement which nonetheless failed to evolve a specific program during these years.

As the organization grew, ideological and factional division developed. Some called upon education to play an active reform role; others insisted that the spirit of Progressivism lay in its emphasis on the child and individual development. The problem was that of finding a rationale, a program, that would be acceptable to a large and unwieldy group more and more composed of professional educators. During the economic crisis of the thirties, some of the Progressives spoke out vehemently for educational reform and particularly for using the school to build a new social order. They offered blueprints of various sorts, and it was largely this question of program that divided the Progressive Education Association.

Above all, change in education was essential; and the teaching profession was called upon to play a more active role. William Kilpatrick, a leading Progressive from Teachers College, called upon the profession to study the social and economic situation and to cooperate with others in intelligent planning in order to evolve a new and inclusive education for all classes. Kilpatrick's concern, like Dewey's, was for making the school more effectively educational and closer to life in order to develop critical intelligence (58). A few years later in 1937, Dewey in "Education and Social Change" restated these views about integrating the schools with social life in order to "share in the construction of a new social order." This is one of the dominant themes of the thirties among one segment of the leadership, some directly involved in the PEA, others on the fringe. They all emphasized the role the schools should play in contributing to social change.

Of the educational programs proposed in this era of crisis, change, and criticism, two stand out because of the extreme nature of the underlying thesis and because of their suggestion that the schools assume an active role and inaugurate drastic changes in the curriculum. These were George S. Counts', "Dare the School Build a New Social Order?" (1932) (59), and the Report of the Commission on the Social Studies of the American Historical Association (1934) (60). Counts, while active in the Progressive Movement, did not sing its praises but rather pointed out its central weakness, lack of a social theory. Progressivism could only be successful if it faced "squarely and courageously every social issue." Activism, acceptance of a central purpose, recognition of the ills of society, and dedication to the welfare of the masses were essential, according to Counts.

The most significant aspect of Counts' and the AHA report is the fact that both questioned the continuation of the existing economic system as perpetuated by the schools and emphasized the need to educate for a new democratic age, not founded on individualism or based on capitalism. This was to be the new role of the school: to offer a new vision of industrial America.

Counts offered an ideology and a program by which the schools could create a democratic society free from the ills of economic depression and crisis. The AHA report presented specific suggestions for remaking the schools and the curriculum. The statement, like Counts', recognized the passing of the older order and criticized the "continued emphasis in education on the traditional values of economic individualism." Such an orientation would intensify the conflicts, contradictions, and maladjustments in society. The school had to recognize the new order and prepare the rising generation to enter it. Thus society would be shaped in accordance with the American ideals of democracy, freedom, and the dignity of man.

Counts' proposals, the AHA report, the writings of Dewey and other critics were the emphatic voices of the 1930s — calling for change and demanding that the schools take an active part in the remaking of America's social and economic order. However, the PEA was reluctant to accept such drastic suggestions as a guiding philosophy. Thus the organization remained without an ideology, and institutional changes followed a vague progressivism rather than a commitment to social reform. Without a platform, but with its radical tinge as a result of the various proposals, Progressivism as an organization and a movement steadily declined. Membership fell off. By 1944 when at last a creed accepting education as a device for social reform was adopted by the Association, it came too late. In 1955 the organization ceased to exist, and two years later the Journal stopped publication.

Progressivism had run its course. It had permeated educational thought and practice; it had helped transform the nineteenth century schools into twentieth century institutions; it had promoted educational reform; it had introduced a new vitality into American educational developments. Perhaps its very success as an organization contributed to its failure as a cause. It began as a spirit and a method; but as the society became formalized, Progressivism sought a program but failed to find one upon which the varied membership could agree. It was pluralistic in its origin, and its wide diversity played a part in its demise.

The role the school should play (or was playing) in promoting American democracy, within the context of the traditional capitalistic system of individualism and the *laissez faire* philosophy and within the framework of the reform impulse, stands out as the significant development of the present century. However, another fundamental problem of education and democracy, that of quality versus mass education, has grown increasingly important. In the nineteenth century universal free education came to be accepted as a right as well as a necessity of democracy. As the ideal becomes a reality in the twentieth century, more concern is evident among educational leaders with the matter of the kind and purpose of training. There is ample evidence of continued recognition of the need for educating all classes, making education available for "every class without distinction."

As a result of the scientific impact on education, the recognition of individual differences, the growing need for specialists, and the democratization of higher education, the period following the depressed thirties and the war years of the forties produced considerable criticism of the long-existing concept of equality of opportunity. Also, the question of the purpose of education and the kind of education — specialization or general, vocational or liberal — is part of the current reevaluation. Harvard University's report, *General Education in a Free Society*, which appeared in

1945, recognized the growing problems of education as a result of the achievement of universal free education on the secondary level (61). Again the traditional faith in American education was voiced; again the school was viewed as the hope of democracy. In addition the writers of the report added a new dimension to the accepted doctrine of equal opportunity. With the attainment of universal education in a complex industrial society, schools in America needed to pursue "two goals simultaneously": to give "scope to ability" and to "raise the average." Thus, as the authors expressed it, the two major strains in American education — Jeffersonian with its emphasis on opportunity to further excellence and Jacksonian with its pursuit of equality — had to be continued. The Harvard report became the basis for a vast revision in college curricula to provide a program of general education; but it was also significant in its recognition of the growing problem of providing universal secondary education, yet opening avenues for promoting excellence and meeting the needs of widely diversified groups in a complex social and economic order.

Progressivism in education, life adjustment, practical and vocational training, all underwent careful scrutiny and criticism in the postwar years. Once again America looked at its education and found it wanting. The "transformation of the school" had occurred, but in the eyes of the critics of the mid-twentieth century, the school was still failing to meet the needs of society — just as the nineteenth century institutions had lagged behind the industrialization and urbanization process. Certainly the new role thrust upon the nation as a world power, as the voice of freedom, and as the prime example of the high achievements of democracy furthered the soul-searching of America's political and intellectual leaders.

Education — the schools in particular — became the single most important agency and institution for promoting national welfare and international awareness. Education was a powerful instrument of national policy. As the sputniks were launched; as the free world sought to confine the encroachment and spread of Communism; as the United States recognized its own failures and shortcomings — the school became both the hope of the nation and the scapegoat for all its ills. Every aspect of education, training, learning, organization and structure of the schools came under the scrutiny of the educational reformers: from Rudolph Flesch's dismay over Johnny's inability to read to Admiral Hyman Rickover's attack on the mediocrity and failure of American education. Once again the critics voiced their concern about mass education versus quality education. Increasingly American educational leaders were tackling the problems evolving from the twentieth century's success in achieving the ideals of equal educational opportunity inherited from the preceding century.

The most vitriolic attack on the existing educational order came from Arthur Bestor, whose series of articles in *The American Scholar*, the *New Republic*, and the *Bulletin* of the American Association of University Professors blasted the life-adjustment movement of Progressivism, teachers' colleges, departments of education, and professional training in general. A historian by profession, Bestor summed up the educational situation as he saw it in the publication in 1953 of *Educational Wastelands*, a title indicative of his interpretation (62). In a sense, a circle had been completed within a half-century. In the 1890s the cry had been for reform of the schools to break the tradition pattern of education; in the 1950s, for the reform of education. Bestor rejected Progressivism and practical training and criticized the separation of the schools from scholarship. Like so many other reformers and critics, from the classical humanists to Robert M. Hutchins, he insisted that the ultimate purpose of education was intellectual rather than practical and that the schools must provide intellectual training through academic discipline not through practical experience.

In considering quality versus mass education, Bestor raised the question whether good education was undemocratic. His answer was "No." He saw intellectual training not as an aristocratic concept, but rather as one that should be part of the democratic ideal. His emphasis was on the need for intellectual and cultural training to promote such developments in society. Bestor states emphatically that twentieth century complexities require broad intellectual training; that the school has to help build a new world order; and that all should receive intellectual training without discrimination. To him democracy is compatible with scientific, scholarly, and artistic achievements.

It is interesting to compare Bestor's mid-twentieth century views on education and democracy with those of the nineteenth century. The idea of the relationship between democracy and education and faith in education are common to both eras. But whereas the reformers of the last century saw education as the means of elevating and improving society, Bestor's principal interest is in the cultural and intellectual quality of society. The earlier generation concerned itself with the problem of providing education for all. Bestor accepts the premise of mass education but wishes to raise it to an intellectual level rather than a practical one. His attack is a scorching indictment of the influence of progressive education and the changes it had brought. In many respects Bestor is typical of a group of critics of this generation who emphasize intellectual training and cultural orientation and reject technical and practical education.

Viewing the sweep of educational developments and issues in the twentieth century in terms of their democratic goals, the role of the federal government in education looms as one of the major developments and one of the most controversial issues of our times. The arguments for federal aid sound similar to those used by the public school advocates of the early nineteenth century: that only through financial assistance by the state could education be extended and made available to all regardless of economic, religious, or social class. Today one looks beyond the confines of the state to the national government; and racial equality is the new dimension.

The question of federal aid is more complicated than that of financing education, but it would be well to trace briefly the role of the federal government and education. As has been pointed out, the Civil War era produced the first real change of national policy in regard to education (Section IV). The Morrill Act, the Freedmen's Bureau, various bills for federal aid, the development of a federal educational policy for Indian tribes, and the creation of a Federal Bureau of Education in 1869 — all directly introduced government into the realm of American education. Not only was a national office established to collect and distribute data and thus crystallize opinion, but more significant is the fact that the national government was supervising and actually providing education for certain groups — for the Negroes in the southern states for a brief period, and for the Indians for more than a half-century on a wide scale (and currently on a more limited basis).

Why the federal government assumed this new role and why such was possible can be answered only in terms of the attitudes and the political climate of the times and the needs of the nation. Need and political policy were the two dominant factors in the educational undertakings of the Freedmen's Bureau. Need and national policy also dictated the federal government's entrance into Indian education. The Indians were wards of the nation; the old removal policy was a failure. Again education was the avenue for assimilating the class, and only the central government could assume the responsibility and expense—so great were both. Though the *laissez faire* doctrine still held sway in the economic sphere, there was a great degree of expansion and extension of federal power in other areas.

There are other examples—successful ones—of federal aid to education in these years, but no general aid for all public education was suggested for decades after the failure of the Republican-sponsored Blair Bill in the eighties. Rather the federal government did step in to promote specialized education: the Hatch Act of 1887 to finance experiment stations in connection with the land grant colleges, the Second Morrill Act of 1890, the Smith-Lever Act of 1914 to assist agricultural and home economics training, and the Smith-Hughes Act of 1917 to provide vocational, agricultural, and trade education in the public schools—attest to the government's active role in education.

The idea of general aid to be distributed to all states and to all public schools made little headway in the early decades of the twentieth century. As the school age was constantly extended and as expansion of the curriculum required greater educational expenditures, the states were unable to keep pace; and once again as in the post-Civil War years aid from the national government seemed the only solution to a national educational problem. However, any suggestion of federal aid in the individualistic society of the twenties immediately brought forth the popular refrain that education was a state and local matter and this was the American way. Both major political parties avoided the issue.

In the 1930s the experimentation in social and economic planning and the spirit of reform and rehabilitation, as well as the expansion of the powers and jurisdiction of the federal agencies ushered in a new era in which the central government assumed a new role in education. The National Youth Administration and the Civilian Conservation Corps were part of the New Deal program of rehabilitating the nation and its youth. Though the two programs were different, both reflected a willingness on the part of the government to assume direct responsibility for promoting education by financing national programs for the improvement of society and the individual.

The New Deal government, while seeking to solve the problems of unemployment, also aided education through the vast building programs of the PWA and WPA. School buildings and other educational facilities were benefiting from government expenditures. In developing job opportunities for every social as well as economic class, the government moved into another educational area for the first time. This was the WPA program aimed at utilizing the talents of the professional and creative classes — artists, writers, musicians, teachers — and thus promoting the cultural and educational life of the nation. The Writers' Project, the Historical Records Survey, the Art Program, and the adult education programs were part of this nationwide undertaking of the federal government. To create jobs and to employ men and women in accordance with their talents and training were the fundamental purposes of the undertaking. The end result of archival surveys, state guides, murals, exhibits have become a permanent cultural and educational contribution of the New Deal era.

In a sense this program in its most idealistic aspects sought to give all Americans the cultural opportunities that had been to a large extent limited to urban dwellers and the more affluent members of society. In the broadest meaning of the word "education," the national government was playing a direct and significant role for the first time in the nation's history. The experiment was a passing one, fading as the economic crisis did, until once again the federal government retreated from direct participation and assistance. The post-Depression era again revealed the deeply entrenched fear over and rejection of the federal government as an agency for educational and cultural promotion; philanthropic foundations again assumed the key position of channeling, promoting, and encouraging education and culture.

As compulsory education laws constantly increased the enrollments of the schools; as the school population steadily grew; and as progressive ideas penetrated the school curriculum and contributed to its diversification, expenditures in education zoomed to unprecedented heights. By the mid-decades of the twentieth century the commitment to the public school ideal created an enormous problem of financing such a program.

In the closing years of the 1940s, the idea of federal aid to the states had once again become a popular issue, with the Democratic Party now assuming the role of leadership. The arguments were practical and realistic ones: need for federal aid because of the great expense and the inability of the states and local communities to finance education adequately; the growing importance of federal taxation; the inequalities in opportunities within the nation. But the opposition won again, and educational bills went down in defeat. There was the fear that federal aid meant federal control and higher taxes; traditionally public education rested on local and state support. Also, the question of parochial schools and their right to federal assistance and the age-old issue of states' rights were brought forth. Yet in these very years when the battles were fought in the news media and the halls of Congress, the federal government continued to give aid to the schools as a result of laws old and new: the vocational education program, ROTC, agricultural extension work, the school lunch program, school transportation. The most significant new role was that of the federal government in providing financial aid to ex-servicemen for furthering their education through the famous "GI Bill." Thus while the opposition cried that federal aid meant federal control, the national government was pouring millions of dollars into public education and was aiding private institutions through direct grants to or for students.

For almost two decades, until the passage of the Elementary and Secondary Education Act of 1965, there was one long debate on the question of federal aid to education. The stumbling blocks for assistance to public schools were more formidable than those obstructing grants to colleges and universities. The problems are complex: states' rights, segregation, private schools, religious education. R. Freeman Butts in his article, "States' Rights and Education," traces the intricacies of the question of federal aid, pointing out the historical development of key issues (63). Also included in this section are the arguments of three Congressmen, each representing a different viewpoint for or against the Kelley Education Bill of 1956, which was defeated (64). Representative John W. McCormack, a Catholic from Massachusetts, argues for federal aid to private schools; Overton Brooks of Louisiana opposes such assistance as a step toward "centralized Federal control of our public schools"; and Harrison A. Williams, Jr. of New Jersey points out the "frightening facts" of need in the states and calls upon the national government to assume responsibility as "the school crisis is a problem common to us all."

By 1956 the desegregation issue in the public schools became the principal barrier to the passage of a federal aid bill. Representative Adam Clayton Powell's amendment to withhold aid to segregated schools contributed in part to the defeat of the national measure. As a result leading educators and politicians sought other solutions to the crisis in education. Economist Beardsley Ruml, among others, offered a solution to the dilemma (65). He suggested granting per capita assistance to states which would in turn administer the funds to "public schools" according to the states' own definition of "public," thus avoiding the problems of desegregation, assistance to private institutions, and the fear of federal control.

The selections by Theodore Brameld and the Study Committee on Federal Responsibility in the Field of Education present two extreme views on the question of federal aid. Brameld rejects outright the argument that federal control is a danger or a handicap to education (66). He represents one side of the question—the necessity and constructive nature of federal aid. He raises the question of whether federal control is intrinsically evil while local control is always good. His cogent statement, arguing for equality in education through federal assistance, is aptly entitled "The Bugaboo of Federal Aid" and represents the continuation of the old principle of equal educational opportunity. The opposite view, rejecting the idea of the necessity of federal assistance, is presented in the report of the Study Committee which emphasizes the importance of state and local responsibility and suggests reduction of federal taxes to give states more resources for educational expenditures (67).

The obstacles to a broad plan of federal assistance were many, and the debate continued. Finally, on April 11, 1965, President Lyndon B. Johnson signed into law the 1.3 billion dollar federal aid program for elementary and secondary schools. The administration's proposal, which passed through both Senate and House without major revisions, had managed to overcome constitutional, religious, sectional, and economic stumbling blocks. The law, the first of its kind in the nation's history, provides for over a billion dollars for school districts according to need in order to meet the national goal of "full educational opportunity." By appropriating one hundred million dollars a year for textbooks and library materials for public institutions (available "on loan" to private schools) and an equal amount for supplementary educational centers (to be shared by private and parochial schools), compromise was possible on the church-state issue. No direct aid will go to church-related schools, nor can federal funds be used for sectarian purposes, according to Section 605. Most significant is that the law makes education a national responsibility. It includes pre-schooling, elementary, secondary and adult education, community programs, and special centers—all aimed at providing education for the masses.

In addition to the introduction from President Johnson's Message to Congress on January 12 outlining the government's goals in education, the selections include examples of both support and criticism which emphasize the controversial nature of federal aid and make clear that the debate has not ended (68). Already the American Jewish Congress has begun the process of testing the constitutionality of the act in the courts on the grounds that it violates the First Amendment. Some religious bodies as well as secular organizations share this view. However, in general, Catholic opinion, as expressed in the Jesuit publication, *America*, does not question the constitutionality of the law and accepts the principle of federal aid to all school children. Such assistance is interpreted as a form of governmental recognition of parochial schools as a part of a pluralistic educational system in the United States.

The opinions of Russell Kirk, the spokesman "From the Academy" in the conservative *National Review*, and of Walter Lippmann, "Dean of the Newspaper Commentators," represent opposite viewpoints and highlight the complexities of the issues surrounding the federal aid program. Kirk, in states' rights fashion, doubts the efficacy of federal funds improving the quality of education. He sets forth the traditional argument that assistance means control, even of church-related schools. Lippmann, on the other hand, sees the measure as "an epoch-making advance toward the improvement of American education" and as an acceptance of parochial schools as American institutions.

The final test is to come, but the commitment of the national government has been made—almost a century after the question of federal responsibility to education was first raised by such men as Senator Justin Morrill and Congressman Gilbert Walker (33, 34). Part of the problem of the federal government's role in education is directly related to the racial question. In 1954 as a result of the Supreme Court's momentous decision in *Brown* v. *Board of Education of Topeka*, the federal government assumed a new and significant role with far-reaching results. The Brown case stands as a landmark in educational as well as civil-rights history, but its true significance must be viewed in historical perspective.

As noted earlier, the system of separate schools for Negroes was widespread throughout the nation in the nineteenth century. Despite the Reconstruction policy with its emphasis on promoting equality for the freedmen through the passage of Constitutional amendments, separate education according to race was maintained with the individual states determining policy. Some northern and western states with a small Negro population admitted them to the public schools without discrimination from the beginning, and others abolished separate schools in the second half of the nineteenth century. Rhode Island, for example, ended the dual system in 1866; but not until 1881 and 1900 did Pennsylvania and New York, respectively, prohibit educational separation of the races. In other non-southern states it has been even more recent. Also, *de facto* segregation, through school districting, has long existed and continues to exist in many parts of the nation. The *Plessy* v. *Ferguson* decision of 1896, which legally recognized the validity of the "separate but equal" doctrine, reinforced the dual school system throughout the first half of the twentieth century.

The subtleties and complexities of the system unfolded as the years passed and other cases made their way to the Supreme Court (69). Included are two excellent examples of the effect the "separate but equal" principle had in the evolution of the southern public school system. In 1899 in *Cumming* v. *Board of Education* (Georgia), the state law providing for separate schools was not questioned, and the United States Supreme Court emphatically stated that "any interference on the part of Federal authority with the management of such schools cannot be justified." Thus both the "separate but equal" concept and the idea of education as a state matter were reconfirmed.

The case of *Lum* v. *Rice* (1927) offers yet another example of the implications of racial segregation in education. Here the child in question, who was of Chinese descent, was seeking admission to a white public school in Mississippi since no school for Chinese children existed. The fact that there was only one school and that the child was not a Negro was the basis of the argument. Here again the Supreme Court affirmed the state's decision and saw no conflict between the denial of rights and the Fourteenth Amendment. The Mississippi Court interpreted the separate school system for the white and colored population as one dividing the races into two categories: white and brown, yellow, or black. Thus the 1927 decision also reconfirmed the existing practice and extended the definition of "colored" to include all who were not "white."

The history of Negro education until the post World War II period was largely one of the acceptance of segregation through a dual school system in the southern states and *de facto* segregation in many of the other areas. With the increase in Negro mobility and the development of Negro leadership and organizations, equal education opportunities came to loom larger and larger in the uphill fight for equal rights for Negroes. Education came to symbolize the first rung in the ladder for greater equality. The Swedish sociologist, Gunnar Myrdal, in his brilliant and perceptive examination of the Negro's position during the period immediately before America's entrance into the war, explains that education for the Negro symbolized their assimilation into the dominant white culture (70). The "magic of education," the belief in the efficacy of education as a means of progress and improvement was deeply ingrained in the mind of the Negro—as it was in other Americans.

The first integration battles of the post-war years were fought in the professional schools and universities. As these were gradually won, through state action, the public schools became the next target. And *Brown* v. *Board of Education of Topeka* was the end result of a long, drawn-out attempt to destroy finally the "separate but equal" doctrine so widely practiced and so frequently reaffirmed. Here the Court's decision was like an echo of the traditional American ideal of equal opportunity. To the question, "Does segregation of children in the public schools solely on the basis of race . . . deprive the children of the minority group of equal educational opportunities," the Court answered: "Separated educational facilities are inherently unequal." It is significant that the Court did not cite historical precedent to support the judgment; little existed in the educational realm of practice and tradition to destroy the "separate but equal" argument. Rather the Court emphasized the nature of the existing public educational system and the importance of education in American life. In many respects the tone and spirit of the 1954 decision were a restatement of the ideals of the schoolmen of the early nineteenth century who had fought for universal free education, though they had not given attention to the problem of racial equality.

The nation divided; it was stunned or exuberant over the decision. The remaining selections are an attempt to view briefly the reactions of the nation to the great educational milestone of 1954. Though the states were given a year in which to prepare arguments to be presented to the Court, the implications were clear. Segregation was being fought not only through the militant organizations and civil-rights legislation, but through the courts as well. The 1899 decision of *Cumming* v. *Board of Education* which had denied federal intervention was superseded by the 1954 decision; but the states' rights argument still had wide popularity, as indicated by the Southern Manifesto of 1956, signed by 96 Southern Representatives and Senators (71). Also, Thomas R. Waring, editor of the Charleston, South Carolina *News and Observer*, provides in "The Southern Case Against Desegregation" a sweeping survey of the conditions and factors in the South that justify and explain southern resistance (72).

It seems fitting to end the volume with a statement by Benjamin E. Mays, President of Morehouse College in Atlanta (73). Though recognizing the moral aspects of the decision, the matter of human rights, and its significance in regard to international affairs, Mays expresses the meaning of the decision and its implications in terms of the traditional American concept of education: the quest for equal opportunities as a challenge to democracy and as a means of promoting the democratic ideal.

CHAPTER 21

EDUCATION AND DEMOCRACY

Democracy . . . must have a distinctive educational system.

Boyd H. Bode, 1938

55. INDIVIDUAL VS. COLLECTIVE EDUCATION (1909)[1]

HERBERT CROLY

Hitherto we have been discussing the ways in which existing American economic and political methods and institutions should be modified in order to make towards the realization of the national democratic ideal. In course of this discussion, it has been taken for granted that the American people under competent and responsible leadership could deliberately plan a policy of individual and social improvement, and that with the means at their collective disposal they could make headway towards its realization. These means consisted, of course, precisely in their whole outfit of political, economic, and social institutions; and the implication has been, consequently, that human nature can be raised to a higher level by an improvement in institutions and laws. The majority of my readers will probably have thought many times that such an assumption, whatever its truth, has been overworked. Admitting that some institutions may be better than others, it must also be admitted that human nature is composed of most rebellious material, and that the extent to which it can be modified by social and political institutions of any kind is, at best, extremely small. Such critics may, consequently, have reached the conclusion that the proposed system of reconstruction, even if desirable, would not accomplish anything really effectual or decisive towards the fulfillment of the American national Promise.

It is no doubt true that out of the preceding chapters many sentences could be selected which apparently imply a credulous faith in the possibility of improving human nature by law. It is also true that I have not ventured more than to touch upon a possible institutional reformation, which, in so far as it was successful in its purpose, would improve human nature by the most effectual of all means—that is, by improving the methods whereby men and

---

[1]Herbert Croly, *The Promise of American Life* (New York: Macmillan, 1910), pp. 399–409.

women are bred. But if I have erred in attaching or appearing to attach too much efficacy to legal and institutional reforms, the error or its appearance was scarcely separable from an analytic reconstruction of a sufficient democratic ideal. Democracy must stand or fall on a platform of possible human perfectibility. If human nature cannot be improved by institutions, democracy is at best a more than usually safe form of political organization; and the only interesting inquiry about its future would be: How long will it continue to work? But if it is to work better as well as merely longer, it must have some leavening effect on human nature; and the sincere democrat is obliged to assume the power of the leaven. For him the practical questions are: How can the improvement best be brought about? and, How much may it amount to?

As a matter of fact, Americans have always had the liveliest and completest faith in the process of individual and social improvement and in accepting the assumption, I am merely adhering to the deepest and most influential of American traditions. The better American has continually been seeking to "uplift" himself, his neighbors, and his compatriots. But he has usually favored means of improvement very different from those suggested hereinbefore. The real vehicle of improvement is education. It is by education that the American is trained for such democracy as he possesses; and it is by better education that he proposes to better his democracy. Men are uplifted by education much more surely than they are by any tinkering with laws and institutions, because the work of education leavens the actual social substance. It helps to give the individual himself those qualities without which no institutions, however excellent, are of any use, and with which even bad institutions and laws can be made vehicles of grace.

The American faith in education has been characterized as a superstition; and superstitious in some respects it unquestionably is. But its superstitious tendency is not exhibited so much in respect to the ordinary process of primary, secondary, and higher education. Not even an American can over-emphasize the importance of proper teaching during youth; and the only wonder is that the money so freely lavished on it does not produce better results. Americans are superstitious in respect to education, rather because of the social "uplift" which they expect to achieve by so-called educational means. The credulity of the socialist in expecting to alter human nature by merely institutional and legal

248

changes is at least equaled by the credulity of the good American in proposing to evangelize the individual by the reading of books and by the expenditure of money and words. Back of it all is the underlying assumption that the American nation by taking thought can add a cubit to its stature,—an absolute confidence in the power of the idea to create its own object and in the efficacy of good intentions.

Do we lack culture? We will "make it hum" by founding a new university in Chicago. Is American art neglected and impoverished? We will enrich it by organizing art departments in our colleges, and popularize it by lectures with lantern slides and associations for the study of its history. Is New York City ugly? Perhaps, but if we could only get the authorities to appropriate a few hundred millions for its beautification, we could make it look like a combination of Athens, Florence, and Paris. Is it desirable for the American citizen to be something of a hero? I will encourage heroes by establishing a fund whereby they shall be rewarded in cash. War is hell, is it? I will work for the abolition of hell by calling a convention and passing a resolution denouncing its iniquities. I will build at the Hague a Palace of Peace which shall be a standing rebuke to the War Lords of Europe. Here, in America, some of us have more money than we need and more good will. We will spend the money in order to establish the reign of the good, the beautiful, and the true.

This faith in a combination of good intentions, organization, words, and money is not confined to women's clubs or to societies of amiable enthusiasts. In the state of mind which it expresses can be detected the powerful influence which American women exert over American men; but its guiding faith and illusion are shared by the most hard-headed and practical of Americans. The very men who have made their personal successes by a rigorous application of the rule that business is business—the very men who in their own careers have exhibited a shrewd and vivid sense of the realities of politics and trade; it is these men who have most faith in the practical, moral, and social power of the Subsidized Word. The most real thing which they carry over from the region of business into the region of moral and intellectual ideals is apparently their bank accounts. The fruits of their hard work and their business ability are to be applied to the purpose of "uplifting" their fellow-countrymen. A certain number of figures written on a check and signed by a familiar name, what may it not accomplish? Some years ago at the opening exercises of the Carnegie Institute in Pittsburg, Mr. Andrew Carnegie burst into an impassioned and mystical vision of the miraculously constitutive power of first mortgage steel bonds. From his point of view and from that of the average American there is scarcely anything which the combination of abundant resources and good intentions may not accomplish.

The tradition of seeking to cross the gulf between American practice and the American ideal by means of education or the Subsidized Word is not be dismissed with a sneer. The gulf cannot be crossed without the assistance of some sort of educational discipline; and that discipline depends partly on a new exercise of the "money power" now safely reposing in the strong boxes of professional millionaires. There need be no fundamental objection taken to the national faith in the power of good intentions and re-distributed wealth. That faith is the immediate and necessary issue of the logic of our national moral situation. It should be, as it is, innocent and absolute; and if it does not remain innocent and absolute, the Promise of American Life can scarcely be fulfilled.

A faith may, however, be innocent and absolute without being inexperienced and credulous. The American faith in education is by way of being credulous and superstitious, not because it seeks individual and social amelioration by what may be called an educational process, but because the proposed means of education are too conscious, too direct, and too superficial. Let it be admitted that in any one decade the amount which can be accomplished towards individual and social amelioration by means of economic and political reorganization is comparatively small; but it is certainly as large as that which can be accomplished by subsidizing individual good intentions. Heroism is not to be encouraged by cash prizes any more than is genius; and a man's friends should not be obliged to prove that he is a hero in order that he may reap every appropriate reward. A hero officially conscious of his heroism is a mutilated hero. In the same way art cannot become a power in a community unless many of its members are possessed of a native and innocent love of beautiful things; and the extent to which such a possession can be acquired by any one or two generations of traditionally inartistic people is extremely small. Its acquisition depends not so much upon direct conscious effort, as upon the growing ability to discriminate between what is good and what is bad in their own native art. It is a matter of the train-

ing and appreciation of American artists, rather than the cultivation of art. Illustrations to the same effect might be multiplied.
The popular interest in the Higher Education has not served to
make Americans attach much importance to the advice of the
highly educated man. He is less of a practical power in the United
States than he is in any European country; and this fact is in itself
a sufficient commentary on the reality of the American faith in
education. The fact is, of course, that the American tendency to
disbelieve in the fulfillment of their national Promise by means of
politically, economically, and socially reconstructive work has
forced them into the alternative of attaching excessive importance
to subsidized good intentions. They want to be "uplifted," and
they want to "uplift" other people; but they will not use their
social and political institutions for the purpose, because those
institutions are assumed to be essentially satisfactory. The "uplifting" must be a matter of individual, or of unofficial associated
effort; and the only available means are words and subsidies.

There is, however, a sense in which it is really true that the
American national Promise can be fulfilled only by education; and
this aspect of our desirable national education can, perhaps, best
be understood by seeking its analogue in the training of the individual. An individual's education consists primarily in the discipline which he undergoes to fit him both for fruitful association
with his fellows and for his own special work. Important as both
the liberal and the technical aspect of this preliminary training is,
it constitutes merely the beginning of a man's education. Its object
is or should be to prepare him both in his will and in his intelligence to make a thoroughly illuminating use of his experience in
life. His experience,—as a man of business, a husband, a father, a
citizen, a friend,—has been made real to him, not merely by the
zest with which he has sought it and the sincerity with which he
has accepted it, but by the disinterested intelligence which he has
brought to its understanding. An educational discipline which has
contributed in that way to the reality of a man's experience has
done as much for him as education can do; and an educational
discipline which has failed to make any such contribution has
failed of its essential purpose. The experience of other people
acquired at second hand has little value,—except, perhaps, as a
means of livelihood,—unless it really illuminates a man's personal
experience.

Usually a man's ability to profit by his own personal experience depends upon the sincerity and the intelligence which he brings to his own particular occupation. The rule is not universal, because some men are, of course, born with much higher intellectual gifts than others; and to such men may be given an insight which has little foundation in any genuine personal experience. It remains true, none the less, for the great majority of men, that they gather an edifying understanding of men and things just in so far as they patiently and resolutely stick to the performance of some special and (for the most part) congenial task. Their education in life must be grounded in the persistent attempt to realize in action some kind of a purpose—a purpose usually connected with the occupation whereby they live. In the pursuit of that purpose they will be continually making experiments—opening up new lines of work, establishing new relations with other men, and taking more or less serious risks. Each of these experiments offers them an opportunity both for personal discipline and for increasing personal insight. If a man is capable of becoming wise, he will gradually be able to infer from this increasing mass of personal experience, the extent to which or the conditions under which he is capable of realizing his purpose; and his insight into the particular realities of his own life will bring with it some kind of a general philosophy—some sort of a disposition and method of appraisal of men, their actions, and their surroundings. Wherever a man reaches such a level of intelligence, he will be an educated man, even though his particular job has been that of a mechanic. On the other hand, a man who fails to make his particular task in life the substantial support of a genuine experience remains essentially an unenlightened man.

National education in its deeper aspect does not differ from individual education. Its efficiency ultimately depends upon the ability of the national consciousness to draw illuminating inferences from the course of the national experience; and its power to draw such inferences must depend upon the persistent and disinterested sincerity with which the attempt is made to realize the national purpose—the democratic ideal of individual and social improvement. So far as Americans are true to that purpose, all the different aspects of their national experience will assume meaning and momentum; while in so far as they are false thereto, no amount of "education" will ever be really edifying. The fundamental process of American education consists and must continue to consist precisely in the risks and experiments which the American nation will make in the service of its national ideal. If the American people balk at the sacrifices demanded by their experiments, or if they attach finality to any particular experiment in the distribution of political, economic, and social power, they will remain morally and intellectually at the bottom of a well, out of which they will never be "uplifted" by the most extravagant subsidizing of good intentions and noble words.

The sort of institutional and economic reorganization suggested in the preceding chapters is not, consequently, to be conceived merely as a more or less dubious proposal to improve human nature by laws. It is to be conceived as (possibly) the next step in the realization of a necessary collective purpose. Its deeper significance does not consist in the results which it may accomplish by way of immediate improvement. Such results may be worth having; but at best they will create almost as many difficulties as they remove. Far more important than any practical benefits would be the indication it afforded of national good faith. It would mean that the American nation was beginning to educate itself up to its own necessary standards. It would imply a popular realization that our first experiment in democratic political and economic organization was founded partly on temporary conditions and partly on erroneous theories. A new experiment must consequently be made; and the great value of this new experiment would derive from the implied intellectual and moral emancipation. Its trial would demand both the sacrifice of many cherished interests, habits, and traditions for the sake of remaining true to a more fundamental responsibility and a much larger infusion of disinterested motives into the economic and political system. Thus the sincere definite decision that the experiment was necessary, would probably do more for American moral and social amelioration than would the specific measures actually adopted and tried. Public opinion can never be brought to approve any effectual measures, until it is converted to a constructive and consequently to a really educational theory of democracy.

Back of the problem of educating the individual lies the problem of collective education. On the one hand, if the nation is rendered incapable of understanding its own experience by the habit of dealing insincerely with its national purpose, the individual, just in so far as he himself has become highly educated, tends to be divided from his country and his fellow-countrymen. On the other hand, just in so far as a people is sincerely seeking the fulfillment of its national Promise, individuals of all kinds will find their most edifying individual opportunities in serving their country. In aiding the accomplishment of the collective purpose by means of increasingly constructive experiments, they will be increasing the scope and power of their own individual action. The opportunities, which during the past few years the reformers have enjoyed to make their personal lives more interesting, would be nothing compared to the opportunities for all sorts of stirring and responsible work, which would be demanded of individuals under the proposed plan of political and economic reorganization. The American nation would be more disinterestedly and sincerely fulfilling its collective purpose, partly because its more distinguished individuals had been called upon to place at the service of their country a higher degree of energy, ability, and unselfish devotion. If a nation, that is, is recreant to its deeper purpose, individuals, so far as they are well educated, are educated away from the prevailing national habits and traditions; whereas when a nation is sincerely attempting to meet its collective responsibility, the better individuals are inevitably educated into active participation in the collective task.

The reader may now be prepared to understand why the American faith in education has the appearance of being credulous and superstitious. The good average American usually wishes to accomplish exclusively by individual education a result which must be partly accomplished by national education. The nation, like the individual, must go to school; and the national school is not a lecture hall or a library. Its schooling consists chiefly in experimental collective action aimed at the realization of the collective purpose. If the action is not aimed at the collective purpose, a nation will learn little even from its successes. If its action is aimed at the collective purpose, it may learn much even from its mistakes. No process of merely individual education can accomplish the work of collective education, because the nation is so much more than a group of individuals. Individuals can be "uplifted" without "uplifting" the nation, because the nation has an individuality of its own, which cannot be increased without the consciousness of collective responsibilities and the collective official attempt to redeem them. The processes of national and individual education should, of course, parallel and supplement each other. The individual can do much to aid national education by the single-minded and intelligent realization of his own specific purposes; but all individual successes will have little more than an individual interest unless they frequently contribute to the work of national construction. The nation can do much to aid individual education; but the best aid within its power is to offer to the individual a really formative and inspiring opportunity for public service. The whole round of superficial educational machinery — books, subsidies, resolutions, lectures, congresses — may be of the highest value, provided they are used to digest and popularize the results of a genuine individual and national educational experience, but when they are used, as so often at present, merely as a substitute for well-purposed individual and national action, they are precisely equivalent to an attempt to fly in a vacuum.

That the direct practical value of a reform movement may be equaled or surpassed by its indirect educational value is a sufficiently familiar idea — an idea admirably expressed ten years ago by Mr. John Jay Chapman in the chapter on "Education" in his "Causes and Consequences." But the idea in its familiar form is vitiated, because the educational effect of reform is usually conceived as exclusively individual. Its *effect* must, indeed, be considered wholly as an individual matter, just so long as reform is interpreted merely as a process of purification. From that point of view the collective purpose has already been fulfilled as far as it can be fulfilled by collective organization, and the *only* remaining method of social amelioration is that of the self-improvement of its constituent members. As President Nicholas Murray Butler of Columbia says, in his "True and False Democracy": "We must not lose sight of the fact that the corporate or collective responsibility which it (socialism) would substitute for individual initiative is only such corporate or collective responsibility as a group of these very same individuals could exercise. Therefore, socialism is primarily an attempt to overcome man's individual imperfections by adding them together, in the hope that they will cancel each other." But what is all organization but an attempt, not to overcome man's individual imperfections by adding them together, so much as to make use of many men's varying individual abilities by giving each a sufficient sphere of exercise? While all men are imperfect, they are not all imperfect to the same extent. Some have more courage, more ability, more insight, and more training than others; and an efficient organization can accomplish more than can a mere collection of individuals, precisely because it may represent a standard of performance far above that of the average individual. Its merit is simply that of putting the collective power of the group at the service of its ablest members; and the ablest members of the group will never attain to an individual responsibility commensurate with their powers, until they are enabled to work efficiently towards the redemption of the collective responsibility. The nation gives individuality an increased scope and meaning by offering individuals a chance for effective service, such as they could never attain under a system of collective irresponsibility. Thus under a system of collective responsibility the process of social improvement is absolutely identified with that of individual improvement. The antithesis is not between nationalism and individualism, but between an individualism which is indiscriminate, and an individualism which is selective.

56. Democracy and Education (1915)[1]

JOHN AND EVELYN DEWEY

The conventional type of education which trains children to docility and obedience, to the careful performance of imposed tasks because they are imposed, regardless of where they lead, is suited to an autocratic society. These are the traits needed in a state where there is one head to plan and care for the lives and institutions of the people. But in a democracy they interfere with the successful conduct of society and government. Our famous, brief definition of a democracy, as "government of the people, for the people and by the people," gives perhaps the best clew to what is involved in a democratic society. Responsibility for the conduct of society and government rests on every member of society. Therefore, every one must receive a training that will enable him to meet this responsibility, giving him just ideas of the condition and needs of the people collectively, and developing those qualities which will insure his doing a fair share of the work of government. If we train our children to take orders, to do things simply because they are told to, and fail to give them confidence to act and think for themselves, we are putting an almost insurmountable obstacle in the way of overcoming the present defects of our system and of establishing the truth of democratic ideals. Our State is founded on freedom, but when we train the State of to-morrow, we allow it just as little freedom as possible. Children in school must be allowed freedom so that they will know what its use means when they become the controlling body, and they must be allowed to develop active qualities of initiative, independence, and resourcefulness, before the abuses and failures of democracy will disappear.

---

[1]John and Evelyn Dewey, *Schools of Tomorrow* (New York: Dutton and Co., 1929), pp. 303–6, 308, 313–16.

The spread of the realization of this connection between democracy and education is perhaps the most interesting and significant phase of present educational tendencies. It accounts for the growing interest in popular education, and constitutes a strong reënforcement to the arguments of science and psychology for the changes which have been outlined. There is no doubt that the text-book method of education is well suited to that small group of children who by environment are placed above the necessity of engaging in practical life and who are at the same time interested in abstract ideas. But even for this type of person the system leaves great gaps in his grasp of knowledge; it gives no place to the part that action plays in the development of intelligence, and it trains along the lines of the natural inclinations of the student and does not develop the practical qualities which are usually weak in the abstract person. For the great majority whose interests are not abstract, and who have to pass their lives in some practical occupation, usually in actually working with their hands, a method of education is necessary which bridges the gap between the purely intellectual and theoretical sides of life and their own occupations. With the spread of the ideas of democracy, and the accompanying awakening to social problems, people are beginning to realize that every one, regardless of the class to which he happens to belong, has a right to demand an education which shall meet his own needs, and that for its own sake the State must supply this demand.

Until recently school education has met the needs of only one class of people, those who are interested in knowledge for its own sake, teachers, scholars, and research workers. The idea that training is necessary for the man who works with his hands is still so new that the schools are only just beginning to admit that control of the material things of life is knowledge at all. Until very recently schools have neglected the class of people who are numerically the largest and upon whom the whole world depends for its supply of necessities. One reason for this is the fact that democracy is a comparatively new thing in itself; and until its advent, the right of the majority, the very people who work with their hands, to supply any of their larger spiritual needs was never admitted. Their function, almost their reason for existence, was to take care of the material wants of the ruling classes. . . .

If schools are to recognize the needs of all classes of pupils, and give pupils a training that will insure their becoming successful and valuable citizens, they must give work that will not only make the pupils strong physically and morally and give them the right attitude towards the state and their neighbors, but that will as well give them enough control over their material environment to enable them to be economically independent. Preparation for the professions has always been taken care of; it is, as we have seen, the future of the worker in industry which has been neglected. The complications of modern industry due to scientific discoveries make it necessary for the worker who aspires to real success to have a good foundation of general education on which to build his technical skill, and the complications of human nature make it equally necessary that the beginner shall find his way into work that is suited to his tastes and abilities. . . .

It is fatal for a democracy to permit the formation of fixed classes. Differences of wealth, the existence of large masses of unskilled laborers, contempt for work with the hands, inability to secure the training which enables one to forge ahead in life, all operate to produce classes, and to widen the gulf between them. Statesmen and legislation can do something to combat these evil forces. Wise philanthropy can do something. But the only fundamental agency for good is the public school system. Every American is proud of what has been accomplished in the past in fostering among very diverse elements of population a spirit of unity and of brotherhood so that the sense of common interests and aims has prevailed over the strong forces working to divide our people into classes. The increasing complexity of our life, with the great accumulation of wealth at one social extreme and the condition of almost dire necessity at the other makes the task of democracy constantly more difficult. The days are rapidly passing when the simple provision of a system in which all individuals mingle is enough to meet the need. The subject-matter and the methods of teaching must be positively and aggressively adapted to the end.

There must not be one system for the children of parents who have more leisure and another for the children of those who are wage-earners. The physical separation forced by such a scheme, while unfavorable to the development of a proper mutual sympathy, is the least of its evils. Worse is the fact that the over bookish education for some and the over "practical" education for others brings about a division of mental and moral habits, ideals and outlook.

The academic education turns out future citizens with no

sympathy for work done with the hands, and with absolutely no training for understanding the most serious of present day social and political difficulties. The trade training will turn future workers who may have greater immediate skill than they would have had without their training, but who have no enlargement of mind, no insight into the scientific and social significance of the work they do, no education which assists them in finding their way on or in making their own adjustments. A division of the public school system into one part which pursues traditional methods, with incidental improvements, and another which deals with those who are to go into manual labor means a plan of social predestination totally foreign to the spirit of a democracy.

The democracy which proclaims equality of opportunity as its ideal requires an education in which learning and social application, ideas and practice, work and recognition of the meaning of what is done, are united from the beginning and for all. Schools such as we have discussed in this book—and they are rapidly coming into being in large numbers all over the country—are showing how the ideal of equal opportunity for all is to be transmuted into reality.

57. PROGRESSIVE EDUCATION AND DEMOCRACY (1938)[1]

BOYD H. BODE

The strongest and most evangelistic movement in American education at the present time is the movement known as progressive education. A visitor to our schools ordinarily has no difficulty in recognizing a so-called progressive school. He can usually tell the difference the moment he opens the door. The progressive school cultivates an atmosphere of activity and freedom which is all its own. In academic language, the progressive school is a place where children go, not primarily to learn, but to carry on a way of life.

THE PROGRESSIVES' PARADOX

In spite of this distinctiveness, however, our visitor, if he is a reflective person, is likely to have peculiar difficulty in defining a progressive school. Any trait or aspect which he may select as a distinguishing characteristic presently turns out to have significant limitations. In other words, we seem to encounter a variety of contradictions when we try to state the qualities of such a school.

It emphasizes freedom, yet it also attaches major importance to guidance and direction. It plays up method, but it is also critical of the content of the more conventional curriculum. It places the individual at the center of the stage; yet it perpetually criticizes the competitive character of the present social order, which indicates that it rejects the philosophy of individualism. It insists that intelligence must be permitted to operate freely; yet it seldom alarms its constituents, who, in the case of private schools, are generally the more prosperous element in society. It commonly

---

[1]Boyd H. Bode, *Progressive Education at the Crossroads* (New York and Chicago: Newson and Co., 1938), pp. 9 –27. Bode made The Ohio State University one of the centers of Progressivism during the twenties and thirties.

regards the college as the citadel of its enemy; yet its chief business is often preparation for college. It holds that learning takes place through doing; yet physical activity tapers off sharply as we go up the educational scale. To the earnest observer all this is very confusing.

These real or apparent contradictions naturally invite the conclusion that the progressive movement draws its chief inspiration from a certain sentimentality about children. This sentimentality, so it appears, leads to a lot of unedifying fussiness, which is camouflaged as "respect for personality," but is not intended to be really subversive. There is no intention of changing the established values of society beyond the point of spreading more sweetness and light. With respect to these values the teachers in our progressive schools are frequently as conventional as the buttons on the sleeve of a man's coat.

A NEW ORGANIZING PRINCIPLE

Such a conclusion, however, would be a bit too simple. The continuing vitality of the progressive movement is evidence that it is based on something of larger significance. The emphasis of progressive education on the individual, on the sinfulness of "imposition," and on the necessity of securing free play for intelligence, whether rightly or wrongly applied, is a reflection of the growing demand, outside of the school, for recognition of the common man. Similarly the confusion in progressive education is a reflection of the confusion in the outside world resulting from this demand.

We are gradually discovering that the admission of the common man to the status of full recognition means more than an extension of privilege. It is not on a par, for example, with opening the doors of an art gallery to all comers, instead of merely to the chosen few. In its application to industry this recognition obviously means an extensive revision of our conception of property rights and of the function of government. As applied to organized religion it means a shift of emphasis from eternal salvation to progress through social control. In relation to the values of scholarship and esthetic appreciation it means a transformation of these values so that they will not remain a detached occupation for a leisure class and for specialists, but will become incorporated in the affairs of everyday

262

experience. In brief, the recognition of the common man—which is what we call democracy—introduces a point of view which is so far-reaching in its implications as to make democracy a distinctive and competing way of life.

Unless progressive education is content to be simply a method which is available to any teacher and for any purpose, it had better play out its string and become the exponent of that specific way of life for which the name "democracy" is perhaps as good as any. The refusal to take this step would leave progressive education with no guiding principle except random interests and hypothetical needs, and so would justify most of the hard things that have been said about it by its critics. On the other hand, taking this step means that the question of reorganizing or reinterpreting the established values and institutions of our civilization must receive major attention. These values took their character and form in large part at a time when the common man had not yet secured a prominent place in the picture. As was intimated a moment ago, there is considerable ground for the suspicion that our concern for the common man will evaporate into idle words and sentiments, unless we gain some perception of what is required to give the common man his proper share in our social and cultural heritage. To leave our conception of this heritage unchanged means that in our attempts to "socialize" the school population we are really practicing "imposition" on the sly.

In a word, the rise of the common man is the disturbing factor, both on the social and on the educational level. As long as he remained submerged, the situation was comparatively simple. It was commonly taken for granted that the higher cultural values were not for him. It was even supposed that he was too earth-earthy to appreciate them. This supposition was refuted as he gained wider opportunities, but it also appears that his scale of values is somewhat different from that of the aristocratic class by which he was ruled so long in the past. This difference is making itself felt in certain areas, such as industrial relations and organized religion, although it is not any too clear as yet just what kind of reorganization in ideals and practice is required in these areas by the application of the principle of democracy. What reorganization the principle of democracy calls for in the field of education is perhaps even more obscure. This problem must be faced, however, if we are to arrive at a significant and defensible conception of the meaning of the progressive movement in education.

THE COMMON MAN AND HIGHER EDUCATION

Perhaps the simplest approach to this whole question can be made by taking a glance at the development of higher education in this country. There was no assurance that the common man would concern himself seriously about the fruits of scholarship and culture, which had been withheld from him so long. In the words of the French writer and traveler, de Tocqueville, written less than a century ago: "It must be confessed that among the civilized peoples of our age there are few in which the highest sciences have made so little progress as in the United States. . . . The future will prove whether the passion for profound knowledge, so rare, and so fruitful, can be born and developed as readily in democratic societies as in aristocracies."

De Tocqueville's comment was pertinent and dispassionate and justified by the facts. With respect to higher education, facilities for advanced study were then almost completely lacking in this country. To cultivate "the passion for profound knowledge" students had to go abroad. Degrees from foreign universities were recognized as an almost indispensable certificate of scholarship. In all the "highest sciences" and arts we leaned heavily on Europe, thus giving color to the suspicion that a democracy is incapable of producing worthy fruits of its own.

This view of the matter was readily accepted by other European writers and travelers, who were less sympathetic than de Tocqueville with the experiment in democracy on these shores. Posing as high priests of culture they took pains to remind us in detail of our deficiencies. This seemed to give them considerable satisfaction and presumably did us no harm. As far as higher learning is concerned, however, the opportunity for invidious comparisons did not last very long. When the Johns Hopkins University led the way, in the 'seventies, in emphasizing graduate work, other institutions speedily followed, with the result that American universities are now competing with old-world institutions on their own terms and in various fields are leading the way.

Perhaps the most striking development in this connection is that which took place in our state universities. In spite of their dependence on public opinion and public appropriations, the more important of these institutions found it possible to advance to a front rank in the cultivation of scholarship and cultural interests. We were presented with the unprecedented spectacle of legislatures composed largely of farmers and small business men appropriating large sums for the promotion of scientific studies ranging all the way from the *mores* and speech habits of primitive peoples to the composition of heavenly bodies so remote as to be invisible to the naked eye. Let me remark in passing that while I have seen this happen over and over again, I still have moments when it seems quite incredible. There is perhaps no more convincing evidence to be had anywhere that our democracy, in spite of all its crudities, has at its core an idealism that is both magnificent and indestructible. As Lord Bryce once said: "There is nothing of which Americans boast less and of which they have more reason to be proud than their universities."

It appears, then, that the question whether "the passion for profound knowledge" can flourish as well in a democracy as in an aristocracy may be regarded as settled. To put it in its lowest terms, our institutions of higher learning have their full quota of men who regard their respective subjects as the supreme achievement of civilization, and whose highest expression of broadmindedness consists in identifying the university with the universe. In the light of this development we are tempted to say that the capacity of the common man to appreciate cultural values was seriously underrated, and to let it go at that.

As was suggested previously, however, there is reason to suspect that the appreciation of the cultural values which we have transplanted with so much apparent success into our civilization is not quite the same thing with us as in the Old World. In the language of evolution, the differences in environment seem to make for a variation from type.

The difference is perhaps most easily indicated by the difference in popular attitude, here and abroad, toward the professor, who is presumably the embodiment or symbol of these cultural values. In the Old World the professor is generally regarded with profound respect. Pre-war Germany was once referred to by Lord Palmerston as "the land of the damned professor." Here we tend to distinguish sharply between faith in education and faith in professors. We have an abiding faith in education; and it may be added that this faith is not merely faith in its utilitarian value. As evidence we may point to the fact that the sporadic attempts to make secondary education consist, for most pupils, in vocational preparation have never made much headway. But the professor, who, after all, does the heavy work in education and who presumably should be regarded as an exemplification of what we mean by education, occupies an equivocal status. We distrust him. It was this distrust which the opponents of the New Deal sought to exploit by their constant harping on the "brain trust" and by their ingenious cartoons of unlovely pedagogs arrayed in cap and gown. The common man as a class is certainly not lacking in the recognition that there are cultural values, but at his profane touch these values seem to have been transmuted into something else.

Somewhere along the line there is a parting of the ways; and to discover just where and how the ways diverge is of essential importance if we are to determine the meaning of democracy as applied to education.

CLEAVAGE BETWEEN INTELLECTUAL AND PRACTICAL

In approaching this problem we may recall de Tocqueville's reminder that "the passion for profound knowledge" was born and developed in the aristocracies of the past, which means that it took on a distinctive quality. Historical aristocracy maintained a cleavage between the cultural and the vocational, between the intellectual and the practical, between the quest for truth and art for their own sake and the recognition of their social significance and responsibility. This cleavage was, of course, a reflection of social organization. Devotion to intellectual and esthetic values was a leisure-time affair, a badge of social distinction. Conversely, practical affairs, and particularly manual labor, were the proper business of slaves and peasants and commoners generally, who were either incapable of, or not destined for, a higher life.

This opposition between the life of leisure and the practical life carried with it momentous consequences, both for social matters and for education. These consequences are symbolized, after a fashion, by the notion that the three R's are just "tool subjects." Perhaps one might say that in the domain of the practical life, insofar as this could be held apart from the higher life of culture, all education was just a tool for getting things done. For a long period it was not considered necessary that the common man should have any formal education at all. Later, as the social order became more complex, it was conceded that a knowledge of reading, writing, and arithmetic was a useful equipment. Beyond that all his knowledge, except what was handed to him on authority, was of a practical kind. He had a store of information about planting and reaping, about the treatment of colds, about how to get along with people, and the like. This kind of knowledge is sometimes called empirical and sometimes called pragmatic. It had a simple test. Knowledge is sound if things work out according to expectations. The common man, for example, could undertake to meet a person at sunrise, and he would consider his knowledge of sunrise valid or true if it served him in such ways. He would not be likely to consider that this knowledge depended on the question whether the sun "really" goes around the earth or *vice versa*.

For the leisure-class person the problem of knowledge and truth was less simple. To him the question of truth was not merely incidental to the business of getting the world's work done. Being separated from the world of practical affairs, he was compelled to contrive for his ideas some other meaning or function than usefulness in the control of experience. Moreover, as long as we make truth dependent on experience, we never get at anything absolute and final. To illustrate, the sun was first supposed to go around the earth; then, it was found that the earth goes around the sun; and no one can say how they will go after a group of relativists, like Einstein, have got in their work. Reliance on experience and practical requirements looked like a degradation of the sacred name of truth. It became necessary, therefore, to go in quest of "absolute" standards.

THE DOMINION OF ABSOLUTES

How this was done is exemplified in simple yet grand fashion by Plato's doctrine of Ideas. According to Plato, the everyday world in which we live is not itself reality, but a fleeting and distorted image or reflection of reality. The real world is supersensuous; it is non-material and unchangeable; it is made up of certain eternal and immutable essences, such as Truth, Goodness, and Beauty. These realities are called Ideas, for want of a better name. The name is perhaps intended to indicate their supersensuous and non-material character. These Ideas furnish us with standards. Our ideas of truth, goodness, and beauty are valid ideas, not by the test of experience but by the test of correspondence or conformity to these supreme essences which go by the same names.

This doctrine of Ideas is of interest to us in the present connection, not because it gives us a better understanding of the world in which we live, but because it shows what happens when men turn their backs on everyday reality and try to lift themselves by their own bootstraps.The creation of this transcendental world was at the same time one of the most brilliant achievements and one of the major tragedies of human civilization. To what extent the intellectual capacity of the race was condemned to speculative sterility by the influence of this doctrine, no one can say. Since the aristocratic form of social organization prevailed practically everywhere during most of the past, some such course of development was perhaps inevitable. The particular form of Plato's doctrine has long been a matter of merely historical interest, but its progeny was legion and is to be found everywhere. The whole tribe of "absolutes" in our Western world can probably claim kinship with these Platonic realities, from notions of absolute property rights to the absolutes of nationalistic or racial dictatorships and to the theological dictum that this vale of wrath and tears is a hopeless mess and heaven alone is our abiding city. Whatever the form, the common man is always told that his little affairs do not count in comparison with these august absolutes.

For a long time these absolutes had things pretty much their own way in the academic world. They had, indeed, frequent squabbles among themselves, but there was little disposition to challenge the principle of absolutism, in spite of the fact that no one has as yet succeeded in giving a convincing account of what an absolute is really like as a "real" thing. Plato was a poet in temperament as well as a philosopher and his access to the world of Ideas seems to have been through a kind of semi-mystical adoration. His successors were often more hard-headed, but they were not any more successful in making these absolutes meaningful; which is perhaps not surprising, since the attempt to get beyond experience seems bound to take us — in Hegelian phrase — into a night where all cows are black.

The common man was, of course, too inarticulate, and at the same time too much in awe of his betters, to challenge the conclusions of the wise men. Since he has been coming into his own, however, he has become more sensitive to the conflict between the aristocratic way of life and the way of life where, as a practical man, he lives and moves and has his being. This sensitiveness makes him more skeptical, even if he cannot match theory with theory; and he has lost his awe sufficiently to engage, on occasion, in ridicule. This perhaps explains the paradoxical attitude which was mentioned previously. Scholarship and culture are prized by him, yet its products are stigmatized with such epithets as "high-brow" and "ivory tower." A highbrow, so we have been told, is a person who has been educated beyond the limits of his intelligence. This is an irreverent way of saying that scholarship and culture tend to become entangled with a mythological realm of trans-experiential reality, which is too remote and too sublime to be checked and tested by ordinary experience. When or insofar as this happens, higher education becomes a kind of cult in which human values evaporate into a set of abstractions. Emphasis on scholarship or theory does not in itself make a person inept, because sound theory always keeps in touch with the relevant facts. But theory which loses this contact by going off in a different direction is deserving of distrust.

The present-day reaction of the common man may perhaps be construed as a hopeful sign that man will presently engage in a direct struggle with himself to keep from being subjugated and exploited by the figments of his own imagination. Nature has proved to be a less formidable enemy than the absolutes which have kept him in bondage from the time of Plato down to our present dictatorships. To use the vernacular, he has never dared to call his soul his own. At the behest of authority he has on occasion repudiated the evidence of science and experience, with all the assurance of the much-quoted rustic who ended his inspection of the giraffe by saying: "There ain't no such animal." The same blind obedience has caused him to believe that fire and slaughter and the degradation of human beings were in accordance with the will of an infinitely tender Providence. In matters of art he—or more frequently she—still struggles pathetically to like the things that have the right labels, even at the cost of those healthy reactions which once prompted Justice O.W. Holmes to say, after he had seen a vaudeville show: "Thank God, I am a man of low tastes."

THE CHOICE REQUIRED

Progressive education is confronted with the choice of becoming the avowed exponent of democracy or else of becoming a set of ingenious devices for tempering the wind to the shorn lamb. If democracy is to have a deep and inclusive human meaning, it must have also a distinctive educational system.

Since the whole weight of tradition is on the side of absolutes, which are abstractions that served to maintain an aristocratic form of society, such a system must have direct and constant reference to the conflict between the aristocratic and the democratic ways of life. It must have a psychology based on the conception of knowledge and truth as functions in the control of experience—the kind of psychology which is pointed toward in what is sometimes called "organismic" psychology. It must have a theory of values which has as its center the continuous improvement of human living through voluntary reciprocity or the constant widening of common interests and common concerns. Lastly, it must undertake to point out how the acceptance of such a standard for growth and progress requires continuous and frequently extensive reconstruction or revision of traditional beliefs and attitudes, in accordance with growing insight and changing circumstances. In a word, progressive education must become clearly conscious of the implications contained in its basic attitude and to use these implications as a vantage point from which to reorganize its thinking and its procedures.

CHAPTER 22

EDUCATION AND SOCIAL CHANGE

Face squarely and courageously every social issue.

George S. Counts, 1932

58. EDUCATION AND THE SOCIAL CRISIS (1932)[1]

WILLIAM H. KILPATRICK

CONCLUSION

We now conclude the special work of the profession of education. It has, first of all, broadened its own outlook beyond mere school-keeping to include a concern for significant educative effects wherever found. The profession will endeavor to use educative procedures to improve any such bad effects and to promote the better. In particular, considering the great significance of the present economic and social situation the profession will join forces with other agencies in the effort to bring about such study of this situation as will mean an increasingly intelligent planning of the social and economic processes to the end that life may be better for all.

As a first step in such a program the profession must re-make its own outlook so as to acquire one and all a truly social point of view. It should then undertake to secure the intelligent study of the social situation both in school and in the adult world in the light of the best that is known, that life may begin at once to be better. Life it must view as one continuous process, with education as the effort at its intelligent direction. Each period of life will show its problems. The aim of education will be to help those of each period so to study its problems that they will more surely act intelligently in both private and public affairs. All must come to expect social changes and adjust their thinking accordingly. If we are to meet the confronting situation, all must wish the common good. All must learn to criticize intelligently both

---

[1]William H. Kilpatrick, *Education and the Social Crisis: A Proposed Program* (New York: Liveright Publishing Corp., 1932), pp. 78 –80. Kilpatrick, born in Georgia in 1871, died in 1965. As a disciple and interpreter of John Dewey, Kilpatrick played an important role in the Progressive Education Movement. He became Professor of Philosophy at Teachers College in 1909, a position he held until his retirement.

existing and proposed institutions. And all must seek, each for himself, a unified outlook on life in place of the conflicts all too common within because they are so deeply at work without.

In particular, in order to help best in the adult world, a new and much more inclusive education must be planned with the aim of reaching all classes of the population in a serious study of life's problems and this in the hope that early steps may be taken to improve our institutional life. Such study among adults should help the schools greatly, partly in relieving the schools of the now impossible task of trying to give an education which will supposedly last for the rest of life. It should further help the schools by making parents and the community in general more intelligent as to what should go on in school and therefore more willing to have the schools undertake a really social program.

The school as we know it must be remade to a more social point of view. Now the aim is too often so to equip each pupil that he may the better get ahead of others. Content and method will need remaking. Much of what is now taught is too largely conventional and all too remote from life. The idea that education consists in the acquisition of stated subject-matter must give way to the study of problems vital within the lives of the young people and to the undertaking of enterprises significant within the community. Only in such way can we hope to get the needed intelligent thinking about social affairs or build adequate social attitudes. As far as the age of the pupils will permit they must become intelligently critical of our, and their, social life and institutions. It is, of course, true that there can be but inefficient social education by the school so long as the institutions of the social and economic world work directly against the effort of the school. But we can do better than we have been doing. With adults working to change our institutions for the better, there will come a better day for the school. When elders are critical of social life about us, that life will have less power to mis-educate the young. As fast as that social life can be changed, the school can become in its own processes more effectively educative. Working thus simultaneously with old and young we may hope to hasten the better day.

59. DARE THE SCHOOL BUILD A NEW SOCIAL ORDER? (1932)[1]

GEORGE S. COUNTS

Like all simple and unsophisticated peoples we Americans have a sublime faith in education. Faced with any difficult problem of life we set our minds at rest sooner or later by the appeal to the school. We are convinced that education is the one unfailing remedy for every ill to which man is subject, whether it be vice, crime, war, poverty, riches, injustice, racketeering, political corruption, race hatred, class conflict, or just plain original sin. We even speak glibly and often about the general reconstruction of society through the school. We cling to this faith in spite of the fact that the very period in which our troubles have multiplied so rapidly has witnessed an unprecedented expansion of organized education. This would seem to suggest that our schools, instead of directing the course of change, are themselves driven by the very forces that are transforming the rest of the social order.

The bare fact, however, that simple and unsophisticated peoples have unbounded faith in education does not mean that the faith is untenable. History shows that the intuitions of such folk may be nearer the truth than the weighty and carefully reasoned judgments of the learned and the wise. Under certain conditions education may be as beneficent and as powerful as we are wont to think. But if it is to be so, teachers must abandon much of their easy optimism, subject the concept of education to the most rigorous scrutiny, and be prepared to deal much more fundamentally, realistically, and positively with the American social situation than has been their habit in the past. Any individual or group that would aspire to lead society must be ready to pay the costs of leadership: to accept responsibility, to suffer calumny, to surren-

---

[1]George Counts, *Dare the School Build a New Social Order?* No. 11 John Day Pamphlets (New York: John Day, [1932]), pp. 3–13, 35–56. Counts early emerged as a principal critic of American education.

der security, to risk both reputation and fortune. If this price, or some important part of it, is not being paid, then the chances are that the claim to leadership is fraudulent. Society is never redeemed without effort, struggle, and sacrifice. Authentic leaders are never found breathing that rarefied atmosphere lying above the dust and smoke of battle. With regard to the past we always recognize the truth of this principle, but when we think of our own times we profess the belief that the ancient rôles have been reversed and that now prophets of a new age receive their rewards among the living.

That the existing school is leading the way to a better social order is a thesis which few informed persons would care to defend. Except as it is forced to fight for its own life during times of depression, its course is too serene and untroubled. Only in the rarest of instances does it wage war on behalf of principle or ideal. Almost everywhere it is in the grip of conservative forces and is serving the cause of perpetuating ideas and institutions suited to an age that is gone. But there is one movement above the educational horizon which would seem to show promise of genuine and creative leadership. I refer to the Progressive Education movement. Surely in this union of two of the great faiths of the American people, the faith in progress and the faith in education, we have reason to hope for light and guidance. Here is a movement which would seem to be completely devoted to the promotion of social welfare through education.

Even a casual examination of the program and philosophy of the Progressive schools, however, raises many doubts in the mind. To be sure, these schools have a number of large achievements to their credit. They have focused attention squarely upon the child; they have recognized the fundamental importance of the interest of the learner; they have defended the thesis that activity lies at the root of all true education; they have conceived learning in terms of life situations and growth of character; they have championed the rights of the child as a free personality. Most of this is excellent, but in my judgment it is not enough. It constitutes too narrow a conception of the meaning of education; it brings into the picture but one-half of the landscape.

If an educational movement, or any other movement, calls itself progressive, it must have orientation; it must possess direction. The word itself implies moving forward, and moving forward can have little meaning in the absence of clearly defined purposes.

We cannot, like Stephen Leacock's horseman, dash off in all directions at once. Nor should we, like our presidential candidates, evade every disturbing issue and be all things to all men. Also we must beware lest we become so devoted to motion that we neglect the question of direction and be entirely satisfied with movement in circles. Here, I think, we find the fundamental weakness, not only of Progressive Education, but also of American education generally. Like a baby shaking a rattle, we seem to be utterly content with action, provided it is sufficiently vigorous and noisy. In the last analysis a very large part of American educational thought, inquiry, and experimentation is much ado about nothing. And, if we are permitted to push the analogy of the rattle a bit further, our consecration to motion is encouraged and supported in order to keep us out of mischief. At least we know that so long as we thus busy ourselves we shall not incur the serious displeasure of our social elders.

The weakness of Progressive Education thus lies in the fact that it has elaborated no theory of social welfare, unless it be that of anarchy or extreme individualism. In this, of course, it is but reflecting the viewpoint of the members of the liberal-minded upper middle class who send their children to the Progressive schools — persons who are fairly well-off, who have abandoned the faiths of their fathers, who assume an agnostic attitude towards all important questions, who pride themselves on their open-mindedness and tolerance, who favor in a mild sort of way fairly liberal programs of social reconstruction, who are full of good will and humane sentiment, who have vague aspirations for world peace and human brotherhood, who can be counted upon to respond moderately to any appeal made in the name of charity, who are genuinely distressed at the sight of *unwonted* forms of cruelty, misery, and suffering, and who perhaps serve to soften somewhat the bitter clashes of those real forces that govern the world; but who, in spite of all their good qualities, have no deep and abiding loyalties, possess no convictions for which they would sacrifice over-much, would find it hard to live without their customary material comforts, are rather insensitive to the accepted forms of social injustice, are content to play the rôle of interested spectator in the drama of human history, refuse to see reality in its harsher and more disagreeable forms, rarely move outside the pleasant circles of the class to which they belong, and in the day of severe trial will follow the lead of the most powerful and respectable forces in society and at the same time find good reasons for so doing. These people have shown themselves entirely incapable of dealing with any of the great crises of our time — war, prosperity, or depression. At bottom they are romantic sentimentalists, but with a sharp eye on the main chance. That they can be trusted to write our educational theories and shape our educational programs is highly improbable.

Among the members of this class the number of children is small, the income relatively high, and the economic functions of the home greatly reduced. For these reasons an inordinate emphasis on the child and child interests is entirely welcome to them. They wish to guard their offspring from too strenuous endeavor and from coming into too intimate contact with the grimmer aspects of industrial society. They wish their sons and daughters to succeed according to the standards of their class and to be a credit to their parents. At heart feeling themselves members of a superior human strain, they do not want their children to mix too freely with the children of the poor or of the less fortunate races. Nor do they want them to accept radical social doctrines, espouse unpopular causes, or lose themselves in quest of any Holy Grail. According to their views education should deal with life, but with life at a distance or in a highly diluted form. They would generally maintain that life should be kept at arm's length, if it should not be handled with a poker.

If Progressive Education is to be genuinely progressive, it must emancipate itself from the influence of this class, face squarely and courageously every social issue, come to grips with life in all of its stark reality, establish an organic relation with the community, develop a realistic and comprehensive theory of welfare, fashion a compelling and challenging vision of human destiny, and become less frightened than it is today at the bogies of *imposition* and *indoctrination*. In a word, Progressive Education cannot place its trust in a child-centered school.

This brings us to the most crucial issue in education — the question of the nature and extent of the influence which the school should exercise over the development of the child. The advocates of extreme freedom have been so successful in championing what they call the rights of the child that even the most skillful practitioners of the art of converting others to their opinions disclaim all intention of molding the learner. And when the word indoctrination is coupled with education there is scarcely

one among us possessing the hardihood to refuse to be horri-
fied. . . .

The issue is no doubt badly confused by historical causes. The
champions of freedom are obviously the product of an age that has
broken very fundamentally with the past and is equally uncertain
about the future. In many cases they feel themselves victims of
narrow orthodoxies which were imposed upon them during childhood and which have severely cramped their lives. At any suggestion that the child should be influenced by his elders they therefore envisage the establishment of a state church, the formulation
of a body of sacred doctrine, and the teaching of this doctrine as
fixed and final. If we are forced to choose between such an unenlightened form of pedagogical influence and a condition of complete freedom for the child, most of us would in all probability
choose the latter as the lesser of two evils. But this is to create a
wholly artificial situation: the choice should not be limited to
these two extremes. Indeed today neither extreme is possible.

I believe firmly that a critical factor must play an important role
in any adequate educational program, at least in any such program
fashioned for the modern world. An education that does not strive
to promote the fullest and most thorough understanding of the
world is not worthy of the name. Also there must be no deliberate
distortion or suppression of facts to support any theory or point of
view. On the other hand, I am prepared to defend the thesis that
all education contains a large element of imposition, that in the
very nature of the case this is inevitable, that the existence and
evolution of society depend upon it, that it is consequently emi-
nently desirable, and that the frank acceptance of this fact by the
educator is a major professional obligation. I even contend that
failure to do this involves the clothing of one's own deepest prejudices in the garb of universal truth and the introduction into the
theory and practice of education of an element of obscurant-
ism. . . .

✢ ✢ ✢

The point should be emphasized, however, that the present
situation is also freighted with hope and promise. The age is
pregnant with possibilities. There lies within our grasp the most
humane, the most beautiful, the most majestic civilization ever
fashioned by any people. This much at least we know today. We
shall probably know more tomorrow. At last men have achieved
such a mastery over the forces of nature that wage slavery can

follow chattel slavery and take its place among the relics of the past. No longer are there grounds for the contention that the finer fruits of human culture must be nurtured upon the toil and watered by the tears of the masses. The limits to achievement set by nature have been so extended that we are today bound merely by our ideals, by our power of self-discipline, by our ability to devise social arrangements suited to an industrial age. If we are to place any credence whatsoever in the word of our engineers, the full utilization of modern technology at its present level of development should enable us to produce several times as much goods as were ever produced at the very peak of prosperity, and with the working day, the working year, and the working life reduced by half. We hold within our hands the power to usher in an age of plenty, to make secure the lives of all, and to banish poverty forever from the land. The only cause for doubt or pessimism lies in the question of our ability to rise to the stature of the times in which we live.

Our generation has the good or the ill fortune to live in an age when great decisions must be made. The American people, like most of the other peoples of the earth, have come to the parting of the ways; they can no longer trust entirely the inspiration which came to them when the Republic was young; they must decide afresh what they are to do with their talents. Favored above all other nations with the resources of nature and the material instrumentalities of civilization, they stand confused and irresolute before the future. They seem to lack the moral quality necessary to quicken, discipline, and give direction to their matchless energies. In a recent paper Professor Dewey has, in my judgment, correctly diagnosed our troubles: "the schools, like the nation," he says, "are in need of a central purpose which will create new enthusiasm and devotion, and which will unify and guide all intellectual plans."

This suggests, as we have already observed, that the educational problem is not wholly intellectual in nature. Our Progressive schools therefore cannot rest content with giving children an opportunity to study contemporary society in all of its aspects. This of course must be done, but I am convinced that they should go much farther. If the schools are to be really effective, they must become centers for the building, and not merely for the contemplation, of our civilization. This does not mean that we should endeavor to promote particular reforms through the educational

279

system. We should, however, give to our children a vision of the possibilities which lie ahead and endeavor to enlist their loyalties and enthusiasms in the realization of the vision. Also our social institutions and practices, all of them, should be critically examined in the light of such a vision.

In *The Epic of America* James Truslow Adams contends that our chief contribution to the heritage of the race lies not in the field of science, or religion, or literature, or art but rather in the creation of what he calls the "American Dream"—a vision of a society in which the lot of the common man will be made easier and his life enriched and ennobled. If this vision has been a moving force in our history, as I believe it has, why should we not set ourselves the task of revitalizing and reconstituting it? This would seem to be the great need of our age, both in the realm of education and in the sphere of public life, because men must have something for which to live. . . .

✿ ✿ ✿

I would consequently like to see our profession come to grips with the problem of creating a tradition that has roots in American soil, is in harmony with the spirit of the age, recognizes the facts of industrialism, appeals to the most profound impulses of our people, and takes into account the emergence of a world society.

The ideal foundations on which we must build are easily discernible. Until recently the very word America has been synonymous throughout the world with democracy and symbolic to the oppressed classes of all lands of hope and opportunity. Child of the revolutionary ideas and impulses of the eighteenth century, the American nation became the embodiment of bold social experimentation and a champion of the power of environment to develop the capacities and redeem the souls of common men and women. And as her stature grew, her lengthening shadow reached to the four corners of the earth and everywhere impelled the human will to rebel against ancient wrongs. Here undoubtedly is the finest jewel in our heritage and the thing that is most worthy of preservation. If America should lose her honest devotion to democracy, or if she should lose her revolutionary temper, she will no longer be America. In that day, if it has not already arrived, her spirit will have fled and she will be known merely as the richest and most powerful of the nations. If America is not to be false to the promise of her youth, she must do more than simply perpetuate the democratic ideal of human relationships: she must make

280

an intelligent and determined effort to fulfill it. The democracy of the past was the chance fruit of a strange conjunction of forces on the new continent; the democracy of the future can only be the intended offspring of the union of human reason, purpose, and will. The conscious and deliberate achievement of democracy under novel circumstances is the task of our generation.

Democracy of course should not be identified with political forms and functions — with the federal constitution, the popular election of officials, or the practice of universal suffrage. To think in such terms is to confuse the entire issue, as it has been confused in the minds of the masses for generations. The most genuine expression of democracy in the United States has little to do with our political institutions: it is a sentiment with respect to the moral equality of men: it is an aspiration towards a society in which this sentiment will find complete fulfillment. A society fashioned in harmony with the American democratic tradition would combat all forces tending to produce social distinctions and classes; repress every form of privilege and economic parasitism; manifest a tender regard for the weak, the ignorant, and the unfortunate; place the heavier and more onerous social burdens on the backs of the strong; glory in every triumph of man in his timeless urge to express himself and to make the world more habitable; exalt human labor of hand and brain as the creator of all wealth and culture; provide adequate material and spiritual rewards for every kind of socially useful work; strive for genuine equality of opportunity among all races, sects, and occupations; regard as paramount the abiding interests of the great masses of the people; direct the powers of government to the elevation and the refinement of the life of the common man; transform or destroy all conventions, institutions, and special groups inimical to the underlying principles of democracy; and finally be prepared as a last resort, in either the defense or the realization of this purpose, to follow the method of revolution. Although these ideals have never been realized or perhaps even fully accepted anywhere in the United States and have always had to struggle for existence with contrary forces, they nevertheless have authentic roots in the past. They are the values for which America has stood before the world during most of her history and with which the American people have loved best to associate their country. Their power and authority are clearly revealed in the fact that selfish interests, when grasping for some special privilege, commonly wheedle and sway the masses by repeating the words and kneeling before the emblems of the democratic heritage.

It is becoming increasingly clear, however, that this tradition, if its spirit is to survive, will have to be reconstituted in the light of the great social trends of the age in which we live. Our democratic heritage was largely a product of the frontier, free land, and a simple agrarian order. Today a new and strange and closely integrated industrial economy is rapidly sweeping over the world. Although some of us in our more sentimental moments talk wistfully of retiring into the more tranquil society of the past, we could scarcely induce many of our fellow citizens to accompany us. Even the most hostile critics of industrialism would like to take with them in their retirement a few such fruits of the machine as electricity, telephones, automobiles, modern plumbing, and various labor-saving devices, or at least be assured of an abundant supply of slaves or docile and inexpensive servants. But all such talk is the most idle chatter. For better or for worse we must take industrial civilization as an enduring fact: already we have become parasitic on its institutions and products. The hands of the clock cannot be turned back.

If we accept industrialism, as we must, we are then compelled to face without equivocation the most profound issue which this new order of society has raised and settle that issue in terms of the genius of our people—the issue of the control of the machine. In whose interests and for what purposes are the vast material riches, the unrivaled industrial equipment, and the science and technology of the nation to be used? In the light of our democratic tradition there can be but one answer to the question: all of these resources must be dedicated to the promotion of the welfare of the great masses of the people. Even the classes in our society that perpetually violate this principle are compelled by the force of public opinion to pay lip-service to it and to defend their actions in its terms. No body of men, however powerful, would dare openly to flout it. Since the opening of the century the great corporations have even found it necessary to establish publicity departments or to employ extremely able men as public relations counselors in order to persuade the populace that regardless of appearances they are lovers of democracy and devoted servants of the people. In this they have been remarkably successful, at least until the coming of the great depression. For during the past generation there have been few things in America that could not be bought at a price.

If the benefits of industrialism are to accrue fully to the people, this deception must be exposed. If the machine is to serve all, and serve all equally, it cannot be the property of the few. To ask these few to have regard for the common weal, particularly when under the competitive system they are forced always to think first of themselves or perish, is to put too great a strain on human nature. With the present concentration of economic power in the hands of a small class, a condition that is likely to get worse before it gets better, the survival or development of a society that could in any sense be called democratic is unthinkable. The hypocrisy which is so characteristic of our public life today is due primarily to our failure to acknowledge the fairly obvious fact that America is the scene of an irreconcilable conflict between two opposing forces. On the one side is the democratic tradition inherited from the past; on the other is a system of economic arrangements which increasingly partakes of the nature of industrial feudalism. Both of these forces cannot survive: one or the other must give way. Unless the democratic tradition is able to organize and conduct a successful attack on the economic system, its complete destruction is inevitable.

If democracy is to survive, it must seek a new economic foundation. Our traditional democracy rested upon small-scale production in both agriculture and industry and a rather general diffusion of the rights of property in capital and natural resources. The driving force at the root of this condition, as we have seen, was the frontier and free land. With the closing of the frontier, the exhaustion of free land, the growth of population, and the coming of large scale production, the basis of ownership was transformed. If property rights are to be diffused in industrial society, natural resources and all important forms of capital will have to be collectively owned. Obviously every citizen cannot hold title to a mine, a factory, a railroad, a department store, or even a thoroughly mechanized farm. This clearly means that, if democracy is to survive in the United States, it must abandon its individualistic affiliations in the sphere of economics. What precise form a democratic society will take in the age of science and the machine, we cannot know with any assurance today. We must, however, insist on two things: first, that technology be released from the fetters and the domination of every type of special privilege; and, second, that the resulting system of production and distribution be made to serve directly the masses of the people. Within these limits, as I see it, our democratic tradition must of necessity evolve and gradually assume an essentially collectivistic pattern. The only conceivable alternative is the abandonment of the last vestige of democracy and the frank adoption of some modern form of feudalism.

The important point is that fundamental changes in the economic system are imperative. Whatever services historic capitalism may have rendered in the past, and they have been many, its days are numbered. With its deification of the principle of selfishness, its exaltation of the profit motive, its reliance upon the forces of competition, and its placing of property above human rights, it will either have to be displaced altogether or changed so radically in form and spirit that its identity will be completely lost. In view of the fact that the urge for private gain tends to debase everything that it touches, whether business, recreation, religion, art, or friendship, the indictment against capitalism has commonly been made on moral grounds. But today the indictment can be drawn in other terms.

Capitalism is proving itself weak at the very point where its champions have thought it impregnable. It is failing to meet the pragmatic test; it no longer works; it is unable even to organize and maintain production. In its present form capitalism is not only cruel and inhuman; it is also wasteful and inefficient. It has exploited our natural resources without the slightest regard for the future needs of our society; it has forced technology to serve the interests of the few rather than the many; it has chained the engineer to the vagaries and inequities of the price system; it has plunged the great nations of the earth into a succession of wars ever more devastating and catastrophic in character; and only recently it has brought on a world crisis of such dimensions that the entire economic order is paralyzed and millions of men in all the great industrial countries are deprived of the means of livelihood. The growth of science and technology has carried us into a new age where ignorance must be replaced by knowledge, competition by coöperation, trust in providence by careful planning, and private capitalism by some form of socialized economy.

Already the individualism of the pioneer and the farmer, produced by free land, great distances, economic independence, and a largely self-sustaining family economy, is without solid foundation in either agriculture or industry. Free land has long since disappeared. Great distances have been shortened immeasurably by invention. Economic independence survives only in the traditions of our people. Self-sustaining family economy has been swallowed up in a vast society which even refuses to halt before the boundaries of nations. Already we live in an economy which in its functions is fundamentally cooperative. There remains the task of reconstructing our economic institutions and of reformulating our social ideals so that they may be in harmony with the underlying facts of life. The man who would live unto himself alone must retire from the modern world. The day of individualism in the production and distribution of goods is gone. The fact cannot be overemphasized that choice is no longer between individualism and collectivism. It is rather between two forms of collectivism: the one essentially democratic, the other feudal in spirit; the one devoted to the interests of the people, the other to the interests of a privileged class.

The objection is of course raised at once that a planned, coordinated, and socialized economy, managed in the interest of the people, would involve severe restrictions on personal freedom. Undoubtedly in such an economy the individual would not be permitted to do many things that he has customarily done in the past. He would not be permitted to carve a fortune out of the natural resources of the nation, to organize a business purely for the purpose of making money, to build a new factory or railroad whenever and wherever he pleased, to throw the economic system out of gear for the protection of his own private interests, to amass or to attempt to amass great riches by the corruption of the political life, the control of the organs of opinion, the manipulation of the financial machinery, the purchase of brains and knowledge, or the exploitation of ignorance, frailty, and misfortune. In exchange for such privileges as these, which only the few could ever enjoy, we would secure the complete and uninterrupted functioning of the productive system and thus lay the foundations for a measure of freedom for the many that mankind has never known in the past. Freedom without a secure economic foundation is only a word: in our society it may be freedom to beg, steal, or starve. The right to vote, if it cannot be made to insure the right to work, is but an empty bauble. Indeed it may be less than a bauble: it may serve to drug and dull the senses of the masses. Today only the

285

members of the plutocracy are really free, and even in their case freedom is rather precarious. If all of us could be assured of material security and abundance, we would be released from economic worries and our energies liberated to grapple with the central problems of cultural advance.

Under existing conditions, however, no champion of the democratic way of life can view the future with equanimity. If democracy is to be achieved in the industrial age, powerful classes must be persuaded to surrender their privileges, and institutions deeply rooted in popular prejudice will have to be radically modified or abolished. And according to the historical record, this process has commonly been attended by bitter struggle and even bloodshed. Ruling classes never surrender their privileges voluntarily. Rather do they cling to what they have been accustomed to regard as their rights, even though the heavens fall. Men customarily defend their property, however it may have been acquired, as tenaciously as the proverbial mother defends her young. There is little evidence from the pages of American history to support us in the hope that we may adjust our difficulties through the method of sweetness and light. Since the settlement of the first colonists along the Atlantic seaboard we have practiced and become inured to violence. This is peculiarly true wherever and whenever property rights, actual or potential, have been involved. Consider the pitiless extermination of the Indian tribes and the internecine strife over the issue of human slavery. Consider the long reign of violence in industry from the days of the Molly Maguires in the seventies down to the strikes in the mining regions of Kentucky today. Also let those, whose memories reach back a dozen years, recall the ruthlessness with which the privileged classes put down every expression of economic or political dissent during the period immediately following the World War. When property is threatened, constitutional guarantees are but scraps of paper and even the courts and the churches, with occasional exceptions, rush to the support of privilege and vested interest.

This is a dark picture. If we look at the future through the eyes of the past, we find little reason for optimism. If there is to be no break in our tradition of violence, if a bold and realistic program of education is not forthcoming, we can only anticipate a struggle of increasing bitterness terminating in revolution and disaster. And yet, as regards the question of property, the present situation has no historical parallel. In earlier paragraphs I have pointed to the possibility of completely disposing of the economic problem. For the first time in history we are able to produce all the goods and services that our people can consume. The justification, or at least the rational basis, of the age-long struggle for property has been removed. This situation gives to teachers an opportunity and a responsibility unique in the annals of education.

In an economy of scarcity, where the population always tends to outstrip the food supply, any attempt to change radically the rules of the game must inevitably lead to trial by the sword. But in an economy of plenty, which the growth of technology has made entirely possible, the conditions are fundamentally altered. It is natural and understandable for men to fight when there is·scarcity, whether it be over air, water, food, or women. For them to fight over the material goods of life in America today is sheer insanity. Through the courageous and intelligent reconstruction of their economic institutions they could all obtain, not only physical security, but also the luxuries of life and as much leisure as men could ever learn to enjoy. For those who take delight in combat, ample provision for strife could of course be made; but the more cruel aspects of the human struggle would be considerably softened. As the possibilities in our society begin to dawn upon us, we are all, I think, growing increasingly weary of the brutalities, the stupidities, the hypocrisies, and the gross inanities of contemporary life. We have a haunting feeling that we were born for better things and that the nation itself is falling far short of its powers. The fact that other groups refuse to deal boldly and realistically with the present situation does not justify the teachers of the country in their customary policy of hesitation and equivocation. The times are literally crying for a new vision of American destiny. The teaching profession, or at least its progressive elements, should eagerly grasp the opportunity which the fates have placed in their hands.

Such a vision of what America might become in the industrial age I would introduce into our schools as the supreme imposition, but one to which our children are entitled—a priceless legacy which it should be the first concern of our profession to fashion and bequeath. The objection will of course be raised that this is asking teachers to assume unprecedented social responsibilities. But we live in difficult and dangerous times—times when precedents lose their significance. If we are content to remain where all is safe and quiet and serene, we shall dedicate ourselves, as teachers have commonly done in the past, to a rôle of futility, if not of positive social reaction. Neutrality with respect to the great issues that agitate society, while perhaps theoretically possible, is practically tantamount to giving support to the forces of conservatism. As Justice Holmes has candidly said in his essay on Natural Law, "we all, whether we know it or not, are fighting to make the kind of world that we should like." If neutrality is impossible even in the dispensation of justice, whose emblem is the blindfolded goddess, how is it to be achieved in education? To ask the question is to answer it.

To refuse to face the task of creating a vision of a future America immeasurably more just and noble and beautiful than the America of today is to evade the most crucial, difficult, and important educational task. Until we have assumed this responsibility we are scarcely justified in opposing and mocking the efforts of so-called patriotic societies to introduce into the schools a tradition which, though narrow and unenlightened, nevertheless represents an honest attempt to meet a profound social and educational need. Only when we have fashioned a finer and more authentic vision than they will we be fully justified in our opposition to their efforts. Only then will we have discharged the age-long obligation which the older generation owes to the younger and which no amount of sophistry can obscure. Only through such a legacy of spiritual values will our children be enabled to find their place in the world, be lifted out of the present morass of moral indifference, be liberated from the senseless struggle for material success, and be challenged to high endeavor and achievement. And only thus will we as a people put ourselves on the road to the expression of our peculiar genius and to the making of our special contribution to the cultural heritage of the race.

60. REPORT OF THE COMMISSION ON THE SOCIAL STUDIES (1934)[1]

PHILOSOPHY AND PURPOSE IN EDUCATION

A.

1. Education is a form of action on the part of some particular social group; it is not a species of contemplation removed from social life and relationships.

2. Education always expresses some social philosophy, either large or small, involves some choices with respect to social and individual action and well-being, and rests upon some moral conception.

3. Conceived in a large and clarified frame of reference, education is one of the highest forms of statesmanship: a positive and creative attack upon the problems generated by the movement of ideas and interests in society.

4. Finding its immediate expression in individuals, education so conceived is concerned with the development of rich and many-sided personalities capable of co-operating in a social order designed to facilitate the creation of the largest possible number of rich and many-sided personalities.

B. EDUCATION AN EXPRESSION OF A PARTICULAR GEOGRAPHICAL AND CULTURAL SETTING

1. Being a form of social action, education always has a geographical and cultural location; it is therefore specific, local, and dynamic, not general, universal, and unchanging; it is a function of

---

[1]"Report of the Commission on the Social Studies of the American Historical Association," *Conclusions and Recommendations of the Commission* (New York and Boston: Charles Scribner's Sons, 1934), pp. 30–43. The Commission was created in 1929 by the American Historical Association and was financed by the Carnegie Corporation.

a particular society at a particular time and place in history; it is rooted in some actual culture and expresses the philosophy and recognized needs of that culture. Contemporary American society of course is of vast proportions and manifests wide-reaching economic and cultural ramifications extending to the most distant parts of the world.

2. Although the basic biological equipment of man seems to be comparatively invariant and may therefore be expected to give certain common elements to education everywhere and at all times, human civilization has characteristics of neighborhood, region, nation, and more extended cultural areas, which lend unique qualities to every working educational program, however persistent and pervasive may be the universal elements entering into it.

3. Since culture plays a dominant role in giving form and substance to education, the formulation of a relevant and effective educational philosophy for a particular society at a particular time and place in history must rest in a large measure upon the findings of the social sciences, findings pertaining to the nature, trends and thought of that society in its regional and world setting.

C. EDUCATIONAL PHILOSOPHY FOR THE UNITED STATES

1. The formulation of an educational philosophy for the United States requires a study of the basic elements, configurations, and trends of American life and culture. The contribution which the social sciences thus make toward shaping the philosophy and purpose of education is as important as any contribution they can make to the content of materials of instruction.

2. Such a study . . . shows that American society during the past hundred years has been moving from an individualistic and frontier economy to a collective and social economy; this trend has steadily gained in momentum, and is strikingly revealed in the contemporary decline of doctrines of *laissez faire* and in the launching of programs of planning and control in local, state, and national economy.

3. Whatever may be the exact character of life in the society now emerging, it will certainly be different in important respects from that of the past. It will be accompanied by many unaccustomed restraints and liberties, responsibilities and opportunities; and

whether it will be better or worse will depend in large measure upon the standards of appraisal applied, the particular choices now made within the limits of the possible, and the education of the rising generation in knowledge, thought, and appreciation of its necessities and potentialities.

4. In two respects education will be challenged: (a) the emerging economy will involve the placing of restraints on individual enterprise, propensities, and acquisitive egoism in agriculture, industry, and labor and generally on the conception, ownership, management, and use of property, as the changing policies of government already indicate; and (b) the emerging economy, by the reduction of hours of labor and other measures, promises to free the ordinary individual from the long working day, exhausting labor and economic insecurity, thus providing him with opportunities for personal development far greater and richer than those enjoyed under the individualistic economy of the eighteenth and nineteenth centuries.

5. The implications for education are clear and imperative: (a) the efficient functioning of the emerging economy and the full utilization of its potentialities require profound changes in the attitudes and outlook of the American people, especially the rising generation—a complete and frank recognition that the old order is passing, that the new order is emerging, and that knowledge of realities and capacity to co-operate are indispensable to the development and even the perdurance of American society; and (b) the rational use of the new leisure requires a cultural equipment which will give strength and harmony to society instead of weakness and discord.

6. Conversely, continued emphasis in education on the traditional ideas and values of economic individualism and acquisitiveness will intensify the conflicts, contradictions, maladjustments, and perils of the transition.

D. GENERAL APPLICATIONS

1. Organized public education in the United States, much more than ever before, is now compelled, if it is to fulfill its social obligations, to adjust its objectives, its curriculum, its methods of instruction, and its administrative procedures to the requirements of the emerging integrated order.

2. If the school is to justify its maintenance and assume its responsibilities, it must recognize the new order and proceed to equip the rising generation to co-operate effectively in the increasingly interdependent society and to live rationally and well within its limitations and possibilities.

3. It thus follows that educators are called upon to examine critically the frame of reference under which they have been operating, and to proceed deliberately to the clarification and affirmation of purpose in the light of the changed and changing social situation and in the light of those facts and trends which remain compelling, irrespective of individual preferences.

4. Educators stand to-day between two great philosophies of social economy: the one representing the immediate past and fading out in actuality, an individualism in economic theory which has become hostile in practice to the development of individuality for great masses of the people and threatens the survival of American society; the other representing and anticipating the future on the basis of actual trends—the future already coming into reality, a collectivism which may permit the widest development of personality or lead to a bureaucratic tyranny destructive of ideals of popular democracy and cultural freedom.

5. If education continues to emphasize the philosophy of individualism in economy, it will increase the accompanying social tensions. If it organizes a program in terms of a philosophy which harmonizes with the facts of a closely integrated society, it will ease the strains of the transition taking place in actuality. The making of choices cannot be evaded, for inaction in education is a form of action.

6. Within the limits of an economy marked by integration and interdependence, many possibilities, many roads stand open before education. The making of choices by either evasion or positive action also cannot be avoided in the development of an educational program.

7. The road which the Commission has chosen . . . is one which, it believes, will make possible the most complete realization, under the changed conditions of life, of the ideals of American democracy and cultural liberty: the recognition of the moral equality and dignity of all men; the abolition of class distinctions and special privileges; the extension to every individual, regardless of birth, class, race, religion, or economic status, of the opportunity for the fullest development of his creative capacities, his

spiritual qualities, his individuality; the encouragement of social inquiry, inventiveness, and tolerance; the protection of all liberties essential to defense against the exercise of brute power; the development of resistance to appeals to racial and religious passion and prejudice; the establishment of those standards and securities set forth in *A Charter for the Social Sciences in the Schools.*

8. Such an affirmation of human values in education, the Commission holds, is peculiarly imperative in a society moving toward economic planning and control. Recognizing the necessity of living in an integrated economy and aware that such economy may be made to serve either some privileged minority or the entire population, the Commission deliberately presents to education, and affirms the desirability of, an economy managed in the interests of the masses, as distinguished from any class or bureaucracy.

9. From this point of view, a supreme purpose of education in the United States, in addition to the development of rich and many-sided personalities, is the preparation of the rising generation to enter the society now coming into being through thought, ideal, and knowledge, rather than through coercion, regimentation, and ignorance, and to shape the form of that society in accordance with American ideals of popular democracy and personal liberty and dignity.

E. IMMEDIATE IMPLICATIONS FOR THE ORGANIZATION AND CONDUCT OF THE SCHOOL SYSTEM

1. In the integrated society now emerging the ideal of individual, institutional, and local advancement will of necessity give way increasingly to considerations of general, national, and world welfare.

2. Since the general social welfare requires the free and full development of all social and creative talents in the individual, the denial of educational opportunity or the submergence of gifts because of circumstances of wealth, family, race, religion, or nationality impoverishes society and is therefore intolerable.

3. In the organization of the life of the school and the conduct of instruction, emphasis will be placed on the development of the social and creative rather than the acquisitive impulses.

4. The materials of instruction will be selected and organized for the purpose of giving to the coming generation the skills,

knowledge, appreciations, and interests necessary to the general understanding and management of an integrated society in its historic and world setting, and of providing all of the special forms of training demanded by a highly complex and differentiated economy.

5. Although the Commission has conceived its work primarily in terms of the necessities and potentialities of American society, it recognizes the growth of world relationships and the urgent need for a better knowledge and appreciation of the common problems of mankind and the significance of international relations.

6. This excludes any commitment of education to either a narrow or an aggressive nationalism and involves a recognition of the fact that any effective world organization must grow with an organization of national and regional unities and with domestic control of outward thrusts of economic, naval, and military power.

7. Moreover, education, being concerned with all cultural interests, not with practical economic interests alone, is compelled to bring into its program of instruction the scientific, intellectual, ethical, and aesthetic ideals, discoveries, and manifestations which give underlying unity to the culture of the Western world and are bringing Asia within a common orbit of civilization.

8. The growing complexity of social relationships, the rapidity of social change, and the consequent social tensions and conflicts in America and throughout the world demand an increased emphasis on social science instruction in the schools and a more realistic approach to the study of society.

9. Also the critical character of the present period in history calls for a far greater stress on the teaching of the social sciences in the schools to-day than in the past; and the difficulties sure to attend the development of an integrated economy, efficiently managed in the interests of the people, will make stress on the social sciences increasingly necessary in the future. There is every reason for believing that this period of adjustment will be prolonged and marked by struggle and uncertainty, by oscillation of action and reaction.

10. For this reason it will be necessary to provide funds, equipment, materials, and training in the social sciences fully adequate to the services they are required to render. Unless the social knowledge and skill required for the operation of the emer-

ging society are forthcoming, the foundations for the support of all cultural interests will crumble away with the disintegration of society itself.

11. The rapid expansion of the secondary and higher schools and the increase in leisure time during the present century give to organized education an unprecedented opportunity and an equally unprecedented responsibility for the preparation of the youth and adults of the nation for the discharge of their social obligations and the exercise and fulfillment of their right to the richness of an abundant life.

CHAPTER 23

MASS VERSUS QUALITY EDUCATION

Excellence and equal opportunity.

Harvard University Committee, 1945

61. GENERAL EDUCATION IN A FREE SOCIETY (1945)[1]

HARVARD UNIVERSITY COMMITTEE

JEFFERSONIANISM AND JACKSONIANISM

. . . Education, like all society's prime needs, changes as society changes. Yet, since the general character of a culture changes more slowly and human nature more slowly still, if at all, there exist also relatively constant elements in education. The most that one can do is therefore, like Long John Silver looking for treasure, to triangulate the major features of the more and the less changing. But to do so is not to find guaranteed solutions: it is only to look in the direction in which they lie.

It was said that the high school's chief problem followed at once from its own explosive growth and from the not less explosive changes taking place outside it. These two categories are not exact; certainly they are not mutually exclusive, and facets of the same historical and social movements appear under both. Yet the consequences for the school system when the attempt was made to realize the ideal of universal free education were in fact immeasurably heightened by the setting of ever-increased urbanization and industrialization in which the attempt was carried out. If related, then, these, as it were, inner and outer movements are distinct in themselves and have raised distinct problems.

The first and inner movement—the sheer numerical growth of the high school at something like thirty times the rate of the country at large—meant that there came into it a number and variety of students far greater than any system had ever before tried to cope with. There were few or no guideposts, and when the traditional academic subjects proved unsuitable for vast numbers of students, the curriculum was widened to include a thousand watered-down versions of these as well as a thousand new vocational and practi-

[1]*General Education in a Free Society* (Cambridge: Harvard University Press, 1945), pp. 31 –35.

cal subjects. The result was, and is, a parceling, an atomization of the curriculum which, if it reflects the actual variations among students, tends if anything to enhance them by dividing man from man in their basic preparations for life. This tendency has been the stronger because the mechanism whereby the stretching of the curriculum was carried out—the course-unit system—likewise emphasized separateness: both a separateness of subject from subject within the high school as a whole, with the resulting presumption that any combination of subjects makes an equally good education; and a separateness of course from course in any student's program, with the resulting danger that it lack rounded-ness and cohesion. The two sides of the problem thus stand forth clearly: on the one, a need for diversity, even a greater diversity than exists at present in the still largely bookish curriculum, since nothing else will match the actual range of intelligence and background among students; and on the other, a need for some principle of unity, since without it the curriculum flies into pieces and even the studies of any one student are atomic or unbalanced or both.

Jointly these opposite needs evidently point to one solution: a scheme of relationship between subjects which shall be similar for all students yet capable of being differently carried out for different students. Within it there must be place for both special and general education: for those subjects which divide man from man according to their particular functions and for those which unite man and man in their common humanity and citizenship. This scheme, further, should provide a continuing bond of training and outlook not only between all members of the high school but also between the great majority who stop at high school and the minority who go on to college, such that their education should not differ in kind but only in degree. It is this scheme, like our society itself, simple in larger outline yet infinitely varied and complex in detail, which it is the main burden of the following chapters to expound.

The second and outer movement—the vast social transformation which attended the lesser, though still great, transformation of the school system—brought sharply forward the question, what is the school's peculiar function in the entirety of a young person's education? It is often despairingly said that the modern school, being expected, like Atlas, to carry the world, is thereby prevented from carrying on its own true work. The question arises out of the inherent specialism of modern and particularly of city life, which leaves few leisurely reaches where young people learn unconsciously from nature and by watching older people. Nature has retreated, and work is for the most part done away from their gaze (with exceptions, notably the mechanic in a small garage, admirable teacher). Hence this extension of the school's activity has come about less in the country than in the city—which is not to say that country schools, for the most part poor and small, do not have their own serious needs, in turn involving the question of federal support. But in the city, well-to-do communities have in fact shown their belief that the school must find and furnish substitutes for what modern life takes away—athletics to replace work and the mere physical struggle for survival, avocations and handicrafts to replace chores and the skill of doing, even a small community in the school to replace the security of church and village. There is no good in complaining that the school is Atlas. People will not let it cease to be such until more generally benign influences surround the young—influences which, in Plato's charming words, "like a wind breathing health from sound regions, insensibly from earliest childhood lead them to likeness and sympathy with the life of reason." The question, rather, is how the school can furnish such influences to the poor as well as to the well-to-do.

There are unquestionable risks in such an extension of scope, the elephantine growth of athletics, for instance, or, in colleges, the strange flourishing of fraternities. You cannot, it is clear, gather together masses of young people and expect them all to behave like young Aristotles. Young people have always brought with them to school the unsettlements and vapors of adolescence, and now when nearly all go to high school the scope of these unsettlements is multiplied geometrically. It is one thing to have a relatively few students of superior gifts and stable backgrounds; it is another to have the present Babel of gifts and backgrounds. Granting, then, that it is at best not easy for the young to see their way through the mists of feeling, it follows that the school cannot hope to accomplish its proper tasks without allowing for and somehow harnessing these feelings. Hence the only way of escaping the excesses of athletics, cliques, and general anti-intellectualism—these gropings, pathetic or harmful, for outlets which neither the community nor the school otherwise provides—is to recognize what the school legitimately should provide. This recognition in turn brings one face to face with teaching in all its varied phases.

It was argued earlier that the low pay of teaching could not be considered as something apart from the caliber and devotion of those who go into it, and that the one would rise only with the other. If the sufferings of our time have shown anything, they have shown that human beings are not led by economic motives alone but equally by visions, however distorted, of causes to be served. The failures of teaching are not therefore ascribable only to the pay, however cryingly it demands improvement, but to the failure of colleges, teachers' colleges, and the country as a whole to make of teaching the high calling that it must be. But, it was further argued, improvement will also depend on a sound and thoroughgoing democracy in the schools. We understand by democracy the interworking of two complementary forces, the Jeffersonian and the Jacksonian, the one valuing opportunity as the nurse of excellence, the other as the guard of equity. If, therefore, equal opportunity no longer lies in the curriculum alone but also in the wider functions which have been cast on the school by the conditions of modern life, the commands of democracy extend to these as well. All are teachers, and all equally necessary, who give to young people through the curriculum or beyond it the opportunity which makes for completeness of life, and improvement in teaching will depend on this wider vision of who the teacher is.

Are Jeffersonianism and Jacksonianism in fact complementary or do they struggle against each other? Much of our future will be written in the answer to this question. The terms are of course vague and relative. Thus we have criticized the school system as too Jeffersonian, because it gives quite different honor to academic and technical subjects from which students go on to relatively assured futures, from any that it gives to subjects pursued by humbler students. The standard of our education is a strongly middle-class standard, which must disappoint and may embitter those (perhaps half of all the students in the high school) who find themselves cast for another role. Their good is still almost wholly to be discovered. On the other hand, it can equally be said that the high school is Jacksonian, in that it largely fails to find and force the able young person. And the same, as has been noted, applies to outer influences, radio and moving picture, which aim, often calculatingly, at the mass. It has been gloomily said that no man and no society can do two things well at the same time. Certainly the human tendency is so to see one goal as to forget the other, and writers on education have not uncommonly erred with this fault, setting either a standard of culture which coolly neglects the great mass or indulging in a flat and colorless egalitarianism. But the belief that one good is purchasable always and only at the expense of another ultimately goes back to a belief in the natural right of the stronger; it runs counter both to religious faith and to the best experience of civilization. The hope of the American school system, indeed of our society, is precisely that it can pursue two goals simultaneously: give scope to ability and raise the average. Nor are these two goals so far apart, if human beings are capable of common sympathies.

62. Is a Good Education Undemocratic? (1953)[1]

ARTHUR E. BESTOR

The American public school system, like the nation itself, is dedicated to the proposition that all men are created equal. Public education is an effort to carry that principle upward into the most complex and exalted realms of human life, those of the mind and spirit.

"We are told," said William Ellery Channing in 1837, "that this or that man should have an extensive education; but, that another, who occupies a lower place in society, needs only a narrow one: that the governor of a state requires a thorough education, while the humble mechanic has need only to study his last and his leather. But why should not the latter, though pursuing an humble occupation, be permitted to open his eyes on the lights of knowledge? Has he not a soul of as great capacity as the former? Is he not sustaining the same relations as a parent, a citizen, a neighbor, and as a subject of God's moral government?"

Democracy, according to this argument, implies the right of every citizen to develop his intellectual powers to the fullest extent possible. It also assumes that intellectual ability is independent of the accidents of wealth and social position. "The poor man," Channing asserted, "as to his natural capacity, does not differ from others. He is equally susceptible of improvement, and would receive as great advantages as others from a well-bestowed education."

Society itself has a stake in education. American institutions, Channing continued, "are for the common mass of the people; and unless the people are educated, they both lose the benefit of these institutions and weaken their power. Liberty requires that every

---

[1]Arthur E. Bestor, *Educational Wastelands. The Retreat from Learning in Our Public Schools* (Urbana: University of Illinois, 1953), pp. 25 –30, 32 –39. A revised and enlarged edition, entitled *The Restoration of Learning,* was published in 1955 by Alfred A. Knopf, New York.

302

citizen, in order to its proper enjoyment, should have the means of elevation."

Nothing that Channing says suggests that the nature, the quality, or the purpose of education should be altered in the process of extending its privileges to the whole body of citizens. To alter, limit, or debase it, in fact, would be to defeat the very object of democratization. Popular education is designed to endow the people as a whole with precisely the kinds of intellectual power that have hitherto been monopolized by an aristocratic few. "In other countries," Channing pointed out, "the class in power have the principal means of knowledge, and, in order to keep the civil power in their hands, their object is to withhold from others the means of mental improvement. But, according to the genius of our government, education must bring all conditions and classes together," until "society, by its general culture, is raised to a higher state of refinement and happiness."

This is the authentic ideal of American democratic education. It inspired the great educational reformers of the nineteenth century, who strove to create for the United States a "single educational ladder," which rich and poor might climb together. "A Public High School," said Henry Barnard in 1848, "is not . . . a public or common school in the sense of being cheap, inferior, ordinary. . . . It must make a good education common in the highest and best sense of the word common—common because it is good enough for the best, and cheap enough for the poorest family in the community."

Today, however, many public school administrators and professors of education are repudiating the position taken by these founders of our public school system. A school which concentrates its effort upon intellectual training, they assert, is an aristocratic school. The views that I am expressing in this book are accordingly said to have "a 'class' character." This curious line of argument can be summed up as follows: Because intellectual training was once monopolized by an aristocracy, it retains its aristocratic character even when extended to the masses of men. To so extend it would be to undermine democracy.

Now it is perfectly true that in a stratified society the only individuals who can hope to receive sound training in the sciences, mathematics, history, and languages—the only ones who can cultivate a knowledge and appreciation of literature, philosophy, and the arts—are those who belong to the aristocratic or wealthy classes. It is equally true, let us remember, that the only persons in such a society who can live in warm and comfortable houses, who can eat and dress well, who can travel freely, and who can enjoy leisure time are men of means or of aristocratic birth. Does it follow from this that democratic housing ought to be drafty and cramped, that a democratic diet should be meagre, that democratic clothing should be shabby and mean, that in a democracy men ought not to have automobiles or time in which to drive them?

In America we have attempted to furnish to every man and woman the advantages and opportunities that were once enjoyed only by an aristocracy. We have supposed that in doing so we were *building* a democratic society, not *undermining* it. The test we have accepted of our achievement in spreading democracy is whether we have given to the many the things that none but the few could once possess.

Why should intellectual values be the exception to this rule? If a privileged class once monopolized for itself the kind of education we call liberal, we are not perpetuating aristocracy but destroying it if we make the same education available to all the people. The way to perpetuate aristocracy is to give sound intellectual training to a minority and to offer the people generally a cheap and shoddy substitute. In a society where only the upper classes can ride, a carriage or an automobile is a symbol of aristocracy. In a society where the masses of men can afford the means of transportation, a crowded parking lot is a symbol of democracy. Now a personal library of good books is a symbol also. If only a few possess and can use one, we have a "class" society. When every family possesses and can use one, we have a democratic society.

Whether our intellectual life is in reality democratic or aristocratic depends on whether the masses of the people, or only a select minority, are reading mature books and handling complex ideas and revealing a profound comprehension of history and science and the arts. The school is not creating a democratic structure of intellectual life merely by gathering all the nation's children within its walls. It becomes an agency of true democratization only if it sends them forth with knowledge, cultural appreciation, and disciplined intellectual power—with the qualities, in other words, that have always distinguished educated men from uneducated ones.

To create a truly democratic cultural and intellectual life is a tremendously difficult task. It requires an organization of economic life so efficient that children can be released from toil and adults can enjoy abundant leisure. This we have at last achieved in the United States. It also requires heavy and continuing expenditures for school buildings, for teachers, and for a host of administrative and auxiliary services. The American people have shown their willingness to underwrite these costs. The preconditions necessary for a democratic school system have been met. But we shall never create a genuinely democratic intellectual and cultural life if, as victory comes almost within our grasp, we repudiate the very purposes we set out to achieve.

When present-day educationists assert that the ideal of rigorous intellectual training throughout the public schools is a false or unattainable ideal, they are taking (whether they realize it or not) precisely the position that was occupied a century ago by the *opponents* of public education. Let us re-examine briefly the traditional anti-democratic arguments against mass education.

Partisans of an aristocratic philosophy of education in the early nineteenth century insisted that literature, philosophy, history, mathematics, science, art, and foreign languages were of concern only to an élite class. Disciplined intellectual training should be reserved for the minority who planned to do advanced study and to enter the learned professions. Such training would be beyond the grasp of the ordinary man, and would be utterly useless to him. The common man should receive only such an education as would fit him for a trade, furnish him with a rudimentary skill in reading, writing, and arithmetic, and give him some helpful guidance, moral, practical, and miscellaneous, in adjusting himself to the way of life he was destined to live. To offer to the masses of men an education which went beyond their immediate practical and personal needs would be futile and wasteful. The common man would see no purpose in it. He would not put the requisite effort into acquiring it. If compelled to master the great intellectual disciplines, he would not appreciate them. He could not use them. And the few who might try to do so would thereby unfit themselves for their practical callings and for a happy life in the station to which society might assign them. . . .

The great American educational reformers committed themselves, in both argument and action, to the view that genuine education, in the sense of intellectual training, was both appropriate and valuable for the common man. They were not inventing something new to which they applied the old and honored name

305

of education. They understood by education what had always been understood by education. They believed in it, and they were anxious that its unquestioned powers should be the possession of every citizen. These democratic writers differed from their aristocratic opponents not because they defined education differently, but because they proposed, quite simply, to make this kind of education available to the many instead of confining it to the few. . . .

In all his efforts for American public education, Horace Mann revealed his fundamental belief in "the inherent superiority of any association or community, whether small or great, where *mind* is a member of the partnership." In every realm of human activity, he asserted, "improvement has advanced in proportion to the number and culture of the minds excited to activity and applied to the work. . . . Succeeding generations have outstripped their predecessors, just in proportion to the superiority of their mental cultivation."

The ideal of Horace Mann, I believe, is as valid today as it was when he set it forth in his great series of reports in the 1830's and 1840's. The need for the kind of education he described is even greater in the complex twentieth-century world than in the relatively simple and relatively peaceful era in which he wrote. The wealth of the nation and the physical facilities of the American school system are far more adequate to the work than there was any hope of their becoming during his lifetime. If we devote ourselves wholeheartedly to the task, I see no reason why the American educational system cannot raise the intellectual and cultural level of the entire nation to as great a height as any people have been able to reach. To do so we must recapture the belief both in democracy and in education that animated the founders of our public schools.

We must remember, at all times, that education is concerned with *improvement*. It undertakes to change a man or a woman from what he or she *is* to what he or she might be and ought to be. Educational policy in a democracy is directed toward *raising* the intellectual standards of the people, just as economic policy is directed toward raising their standard of living. Poverty and ignorance were the lot of the common man in the past. The elimination, not the perpetuation, of poverty and ignorance is the mission of democracy.

To say this is not to cast a slur upon democracy. If the common man has been ignorant in the past, it is because he has never been offered an opportunity to learn. If he has been indifferent to intellectual effort, it is because he has never been shown its value. These shortcomings have not been his fault, but they are nonetheless shortcomings. They are not attitudes and qualities to be accepted and respected. They are characteristics which an educational system is designed to destroy.

Educators may not take popular indifference to intellectual training as a mandate to guide them in the discharge of their public duties. Their mandate is the opposite. They are professionally obligated to oppose anti-intellectualism, no matter how powerful a majority it may command. Democracy does not require of its servants the abdication of professional responsibility. Every professional man has the duty—the democratic duty—of seeking to guide public opinion not of succumbing to it. A public health officer may not pronounce polluted water safe when he discovers that his community is unwilling to pay for a proper filtration plant. His duty is to take a bacterial count, not a public-opinion poll, and to explain clearly what it signifies, whether the community likes the conclusion or not. So it is with the educator. If the community prefers trivia to sound learning in its schools, the educator cannot compel it to choose otherwise. But he has the solemn duty of pointing out with absolute clarity that training in trivia is not education and cannot produce the results that the community expects to derive from its educational investment.

Democratic education differs from aristocratic education in terms of the persons it deals with, not in terms of the values it seeks to impart. One of the most dangerous fallacies propagated today by certain groups of professional educationists is the assertion that intellectual training, while "functional" in an aristocratic society, is not "functional" for the citizen of a democratic state. This argument overlooks the fundamental fact that when a government of the few is transformed into a government of the many, the functions of an aristocracy become the functions of citizens at large. What the few once needed, the many now need. The constituency of the school changes, but not its basic purposes. The men who govern a nation must be informed and intelligent, whether the governors be the few or the many. Science is a source of power, whatever be the organization of the state. Literature, philosophy, and the arts are measures of the greatness of a civilization, be it aristocratic or democratic. The question in any society is how to produce these universally valued qualities of mind in the group of young people—whether they comprise a small number or a large—which it chooses to educate. Intellectual training itself is "functional" to any civilized and organized society, not just to an aristocratic one.

A variant of this fallacy asserts that intellectual training is "functional" in the life of an individual member of an aristocracy but not in the life of an individual citizen in a democracy. This involves a most curious assumption about the life of an aristocrat. Are we to suppose that a country gentleman needs to know Greek in order to collect his rents? Does a nobleman owe his social position to his learning rather than his birth? Does a young man, because he is well born, rush to grammar and mathematics as a lover to the arms of his mistress? Is the life of an aristocratic society so austere that it offers no dissipations that might distract a wealthy young blade from his books?

If we think about the matter, how absurd this argument turns out to be! Intellectual and cultural pursuits are of no more "practical" value to a nobleman than to a commoner. *Every* member of the race has the same great *humane* reason for wishing to cultivate his highest powers. And if "practical" reasons are needed, it is actually the democratic society, rather than the aristocratic one, which furnishes them. Recollect that it is not the aristocrat, but the man without inherited advantages, whose social position and income depend upon his education. The latter has the truer need for intellectual training and potentially the stronger motive for intellectual exertion.

If certain aristocratic societies have been distinguished for literature, art, and philosophy, it is because those societies have deliberately cultivated a regard for such values, in and for themselves. It is a mistake to assume that the intellectual and cultural tradition of an aristocracy was created without effort. Education is a serious business in any society, and it requires serious and sustained effort on the part of any man, whatever his birth. The ruling classes of the past began as quasi-barbaric military chieftains. They were slowly and painfully disciplined, through centuries of time, before they acquired that respect for cultural and intellectual values which we sometimes assume was inborn in them. They perpetuated that tradition by rigorous self-discipline, and by steadily directed effort in the education of each new generation. Any society can do this. And the ruling classes of the present—the people as a whole—must adopt similar means if they are to preserve their own civilization against decay and destruction.

I am not seeking to minimize the difficulty of giving to the children of all the people the intellectual and cultural background that belonged in the past only to those brought up in surroundings of opulence, leisure, and privilege. I am merely asserting that to do this was precisely the task which a democratic educational system assumed. And I am insisting that the school must devote its resources wholeheartedly to this end, for to do otherwise would be to betray the very ideal which created it.

We must, in particular, guard against the danger of confusing lack of cultural background with lack of intellectual ability. These are distinctly different matters. Much is made of the fact that the students in an aristocratic school system were a selected group, while those in the American public schools of today are not. But much of the force of this argument vanishes once one recognizes the fact that the aristocratic few were selected for reasons totally unconnected with intellectual capacity. Inherited wealth and social position are no guarantees of mental ability. The school-master in an aristocratic society has the problem of individual differences thrust upon him just as truly as the teacher of a country school. There is no reason whatever for assuming that the schools of today have a smaller proportion of students of high innate ability, merely because they are drawing more students from families low on the income scale. To assert that intellectual capacity decreases as one reaches down into lower economic levels of the population is to deny, point-blank, the basic assumptions of democratic equalitarianism.

Within any given class of the population, there are *individual* differences. But as democratic educators we have no right and no reason to assume that there are *class* differences in intellectual ability as well. The student from a wealthy home does differ from the student whose family lives on the edge of poverty. But this is not a matter of innate intellectual ability; it is a difference of background, pure and simple. One child will probably have read many books, the other few or none. One will have caught glimpses of the larger world of thought and art—through discussion, through travel, through intelligent parental guidance. The other may have been deprived of all these advantages. Environment, not inherited capacity, is responsible for the difference. And the effects of environment are effects we can do something to cure—in

309

the long run by altering the environment, in the short run by remedying the deficiencies which the environment has produced.

What is the duty of the school in this situation? The answer ought to be clear. It must make up, so far as it is able, the deficiencies of background which it finds in its students. Both in the short run and in the long, the democratic school must concentrate, as never before, upon the task of intellectual training. Intellectual effort must be made the central, inspiring ideal of the school's life. The intellectual seriousness missing in the home must be deliberately cultivated in the schoolroom. The important books must be read there. Fundamental problems must be *studied,* not merely talked about. The basic scientfic and scholarly disciplines must be presented, not as mere repositories of information, but as systematic ways of thinking, each with an organized structure and methodology of its own. The student who has been deprived of intellectual and cultural background at home must receive full restitution in the school.

The public schools of today possess many resources that can be effectively devoted to this end. They make use of buildings, equipment, books, and teaching aids far more costly, varied, and efficient than those available to the wealthiest schools of the aristocratic past. They bring the average child under academic discipline for a longer span of time than that usually devoted to formal education by the privileged youths of former ages. Knowledge of the psychology of learning has greatly increased. If properly and intelligently applied in teaching, it is capable of arousing an interest in intellectual and cultural matters among persons who were beyond the reach of the cruder pedagogy of earlier days.

What seems to be lacking is a faith in the value of intellectual endeavor among those who are making American educational policy. Restore that faith, and I believe that American schools can provide the overwhelming majority of our children with the kind of disciplined education which this book describes. To those of lower mental ability, special treatment must be accorded. Most of them, I believe, can be brought at a slower pace along the same route. As before, what is necessary is faith in the value and importance of the end in view, even if incompletely attained. For those completely beyond intellectual salvation, I grant that the school must offer something completely different. But the question of what that training should be is, in my judgment, a matter to be deferred until such time as the public schools shall have made a far more determined effort than any they are currently making to guide and direct the masses of American children along the path of genuine liberal education. I suspect that fewer will fall by the wayside than most educationists assume.

To accomplish these high ends, the school must transmit to the public at large, not merely to its own students, a respect for knowledge and cultural achievement. If we are to have an intellectual life that is both democratic and worthy of democracy, the school must uphold for all men the ideal of disciplined intellectual effort. In a manifesto published some years ago, an eminent American educator asked the question "Dare the school build a new social order?" I would answer in the affirmative, but in a somewhat different sense from the author. The American public school was created to build a new social order, a social order in which intellectual training would be offered without discrimination to every citizen, in which respect for the highest cultural values would be universal, in which every man would be expected to bring trained intelligence to bear on personal and public problems, and in which scientific and scholarly effort would be so valued that assaults upon intellectual freedom would be impossible. Only the school can build this kind of social order. This is its great task in a democracy.

The American people, to their eternal credit, accepted this ideal, which the founders of our public school system held up to them. As a people they labored to carry the implications of the democratic philosophy from politics into ever wider areas of national life. In their ideal of equal opportunity, the life of the mind was included. Americans valued democracy too highly to believe for a moment that a democratic society had to be inferior in any respect to societies otherwise constituted. To them democracy was not a sacrifice but an enlargement of values. Equality of opportunity did not mean its diminution. The *opponents* of the American experiment were the ones who said that men would have to choose between democracy and literary cultivation, between democracy and scientific eminence, between democracy and intelligently conducted government. To the American people, however, democracy was perfectly compatible with the highest scientific, scholarly, and artistic achievement.

When Americans, a century or so ago, committed themselves to the ideal of universal democratic education, they were not thinking in terms of the trivia that fascinate many present-day educationists. They did not intend, by making education universal, to debase and destroy it. They were not seeking to water down the great tradition of disciplined and liberal study. They were undertaking the heroic task of raising an entire nation to the highest attainable level of intellectual competence.

Liberal education, they believed, was not and should not be the exclusive prerogative of the aristocratic few. Even the humblest man, whatever his trade, was capable of a liberal education. In a democracy he was entitled to it. His intellectual horizon should not be limited, as it had been for the lower classes in times gone by, to his occupation and to the routine details of his everyday life. He should receive training for his occupation, true. But far more important than that, he should be given the opportunity to develop his mind to the fullest extent possible. He should be given command of the intellectual resources that had once been the badge—and one of the principal bulwarks—of aristocracy. His mind furnished with the knowledge and disciplined to the strength that had made the old ruling classes great and powerful, the American freeman would be in a position to rule himself. And the civilization he built would be a humane and magnificent civilization because it would offer to every man not only equality before the law, not only the right to vote and to work, but, most precious of all, the opportunity to develop through liberal education his own highest qualities of manhood.

Let us never be satisfied with less.

CHAPTER 24

FEDERAL AID AND STATES' RIGHTS

To guarantee decent standards of education to every citizen.

Theodore Brameld, 1952

63. States' Rights and Education (1957)[1]

R. FREEMAN BUTTS

We Americans have traditionally had the comfortable feeling that education is above and beyond politics, but we can no longer escape the clear fact that education keeps pushing itself insistently and uncomfortably into the center of public attention. It is now in the middle of politics as it has never been before.

This fact should not be startling to those who have kept abreast of developments in American life and education during the post-war period, but the uncertainty, confusion, and controversy surrounding education have been highlighted in recent months and they promise to be in the center of the stage in the months ahead.

In July, 1956, the Federal aid to education bill was defeated in the House of Representatives after a complicated parliamentary debate in which segregation, civil rights, religion, and the private-school issue were all mixed up with partisan politics and economy drives.

The Supreme Court recessed for the summer under bitter attack for infringing on states' rights in its decisions on desegregation in schools and on sedition procedures in the states. Manifestoes by Southern Senators and Representatives called for curbs on the Supreme Court, maintenance of segregated schools, and opposition to civil-rights legislation. The Administration's civil-rights bill died in the closing week of Congress, to the evident relief of some members of both parties.

On the other hand, civil-rights groups hammered away at both parties with demands for stronger civil-rights planks in their platforms for the campaign—and education was their chief concern.

The Democratic nominees for President and Vice President criticized the Eisenhower Administration for a weak stand on desegregation in the schools and supported the Supreme Court's

---

[1]*Teachers College Record*, Vol. 58 (Jan. 1957), 189–97. Butts is Professor of Education and Director of International Studies, Teachers College, Columbia.

decision, but the Southern delegations at both conventions tried to soften the civil-rights pledges, and with some success.

In the course of the political campaign each presidential candidate tried to fasten upon the other party responsibility for killing Federal aid in the previous session of Congress. Both candidates dealt with education as an issue of high priority in their domestic programs. With the opening of the new session of Congress in January, education is bound to reappear upon the national political stage with renewed intensity.

To make matters worse, our domestic record of confusion and uncertainty is now a matter of international concern. Some months ago, when a prominent Soviet educator challenged the United States to a competition in the field of education, *The New York Times* reported that there was no United States reponse to the Soviet suggestion.

At a time when America's status in the world may well depend on our educational, cultural, and economic policies as well as our military and diplomatic relations with other countries, it behooves the American people to become very clear about public decisions in education and politics. Moreover, what we decide in the near future may determine for years to come the fate of the American public-school system and, indeed, the nature of American society itself.

With the world's eyes on us, we face these four inflammatory educational issues: desegregation in the public schools, the relation of private and public schools, the role of religion in education, and Federal aid to education. My main point is that these four issues are interlocked and must be viewed as parts of a single problem. What we decide regarding one will have serious repercussions for the others. Together, these four bitterly fought issues add up to one of the central political questions of our time: What are the rights of the states with respect to education? Unless we answer this question definitely and conscientiously, in accordance with the best of our traditions, we will only contribute to the confusion and uncertainty.

STATES' RIGHTS AND SEGREGATION IN SCHOOLS

Racial segregation in American schools dates from a time when some states prohibited the instruction of Negroes or required that they be taught in separate schools. An early challenge to separate schools for Negro and white children arose when the case of Roberts *vs.* City of Boston came up in the Supreme Court of Massachusetts in 1849. Charles Sumner argued that separate schools for Negroes violated the Massachusetts Constitution's declaration that all men are born free and equal and have certain natural, essential, and unalienable rights. The court, however, decided that the races should be segregated and that schools could be separate yet equal.

This "separate but equal" doctrine was later affirmed by the United States Supreme Court in Plessy *vs.* Ferguson in 1896. During the past twenty years the Supreme Court, applying the Fourteenth Amendment, has required several states to provide equal facilities for Negroes in institutions of higher education, but in doing so the Court did not disturb the basic doctrine.

Finally, in 1954, when the Supreme Court faced squarely the "separate but equal" doctrine, it just as squarely rejected it on the grounds that separate educational facilities are inherently unequal and deprive Negro children of equal educational opportunity. Segregated school systems were thus declared unconstitutional under the injunction that no state could deny to any person the equal protection of the law guaranteed by the Fourteenth Amendment. This means that Federal authority can limit the powers of the states over education when the principle of *equality* is involved.

Now, several of the Southern states are trying desperately to find ways to avoid or nullify the Supreme Court's ruling. Some states have started procedures to abolish their public school systems, to create private corporations that may continue segregation, and to give public funds to these corporations to carry out their purposes. The idea of a free private-school system has thus been designed to replace the American tradition of a free public-school system.

In 1956 Virginia, for example, amended its Constitution so that local school districts might decide for themselves what to do about segregation. If a district wished to abolish its public schools, it could do so, and the state would pay the tuition of all children to attend private and segregated schools. If, on the other hand, a district wanted to maintain desegregated public schools, it could do so, but those parents who wished to receive state funds to aid their children to attend private, segregated schools were entitled to them.

It is interesting to note what was involved in the court case which led to the amendment of Virginia's Constitution. In November, 1955, the Supreme Court of Virginia, in Almond *vs.* Day, ruled that under Virginia's Constitution as it then stood, the state could *not* pay tuition or maintenance grants for children to attend private schools.

Here was a case brought on by the *private-school* issue. Most of the winning argument rested on a historical analysis of the religious and *church-state* issue. The real but unstated purpose, however, was to avoid *desegregation,* and the question of *Federal aid* was in the background. This illustrates precisely my main thesis: that all four of these educational issues are now closely interrelated and must be considered as part of one problem.

If we permit the use of public funds to establish free private schools to maintain segregation, we will destroy our ideal of a genuinely free and equal system of common schools open freely and equally to all children, irrespective of race, color, creed, or national origin. The common, or public school, has been part of the American tradition for the past one hundred years. If we try to maintain the separation of children according to race, by dividing them among private or sectarian schools, we run the risk of creating still greater divisions among us along class or religious lines.

STATES' RIGHTS AND PRIVATE AND PUBLIC SCHOOLS

The first colonial laws in Massachusetts, in 1642 and 1647, stated the principle that education of children was necessary for the benefit of the commonwealth and the church. The church was included because it was then considered part of government, as established by law.

These early laws expressed the view that parents were *not* free to let their children go uneducated, but that government had the right to set up schools or exert its authority to provide the education that would protect the state from mischief as well as benefit the individual.

Private schools, as we know them in the United States today, generally appeared from fifty to one hundred years *after* town-supported schools and government-licensed teachers were in the field. The eighteenth century, not the seventeenth, witnessed their real growth. These schools, whose corporate existence con-

tinues beyond the lifetime of a single teacher or owner, are creatures of the state. They derive their powers and rights by delega-
tion of authority from the state in their corporate charters. After all,
the state grants the authority by which a private, corporate school
teaches. It is not the private corporation or a church that grants the
state the right to conduct schools.

Today the Federal Government has limited the power of the
states over private schools. This limitation was first defined in the
Dartmouth College case in 1819. In that case, the Supreme Court
ruled that the State of New Hampshire could not alter the corporate charter of Dartmouth College and change the College from a
private to a public corporation, because its charter was a contract
whose obligation could not be impaired by the state under the
United States Constitution.

The Dartmouth College case is thus properly taken as a charter
of freedom for private, corporate educational institutions. But too
little attention has been paid to the fact that this case asserted that
if "the funds of the college be public property," then the state
legislature *could* have exerted control over Dartmouth College.

Perhaps the private-school people who today want public
funds for their own use, but do not want state control, should look
at this case again. I believe it means at least this—where public
funds go, public control may follow.

It will be well to keep the decisions in two other historic cases
in mind—Meyer *v.* Nebraska, in 1923, and the Oregon Case,
in 1925. These are taken to mean, and properly so, that parents
may have a say in the education and upbringing of their children.

The most famous passage in the Oregon Case is this:

> The fundamental theory of liberty under which all
> governments in this Union repose excludes any general
> power of the State to standardize its children by forcing
> them to accept instruction from public teachers only.
> The child is not the mere creature of the State; those
> who nurture him and direct his destiny have the right,
> coupled with the high duty, to recognize and prepare
> him for additional obligations.

Perhaps a prior passage in the Oregon Case should now become equally famous:

> No question is raised concerning the power of the
> State reasonably to regulate *all* schools, to inspect, su-
> pervise and examine them, their teachers and pupils; to

require that all children of proper age attend *some* school, that teachers shall be of good moral character and patriotic disposition, that certain studies plainly essential to good citizenship must be taught, and that nothing be taught which is manifestly inimical to the public welfare.

The decision in Meyer *v.* Nebraska had earlier been even more definite on the point that no challenge had been made of "the states' power to prescribe a curriculum for institutions which it supports."

So Dartmouth, Meyer, and Oregon all set limits on the states' powers over purely private schools. The states cannot eliminate qualified private teachers or abolish private schools, and they cannot require all children to attend public schools. I believe this is a wise and sound part of our tradition. But I think these cases can also be read to mean that if the states *support* private schools, they take on one vital characteristic of public schools and *can* then be controlled by the state. Their teachers, their curriculum, and their facilities can be regulated, supervised, inspected, and examined by the state. If the private schools be religious schools, and most of them are, we then face the problem of the separation of church and state.

STATES' RIGHTS IN RELIGION AND EDUCATION

A key issue in recent years has been the meaning of the clause in the First Amendment which reads: "Congress shall make no law respecting an establishment of religion." Many have contended that this simply means that there shall be no single established church in the nation, but that the Federal Government and state governments may cooperate with all churches on a non-discriminatory basis.

The proponents of this point of view hold that no special privilege or preference can be given to one church or religion, but if all churches and all religions are treated fairly and equally, then the states may aid the churches, either by financial support for their religious schools or by helping them to promote religion in general through the public schools.

Others have argued that our historic tradition means that the Federal and state governments must be separated from the churches to the extent that government may not aid one church, several churches, or all churches, even though all are treated equally. The state as a civil agency must remain neutral with respect to religion in general as well as with respect to any specific religion.

My own reading of history is something like this. For nearly one hundred and fifty years, from the latter part of the eighteenth century to the early twentieth century, there was a fairly recognizable and steady movement away from state-established religion toward separation of church and state. By the beginning of the twentieth century, this movement to protect religious freedom included two widely agreed-upon principles: first, that public funds should not be used to aid religious schools, and, second, that there should be minimum attention to religious instruction or observance in the public schools.

Before 1950, the Supreme Court, in the Everson and McCollum cases, accepted the historical interpretation which I believe to be accurate: that the principle of separation widely prohibited the states from giving financial aid to religious schools or promoting religion through the public schools.

The Court has made an exception in the case of public funds for free textbooks and transportation of children to parochial schools by bus. The grounds for these exceptions are that these services are simply public-welfare benefits to which all children are entitled.

In the last half dozen years, however, the argument for greater cooperation between church and state has gone through a subtle change. The dominant argument for cooperation now rests on a generalized historical assumption that "We are a religious people," or "We are a religious nation," or "Our institutions presuppose a Supreme Being." It is therefore argued that it is legitimate for public education, as an agency of the state, to promote a generalized belief in God.

I believe it is an unwarranted leap of logic and of history to say that *because* we are a religious people or a religious nation, *therefore* our *government* rests on religion.

Let us look again at the Zorach case, hailed by some religious groups as a change of heart by the Supreme Court because it permitted released-time religious instruction outside schoolbuildings in New York City. To be sure, Justice Douglas said in the decision, "We are a religious people whose institutions presuppose a Supreme Being." But he also distinguished between "we as a people" and "we as a government" when he said, "Government may not finance religous groups nor undertake religious instruction nor blend secular and sectarian instruction or use secular institutions to force one or *some* religion on any person."

This surely defines government and public schools as secular institutions, and Douglas said further that government must be neutral. "It may not thrust any sect on any person," he wrote. "It may not make a religious observance compulsory." And he added that it may not coerce or persuade students to "take religious instruction." In view of this, can we possibly use the schools to encourage belief in God or promote religion among the people without persuading students to take religious instruction? I think not.

If the states cannot promote religion, what shall we say of *Federal* funds for the states? Can Federal funds be used by the states to promote religion, or aid private schools, or maintain segregated schools? I believe not.

STATES' RIGHTS AND FEDERAL GOVERNMENT

Our traditional assumption has been that education should be under state control, rather than Federal control. This is a long and commonly accepted tradition. It is one of our strongest assurances against the potential excesses, uniformities, and rigidities of a highly centralized system of education for the whole country.

There is wide agreement that the failure of the Constitution to specify education as a power of the Federal government reserves education to the states, or to the people, under the Tenth Amendment. The states have certainly acted on this principle, for in time every state has put in its Constitution provisions that require the legislature to establish and maintain a public school system. The body of court decisions raises no substantial question about the rights of states to undertake the educational enterprise as an integral function of state government.

But now two extraordinarily important questions arise. The first is this: Granted that the states have the right to conduct public school systems, are they free, in every and all respects, to conduct their public school systems as they see fit? The answer is now clearly No. The states do not have unlimited power over education within their jurisdiction. The states' power over education is limited in those arenas where the Federal Government has power to protect the *liberty* and promote the *equality* of all persons in the United States.

The Federal Government acquires this power from the First and Fourteenth Amendments to the United States Constitution: Neither the Federal Government nor state governments can deprive any person of life, *liberty* or property without due process of law, nor deny him the *equal* protection of the law. This limit on the rights and powers of the states in educational matters, then, has had to do principally with the three questions of segregated, private, and religious schools.

The second question is: Can the states legally abolish their public school systems? This question is important for obvious reasons. The fate of our public-school system is now at stake as some Southern states threaten to interpose their powers between the Federal Government and the people of their states to avoid the Supreme Court's order to end segregation in their public schools.

Some of the states are now saying, "If we can't conduct our public schools in the way we wish, we won't have any public schools at all."

Must a state operate a public-school system for its people? *Can* a state abolish something it has the *right* to maintain, but no longer *wishes* to maintain? Does a state have the *obligation* to conduct a public-school system as an essential function of its very nature as a government?

If a state can abolish its public-school system by amending its Constitution, what other governmental functions can it abolish? Its parliamentary forms? Its free elections? Its courts? Its police? Are public schools as essential to a free government as these other functions, without which it is no longer a free government? These and similar questions are as fundamental to our political theory and practice as any I can think of.

Here again, I believe we must look at the obligations as well as the rights of states with respect to education. Here again, we need to re-examine the United States Constitution to see what obligations the Federal Government may lay on the states with respect to what they *should* do to promote freedom and equality, as well as the things that they *cannot* do, lest they infringe on freedom and equality.

Can we say, for example, that the guarantees of liberty and

equality in the First and Fourteenth Amendments can be interpreted to mean that the Federal courts or Congress can require the states to maintain public education if we are to protect and promote liberty and equality in our society? I hope so, but this raises serious questions relating to the means by which such requirements could be enforced.

Or, what about Article 4, Section IV, of the Constitution, which reads, "The United States shall guarantee to every State in the Union a republican form of government?" Can this be interpreted to mean that the Federal Government can require the states to maintain public school systems, without which they are no longer republican in form?

Historically, we can show clearly that the founders of the public-school systems, in the nineteenth century, argued well that a republican government *did* require a public-school system if it were to promote freedom and equality. The states accepted this view when they incorporated public-school systems into their constitutional structures.

But what if the states now decide to go back and repudiate their historic tradition? Can the Federal Government say to the states, "Oh, no you don't. This is an irrevocable commitment, and Article 4 obligates Congress and the Federal courts to see that you do not take this step"?

Again, I hope so, but even if the legal question were clear, the problem of political and moral enforcement would remain. It should be remembered here that Congress has already required all states admitted to the Union since 1876 to make irrevocable provisions in their constitutions for a system of public schools, free from sectarian control.

I do not pretend to know the final answer to these questions, and some constitutional lawyers say that they are purely academic, not subject to judicial interpretation, but I think the problem is now so important that we should be aware of the range of alternatives.

If the issue comes to a showdown, and I hope that it does not, we can simply say, at one extreme, that the principle of states' rights permits the states to abolish their public schools, for the Federal Government has no power to prevent it. Or, at the other extreme, we can amend the United States Constitution, giving Congress clear power to require the states to maintain public schools. Or, we can give to Congress, by amendment or statute, the power to establish a Federal system of public schools wherever

323

they are not genuinely maintained by the states, as was proposed in the nineteenth century. These alternatives do not sound very likely or palatable.

I believe it would be better if the Constitution, as it stands, could be interpreted by the courts to mean that the states cannot legally abolish their public-school systems. I believe it would be still better for all concerned if the people of the states and of the nation could be persuaded that our historic traditions should be honored and that all the states should and must maintain public-school systems based on liberty and equality.

As a step toward clarifying our national policy and achieving common agreement, I propose that the following principles should be the basis for solving the problems of states' rights and education:

1. States have the right and power to establish public schools, but this right is limited by the Federal Constitutional concern for liberty and equality.

The principle of liberty requires that public schools must be free of sectarian religious control and must not promote sectarian religion; even the effort to promote religion in general is a threat to the religious freedom of some. Public schools should not be hostile toward religion in particular, nor should they promote religion in general.

The principle of equality requires that public schools do not discriminate against or segregate pupils on the basis of race, creed, religion, or national origin. In other words, public schools must be common schools, freely and equally available to all.

2. States cannot create a monopoly for public education by destroying private schools, nor can they create a monopoly for private schools by undermining or destroying their own public schools.

The principle of freedom works both ways: properly approved private schools are free to exist and parents are free to send their children to them; public schools must be maintained by the states to give a common, free, and equal education to all.

3. States can and must have the right to support public schools by general taxation to assure that a good education is available freely and equally to all.

But states should not have the right to use public funds to support segregated, private, or religious schools, either directly by grants to the schools themselves, or indirectly by grants to pupils or parents as aid in attending such schools. Once financial grants

324

by the states are made to private schools for *some* purposes, there is no reasonable place to stop—short of undermining the public schools themselves. Undermining or abolishing our public-school system contributes to undermining representative government itself.

4. States can and should have the right to exert considerable control over their public-school systems, but our experience has shown that it is desirable for the states to delegate considerable freedom and initiative to local school units in the actual day-to-day management of schools.

Our experience has also shown that equality of opportunity can be jeopardized by delegating too much freedom to local districts to do as they please. The states must therefore exert over-all authority to preserve freedom and achieve equality of opportunity throughout a state.

States also have considerable power to exercise control and supervision over private schools, but our experience again has shown that such control should be kept to the minimum necessary to guarantee that private schools serve the principles of freedom and equality and meet minimum educational standards. Granting public funds to private schools would warrant state control of private schools.

5. The Federal Government does not have the right to exert direct control over state schools except to protect the principles of freedom and equality, as already indicated. On the other hand, our experience shows that, while the Federal Government does not have the right to manage state school systems, it does have the right and power to give financial support to the states for their public schools, to enable them more fully to enhance the liberty and the equality of educational opportunity in the nation as a whole. Federal aid should not go to segregated, private, or religious schools for the same reasons that state aid should not go to such schools.

These principles, I believe, point to the best of our historic traditions of states' rights in education and give fair guidance for the fulfillment of our highest aspirations for a democratic society based on freedom and equality.

These are principles we could be proud to proclaim to the world as distinctively American. With full faith and confidence in their right and justice, we could welcome educational competition from any source.

64. Arguments For and Against Federal Aid (1956)[1]

THREE CONGRESSMEN

CONGRESSMAN JOHN McCORMACK OF MASSACHUSETTS

I am impressed by the convincing evidence that our public schools need more classrooms. Many schools in almost every part of the United States are overcrowded; others are obsolete and should be replaced by modern, safe school buildings; new schools are needed everywhere to take care of the thousands and thousands of babies born during the past decade.

I am dismayed to hear some people talk about our high birthrate as though it were a calamity. There is too much talk about the crisis in our schools, the desperate need for teachers, the horrible shortage of classrooms. These sad cries of alarm and disaster should stop. There is no sense to such thought or argument.

These children are a blessing of God upon our Nation. To provide good schools for them is not a backbreaking burden; it is a grand and wonderful opportunity and privilege to be able to prepare them for good citizenship in our great Nation.

This is no time to wring our hands in fretful worry about the cost of education. This is the time to roll up our sleeves and get to work on new schools. Every penny spent for education is a solid investment in the future of our Nation. In a Nation as wealthy as ours pennypinching with regard to education has no place.

The American people want good schools and are willing to pay the price. Time and time again they have voted for increases in their taxes for educational purposes. They expect the Federal Government to help out whenever this is necessary to guarantee a child a reasonable opportunity for a decent education. Across the whole Nation there is widespread support and enthusiasm for the legislation before us.

---

[1]*Congressional Record.* 84th Congress, House of Representatives, 102:9 (July 5, 1956), pp. 11843–47. The Kelley Education Bill was being debated.

Today I want to pay particular tribute to some people whose generous support of education in our country is frequently overlooked or even ignored. I refer to the parents and guardians of children attending private and parochial schools. I also refer to those religious groups which operate the parochial schools which so many of us appreciate and admire.

At their own expense these good people now provide excellent grade and high schools for about 4,400,000 pupils. At least 12 percent of the Nation's schoolchildren attend private and parochial schools. Three million, nine hundred thousand of these children are enrolled in the parochial schools of the Catholic Church.

In Massachusetts, 23 percent of the children attend private and parochial schools; in Rhode Island, 28 percent; in New Hampshire, 25 percent; in New York, 25 percent; in New Jersey, 21 percent; in Pennsylvania, 20 percent; in Illinois, 22 percent.

In these States as in every other State, private and parochial schools are an essential part of our educational enterprise. Without them the public schools today would be burdened to a much greater degree. In many places it would be impossible for our crowded public schools to accommodate even a small part of the thousands of children in private and parochial schools. These schools, therefore, are an indispensable part of the Nation's school system. We simply could not get along without them.

These private and parochial schools save the Nation's taxpayers a tremendous sum of money. Using a conservative estimate, I would say these schools are saving the taxpayers at least $1,210,-000,000 maintenance and operating costs a year, money which would be added to our tax bills if the children in private and parochial schools had to be accommodated in public schools. Imagine the increase in taxes if all the private and parochial schoolchildren in States like New York, Massachusetts, California, and Illinois—to name a few—were transferred to public schools. These are facts we ought to remember when we talk about spending Federal money for education.

Operating these private and parochial schools costs money. We do not have an exact per capita cost of operating a private or parochial school, but I would estimate that on the average it would be in the neighborhood of $200 per student per year. Multiply $200 by 4,400,000 pupils and you will find that the annual cost of operating these schools is $880 million a year, $440 million more than the annual authorization for Federal grants for school construction in the bill before us. Moreover, people supporting these private and parochial schools will be expected to pay interest on school-building debts, to pay off part of the principal, and after all this, to pledge even greater donations to finance new building to take care of the huge increases in enrollment anticipated during the coming decade.

The United States Office of Education predicts that by 1960 private and parochial schools will enroll in excess of 5 million pupils, at least 600,000 more pupils than were enrolled during the school year 1955–56. At a very minimum, therefore, these schools will need 15,000 new classrooms by 1960. To build them they will need a minimum of $400 million, about $100 million a year for the next 4 years.

The children destined for enrollment in private and parochial schools in 1960 are already born. The need for new classrooms, therefore, is compelling and urgent. People who believe in these schools will have to provide the necessary funds for these school facilities. This applies to our whole educational system, whether public or private.

I want to point out that, despite the heavy burden of financing their own schools, those who support private and parochial schools have not complained about the cost of public education. On the contrary, they want good public schools and are willing to pay the price. All one has to do is to read the hearings on Federal aid for school construction and you will find no complaints, no opposition, no obstructionist proposals that have come from private or parochial school sources. For the most part, people who generously supported private or parochial schools have refrained from any action that might impede passage of this bill even though it will bring no direct benefit to their schools. These people have an unselfish, statesmanlike attitude. Their reasoning is that, if this bill and the money it authorizes are proven to be essential for the general good of the Nation's public school children, they do not want to stand in its way. That, I say, is an attitude deserving of highest commendation. It is big, noble, and generous.

I cannot help but recall that a few years ago some of us wanted to help the public schools with their operating expenses, particularly with better salaries for teachers. Most private and parochial school representatives were willing to go along. They did not want to stand in the way of legislation that would help public school children. Some of us, however, wanted to use a little part of the money for health and safety services, like polio shots or bus rides, for nonpublic school children. What happened? Public school devotees descended upon us en masse. They opposed our giving millions of dollars to the public schools if at the same time we were to spend a few thousand dollars for the health and safety of private and parochial school children for auxiliary services. They would not listen to reason. Better to have no Federal aid at all, they said, than to give a penny to a private or parochial school child. This was their unthinking, and in fact and effect, selfish and belligerent attitude. The result of their attitude was inaction in this important field.

I do not know whether we shall again need to consider Federal aid for current expenditures. If we do, I hope we will be spared a repetition of the ordeal of a few years ago. I hope public-school authorities will have a tolerant, cooperative attitude if an effort is made to try in a small way to help private and parochial school children by giving them health and safety services clearly allowable under the Federal Constitution as interpreted by the Supreme Court of the United States. If these public-school authorities want to see a good example of a cooperative, constructive attitude, I suggest they examine the attitude which many private and parochial school authorities have shown toward the legislation before us today.

Public, private, and parochial school children are equally precious in the sight of God, their Father. All are citizens of this blessed land. All deserve fair consideration that can be given them under the laws of our Government. . . .

CONGRESSMAN OVERTON BROOKS OF LOUISIANA

I am deeply in favor of helping our public schools. I am, at the same time, just as strongly against Federal control of our State school system. I have supported programs of limited nature for our public schools in the past. At the same time, any program which is general in scope and which threatens to become a permanent one fills me with fear of Federal and bureaucratic control.

The other day, one of my colleagues held up a thick book and shouted on this floor that "this is a volume of all of the Federal laws and regulations in aid of our public schools" and he drew the inference from this large book of laws and regulations that Federal aid is possible without Federal control. Such is, of course, the case; but as we approach nearer the program of our State-controlled public schools, we come closer to the point where State control leaves off and Federal control begins. Inversely, the more we depend upon Federal Government for help for our public schools, the greater is the threat of Federal control of them.

No one has to be persuaded of the bad effects of centralized Federal control of our public schools. Such a program will be disastrous to us and to our type of government. Dictatorships first attempt to gain control of the school systems before consolidating themselves in complete control of government. Centralized control of education means regimented control of education. It easily follows that education then becomes a mass, uniform, orthodox type of learning, without innovations and without competition and without the yearning for change and advance which we find so evident in our State-controlled school system.

This bill presents a 4-year program of $100 million per year. This money is to be used for the building of classrooms which may cost about $32,000 per classroom. The need for classrooms is terrific; and it is very apparent that 4 years of this type of program will not be sufficient to meet the current needs for new buildings and new classrooms. Four years of the program will mean an expenditure of $1.6 billion. There are 63,000 public schools in the United States; and according to the committee report, it will cost from ten to twelve billion dollars to provide adequate classrooms for children currently enrolled in public schools throughout the country.

All of this means simply that we will have a continuing program from now on out. Four years of this aid will not be sufficient. States and parishes and counties under this program will await the coming of Federal money with which to build classrooms; and this delay will hold up the entire program in some communities. It will mean the classroom shortage will not be overcome for many years, during which time we will have had a fixed program saddled to the backs of our State public schools.

During past years I have seen many temporary programs which have become permanent. The defense impact public school program is one of them. I have supported this defense impact program because it was promised to be temporary and because it was limited in scope to a relatively few schools in defense areas throughout the country. It looks to me as though this has now become a permanent school program, and more and more our States are being encouraged to depend upon it for aid. A general program of a permanent nature may be disastrous.

I am concerned a great deal with regulations and restrictions placed in the bill. The old adage of, "He who pays the piper calls the tunes" applies today with great force. Over the years, that government which puts up the money to support a permanent school policy will exert its control over our public educations. Of course, integration in our public schools in the South is unthinkable; and with or even without the amendment, under Federal control such is possible and could be expected. With the stipulations recently placed in this bill, it will integrate our schools and this Louisiana will not tolerate. . . .

CONGRESSMAN HARRISON A. WILLIAMS, JR., OF NEW JERSEY

The fact that the public schools of our Nation are facing the greatest crisis in our history is no longer surprising news. Nor are some of these facts — that 18 percent of our schools are fire hazards, a third are health and safety hazards, and thousands of school buildings are more than 50 years old. We are no longer astonished to hear that the school enrollment figure in 1955–56 was 1,675,000 over that of the previous year, or that the Nation faces a shortage of hundreds of thousands of classrooms. All of these frightening facts have become almost old hat, incredibly enough. What is even more incredible is that all this is true at a time when our gross national product is over $400 billion a year and is rising continuously; when our Nation has at its command resources of unparalleled magnitude; when we could solve any domestic problem confronting us by making the concerted decision to do so — and then going ahead and solving it.

The Kelley bill will not of itself solve our desperate school crisis. But it represents a step of major significance. The Kelley bill represents national recognition that the school crisis is a problem common to us all. It makes concrete the widespread sentiment of parents throughout the country that the fiscal resources not only of local communities and the States but of the Federal Government must be tapped to finance a frontal assault on a situation which is perilously close to being a national disaster. It

331

is genuinely realistic thinking about the needs of this Nation at a time when domestic conditions and world leadership are inseparable from each other.

A vivid illustration of why this measure is so vital is found in my own State of New Jersey. New Jersey has 547 administrative school units. Of these, 395—or 72½ percent—have exhausted their statutory bonding capacity. Half of these 395 districts, in turn, have obtained the permission of the State to exceed their statutory bonding limits. In my own congressional district, Union County, 12 out of 21 school districts have reached their statutory limits; and 29 applications have been made by those 12 school districts for permission to exceed the limits. Among the communities which have made such applications are several of the highest income suburban towns in the area.

What this indicates is that school needs have pyramided so rapidly that the dependence of our schools for a major portion of their revenues on the fiscal resources of local communities has become an anachronism. The theory that school revenues should be drawn largely from property taxes is one of the roots of our present school crisis since, as we well know, property assessments have hardly begun to keep pace with real values. Another of the roots of this crisis is that the Nation's tax structure has undergone a complete revision in the past generation. Three out of every 4 tax dollars now go to the Federal Government, rather than to State and local governments. While some people may label this an illustration of Federal aggrandizement, I think a realistic examination of our tax structure will reveal quite the reverse—namely, that States and local communities have not been adjusting progressively to the burgeoning needs of a Nation whose rising population and productivity have made it a giant of the modern world.

As has been pointed out to me by members of the New Jersey Department of Education, the Kelley bill will not only be helpful in meeting the immediate school shortages, but it also has the advantage of being, in the long run, a less costly source of revenue to the local community. While it is true that New Jersey's contribution to the Federal Treasury will be greater than the grants it will receive if the Kelley bill passes, those grants will not be saddled by the interest and financing charges which attach to local bond issues.

The Kelley bill would yield New Jersey a significant amount of help toward a solution to its school problems. A projected 5-year program for additions to existing schools and construction of new schools would cost an estimated $478 million; applications to the State by local communities for permission to exceed their statutory bond limits amounted to $81 million in the 1955–56 school year. While New Jersey is neither a poor nor a backward State, the impact of new population moving into our urban and suburban communities has been accelerating at such a pace that our needs are quite as pressing as those of States whose economic development is behind New Jersey's. And because school construction is a lengthy process—taking 2 to 3 years to plan and build a new school—States like New Jersey, undergoing the steady assault of population growth, must be helped as rapidly as possible.

There is one more point that I want to make about this bill. As a member of the Committee on Foreign Affairs, our world leadership position is never far from my mind. I cannot help being disturbed when I read that while the United States spends $8 billion a year on its public schools, the Soviet Union spends 16 billion. There is no reason to doubt that with our ingenuity and inventive capacity we can continue to stay far ahead of the Soviets in technological and scientific development. I believe that in any competition with the Soviets we can win. But to win this technological, scientific, and industrial competition we must have people adequately trained for their tasks. A recent congressional study shows that we are scarcely even with the Soviet Union as regards numbers of engineers and have only a slight lead in numbers of scientists. In 1954 we graduated only half as many college-trained specialists in engineering and science as we did in 1950. In the same year the Soviets turned out more than twice as many as we did. Allen Dulles, Director of the Central Intelligence Agency, recently warned that in this present decade the Soviet Union will graduate 1,200,000 university students in the basic physical sciences, while we will graduate only 900,000.

If this Congress passes the Kelley bill it will mean that we recognize the imperative need to face the school crisis as a national crisis. It means a first step toward national acceptance of the fact that the Soviet lead in training specialists must be faced and dealt with as a basic phase of our national security effort. It means, too, that, although this would be the first general school bill passed by Congress, we would in reality be continuing our faithfulness to the basic principles of our Nation. Our public schools are the very pedestal of our democracy, as our Founding Fathers knew, since

Federal aid to education preceded even George Washington's inauguration with the passage of the Land Grant Act of 1787. The Kelley bill would be the most recent link in a long chain of legislation to support a school system which can transmit to our children the skills, techniques, moral principles, and ideals which are the core of America.

The record is clear on the demonstrated need for this school legislation. It also seems manifest that we will not achieve this legislation during the current session of Congress if the so-called Powell amendment is attached. And here we come to the real dilemma. Many in this body are sincerely troubled over this problem, and no one could question their obvious sincerity in arguing for the Powell amendment. I share their ardent desire to see full and equal opportunity extended to all American citizens at the earliest possible time. As a matter of fact, I yield to no one in my deep-seated desire to see the end of the awful practices of segregation and discrimination. I will continue to devote my energies to advancing the cause of civil rights and welcome the opportunity which we in the House will shortly have to vote on a straight civil-rights measure.

But this question is posed: What will be gained by the passage of the Powell amendment? The clear answer is that nothing will be gained. No responsible person would suggest that this bill will become law if the Powell amendment is included. Not only would inclusion of the amendment kill the bill, it would set back the possibility of adequate aid to schools possibly for years to come, while our public school system will continue to deteriorate.

From a practical point of view, there are already signs that many who are relatively neutral on the question of civil rights but deeply concerned about the school crisis may well become hostile to civil-rights legislation if we permit this measure to die over the question of the Powell amendment. The amendment's adoption will not only defeat much-needed school legislation but will set back the possibility of meaningful civil-rights legislation. This seems to me far too high a price to pay.

Many may argue that in a district such as mine a vote against the Powell amendment could mean political suicide. But this underestimates the intelligence of people who are interested in advancing the cause of civil rights. Our real goal is respect for individual integrity and the provision for equal opportunity in a meaningful fashion rather than making a futile gesture.

334

Finally, let me make this other point. The Supreme Court has spoken on this subject. Progress toward desegregation is mandatory under the law. I recognize that there is opposition to the Court's decision, and in several States no progress is being made. This is a thoroughly deplorable fact. But it does not set aside the law of the land. We must move toward compliance with the Supreme Court decision, perhaps not as rapidly as some of us would like, but we must move ahead. Given sympathetic administration of a Federal-aid-to-school-construction program, there is no doubt that progress can be made in accordance with the Court's decision. Therefore, I suggest that we who are interested both in helping our schools and moving forward in civil rights pass this measure without the Powell amendment and that we give scrupulous attention to the aid program to assure that it is not used to frustrate implementation of the Supreme Court decision. Let us not permit the people of good faith who are interested in school legislation or in civil rights legislation to become embroiled with each other in futile argument. Let us not permit the friends of sound progress to dissipate their energies by fighting each other.

65. FEDERAL SUPPORT FOR THE PUBLIC SCHOOLS (1957)[1]

BEARDSLEY RUML

A federal duty to support the public schools flows both from the national interest and from the fact that access to the growing income of the country is most directly and most equitably imposed through the federal income tax.

Support implies interest and duty. Certainly we have a federal interest in making certain that our future citizens can communicate and can compute. These are the basics on which our society rests; and having a federal society as we do, a federal interest as well as a federal duty in safeguarding the basics of education follows inescapably.

State and local bodies will add to the foundation of support built federally as their vision, conscience, and means provide. However, there is neither prudence nor equity in making plans such that the basic requirement of the public schools would have to be met from resources to which state and local bodies have access.

The phrase, "federal support for the public schools," deliberately uses the term "public schools" rather than the broader term "education." The public schools are an essential but not an exclusive instrument in the nation's educational program. State and local bodies, private schools, churches, families, formal and informal voluntary agencies, will have plenty to do in expressing the variety of their own insights in the general educational fabric of which the public schools are a part. Federal support for the public schools should therefore provide the more formal important substance to every community's education program without the rigidity and interference usually associated with responsible use of federal funds.

---

[1]Beardsley Ruml, "A Plan That Will Work: Federal Support for the Public Schools," *Phi Delta Kappan*, XXXVIII (April 1957), 261–65. Ruml, an economist, is well known as the originator of the "pay as you go" income tax scheme.

The question immediately arises, "Can federal support for the public schools be provided in a form that carries no danger of objectionable interferences?" I believe that federal support can be so provided once the point of view of "aid" and the "means test" is set aside.

Most suggestions that have been made for federal support of education involve some kind of equalization formula to distinguish between the richer and the poorer states, and also some test as to whether any particular state was doing its full part in the support of its schools.

Equalization, involving as it does some measures and tests of need, ability, and willingness to meet need, always threatens to bring about federal dominance or control of education. The possibility of the federal government coercing the states in education matters would always exist. This should be avoided and it could be avoided by distributing federal support for the public schools on a per capita, school age child basis. Each state government would receive this money each year upon certification that the funds would be spent that year for the support of public schools as defined by the state.

If federal funds are distributed on a per capita basis, the definition of public school to be made by each particular state, then the wealthier states that now pay the larger share of the federal income tax might be expected to be able to take care of public education on any level they feel suitable, and indefinitely. This I doubt; but even if it were so, it still remains true that a child in a wealthier state is also at the same time a child of the United States and deserves equal federal support for the basic costs of his school system.

* * *

Although at the level of broad purpose and policy federal support for the public schools on a per capita basis offers no difficulty except the effort to get it going, there are nevertheless several sensitive points that must be anticipated and dealt with. Of these I shall mention five.

First, the definition of what is a "public school" must be left to the individual state. The definitions will vary and will seem to some fanciful and even inconsistent with prevailing notions of what a public school really is. Some will define a public school in terms of its top controlling board, some in terms of its availability to students, some in terms of the character of its support. Some

337

states will define parochial schools as public schools, others will not. Latitude must be given to the state to define "public school" as it sees fit. This is a prime consideration for state freedom from federal control.

Second, there must be a definition of what is a "child in school." This is the unit in terms of which support will be given. Here are some of the questions: What is a child, that is, from what age to what age is the child to be counted as such? When is he in school, that is, how many days a year, how many hours a day? Must he be on the school premises, or only under school supervision? These points as a statement of minimum standards should be a matter of federal determination.

Third, what about present funds now going to the schools from state and local bodies? Must they be maintained? My answer here is that the maintenance of existing funds should not be required, otherwise the federal support is not really the discharge of a federal responsibility, and the state would be coerced as a result of a history that may or may not be currently in tune with overall needs as the state itself presently appraises them.

Fourth, what about de-segregation? I feel that aid should be given to all states on a per capita basis without regard to how the administration of the public schools is currently handled. Law enforcement of national policy is in the hands of the courts. Improved educational opportunity will be a powerful force in aiding the establishment of a rational and humane democracy.

THE DESEGREGATION ISSUE

A special problem arises, however, if a state defines what is ordinarily considered to be a "public" school as a "private" school for purposes of evading the intent of national desegregation policy. Should a state be permitted to define "public school" in one way for the Supreme Court and another way for the comptroller general? Personally, I feel that one definition is enough, and "public school" once being defined, that concept should prevail uniformly in all judicial and administrative matters where the public school as such is involved.

Fifth, what about current proposals for federal aid to states and communities for the building of schools? The best that can be said for them is that they are harmless and gestures of good intent. The worst that can be said is that they are wholly inadequate, expensive, and that they evade the central duty of federal support for the public schools.

Per capita appropriations to the states will permit them to finance the schools they believe they need, and to determine for themselves the balance locally desirable between educational structures and teaching functions.

Finally, the dreary question of accounting and auditing. Here I feel that the accounting should be done by the state, certified to by some high agency other than the school authority. The auditing should be done by an agency of the federal government, and the rules of the audit should provide whatever uniformity and flexibility in accounting the state machinery will use as its guide to procedure and to form. Such federal supervision is not an interference with the educational program of the state, it is only the assurance that the declared policy of the state has been performed in terms that reflect federal responsibility and accountability.

THE OTHER STATE RESPONSIBILITIES

Opposition to federal support for the public schools is rarely heard on economic grounds, that the burden on the federal budget would be too great. It is frequently contended that the states could do more if they only wanted to, by means of re-assessments, higher rates of real estate taxes, higher general and specific sales taxes, new taxes on business turnover, and the like. There is no doubt some truth in these contentions; but what is not always recognized is that states and local communities have many public responsibilities other than the schools, and that growth and shifts of population have created many a new problem for local government. In any case, catching up with school necessities and keeping up with school demands will require more state and local funds than have ever been planned for, even with moderate assistance in federal support.

The most vocal opposition to federal support for the public schools comes as expressed apprehension that federal money means federal interference and ultimate federal control of education. The right of each state to determine what kind of education it wants is constantly asserted, a somewhat legalistic position considering the interference of the state in the educational affairs of local communities and of both in the decisions of the individual family, which after all should have some final rights as to how the children should be brought up.

It is true that the protestations of fear of federal interference are mostly based on the assumption of an equalization formula, of the means test, hand-out policy which always presented a potential danger. If, however, the measure of federal support is on a per capita child in public school basis, the only federal concern would be to prevent false reporting or fraud of other kinds.

PROPOSAL WILL BRING NEW OPPONENTS

The opposition will now come from those who favor federal aid because they expect at the same time to get federal influence on local educational policies and standards. This opposition feels that working through local citizens groups is too slow and too uncertain, and that unless there is conformance to federal standards there should be no federal aid. Whether or not this group is large, it is extremely vocal; and recent disclosures as to what the Soviet Union has been able to accomplish educationally by means of central expenditure and central control makes this group understandably impatient with the slower policies of popular consent and popular will.

There is, however, another angle to this controversy — one that is very old and very deep. Briefly, it is the question of whether the burden of social programs, such as education, should be borne by a tax on real property or by a tax on income.

This issue was brought home to me very vividly in 1931 when I was a dean at the University of Chicago. Professor Charles H. Judd had just returned from New York, where he had attended a small private meeting of businessmen and educators. The subject under discussion was increasing the required age of school attendance. I asked him how the meeting went. He said, "Fine. There was unanimous agreement that the compulsory school attendance age should be raised." I was surprised and asked him to explain. "Well," said Judd, "the educators and the businessmen have a common interest. The educators want more children to teach and the businessmen want to put the burden of unemployment on real estate."

              *   *   *

THE NEW NECESSITIES OF EDUCATION

We are now in a time of historic change in education. The old traditions are falling apart under the pressure of the new necessities. And in a curious way the new necessities derive from a will to provide for all children the educational opportunities which the old traditions were designed to give the few.

The period from 1929 to 1939 was a period of economic disorder. The institutional pattern was no longer able to support the basic demands of production and distribution. We were confronted for a decade with the paradox of need for goods and need for work in a setting of abundance of raw materials and the highest technical competence the world had at that time known. Later the folly of war revealed the folly of the old economic and financial traditions. The reluctantly adopted palliatives of the early thirties became established as the guides to institutional economic reform.

In 1946, after fifteen years that were marked by both depression and war, a national policy was formulated in the simple preamble to the Employment Act of 1946. This policy has become more creative as the years have passed. It declared that the federal government has responsibility, consistent with a fundamental belief in free, competitive enterprise, to "utilize all its plans, functions, and resources for the purpose of creating and maintaining conditions under which there will be afforded useful employment opportunities, including self-employment, for those able, willing, and seeking to work."

At the time the Employment Act was passed, there were misgivings, even fears. The *New York Herald Tribune* on June 14, 1946, spoke of the act as "perhaps the most serious threat to free enterprise and democracy with which the country has been confronted in the 170 years of its existence." But today the act has bi-partisan support at the highest levels, and all sectors of the economy recognize its policy as a necessary element in protecting the national welfare.

THE EDUCATION ACT OF 195X

The period from 1949 to 1959 is a period of educational disorder. The old institutional structure can no longer contain the urgent demand for general and selective educational opportunity.

The public schools in 1957 are in the same position that the banks were in 1931. In a year or two or three, more and more public schools will become educationally insolvent. Unfortunately, or perhaps fortunately, there can be no run on the schools that will force them to close. But the present inadequacies will become more apparent as the needs become more acute, and we can look forward to an Education Act of 195x whose preamble may well be a paraphrase of that of the Employment Act of 1946.

Such a preamble to the Education Act of 195x might read in part as follows: "There is a federal responsibility, consistent with the constitutional rights, the privileges and the duties of the states, to utilize all its plans, functions, and resources for the purpose of creating and maintaining conditions under which there will be afforded useful educational opportunities, including self-education, for those able, willing, and seeking to learn."

66. THE BUGABOO OF FEDERAL CONTROL (1952)[1]

THEODORE BRAMELD

1.

If American education is to move in the direction of a more inclusive community approach to educational needs and aims, then it should concern itself even more directly than hitherto with the most controversial social, economic, and political issues confronting our democracy. Not only should it concern itself in an academic sense; it should seek through frank debate on the part of the largest possible number to clarify and then to act vigorously according to its judgments.

One of these issues is federal aid and control of public education. According to all indications, including a public opinion poll, a large proportion of informed teachers and citizens would endorse some kind of federal educational *aid*. What we have not considered with equal care is the other pole of the federal equation. We have not, that is to say, analyzed realistically the issue of federal *control*.

Even our more thoughtful educational leaders often tend to separate the one sharply from the other — to regard federal aid as something virtuous, control as something wicked. We have, it seems, tended to make "control" an emotive word no more specifically meaningful to us than "collectivism" is to an archconservative in politics.

As a matter of fact, the word "control" is entirely amoral. It connotes neither the good nor the bad as such. It becomes good or bad only in the context of specific methods and purposes — in other words, according to *how* control is exercised and for *whose* purposes. Thus localized controls are by no means always good: if we assume that one test of desirable education is wide participation by students, teachers, and parents in program-making, then great

---

[1]Theodore Brameld, *Education for the Emerging Age: Newer Ends and Stronger Means* (New York: Harper and Brothers, 1961), pp. 145–51. Brameld is Professor of Philosophy of Education at Boston University.

numbers of schools dominated by autocratic local boards and administrators are very bad indeed. On the other hand, it is far from established that federal directives have invariably been inimical to worth-while processes and goals. For example, the Smith-Hughes Act (providing federal funds to industrial and home-economics education) is accompanied by standards of implementation applicable to all recipients. So, too, is the GI Bill of Rights that has made educational attainment possible for vast numbers of recent war veterans. Yet opponents of federal control would be ridiculed by the typical beneficiary of such programs were they to argue that the total educational effect has been more injurious than beneficial to the millions of students and thousands of teachers involved in them. Despite inevitable red tape, approval has been exceedingly high, and in terms of educational advancement, rightly high.

Such examples lead to the contention that the whole matter of federal control needs to be reviewed in terms of cultural and ethical presuppositions. Until this is done, neither we as a profession nor the public at large will be sufficiently settled in our minds to unite around a policy and a program that can defeat the enemies of generous, free public education — enemies of whom, unfortunately, there are many in places of power and prestige.

2.

It would be enlightening to contrast critically the premises of those who oppose and those who favor federal intervention. The most we can do is to imply the former by considering the latter — that is, by considering three premises which, among others, underlie the case not only for federal aid but for control as well. These are (1) the desirability of equal educational opportunity for all citizens, regardless of race, creed, or economic status; (2) the necessity of an educated citizenry for the nation as a whole; and (3) the increasingly unified structures of modern culture.

Now there is no doubt that some educators, in common with some citizens, would profess to accept each of these premises while emphatically denying that either federal aid or federal control of the schools is a proper conclusion from them. Actually, however, by that denial they also tacitly distrust all three premises.

To take the first, if any fact is established by our present economy, it is that educational equality is not and cannot be provided in large sections of the country—especially the South—unless the states are assisted by federal funds. Their own resources simply will not allow such equality with the richer states.

Here, of course, is the chief argument of those who now support the need for federal aid; and in doing so, they certainly cannot be accused of paying mere lip service to the first of the three premises. Yet the question arises whether even they, if and when they continue to insist that such equality should be achieved without federal control, are not still guilty of lip service at least toward both the other premises.

For if, to consider the second premise next, it is true that an educated people is a *national* necessity—if, for example, the country *as a whole* has been weakened by the ignorance of *some parts* of the population—then surely it also becomes an obligation of the nation to guarantee decent standards of education to every citizen in the interests of the whole.

Yet if federal funds are simply handed over to the states and districts, what assurance is there that this kind of education will result at all? Vast amounts of money can be spent by ingenious but irresponsible public officials without any certainty that the children and adults for whose benefit it is intended will enjoy plentiful and excellent textbooks, well-trained and well-paid teachers, or up-to-date equipment. It is not impossible, under some of the bills that have been proposed, that states could manage to reduce their own expenditures and substitute federal funds so that educationally they would be little better off than they were before. And if such subterfuges are to be prevented, so that every state is compelled to spend federal funds for the sole purpose of raising standards of their schools, then already federal control must obviously function in some specified degree in order to make sure all regulations are properly enforced.

Indeed, it is just because certain educators have seen that any kind of workable support must be, as it has always been, accompanied by definite controls that they have preferred what they regard as the lesser of two evils—no federal aid at all. But these educators, while more consistent than some of their colleagues, are themselves likely to be caught on the horns of a dilemma. If they deny federal aid, they deny equality of educational opportunity, for they usually admit such opportunity can be assured in no other practical way; but if they approve of federal aid, then they yield to federal control, for they see clearly that to be effective, any kind of aid must necessarily be so accompanied.

The resolution of the dilemma is to recognize frankly that those educational standards which, with our second premise, we concede are needed for the nation as a whole can only be safeguarded by a measure of federal authority. For the fact is that even our first premise might mean little in practice so long as it were possible to siphon off federal support in the absence of sufficient supervision to insure that it was actually used for the educational improvement of *all* the common people of any state or region.

The third premise, however, generates the strongest need for reconsideration of the problem of control. That our entire culture has been undergoing a breathlessly swift transition from independent, decentralized traditions and practices toward new methods and institutions which are just as strongly interdependent and centralized is a fact no one can any longer overlook. Yet while we now accept this fact as a matter of course in speaking of economic relations or even of such potent educational media as television, many of us still revert to the precious beliefs of our forefathers the moment we begin to consider public education. The sacredness of "states' rights," the horrors of "bureaucracy," and other typical shibboleths of the nineteenth century are brought out of storage and hauled creakingly to the battlefronts of professional debate whenever the question is raised whether, just possibly, interdependence and centralization might have some bearing upon the schools as well.

And what bearing might they have? The connection of our third premise with the first and second here becomes significant. With the first, because concern with *equality* of opportunity rather than so exclusively with the more individualistic value of *liberty* is a token of our growing regard for human *similarities* as well as *differences* — similarities of which we are more and more conscious as our industrial and agricultural occupations become increasingly integrated and systematized through the power especially of technology. With the second, because the recognition that good education is a *total* necessity of our national life is itself an indication that today we are becoming much too closely knit as a people to run the risk of neglecting any considerable number of us for any length of time.

It is, of course, precisely because many of our gravest problems have become national rather than local in character that often in recent years they have been met most successfully through the instrumentality of federal legislation. The history of the New Deal disproves an old notion that decentralized controls always carry out the wishes of the people more efficiently than centralized controls. When a problem like old-age security is national in scope, the mutual concern of citizens to find a solution may crystallize more quickly and successfully into federal legislation just because it is so all-pervading. Thus we have seen on several recent occasions that the voice of fifty million citizens or more may be considerably more insistent and harmonious than the discordant voices of groups, communities, even whole states.

"Democratic centralism," as it is sometimes called, expresses in a phrase the realization that there are times — and now evidently a great many times — when the similar needs of similar people may be satisfied better by federal centers of delegated authority responsible to the great majority than by any other means at present available.

3

The difficulties raised by this analysis are great. If, however, I am thus far even roughly correct, then it follows that federal control of education not only will not be incompatible with American well-being in the years just ahead, but may actually enhance it much more rapidly than the types to which we are habituated by routine, ideology, and perhaps timidity.

This is not to say, certainly, that central authority subject to popular consent would always and necessarily meet the educational requirements of our interdependent nation more competently than any other kinds. Just as we oversimplify by sharply separating aid from control, so we oversimplify, too, by taking an "either-or" attitude toward federal and local authority.

It still remains true, for example, that a more efficient and rewarding job can and should be done on local and state levels than is now being done. It is true, also, that a crucial test of democracy in action is the degree to which ordinary people participate in its operations. But the means by which they do so are likely to change with other changes in social evolution; and it is just because you and I often are no longer able to do so fruitfully on a merely local basis that new techniques of participation — new formulae for building two-way ladders between ourselves at the base of the democratic pyramid and our chosen leaders at its apex—are required at this juncture of our history.

4

Here are two suggestions through which such ladders could be built. The first is a neglected proposal made years ago by the John Dewey Society that a "national emergency educational board" be set up, representing not only the teaching profession, but business-men, industrial workers, farmers, minority groups, and youth. The board would have several functions: to develop a grand conception of education for the American people, to translate this conception into a national program for the schools, to coordinate its program with non-school educational agencies such as the press, and to formulate a plan for federal support. The proposal skirts the pain-ful question of how recognition of the need for nation-wide stand-ards could become something more than "suggestive and stimu-lating" to localities that might prefer to ignore them entirely. Even so, it deserves more careful consideration than it has ever received.

A second suggestion arises from the experience of the Tennes-see Valley Authority. The TVA proves that, even in a complex society like ours, it is thoroughly practical to combine *centralized authority* and *decentralized administration* in a working synthe-sis. The people of the valley have participated constantly and enthusiastically at many crucial points of its development; yet if strong directives were not provided by the federal government, such participation would not have been forthcoming.

This second suggestion has, therefore, two facets. It implies, on the one hand, that federal control of education is bound up with the entire planning of American economic and cultural life—that there is pressing need, especially, for experiments comparable to, though not identical with, the TVA in *every* region of the country, not just in one alone. But the suggestion implies, on the other hand, that even while we are working toward such social objec-tives in a comprehensive sense, we should carefully explore the formula of "centralized authority—decentralized administration" as an educational objective in a more specific sense. In a word, it is more than likely that, if we but insisted strongly enough, we could construct for America an "educational TVA" on a national scale.

Here is where professional and lay organizations concerned with the problem could perform a service. With need for federal assistance as much alive as ever, a conference of representatives of these organizations should be called as soon as possible for the purpose of framing a new bill and organizing a campaign for its passage into law. This conference should reconsider the provisions of bills recently proposed. Also, it should at last come to grips with the issue of federal control. For if it is true that control by desirable means and for desirable ends is, after all, integral with effective aid, then we do injustice, not only to ourselves as teachers but to the American people whom we serve, when we evade the issue largely because it has become a bugaboo.

67. Federal Responsibility in the Field of Education (1955)[1]

Adequate education of all American youth is essential to the preservation of the Republic and to the welfare of the nation in peace and war. The country's most important resource lies in its citizens more than in its soil or climate or extent of territory. Full development of this resource is dependent upon solutions to a number of pressing problems. An unprecedented rise in school enrollment presents a monumental task for our vast elementary and secondary school system; it will in the 1960's pose a problem of similar magnitude to the institutions of higher learning. A current shortage of teachers may become increasingly serious as enrollments grow. Years of depression and war have left a grossly inadequate school plant, and our competition with communism obliges us to utilize our human resources to a greater extent than ever before in our history.

These problems combine to emphasize that the financial needs of education are on the rise. We believe that the American people can and will devote an increasing share of their income to education. The question is not whether the United States can afford to spend more on education than it does now, but how the needed funds can best be raised. We have sought the answer to this question within the framework of the traditions of American development though it would have been simpler had we accepted the easier and often urged alternative of passing the problem to the federal government for solution. It is necessary to remind ourselves that our primary interest in the immediate schooling of the child must not overwhelm our responsibility to preserve for him a pattern of political and social organization which has values beyond the immediate needs of education. His heritage of individual liberty is a sacred obligation. . . .

[1]*Federal Responsibility in the Field of Education* (Washington: GPO, 1955), pp. 5 –9, 19 –20. The Committee appointed by President Eisenhower submitted its report to the Commission on Intergovernmental Relations.

While it is perfectly apparent that the Founding Fathers intended that the federal government should have minimal powers in education, we are nevertheless satisfied that the Supreme Court subsequently has authorized congressional action in the field of education which would transcend the claims of the most ardent of the "federal aid" supporters. We think it perfectly clear that the power of Congress to use its taxing authority for the general welfare is limited only by its own discretion. Our problem thus becomes a matter of congressional discretion, rather than of constitutional authority. Thus, it is to the issue of the wisdom of federal government participation in education that we must turn. Varying and often conflicting values have impressed themselves upon us. Dominant among them, of course, are the questions of fiscal capacity. Not to be lightly dismissed are larger questions of a total governmental structure and a philosophy of social growth and organization. [In seeking solutions to the compelling educational problems of the Nation, we have extracted these] principles to serve as guides for our appraisal of the wisdom of retaining or embarking upon specific programs of federal aid to education.

1. Every child has a right to an education commensurate with his capacity.

2. The purposes of a universal education include not only personal growth but also service to the community and training for responsibility in a free world.

3. Educational responsibility rests initially with the parent, but is shared with the community, the state, and the nation. It is a function both of government and of private groups. It cannot be allocated to any one level of government, but should be undertaken at the lowest level capable of its satisfactory performance. The presumption must be that responsibility remains within the lesser unit until there is clear demonstration of the necessity of its transfer from one to another.

4. A viable federalism presumes, not only a restraint on the part of the federal government, but a full assumption of initiative and responsibility on the part of parents, the localities, and the states. If there is a disturbing tendency of the federal government to assume disproportionate powers, we feel there is an equally dangerous tendency of the states and the communities to neglect, and even abandon, their proper roles. Delinquency in the latter can be quite as serious as an excessive ambition in the former.

5. The educational system, like other institutions in a free

society, should be responsive to the desires of the people it serves. Because democracy possesses vitality to the extent that individual citizens are convinced that their choices make a difference, it is most frequently manifested at the local level, where the individual voice has a chance to be heard. Furthermore, the closer the relationship between means and end—between the cost of education and the services received—the greater the sense of responsibility toward both.

6. Fundamental values in our educational system must be a compound of diversity and variety on the one hand and a certain amount of uniformity on the other. The pressures for standardization are clear and often compelling. Yet the traditions of pluralism retain their meaning and essential importance in a democratic society. The preservation of a concept of the multiple sources of truth is peculiarly the responsibility of education, for here we are concerned, not only with the maintenance of diverse points of view in education which is but one area of public policy, but with the preservation of the fundamental concept that a calculated diversity is a major protection against the compulsions of a sterilizing orthodoxy and a paralyzing absolutism. The urgent demand for uniformity of standards must modify rather than parallel this basic pluralist assumption.

7. Extensive citizen participation in public education at the local level provides an important training in self-government. While derivative from the immediate purposes of the educational system, this is nonetheless a feature of our present structure worthy of careful conservation.

8. Governmental structure is not an end in itself, but a vehicle for the realization of community purposes. While it serves its purpose it should be assiduously preserved, but when it is no longer adequate, it must be replaced. Preservation of structures and practices as ends in themselves militates against the maintenance of a viable federalism.

9. The tendency of responsible legislators is to attach restrictions to the expenditures of funds they appropriate. . . . To the extent that the federal government supplies funds such restrictions are therefore likely to increase.

10. Population mobility, the necessity of reasonable equality in economic position and cultural maturity of residents of the United States, and current international competitive realities have created a national interest in an adequate education for all of our citizens.

These same considerations require a higher level of public expenditure for education than has heretofore been made.

11. Fiscal capacity for the performance of a function of government should not be measured in terms of revenues actually available, but in terms of basic resources upon which the unit of government may draw, if it is willing to do so. Nor do we believe that a desirable pattern of governmental activity should be compromised or abandoned because it may be administratively more convenient or publicly more palatable to collect revenues through central facilities.

Education being a function of government which is particularly suited to local control, unused state and local tax capacity and new fiscal resources should be available for educational purposes before being utilized for other functions of government. . . .

The federal government could not achieve universal educational opportunity by appropriating money to the states to be distributed at their discretion. Federal action could bring about universal educational opportunity only if grants-in-aid were conditioned upon control of distribution of both state and federal funds. Such control is contrary to the established principle of state and local school control and probably unacceptable to the states.

The costs of the expansion in enrollment in the next ten years can be taken care of by state and local governments if they continue to increase their school contributions at the rate at which they have been boosting them in recent years. To improve standards at the rate at which they have been advancing in the last few decades will require greater efforts. An effective way in which the federal government can aid this effort is to reduce its tax bill. Such action should make it easier for state and local governments to raise additional funds for the schools without increasing the total tax burden of their citizens.

Research does not sustain the contention that federal funds are essential to support the elementary and secondary school system. All economic resources in the United States, all wealth and income, are within the borders of the 48 states and subject to their taxing powers. There is no magic in the United States Treasury. Federal support for education can come, in the last analysis, only from the same basic resources which are available to states and local governments. . . .

Schools have been a state and local responsibility by longstanding and firmly embedded tradition. They should so remain.

We have not been able to find a state which cannot afford to make more money available to its schools or which is economically unable to support an adequate school system. . . .

[We conclude] that federal aid is not necessary either for current operating expenses for public schools or for capital expenditures for new school facilities. Local communities and states are able to supply both in accordance with the will of their citizens.

68. Elementary and Secondary Education Act: Supporters and Critics (1965)[1]

PRESIDENT LYNDON B. JOHNSON: MESSAGE TO CONGRESS

To the Congress of the United States:

In 1787, the Continental Congress declared in the Northwest Ordinance:

"Schools and the means of education shall forever be encouraged."

America is strong and prosperous and free because for 178 years we have honored that commitment.

In the United States today —

One-quarter of all Americans are in the Nation's classrooms.

High school attendance has grown eighteenfold since the turn of the century — six times as fast as the population.

College enrollment has advanced eightyfold. Americans today support a fourth of the world's institutions of higher learning and a third of its professors and college students.

In the life of the individual, education is always an unfinished task.

And in the life of this Nation, the advancement of education is a continuing challenge.

There is a darker side to education in America:

One student out of every three now in the fifth grade will drop out before finishing high school if the present rate continues.

Almost a million young people will continue to quit school each year — if our schools fail to stimulate their desire to learn.

Over 100,000 of our brightest high school graduates each year will not go to college — and many others will leave college — if the opportunity for higher education is not expanded.

---

[1]U.S. House of Representatives, 89th Cong., 1st sess., Doc. No. 45, Message from the President of the United States Transmitting Education Program (Washington D.C.: GPO, 1965), pp. 1 –3; "Tarnished Aid to Education" (Editorial), *Congress bi-Weekly,* 32 (Feb. 15, 1965), 3; "Federal Aid at Last" (Editorial), *America,* 112 (April 24, 1965), 602; Russell Kirk, "Who Will Be Aided by Federal Aid?" *National Review,* XVII (May 4, 1965), 378; Walter Lippmann, "On Aid to Religious Schools," *The Washington Post,* April 15, 1965.

The cost of this neglect runs high—both for the youth and the Nation:

Unemployment of young people with an eighth grade education or less is four times the national average.

Jobs filled by high school graduates rose by 40 percent in the last 10 years. Jobs for those with less schooling decreased by nearly 10 percent.

We can measure the cost in even starker terms. We now spend about $450 a year per child in our public schools. But we spend $1,800 a year to keep a delinquent youth in a detention home, $2,500 a year for a family on relief, $3,500 a year for a criminal in State prison.

The growing numbers of young people reaching school age demand that we move swiftly even to stand still.

Attendance in elementary and secondary schools will increase by 4 million in the next 5 years; 400,000 new classrooms will be needed to meet this growth. But almost one-half million of the Nation's existing classrooms are already more than 30 years old.

The post-World War II boom in babies has now reached college age. And by 1970, our colleges must be prepared to add 50 percent more enrollment to their presently overcrowded facilities.

In the past, Congress has supported an increasing commitment to education in America. Last year, I signed historic measures passed by the 88th Congress to provide—

Facilities badly needed by universities, colleges, and community colleges;

Major new resources for vocational training;

More loans and fellowships for students enrolled in higher education; and

enlarged and improved training for physicians, dentists, and nurses.

I propose that the 89th Congress join me in extending the commitment still further. I propose that we declare a national goal of

FULL EDUCATIONAL OPPORTUNITY

Every child must be encouraged to get as much education as he has the ability to take.

We want this not only for his sake—but for the Nation's sake.

Nothing matters more to the future of our country: not our military preparedness, for armed might is worthless if we lack the brainpower to build a world of peace; not our productive economy, for we cannot sustain growth without trained manpower; not our democratic system of government, for freedom is fragile if citizens are ignorant.

We must demand that our schools increase not only the quantity but the quality of America's education. For we recognize that nuclear age problems cannot be solved with horse-and-buggy learning. The three R's of our school system must be supported by the three T's—teachers who are superior, techniques of instruction that are modern, and thinking about education which places it first in all our plans and hopes.

Specifically, four major tasks confront us—

to bring better education to millions of disadvantaged youth who need it most;

to put the best educational equipment and ideas and innovations within reach of all students;

to advance the technology of teaching and the training of teachers; and

to provide incentives for those who wish to learn at every stage along the road to learning.

Our program must match the magnitude of these tasks. The budget on education which I request for fiscal year 1966 will contain a total of $4.1 billion. This includes $1.1 billion to finance programs established by the 88th Congress. I will submit a request for $1.5 billion in new obligational authority to finance the programs described in this message. This expenditure is a small price to pay for developing our Nation's most priceless resource.

In all that we do, we mean to strengthen our State and community education systems. Federal assistance does not mean Federal control—as past programs have proven. The late Senator Robert Taft declared:

Education is primarily a State function—but in the field of education, as in the fields of health, relief, and medical care, the Federal Government has a secondary obligation to see that there is a basic floor under those essential services for all adults and children in the United States.

In this spirit, I urge that we now push ahead with the No. 1

business of the American people—the education of our youth in preschools, elementary and secondary schools, and in the colleges and universities.

✿ ✿ ✿

CONGRESS bi-WEEKLY: TARNISHED AID TO EDUCATION

Two American Jewish Congress spokesmen—Howard M. Squadron, chairman of AJCongress' Commission on Law and Social Action, and Harrison J. Goldin, executive chairman of Congress' New York Metropolitan Council—testifying before House and Senate subcommittees on the school aid bill, gave pointed expression to the fears troubling many Americans that certain provisions of the bill would violate the constitutional principle of church-state separation. Both AJCongress spokesmen strongly urged the use of federal funds to strengthen public education and fight poverty, but saw no need for extending such aid in violation of the First Amendment.

They singled out as particularly objectionable the bill's requirement that, where there are underprivileged children attending non-public schools, "shared time" programs must be established as a condition for the public school system to receive a basic or special incentive grant; the use of federal funds to provide books and other materials to parochial schools; and the plan for "consortiums" or partnerships between public officials and religious authorities to operate supplementary educational centers.

It is astonishing that these features of the bill have not given greater pause to those who have rallied to the support of the bill without reservation and who, in other years, were zealous about safeguarding church-state separation. That those provisions could be swallowed without hesitation by well-intentioned groups we can only attribute to the fact that they have wearied of the struggle to obtain the massive aid public education sorely requires without making concessions to those who have blocked such programs unless parochial schools were included. It is simple to assert that these concessions are a small price to pay for the funds that will flow to needy children. But is the price, in fact, small? Are there no dangers apart from flouting sacred constitutional principles—a grave enough evil?

To these questions, it seems to us, Mr. Squadron returned answers which should give food for reflection to those who have made light of the concessions that are being offered to obtain the favor of the parochial school-aid proponents. The provisions of the bill, he noted, jeopardize the public school system they are designed to strengthen. "Our public school system," he declared, "in desperate need of funds for its own vitality, will be gravely threatened if tax-raised funds are made available for the support of private schools." He went on to cite the collapse of the public school system in the Netherlands where only 20 percent of Dutch children attended church schools before tax-raised funds were made available to them, but the ratio was almost reversed when the Dutch constitution was changed to provide for governmental subsidy.

The Dutch experience may appear a remote contingency, but it does effectively illustrate the dangers implicit in a situation where the availability of federal funds may entice many of the 250 religious denominations in the U.S. to establish their own separate school systems. Surely, no one can contemplate with equanimity the distinct possibility that a rivalry between public and parochial schools will be generated as each seeks, in Mr. Squadron's words, "a fair share of the pie."

We do not share the widespread belief that President Johnson's "canny" formula of grants to students instead of schools really gets around the constitution, or that it will promote general harmony and mutual satisfaction. We believe that so far from accomplishing the latter aim it will, in the end, foster discord and bitter competition for public funds. As for the constitutional aspects of the proposals, it will be wise for Congress to add a provision for judicial review if it passes the bill in its present form. This provision would expedite a decision by the Supreme Court on the measure's constitutionality.

We hope that the enthusiasm generated in favor of supplying massive aid to public school education will continue, but that it will not obscure or block out from consciousness either the great principle of church-state separation or the pragmatic difficulties that must inevitably arise by pitting public and private schools in the competition for federal funds.

* * *

AMERICA: FEDERAL AID AT LAST

On Sunday, April 11, in the old country school in Texas where he had learned his first lessons, President Johnson signed into law the Elementary and Secondary Education Act of 1965. It was the first major, general Federal aid to education measure to get through a Congress split by political, economic, sectional and religious divisions. It was also the first such measure to include some degree of aid to pupils in private, even religiously affiliated, nonprofit schools.

This law is more than a milestone in the progress of education in the United States. It is a distinct turn in the road, which opens new vistas. The future is never fully predictable, but one can already discern several features of the educational scene in the years ahead.

Federal aid to education will become a permanent part of American education finance. And Federal aid will increase rather than decrease. The Federal government will never bear the major cost of education; those who have nightmares in which the States vanish into the maw of the Federal octopus may relax. But the Federal government is in the business of financing education to stay, and in a big way.

The character of Federal aid to education will change, too. The present law is designed mainly to furnish special and supplementary aid to schools, and to do this chiefly for the benefit of children from the lowest income groups. But the pressure to involve the Federal government in paying for school construction and higher teachers' salaries will continue relentlessly. In the end, it will probably prevail.

The new Federal education act also recognizes the existence of what are usually called parochial schools. On the elementary level, most of them are in fact Catholic schools attached to parishes (which is what "parochial" means). But there are also Christian Reformed, Lutheran, Episcopalian, Seventh Day Adventist, Jewish and other nonprofit schools outside the system of schools owned and operated by the state. It is a misnomer to call them all indiscriminately parochial schools.

Not that it matters greatly what they are called. All that really matters is that they are educating children and cannot be omitted from any program of public spending that seriously intends to aid education and not just public schools.

Now, the new Federal law does nothing at all to help private schools directly. It gives them no money; it vests no property in them. Every benefit conferred on their pupils comes to them through the public school system. Even the textbooks that will be put into their pupils' hands will remain the property of public school districts.

But the new law at least recognizes that these schools exist and are educating children. In a variety of ways, it proposes to assist and improve the education of these children. The aid is, in every instance, directly to the child rather than to the school he attends. But it is aid, and it holds a promise for the future of a truly pluralistic school system.

The "child benefit" principle is capable of being extended to every phase of education other than the directly religious. It could well justify tuition grants to the parents of children in any nonprofit school that the state recognizes as giving an acceptable general education. Here, as with Federal aid to public schools, the Elementary and Secondary Education Act is a beginning rather than an end.

✻   ✻   ✻

RUSSELL KIRK: WHO WILL BE AIDED BY FEDERAL SCHOOL AID?

For two decades, the National Education Association and its affiliates have lobbied belligerently for such "aid to public schools." At last they have succeeded, although only through President Johnson's masterful clutch upon Congress. Members of the National School Boards Association, long opposed to such subsidy because it must mean federal control of schools, are correspondingly disheartened; some think that we must now accept eventual centralization of the public educational system.

What, after all, will these $1.3 billion accomplish?

Some $1.06 billion go for assistance to "poor" school districts. These "poor" districts can use their subsidies to increase the pay of teachers and administrators, erect new buildings, and whatever else they like. This sounds promising; yet the problems of even our slum schools and "gray area" schools are not really fiscal. Their present buildings are adequate, in most districts, and sometimes are less crowded than those of suburban schools. Their teachers ordinarily benefit, already, from citywide pay scales that do not discriminate between prosperous and poor neighborhoods.

More than anything else, what these troubled "poor" districts need is courageous and imaginative administrators, and competent and energetic teachers. At the average "gray area" school today, discipline and the level of instruction are inferior because, in considerable part, of listless administration (soothed by the slogans and jargon of yesteryear) and uninspired pedagogical approaches. Mere subsidies will not alter this condition; indeed, subsidies may entrench in power the very people who have failed to respond to the challenge of rootless megalopolis.

Under the new act, a hundred million dollars will be spent for library materials and textbooks—including the lending of some of these books to parochial and private schools. But few districts have actually been unable to afford to buy books in the past; one encounters new schools in which the library shelves are almost empty—not because the district is impoverished, but because their school administrators and school boards have very little interest in so obsolescent a thing as *book*-learning.

Another hundred million dollars will go for "supplementary educational centers," to entice adults and school drop-outs into the academy. The response, one suspects, will be discouraging, for a primary difficulty of American public schooling is the boredom of most courses. Compulsion lacking, adult and drop-out pupils will be scarce.

The sum of $22.5 million is allotted for creation of national and regional "educational research centers," and for subsidies to other research programs. Finally, $25 million dollars will be spent upon "strengthening state departments of education." Certainly the great majority of such departments of public instruction are now dull as dishwater, hostile toward genuinely qualitative reform, and staffed by remarkably mediocre members of the educationist "establishment."

Do these vast subsidies—spread somewhat thinly across the nation—actually accomplish aught toward improving the *quality* of primary and secondary instruction? We Americans have long spent, per capita, twice as much upon schooling as do our nearest rivals in educational expenditure, the Russians. What we require, in the schools, is a change of heart and an elevation of mind. How will these subsidies practically attract and instruct better teachers? How will they give us better school administrators? How will they improve the basic educational disciplines? How will they inspire better methods in the teachers' colleges and departments of education? How will they restore norms, standards, to the curriculum?

How will they remedy the anarchy of the slum school? These are awkward questions—and President Johnson, self-described as "a nut on education," is one of the gentlemen least qualified to answer them.

Catholic leaders who supported this school-subsidy act in the expectation of refreshing draughts of public money may find that they have exchanged their birthright for a mess of pottage. For parochial schools are cast only the small sop—which will be challenged in the federal courts—of using some limited facilities at neighboring public schools, and the loan of some library volumes and textbooks. For these tiny and questionable benefits, Catholic and other church going taxpayers who support parochial schools will have to foot their share of the national cost of school subsidies.

Also the specter of federal interference with church-connected schools begins to materialize. An officer of a "Protestants and Others" group writes to me that he welcomes this federal subsidy, as a chance to abolish "bigoted" Catholic school textbooks and replace them with sound Deweyite doctrine. John Henry Newman is not much in favor at the federal Office of Education. Look to King Stork, my masters.

§ § §

WALTER LIPPMANN: ON AID TO RELIGIOUS SCHOOLS

Near the end of the debate in the Senate on the education bill, Senator Morse, who is chairman of the Education subcommittee in the Senate, said: "Let us face it. We are going into federal aid for elementary and secondary schools . . . through the back door."

Senator Morse went on to say that the back door was to give federal aid "for 11 per cent of the school children of America who are deprived," and that the back door selected was "entirely constitutional". There were, quite naturally, senators who doubted or denied this, and there was some argument about how the constitutionality of the act could be tested in the courts. The argument was, however, procedural and technical and not substantial.

Senator Morse and the other proponents of the bill agreed entirely with the opponents and the skeptics that the bill should be reviewed in the courts. Senator Morse said that "in the not-too-distant future a decision will be rendered 'on the nose,' as we lawyers say, by the Supreme Court, telling Congress how far it can go under the First Amendment in giving aid to religious schools."

The bill which Congress has passed contains in itself a statement of the limits beyond which Congress does not wish to go. Section 605 says that "Nothing contained in this act shall be construed to authorize the making of any payment under this act, or under any act amended by this act, for religious worship or instruction."

Thus, subject to a judicial review, the principle affirmed by the Congress and the President is that religious schools are schools which offer their pupils not only religious worship and instruction but also education.

Admittedly, the boundary line between religious and non-religious instruction is in part not black and white but gray, notably in the study of history, literature and philosophy. But granting that there is a gray zone, there is also a great deal of education, for example in the physical sciences and mathematics, which is theologically neutral.

There is here a very considerable ground which is common to the public and the religious schools, and here, say the proponents of the act, it is constitutional to provide federal aid.

Without presuming to anticipate the decision of the Supreme Court, we may justly ask ourselves what is the sound public policy. The act is a breakthrough. The federal aid to religious schools which it authorizes is, to be sure, not wholly without any precedent. There have been in recent years certain fringe benefits accorded to the religious schools. But in the field of national policy, the act is a great innovation.

What is novel in it and highly significant is the recognition by Congress that religious schools are American schools, that they are an essential part of the American school system. Inasmuch as the religious schools instruct in religion, they cannot be given federal aid without contravening the First Amendment. But insofar as they provide education which is nonreligious, they are entitled to receive federal aid.

It has long seemed to me that the public policy of the act can be stated in the following way. It is a fundamental principle of American society that education is so indispensable that government rightly makes it compulsory. At all levels of government, the nation since it was founded has promoted education in schools and colleges.

It has never been the rule or the practice to make it compulsory that children be educated in public schools alone. From the beginning, American governments have accepted religious and private schools as educational agencies, provided they met certain standards of educational efficiency.

If, then, private schools are legitimate and recognized institutions, then justice demands and the public interest requires that they receive public assistance, outside the prohibitions of the First Amendment. A parochial school is an American school, and those who would deny it any public assistance ought, if they had the courage of their convictions, to ask that parochial schools be outlawed.

In fact, parochial schools are regarded as legitimate educational facilities, and in actual practice they have long been helped in one way or another by state and local authorities.

Those of us who believe in the act take as our major premise the paramount importance of educating the young. However, without a very substantial increase in the money available for education, we shall not be able to make progress in the attempt to educate the masses of our large and growing population.

There are, to be sure, many things besides money that must be provided in order to improve American education, to raise it from backwardness in the backward areas to an average level and to bring it in sight of excellence. But since it is not possible to raise enough money through state and local governments, the paramount principle requires that the federal government, with its far greater financial resources, be brought in to help. This makes the act an epoch-making advance towards the improvement of American education.

CHAPTER 25

THE ISSUE OF INTEGRATION

Separate educational facilities are inherently unequal.

Brown v. Board of Education of Topeka, 1954

69. The Supreme Court and Education (1899, 1927, 1954)[1]

CUMMING V. BOARD OF EDUCATION (1899)

[Mr. Justice Harlan delivered the opinion of the Court.]

. . . The constitution of Georgia provides: "There shall be a thorough system of common schools for the education of children in the elementary branches of an English education only, as nearly uniform as practicable, the expenses of which shall be provided for by taxation or otherwise. The schools shall be free to all children of the State, but separate schools shall be provided for the white and colored races."

It was said at the argument that the vice in the common school system of Georgia was the requirement that the white and colored children of the State be educated in separate schools. But we need not consider that question in this case. No such issue was made in the pleadings. Indeed, the plaintiffs distinctly state that they have no objection to the tax in question so far as levied for the support of primary, intermediate and grammar schools, in the management of which the rule as to the separation of races is enforced. We must dispose of the case as it is presented by the record.

The plaintiffs in error complain that the Board of Education used the funds in its hands to assist in maintaining a high school for white children without providing a similar school for colored children. The substantial relief asked is an injunction that would either impair the efficiency of the high school provided for the white children or compel the Board to close it. But if that were done, the result would only be to take from the white children educational privileges enjoyed by them, without giving to colored children additional opportunities for the education furnished in high schools. The colored school children of the county would not be advanced in the matter of their education by a decree compelling the defendant Board to cease giving support to a high school

---

[1] *Cumming* v. *Board of Education* (175 U.S. 528); *Gong Lum* v. *Rice* (275 U.S. 78); *Brown* v. *Board of Education* (347 U.S. 483).

for white children. The Board had before it the question whether it should maintain, under its control, a high school for about sixty colored children or withhold the benefits of education in primary schools from three hundred children of the same race. It was impossible, the Board believed, to give educational facilities to the three hundred colored children who were unprovided for, if it maintained a separate school for the sixty children who wished to have a high school education. Its decision was in the interest of the greater number of colored children, leaving the smaller number to obtain a high school education in existing private institutions at an expense not beyond that incurred in the high school discontinued by the Board.

We are not permitted by the evidence in the record to regard that decision as having been made with any desire or purpose on the part of the Board to discriminate against any of the colored school children of the county on account of their race. But if it be assumed that the Board erred in supposing that its duty was to provide educational facilities for the three hundred colored children who were without an opportunity in primary schools to learn the alphabet and to read and write, rather than to maintain a school for the benefit of the sixty colored children who wished to attend a high school, that was not an error which a court of equity should attempt to remedy by an injunction that would compel the Board to withhold all assistance from the high school maintained for white children. If, in some appropriate proceeding instituted directly for that purpose, the plaintiffs had sought to compel the Board of Education, out of the funds in its hands or under its control, to establish and maintain a high school for colored children, and if it appeared that the Board's refusal to maintain such a school was in fact an abuse of its discretion and in hostility to the colored population because of their race, different questions might have arisen in the state court.

The state court did not deem the action of the Board of Education in suspending temporarily and for economic reasons the high school for colored children a sufficient reason why the defendant should be restrained by injunction from maintaining an existing high school for white children. It rejected the suggestion that the Board proceeded in bad faith or had abused the discretion with which it was invested by the statute under which it proceeded or had acted in hostility to the colored race. Under the circumstances disclosed, we cannot say that this action of the state court was, within the meaning of the Fourteenth Amendment, a denial by the State to the plaintiffs and to those associated with them of the equal protection of the laws or of any privileges belonging to them as citizens of the United States. We may add that while all admit that the benefits and burdens of public taxation must be shared by citizens without discrimination against any class on account of their race, the education of the people in schools maintained by state taxation is a matter belonging to the respective States, and any interference on the part of Federal authority with the management of such schools cannot be justified except in the case of a clear and unmistakable disregard of rights secured by the supreme law of the land. We have here no such case to be determined; and as this view disposes of the only question which this court has jurisdiction to review and decide, the judgment is

Affirmed.

GONG LUM V. RICE (1927)

[Mr. Chief Justice Taft delivered the opinion of the Court.]

This was a petition for mandamus filed in the state Circuit Court of Mississippi for the First Judicial District of Bolivar County.

Gong Lum is a resident of Mississippi, resides in the Rosedale Consolidated High School District, and is the father of Martha Lum. He is engaged in the mercantile business. Neither he nor she was connected with the consular service or any other service of the government of China, or any other government, at the time of her birth. She was nine years old when the petition was filed, having been born January 21, 1915, and she sued by her next friend, Chew How, who is a native born citizen of the United States and the State of Mississippi. The petition alleged that she was of good moral character and between the ages of five and twenty-one years, and that, as she was such a citizen and an educable child, it became her father's duty under the law to send her to school; that she desired to attend the Rosedale Consolidated High School; that at the opening of the school she appeared as a pupil, but at the noon recess she was notified by the superintendent that she would not be allowed to return to school; that an order had been issued by the Board of Trustees, who are made defendants, excluding her from attending the school soley on the ground that she was of Chinese descent and not a member of the white or Caucasian race, and that their order had been made in pursuance to instructions from the State Superintendent of Education of Mississippi, who is also made a defendant.

The petitioners further show that there is no school maintained in the District for the education of children of Chinese descent, and none established in Bolivar County where she could attend.

The Constitution of Mississippi requires that there shall be a county common school fund, made up of poll taxes from the various counties, to be retained in the counties where the same is collected, and a state common school fund to be taken from the general fund in the state treasury, which together shall be sufficient to maintain a common school for a term of four months in each scholastic year, but that any county or separate school district may levy an additional tax to maintain schools for a longer time than a term of four months, and that the said common school fund shall be distributed among the several counties and separate school districts in proportion to the number of educable children in each, to be collected from the data in the office of the State Superintendent of Education in the manner prescribed by law; that the legislature encourage by all suitable means the promotion of intellectual, scientific, moral and agricultural improvement, by the establishment of a uniform system of free public schools by taxation or otherwise, for all children between the ages of five and twenty-one years, and, as soon as practicable, establish schools of higher grade.

The petition alleged that, in obedience to this mandate of the Constitution, the legislature has provided for the establishment and for the payment of the expenses of the Rosedale Consolidated High School, and that the plaintiff, Gong Lum, the petitioner's father, is a taxpayer and helps to support and maintain the school; that Martha Lum is an educable child, is entitled to attend the school as a pupil, and that this is the only school conducted in the District available for her as a pupil; that the right to attend it is a valuable right; that she is not a member of the colored race nor is she of mixed blood, but that she is pure Chinese; that she is by the action of the Board of Trustees and the State Superintendent discriminated against directly and denied her right to be a member of the Rosedale School; that the school authorities have no discretion under the law as to her admission as a pupil in the school, but that they continue without authority of law to deny her the right to attend it as a pupil. For these reasons the writ of mandamus is prayed for against the defendants commanding them and each of them to desist from discriminating against her on account of her race or ancestry and to give her the same rights and privileges that other educable children between the ages of five and twenty-one are granted in the Rosedale Consolidated High School.

The petition was demurred to by the defendants on the ground, among others, that the bill showed on its face that plaintiff is a member of the Mongolian or yellow race, and therefore not entitled to attend the schools provided by law in the State of Mississippi for children of the white or Caucasian race.

The trial court overruled the demurrer and ordered that a writ of mandamus issue to the defendants as prayed in the petition.

The defendants then appealed to the Supreme Court of Mississippi, which heard the case. In its opinion, it directed its attention to the proper construction of §207 of the State Constitution of 1890, which provides:

"Separate schools shall be maintained for children of the white and colored races."

The Court held that this provision of the Constitution divided the educable children into those of the pure white or Caucasian race, on the one hand, and the brown, yellow and black races, on the other, and therefore that Martha Lum of the Mongolian or yellow race could not insist on being classed with the whites under this constitutional division. The Court said:

"The legislature is not compelled to provide separate schools for each of the colored races, and, unless and until it does provide such schools and provide for segregation of the other races, such races are entitled to have the benefit of the colored public schools. Under our statutes a colored public school exists in every county and in some convenient district in which every colored child is entitled to obtain an education. These schools are within the reach of all the children of the state, and the plaintiff does not show by her petition that she applied for admission to such schools. On the contrary the petitioner takes the position that because there are no separate public schools for Mongolians that she is entitled to enter the white public schools in preference to the colored public schools. A consolidated school in this state is simply a common school conducted as other common schools are conducted; the only distinction being that two or more school districts have been consolidated into one school. Such consolidation is entirely discretionary with the county school board having reference to the condition existing in the particular territory. Where a school district has an unusual amount of territory, with an unusual valuation of property therein, it may levy additional taxes. But the other common schools under similar statutes have the same power.

"If the plaintiff desires, she may attend the colored public schools of her district, or, if she does not so desire, she may go to a private school. The compulsory school law of this state does not require the attendance at a public school, and a parent under the decisions of the Supreme Court of the United States has a right to educate his child in a private school if he so desires. But plaintiff is not entitled to attend a white public school."

As we have seen, the plaintiffs aver that the Rosedale Consolidated High School is the only school conducted in that district available for Martha Lum as a pupil. They also aver that there is no school maintained in the district of Bolivar County for the education of Chinese children and none in the county. How are these averments to be reconciled with the statement of the State Supreme Court that colored schools are maintained in every county by virtue of the Constitution? This seems to be explained, in the language of the State Supreme Court, as follows:

"By statute it is provided that all the territory of each county of the state shall be divided into school districts separately for the white and colored races; that is to say, the whole territory is to be divided into white school districts, and then a new division of the county for colored school districts. In other words, the statutory scheme is to make the districts outside of the separate school districts, districts for the particular race, white or colored, so that the territorial limits of the school districts need not be the same, but the territory embraced in a school district for the colored race may not be the same territory embraced in the school district for the white race, and *vice versa*, which system of creating the common school districts for the two races, white and colored, does not require schools for each race as such to be maintained in each district, but each child, no matter from what territory, is assigned to some school district, the school buildings being separately located and separately controlled, but each having the same curriculum, and each having the same number of months of school term, if the attendance is maintained for the said statutory period, which school district of the common or public schools has certain privileges, among which is to maintain a public school by local taxation for a longer period of time than the said term of four months under named conditions which apply alike to the common schools for the white and colored races."

We must assume then that there are school districts for colored children in Bolivar County, but that no colored school is within the limits of the Rosedale Consolidated High School District. This is not inconsistent with there being, at a place outside of that district and in a different district, a colored school which the plaintiff Martha Lum, may conveniently attend. If so, she is not denied, under the existing school system, the right to attend and enjoy the privileges of a common school education in a colored school. If it were otherwise, the petition should have contained an allegation showing it. Had the petition alleged specifically that there was no colored school in Martha Lum's neighborhood to which she could conveniently go, a different question would have been presented, and this, without regard to the State Supreme Court's construction of the State Constitution as limiting the white schools provided for the education of children of the white or Caucasian race. But we do not find the petition to present such a situation.

The case then reduces itself to the question whether a state can be said to afford to a child of Chinese ancestry born in this country, and a citizen of the United States, equal protection of the laws by giving her the opportunity for a common school education in a school which receives only colored children of the brown, yellow or black races.

The right and power of the state to regulate the method of providing for the education of its youth at public expense is clear. In *Cumming* v. *Richmond County Board of Education* persons of color sued the Board of Education to enjoin it from maintaining a high school for white children without providing a similar school for colored children which had existed and had been discontinued. Mr. Justice Harlan, in delivering the opinion of the Court, said:

"Under the circumstances disclosed, we cannot say that this action of the state court, was within the meaning of the Fourteenth Amendment, a denial by the State to the plaintiffs and to those associated with them of the equal protection of the laws, or of any privileges belonging to them as citizens of the United States. We may add that while all admit that the benefits and burdens of public taxation must be shared by citizens without discrimination against any class on account of their race, the education of the people in schools maintained by state taxation is a matter belonging to the respective States, and any interference on the part of Federal authority with the management of such schools can not be justified except in the case of a clear and unmistakable disregard of the rights secured by the supreme law of the land."

The question here is whether a Chinese citizen of the United States is denied equal protection of the laws when he is classed among the colored races and furnished facilities for education equal to that offered to all, whether white, brown, yellow or black. Were this a new question, it would call for very full argument and consideration, but we think that it is the same question which has been many times decided to be within the constitutional power of the state legislature to settle without intervention of the federal courts under the Federal Constitution.

In *Plessy* v. *Ferguson,* in upholding the validity under the Fourteenth Amendment of a statute of Louisiana requiring the separation of the white and colored races in railway coaches, a more difficult question than this, this Court, speaking of permitted race separation, said:

"The most common instance of this is connected with the establishment of separate schools for white and colored children, which has been held to be a valid exercise of the legislative power even by courts of States where the political rights of the colored race have been longest and most earnestly enforced."

The case of *Roberts* v. *City of Boston* in which Chief Justice Shaw of the Supreme Judicial Court of Massachusetts, announced the opinion of that court upholding the separation of colored and white schools under a state constitutional injunction of equal protection, the same as the Fourteenth Amendment, was then referred to, and this Court continued:

"Similar laws have been enacted by Congress under its general power of legislation over the District of Columbia as well as by the legislatures of many of the States, and have been generally, if not uniformly, sustained by the Courts," citing many of the cases above named.

Most of the cases cited arose, it is true, over the establishment of separate schools as between white pupils and black pupils, but we can not think that the question is any different or that any different result can be reached, assuming the cases above cited to be rightly decided, where the issue is as between white pupils and the pupils of the yellow races. The decision is within the discretion of the state in regulating its public schools and does not conflict with the Fourteenth Amendment. The judgment of the Supreme Court of Mississippi is

Affirmed.

BROWN V. BOARD OF EDUCATION OF TOPEKA (1954)

[Mr. Chief Justice Warren delivered the opinion of the Court.]

These cases come to us from the States of Kansas, South Carolina, Virginia, and Delaware. They are premised on different facts and different local conditions, but a common legal question justifies their consideration together in this consolidated opinion.

In each of the cases, minors of the Negro race, through their legal representatives, seek the aid of the courts in obtaining admission to the public schools of their community on a nonsegregated basis. In each instance, they had been denied admission to schools attended by white children under laws requiring or permitting segregation according to race. This segregation was alleged to deprive the plaintiffs of the equal protection of the laws under the Fourteenth Amendment. In each of the cases other than the Delaware case, a three-judge federal district court denied relief to the plaintiffs on the so-called "separate but equal" doctrine announced by this Court in *Plessy* v. *Ferguson*. Under that doctrine, equality of treatment is accorded when the races are provided substantially equal facilities, even though these facilities be separate. In the Delaware case, the Supreme Court of Delaware adhered to that doctrine, but ordered that the plaintiffs be admitted to the white schools because of their superiority to the Negro schools.

The plaintiffs contend that segregated public schools are not "equal" and cannot be made "equal," and that hence they are deprived of the equal protection of the laws. Because of the obvious importance of the question presented, the Court took jurisdiction. Argument was heard in the 1952 Term, and reargument was heard this Term on certain questions propounded by the Court.

Reargument was largely devoted to the circumstances surrounding the adoption of the Fourteenth Amendment in 1868. It covered exhaustively consideration of the Amendment in Congress, ratification by the states, then existing practices in racial segregation, and the views of proponents and opponents of the Amendment. This discussion and our own investigation convince us that, although these sources cast some light, it is not enough to resolve the problem with which we are faced. At best, they are inconclusive. The most avid proponents of the post-War Amendments undoubtedly intended them to remove all legal distinctions among "all persons born or naturalized in the United States." Their opponents, just as certainly, were antagonistic to both the letter and the spirit of the Amendments and wished them to have the most limited effect. What others in Congress and the state legislatures had in mind cannot be determined with any degree of certainty.

An additional reason for the inconclusive nature of the Amendment's history, with respect to segregated schools, is the status of public education at that time. In the South, the movement toward free common schools, supported by general taxation, had not yet taken hold. Education of white children was largely in the hands of private groups. Education of Negroes was almost non-existent, and practically all of the race were illiterate. In fact, any education of Negroes was forbidden by law in some states. Today, in contrast, many Negroes have achieved outstanding success in the arts and sciences as well as in the business and professional world. It is true that public school education at the time of the Amendment had advanced further in the North, but the effect of the Amendment on Northern States was generally ignored in the congressional debates. Even in the North, the conditions of public education did not approximate those existing today. The curriculum was usually rudimentary; ungraded schools were common in rural areas; the school term was but three months a year in many states; and compulsory school attendance was virtually unknown. As a consequence, it is not surprising that there should be so little in the history of the Fourteenth Amendment relating to its intended effect on public education.

In the first cases in this Court construing the Fourteenth Amendment, decided shortly after its adoption, the Court interpreted it as proscribing all state-imposed discriminations against the Negro race. The doctrine of "separate but equal" did not make its appearance in this Court until 1896 in the case of *Plessy* v.

Ferguson involving not education but transportation. American courts have since labored with the doctrine for over half a century. In this Court, there have been six cases involving the "separate but equal" doctrine in the field of public education. In *Cumming* v. *County Board of Education* and *Gong Lum* v. *Rice* the validity of the doctrine itself was not challenged. In more recent cases, all on the graduate school level, inequality was found in that specific benefits enjoyed by white students were denied to Negro students of the same educational qualifications. In none of these cases was it necessary to re-examine the doctrine to grant relief to the Negro plaintiff. And in *Sweatt* v. *Painter* the Court expressly reserved decision on the question whether *Plessy* v. *Ferguson* should be held inapplicable to public education.

In the instant cases, that question is directly presented. Here, unlike *Sweatt* v. *Painter*, there are findings below that the Negro and white schools involved have been equalized, or are being equalized, with respect to buildings, curricula, qualifications and salaries of teachers, and other "tangible" factors. Our decision, therefore, cannot turn on merely a comparison of these tangible factors in the Negro and white schools involved in each of the cases. We must look instead to the effect of segregation itself on public education.

In approaching this problem, we cannot turn the clock back to 1868 when the Amendment was adopted, or even to 1896 when *Plessy* v. *Ferguson* was written. We must consider public education in the light of its full development and its present place in American life throughout the Nation. Only in this way can it be determined if segregation in public schools deprives these plaintiffs of the equal protection of the laws.

Today, education is perhaps the most important function of state and local governments. Compulsory school attendance laws and the great expenditures for education both demonstrate our recognition of the importance of education to our democratic society. It is required in the performance of our most basic public responsibilities, even service in the armed forces. It is the very foundation of good citizenship. Today it is a principal instrument in awakening the child to cultural values, in preparing him for later professional training, and in helping him to adjust normally to his environment. In these days, it is doubtful that any child may reasonably be expected to succeed in life if he is denied the opportunity of an education. Such an opportunity, where the state

377

has undertaken to provide it, is a right which must be made available to all on equal terms.

We come then to the question presented: Does segregation of children in public schools solely on the basis of race, even though the physical facilities and other "tangible" factors may be equal, deprive the children of the minority group of equal educational opportunities? We believe that it does.

In *Sweatt* v. *Painter* in finding that a segregated law school for Negroes could not provide them equal educational opportunities, this Court relied in large part on "those qualities which are incapable of objective measurement but which made for greatness in a law school." In *McLaurin* v. *Oklahoma State Regents* the Court, in requiring that a Negro admitted to a white graduate school be treated like all other students, again resorted to intangible considerations: ". . . his ability to study, to engage in discussions and exchange views with other students, and, in general, to learn his profession." Such considerations apply with added force to children in grade and high schools. To separate them from others of similar age and qualifications solely because of their race generates a feeling of inferiority as to their status in the community that may affect their hearts and minds in a way unlikely ever to be undone. The effect of this separation on their educational opportunities was well stated by a finding in the Kansas case by a court which nevertheless felt compelled to rule against the Negro plaintiffs:

> Segregation of white and colored children in public schools has a detrimental effect upon the colored children. The impact is greater when it has the sanction of the law; for the policy of separating the races is usually interpreted as denoting the inferiority of the negro group. A sense of inferiority affects the motivation of a child to learn. Segregation with the sanction of law, therefore, has a tendency to [retard] the educational and mental development of negro children and to deprive them of some of the benefits they would receive in a racial [ly] integrated school system.

Whatever may have been the extent of psychological knowledge at the time of *Plessy* v. *Ferguson,* this finding is amply supported by modern authority. Any language in *Plessy* v. *Ferguson* contrary to this finding is rejected.

We conclude that in the field of public education the doctrine of "separate but equal" has no place. Separate educational facilities are inherently unequal. Therefore, we hold that the plaintiffs and others similarly situated for whom the actions have been brought are, by reason of the segregation complained of, deprived of the equal protection of the laws guaranteed by the Fourteenth Amendment. This disposition makes unnecessary any discussion whether such segregation also violates the Due Process Clause of the Fourteenth Amendment.

Because these are class actions, because of the wide applicability of this decision, and because of the great variety of local conditions, the formulation of decrees in these cases presents problems of considerable complexity. On reargument, the consideration of appropriate relief was necessarily subordinated to the primary question—the constitutionality of segregation in public education. We have now announced that such segregation is a denial of the equal protection of the laws. In order that we may have the full assistance of the parties formulating decrees, the cases will be restored to the docket, and the parties are requested to present further argument on Questions 4 and 5 previously propounded by the Court for the reargument this Term. The Attorney General of the United States is again invited to participate. The Attorneys General of the states requiring or permitting segregation in public education will also be permitted to appear as *amici curiae* upon request to do so by September 15, 1954, and submission of briefs by October 1, 1954.

70. THE NEGRO AND EDUCATION (1944)[1]

GUNNAR MYRDAL

I. NEGRO EDUCATION AS CONCERTED ACTION

The trend toward a rising educational level of the Negro population is of tremendous importance for the power relations discussed in this Part of our inquiry. Education means an assimilation of white American culture. It decreases the dissimilarity of the Negroes from other Americans. Since the white culture is permeated by democratic valuations, and since the caste relation is anything but democratic, education is likely to increase dissatisfaction among Negroes. This dissatisfaction strengthens the urge to withdraw from contact with prejudiced whites and causes an intensified isolation between the two groups. Increasing education provides theories and tools for the rising Negro protest against caste status in which Negroes are held. It trains and helps to give an economic livelihood to Negro leaders.

In the Negro community, education is the main factor for the stratification of the Negro people into social classes. The professionals who base their status upon having acquired a higher education form a substantial part of the Negro upper classes. And even in the middle and lower classes, educational levels signify class differences in the Negro community. In addition, education has a symbolic significance in the Negro world: the educated Negro has, in one important respect, become equal to the better class of whites.

These tendencies are most unhampered in the North. There Negroes have practically the entire educational system flung open to them without much discrimination. They are often taught in

---

[1] Gunnar Myrdal: *An American Dilemma. The Negro Problem and Modern Democracy* (New York: Harper and Brothers, 1944), pp. 879 – 82, 883 – 84, 893 – 96, 900 – 02. This monumental study, financed by the Carnegie Corporation, attempted to analyze and interpret the place of the Negro in American life. Myrdal, a Swedish social economist, was "imported" to direct the project in order to bring to the study a fresh outlook not influenced by traditional attitudes.

mixed schools and by white teachers; some of the Negro teachers have white pupils. Little attempt is made to adjust the teaching specifically to the Negroes' existing status and future possibilities. The American Creed permeates instruction, and the Negro as well as the white youths are inculcated with the traditional American virtues of efficiency, thrift and ambition. The American dream of individual success is held out to the Negroes as to other students. But employment opportunities – and, to a lesser extent, some other good things of life – are so closed to them that severe conflicts in their minds are bound to appear.

Their situation is, however, not entirely unique. Even among the youths from other poor and disadvantaged groups in the North the ideals implanted by the schools do not fit life as they actually experience it. The conflicts are, of course, accentuated in the case of Negroes. Often they become cynical in regard to the official democratic ideals taught by the school. But more fundamentally they will be found to have drunk of them deeply. The American Creed and the American virtues mean much more to Negroes than to whites. They are all turning into the rising Negro protest.

The situation is more complicated in the South. The Negro schools are segregated and the Negro school system is controlled by different groups with different interests and opinions concerning the desirability of preserving or changing the caste status of Negroes. Looked upon as a "movement," Negro education in the South is, like the successful Negro organizations, an interracial endeavor. White liberals in the region and Northern philanthropists have given powerful assistance in building up Negro education in the South. They have thereby taken and kept some of the controls. In the main, however, the control over Negro education has been preserved by other whites representing the political power of the region. The salaried officers of the movement – the college presidents, the school principals, the professors, and the teachers – are now practically all Negroes; in the elementary schools and in the high schools they are exclusively Negroes. With this set-up, it is natural and, indeed, necessary that the Negro school adhere rather closely to the accommodating pattern.

Negro teachers on all levels are dependent on the white community leaders. This dependence is particularly strong in the case of elementary school teachers in rural districts. Their salaries are low, and their security as to tenure almost nothing. They can be used as disseminators of the whites' expectations and demands on the Negro community. But the extreme dependence and poverty of rural Negro school teachers, and the existence of Negroes who are somewhat better off and more independent than they, practically excluded them from having any status of leadership in the Negro community. In so far as their teaching is concerned, they are, however, more independent than it appears. This is solely because the white superintendent and the white school board ordinarily care little about what goes on in the Negro school. There are still counties where the superintendent has never visited the majority of his Negro schools. As long as Negro stool pigeons do not transfer reports that she puts wrong ideas into the children's heads, the rural Negro school teacher is usually ignored.

In cities the situation is different. Negro elementary and high schools are better; teachers are better trained and better paid. In the Negro community teachers have a higher social status. As individuals they also achieve a measure of independence because they are usually anonymous to the white superintendent and school board. In the cities, the white community as a whole does not follow so closely what happens among the Negroes. The Negro principal in a city school, however, is directly responsible to white officials and watches his teachers more closely than do superintendents of rural schools.

In state colleges the situation is similar, except that the professors have a still higher social status in the Negro community and except that the college tends to become a little closed community of its own, with its own norms, which tends to increase somewhat the independence of the teachers.

In the private colleges there is much more independence from local white opinion within the limits of the campus. A friendly white churchman belonging to the interracial movement recently told the students of Atlanta University, in a commencement address, that the teachers there enjoyed greater academic freedom than their white colleagues at the Georgia state institutions, and this is probably true. The influence exerted by the Northern philanthropists and church bodies who have contributed to the colleges — often exercised through Southern white liberals and interracialists and through outstanding conservative Negro leaders — is, to a great extent, effective as a means of upholding the independence of Negro college presidents and professors.

As conditions are in the South, it is apparent that this influence is indispensable for this purpose. Neither the Negro teachers themselves nor any outside Negro institution could provide a power backing effective enough to keep off local white pressure. This outside white control gives the Negro teachers a considerably greater freedom even to inculcate a protest attitude — if it is cautiously done — than is allowed in publicly supported educational institutions. But it is inherent in the Southern caste situation, and in the traditions of the movement to build up Negro education in the region, that even this control is conservatively directed when compared with Northern standards.

In spite of these controls, strongest at the bottom of the educational system but strong also in the higher institutions, there is no doubt, however, that *the long-range effect of the rising level of education in the Negro people goes in the direction of nourishing and strengthening the Negro protest.* Negro-baiting Senator Vardaman knew this when he said:

What the North is sending South is not money but dynamite; this education is ruining our Negroes. They're demanding equality.

This would probably hold true of any education, independent of the controls held and the direction given. An increased ability on the part of the Negroes to understand the printed and spoken word cannot avoid opening up contact for them with the wider world, where equalitarian ideas are prevalent. But in the South there is not much supervision of Negro schools. And as we shall see later, Southern whites have been prohibited by their allegiance to the American Creed from making a perfected helot training out of Negro education.

✻   ✻   ✻

The duty of society to provide for public education was early established in America, and private endowments for educational purposes have been magnificent. America spends more money and provides its youth, on the average, with more schooling than any other country in the world. America has also succeeded in a relatively higher degree than any other country in making real the old democratic principle that the complete educational ladder should be held open to the most intelligent and industrious youths, independent of private means and support from their family. Education has been, and is increasingly becoming, a chief means of climbing the social status scale. It is entirely within this great American tradition when white people, who have wanted to help the Negroes, have concentrated their main efforts on improving Negro education.

American Negroes have taken over the American faith in education. Booker T. Washington's picture of the freedmen's drive for education is classical:

> Few people who were not right in the midst of the scenes can form any exact idea of the intense desire which the people of my race showed for education. It was a whole race trying to go to school. Few were too young, and none too old, to make the attempt to learn. As fast as any kind of teachers could be secured, not only were day-schools filled, but night-schools as well. The great ambition of the older people was to try to learn to read the Bible before they died. With this end in view, men and women who were fifty or seventy-five years old, would be found in the night-schools. Sunday-schools were formed soon after freedom, but the principal book studied in the Sunday-school was the spelling-book. Day-school, night-school, and Sunday-school were always crowded, and often many had to be turned away for want of room.

. . . As self-improvement through business or social improvement through government appeared so much less possible for them, Negroes have come to affix an even stronger trust in the magic of education. It is true that some Negroes may lately have lost their faith in education, either because the schools available to them —in the South—are so inadequate or—in the North—because they achieve education but not the things they hoped to do with it. This attitude of dissatisfaction is probably part of the explanation why Negro children tend to drop out of high school more than do whites. If both sources of dissatisfaction could be removed, there is reason to believe that American Negroes would revert to their original belief in education. And, aside from such dissatisfaction and even cynicism, the masses of Negroes show even today a naïve, almost religious faith in education. To an extent, this faith was misplaced: many Negroes hoped to escape drudgery through education alone. But it is also true that this faith has been justified to a large extent: education is one of the things which has given the Negroes something of a permanent advance in their condition.

✧ ✧ ✧

THE WHITES' ATTITUDES TOWARD NEGRO EDUCATION

There are apparent conflicts of valuations between whites and Negroes in regard to Negro education. These conflicts, the interests involved, and the theories expressing them determine the forms of Negro education. But the situation is not so simple as just a difference of opinion. In fact, many whites are as eager to improve Negro education as is any Negro, and there are some Negroes who are rather on the other side of the fence, at least for the purpose of an opportunistic accommodation. The situation is complicated by the fact that both whites and Negroes are divided in their own minds. They harbor conflicting valuations within themselves. Only by keeping this constantly in mind can we understand the development of Negro education and correctly evaluate future prospects.

The American Creed definitely prescribes that the Negro child or youth should have just as much educational opportunity as is offered anyone else in the same community. Negroes should be trained to become good and equal citizens in a democracy which places culture high in its hierarchy of values. This equalitarian valuation is strong enough to dominate public policy in the North, in spite of the fact that probably most white people in the North, too, believe the Negroes to be inferior and, anyhow, do not care so much for their potentialities and possibilities as for those of whites. In the South the existing great discrimination in education is an indication that another valuation is dominating white people's actions. But it is a great mistake to believe that the American Creed is not also present and active in the motivations of Southern whites. Behavior is as always a moral compromise. Negroes would not be getting so much education as they are actually getting in the South if the equalitarian Creed were not also active.

By itself, the interest of upholding the caste system would motivate Southern whites to give Negroes practically no education at all or would restrict it to the transmission of only such lowly skills as would make Negroes better servants and farm hands. There is no mistake about this interest; it is real and has economic importance.

✣   ✣   ✣

The poorer classes of whites in this respect have interests similar to those of the planters. They are in competition with

Negroes for jobs and for social status. One of the things which demarcates them as superior and increases the future potentialities of their children is the fact that white children in publicly supported school buses are taken to fine consolidated schools while often Negro children are given only what amounts to a sham education in dilapidated one-room schools or old Negro churches by underpaid, badly trained Negro teachers. The observer, visiting Southern rural counties, gets clear statements of these interests on the part of all classes of whites who want to preserve the traditional caste order. The segregated school system of the South, in addition, allows a substantial saving by keeping Negro education low.

The caste interest is not merely economic. The whites have told themselves that education will make the Negro conscious of "rights" which he should not know about. It will make him dissatisfied where he has been happy and accommodated. It will raise some Negroes above many whites in culture. It will make many more Negroes "uppity" and obnoxious. The supremacy of individual whites is bound up with Negro ignorance. If the Negro stays in the only "place" where he should be, then he does not need any education. These opinions also make sense in the light of the white caste's undoubted interest in keeping education away from the Negroes.

The white people have among themselves all the power, and so their convergent interests have molded Negro education in rural districts. The low standard of Negro schools is the result. But even in the rural South the observer sees the impact of the American Creed. Often it is revealed only in a bad conscience. This is apparent everywhere. In most localities there also seems to be a gradual improvement of Negro schools. In practically all places no obstacles are placed in the way of outside help if it observes the proper Southern forms, and it will even be encouraged either verbally or by "matching" it with local financial support. The scattering around the entire region of the Rosenwald schoolhouses is a case in point. Exertions by the Negroes to collect money among themselves for educational purposes are never discouraged but applauded by almost everybody. This is not said by way of excusing the bald and illegal discrimination in the rural school systems in the South, but only to stress the fact that the white caste interests are practically never driven to their logical end.

In the urban South, whites of the employing class do not have the same material interests in keeping the Negroes ignorant. They have rather to gain if their Negro servants and laborers have at least some education. The poorer classes of white have scarcely any such gains to reap, however. They are interested in keeping Negroes as much as possible out of competition on the labor market. The general interest of keeping the Negroes down to preserve the caste order intact is present in the cities too. It is shared by all classes, but, of course, felt most strongly by the poorer whites. City populations are, however, more closely integrated in the life of the nation: the regional traditions are somewhat weaker, the cultural level among whites is higher, and American Creed is stronger. So we find that Southern cities offer the Negroes a substantially better education. In the Border states the integration in the national life and the strength of the American Creed are still stronger, and we find also that the educational facilities available to Negroes are more nearly equal to those of the whites.

The primary rationalization of this gradual deviation in the South from the policy representing the crude caste interest is usually phrased in the popular theory of the American Creed—that education of the youths of the poorer classes is beneficial not only to themselves but to society. Thomas Nelson Page presented the liberal Southerners' attitude toward the education of the Negro masses many years ago:

There is much truth in the saying that unless the whites lift the Negroes up, the Negroes will drag them down, though it is not true in the full sense in which it was intended. It is not true to the extent that the white must lift the Negro up to his own level; it is true to the extent that he must not leave him debased—at least must not leave him here debased. If he does, then the Negro will inevitably hold him, if not drag him down. No country in the present stage of the world's progress can long maintain itself in the front rank, and no people can long maintain themselves at the top of the list of peoples if they have to carry perpetually the burden of a vast and densely ignorant population, and where that population belongs to another race, the argument must be all the stronger. Certainly, no section can, under such a burden keep pace with a section which has no such burden. Whatever the case may have been in the past,

the time has gone by, possibly forever, when the ignorance of the working-class was an asset. Nations and
peoples and, much more, sections of peoples, are now
strong and prosperous almost in direct ratio to their
knowledge and enlightenment. . . .

Viewing the matter economically, the Negro race,
like every other race, must be of far more value to the
country in which it is placed, if the Negro is properly
educated, elevated, and trained, than if he is allowed to
remain in ignorance and degradation. He is a greater
peril to the community in which he lives if he remains
in ignorance and degradation than if he is enlightened.
If the South expects ever to compete with the North, she
must educate and train her population, and, in my judgment, not merely her white population but her entire
population.

This has been the main argument through decades for improving the educational facilities for Negroes in the South. Usually it is
restricted by assertion of their lower capability of responding to
education. Usually also it is qualified by the insistence on a particular kind of education as more suitable for Negroes.

There is petty pressure on Negro education in the South, but
the truth is that the *Southern whites have never had the nerve to
make of Negro education an accomplished instrument to keep the
Negroes in their caste status.* It would have been possible, but it
has not been done. The Southern whites' caste policy has been
halfhearted all through, but particularly so in education. The
explanation is again that they are also good Americans with all the
standardized American ideals about education. The interest of
educating the Negroes to become faithful helots has been obvious,
but the Southern whites have not even attempted to make it effective in practice. Instead, they have merely kept Negro education
poor and bad. And even on that point they have been gradually
giving up resistance to the command of the Creed. This is the
deeper dynamics of Negro education.

✸ ✸ ✸

NEGRO ATTITUDES

The attitudes of the whites are of greatest importance for the
growth of Negro education, as they have all the power. The Ne-

groes are, however, not without influence, partly because the whites are divided among themselves and divided in their own conscience. The remarkable thing is that the Negroes are split in much the same way and on the same issues.

It is natural, to begin with, that the American Creed interest is more stressed with the Negroes. Deep down in their souls practically all Negroes feel that they have the right to equal opportunities for education. And the sanctity of the American Creed gives them the opportunity to express this opinion and to press the whites for concessions. The stress on education in American culture makes the Negro protest most respectable. But the observer finds also that there are a few upper class Negroes who express about the same opinion as whites, that common Negroes do not need and should not have much education. This is rare, however, and the opinion has to be concealed.

Much more important is the split in the Negro world as to what kind of education is desirable. On the one hand, they sense the caste motivation behind most whites' interest in industrial education for Negroes. They know also that they can hope to win the respect of the whites and take their place as equal citizens in American democracy only if they are educated in the nonvocational cultural values of the broader society. On the other hand, they see the actual caste situation as a reality and know that many lines of work are closed to them. In order to utilize fully the openings left, and in order eventually to open up new roads into industrial employment, they often conclude that Negroes are in particular need of vocational training. They realize also that the great poverty and cultural backwardness of their people motivate a special adaptation of Negro education. On this point there is a possibility of striking a compromise with the liberal white man. In the North most Negroes will not make this concession, and by no means all Negroes, perhaps not even a majority, in the South are prepared to take the stand. Even the ones who do, stress at the same time the necessity of raising educational opportunities and of improving the schools.

Concerning the content of teaching in other respects, Negroes are also divided. On the one hand, they are inclined to feel that the Northern system, where a standardized teaching is given students independent of whether they are whites or Negroes, is the only right thing. On the other hand, they feel that the students get to know too little about Negro problems. They thus want an

389

adjustment of teaching toward the status of Negroes, usually not in order to make the Negroes weak and otherwise fit into the white man's wishful picture about "good niggers" but, on the contrary, to make Negroes better prepared to fight for their rights. They feel that education should not only be accepted passively but should be used as a tool of concerted action to gain the equal status they are seeking. For this reason many, if not most, Negro leaders desire that Negro students should get special training in Negro problems.

Du Bois, who originally was the most uncompromising advocate of the idea that no difference at all should be made in teaching Negro and white students, later came out with the opinion that the Negro student should not only be taught general history and social subjects as they were taught to white students, but also Negro history and Negro problems and, indeed, a special race strategy for meeting their individual and collective problems in America. Negro youth should even be taught to have pride in Africa.

This opinion, except perhaps for the last point, is now commonly shared by most Negro intellectuals. The institution of "Negro History Week" has emanated from such attitudes. Negro colleges and high schools are devoting an increasing interest to Negro problems. White interracialists condone these things. Other whites do not care but feel, as we have said, that it is the Negroes' right to discuss their own problems if they want to.

There is a further controversy as to whether Negro education ought to be segregated or not. In the North the official opinion among whites is that segregation is not compatible with equality, but, as we have seen, much segregation is actually in effect as a consequence of residential segregation and of gerrymandering districts and granting permits to transfer. In the South direct segregation in schools is a necessary means of keeping up the tremendous financial discrimination against Negro schools. In recent years not even Southern liberals—with some rare exceptions—have stated that they favored mixed education. Segregation is usually not motivated by financial reasons but as a precaution against social equality.

Negroes are divided on the issues of segregated schools. In so far as segregation means discrimination and is a badge of Negro inferiority, they are against it, although many Southern Negroes would not take an open stand that would anger Southern whites. Some Negroes, however, prefer the segregated school, even for the North, when the mixed school involves humiliation for Negro students and discrimination against Negro teachers. . . . Other Negroes prefer the mixed schools at any cost, since for them it is a matter of principle or since they believe that it is a means of improving race relations.

71. A Southern Declaration
of Constitutional Principles (1956)[1]

The unwarranted decision of the Supreme Court in the public school cases is now bearing the fruit always produced when men substitute naked power for established law.

The Founding Fathers gave us a Constitution of checks and balances because they realized the inescapable lesson of history that no man or group of men can be safely entrusted with unlimited power. They framed this Constitution with its provisions for change by amendment in order to secure the fundamentals of government against the dangers of temporary popular passion or the personal predilections of public officeholders.

We regard the decision of the Supreme Court in the school cases as clear abuse of judicial power. It climaxes a trend in the Federal judiciary undertaking to legislate, in derogation of the authority of Congress, and to encroach upon the reserved rights of the states and the people.

The original Constitution does not mention education. Neither does the Fourteenth Amendment nor any other amendment. The debates preceding the submission of the Fourteenth Amendment clearly show that there was no intent that it should affect the systems of education maintained by the states.

The very Congress which proposed the amendment subsequently provided for segregated schools in the District of Columbia.

When the amendment was adopted in 1868, there were thirty-seven states of the Union. Every one of the twenty-six states that had any substantial racial differences among its people either approved the operation of segregated schools already in existence or subsequently established such schools by action of the same law-making body which considered the Fourteenth Amendment.

---

[1]Referred to as the "Southern Manifesto," this statement of constitutional principles was signed by 96 Senators and Representatives from the Southern states. *New York Times,* March 12, 1956, p. 19.

As admitted by the Supreme Court in the public school case (Brown v. Board of Education), the doctrine of separate but equal schools "apparently originated in Roberts v. City of Boston (1849), upholding school segregation against attack as being violative of a state constitutional guarantee of equality." This constitutional doctrine began in the North—not in the South—and it was followed not only in Massachusetts but in Connecticut, New York, Illinois, Indiana, Michigan, Minnesota, New Jersey, Ohio, Pennsylvania and other northern states until they, exercising their rights as states through the constitutional processes of local self-government, changed their school systems.

In the case of Plessy v. Ferguson in 1896 the Supreme Court expressly declared that under the Fourteenth Amendment no person was denied any of his rights if the states provided separate but equal public facilities. This decision has been followed in many other cases. It is notable that the Supreme Court, speaking through Chief Justice Taft, a former President of the United States, unanimously declared in 1927 in Lum v. Rice that the "separate but equal" principle is ". . . within the discretion of the state in regulating its public schools and does not conflict with the Fourteenth Amendment."

This interpretation, restated time and again, became a part of the life of the people of many of the states and confirmed their habits, customs, traditions and way of life. It is founded on elemental humanity and common sense, for parents should not be deprived by Government of the right to direct the lives and education of their own children.

Though there has been no constitutional amendment or act of Congress changing this established legal principle almost a century old, the Supreme Court of the United States, with no legal basis for such action, undertook to exercise their naked judicial power and substituted their personal political and social ideas for the established law of the land.

This unwarranted exercise of power by the court, contrary to the Constitution, is creating chaos and confusion in the states principally affected. It is destroying the amicable relations between the white and Negro races that have been created through ninety years of patient effort by the good people of both races. It has planted hatred and suspicion where there has been heretofore friendship and understanding.

Without regard to the consent of the governed, outside agitators are threatening immediate and revolutionary changes in our public school systems. If done, this is certain to destroy the system of public education in some of the states.

With the gravest concern for the explosive and dangerous condition created by this decision and inflamed by outside meddlers:

We reaffirm our reliance on the Constitution as the fundamental law of the land.

We decry the Supreme Court's encroachments on rights reserved to the states and to the people, contrary to established law and to the Constitution.

We commend the motives of those states which have declared the intention to resist forced integration by any lawful means.

We appeal to the states and the people who are not directly affected by these decisions to consider the constitutional principles involved against the time when they too, on issues vital to them, may be the victims of judicial encroachment.

Even though we constitute a minority in the present Congress, we have full faith that a majority of the American people believe in the dual system of government which has enabled us to achieve our greatness and will in time demand that the reserved rights of the states and of the people be made secure against judicial usurpation.

We pledge ourselves to use all lawful means to bring about a reversal of this decision which is contrary to the Constitution and to prevent the use of force in its implementation.

In this trying period, as we all seek to right this wrong, we appeal to our people not to be provoked by the agitators and troublemakers invading our states and to scrupulously refrain from disorder and lawless acts.

[Signed by 19 Senators and 77 Representatives from Southern states].

72. The Southern Case Against Desegregation (1956)[1]

THOMAS R. WARING

Although the Supreme Court has declared that separation of the races in public schools is unconstitutional, few white Southerners are able to accept the prospect of mingling white and Negro pupils. Resistance to the court decree is stiffening throughout the region.

Many white Northerners are unable to understand the depth of feeling in the Southern states, whose area is about a sixth of the nation and whose population is roughly a fourth of the total. The purpose of this article is to try to put before the open-minded readers of this magazine the point of view of the Southerner — whom the rest of the United States apparently cannot believe to be open-minded at all on the subject of race.

At the outset it is only fair to warn the Northern reader that he may be infuriated long before he reaches the end. This, I suspect, is just as inevitable as the outraged feelings of the Southerner when he reads the Northern press with its own interpretation of the American dilemma. Both sides have been shouting at each other so loudly that it is difficult any longer to hear facts through the din of name-calling. If, in the course of speaking for the South, I should raise blood pressure among some Northerners, I apologize for causing pain — with the hope that I may be able to reach Northern minds that are truly open so that some good may come along with the discomfort.

The reader outside the South may, unfortunately, react in still another way. He may find it difficult, if not impossible, to believe much of what I say. To this I can only reply that as editor of a South Carolina newspaper with a circulation of 56,000, with twenty-eight years of journalistic experience in both the North and

---

[1] *Harpers' Magazine* (Jan. 1956), pp. 39–45.

the South, I have had to be in possession of accurate information on this as on any other subject covered in my work. Across an editor's desk pass, day by day and year after year, reports, letters, statistics — in other words, facts. By means of these facts, plus personal conversations with people from all over the world, an editor manages to keep in touch with public opinion.

It is the public opinion of the South that I am about to report. That opinion is a fact. It exists, and can be demonstrated. What I am saying is documented by facts and statistics. If these should seem to the reader to add up merely to bias, bigotry, and even untruth, I shall regret it. Facts, however, remain facts.

One of the reasons these facts may be unfamiliar — and therefore incredible — is the almost unanimous attitude of the national press — daily and weekly — toward the subject of race. I read many newspapers and news magazines, and people send me clippings from others that I do not see regularly. From my observation, the testimony these publications print is almost entirely one-sided. While less violent than the Negro press — which understandably presents only the militant anti-segregation case — the metropolitan press almost without exception has abandoned fair and objective reporting of the race story. For facts it frequently substitutes propaganda.

Furthermore, with the exception of a small coterie of Southern writers whom Northern editors regard as "enlightened," spokesmen for the Southern view cannot gain access to Northern ears. This article will be one of the few of its kind published in a magazine of national circulation. The South, alas, lacks a magazine or other organ with nationwide distribution.

Perhaps my first assertion of a seldom realized truth will be the most difficult to believe. This statement is that white Southerners of good will — and the percentage of decency runs about the same in the South as anywhere else — favor uplift of the Negro, and that these white Southerners are in the vast majority. If it is impossible to prove the percentage of decency among Southerners, it is equally impossible to show that people in the North — or any other region — have a monopoly of it. But the South fears, and with reason, that the uplift is being forced at too fast a pace. The vagaries of custom and race taboos have many inconsistencies. The rules of segregation, both written and unwritten, change with conditions. And the sudden rewriting by the Supreme Court of regional laws and state constitutions has stirred as much resentment in Southern breasts as would be aroused among Northerners if suddenly their own freedom from race restrictions were denied by federal fiat. (Do I hear a muffled cheer from one or two Northerners who may take a dim view of mingling the races?)

Interference with sovereignty usually produces rage. In matters of education, the states long have been sovereign—until suddenly nine men have held otherwise.

Is it any wonder that the Southerner is bitter over what he believes to be a flouting of the Constitution for political reasons?

Aside from legal questions—and they are deep and broad—the Southerner believes that as a practical matter, he is better equipped by experience to cope with race problems than people from other regions, no matter what their intellectual or political attainments. One of the proofs that this belief is founded not merely on pride or emotional prejudice lies in the fact that Northerners who spend some time in the South—not tourists or weekend visitors, but people who make their homes here—come rather sooner than later to agree that this is so. These transplanted Northerners come to see that there are far more bonds of friendship and active, productive good will between the white Southerner and his Negro neighbor than they had believed—or could believe until they became eye-witnesses and partakers of this relationship.

Although the South is both willing and eager to have the Negro earn greater acceptance on many levels—especially economic—it does not consider, for reasons that I shall submit, that mixed education is the way to achieve this acceptance—certainly not at this stage of affairs.

What may lie in the distant future is more than any of us can predict with accuracy. Southerners know that race problems are as old as history. While views and philosophies may change through the ages, some basic truths stand out like the Ten Commandments. Southerners are not yet ready to accept an eleventh, "Thou shalt not protect the purity of thy race."

THE CLASH OF CULTURES

Before going into the actual reasons for the Southerner's objections to mixed education—before asking the burning question, how can the races best live together—let us examine for a moment the pattern of separation. It is a pattern that Thomas Jefferson, Abraham Lincoln, and at one time Dwight D. Eisenhower have favored as best for both races. In 1888, Henry W. Grady, Atlanta editor — described by Don Shoemaker of the Southern Education Reporting Service as a Southern "liberal" of his time — summed up the situation as follows:

> Neither "provincialism" nor "sectionalism" holds the South together but something deeper than these and essential to our system. The problem is how to carry within her body politic two separate races, and nearly equal in numbers. [Since Grady spoke, the whites in the South have come to outnumber the Negroes four to one, but the proportions vary greatly by neighborhoods.] She must carry these races in peace — for discord means ruin. She must carry them separately — for assimilation means debasement. She must carry them in equal justice — for to this she is pledged in honor and gratitude. She must carry them to the end, for in human probability she will never be quit of either.

While Grady's statements were made nearly seventy years ago and therefore are subject to the criticism that they do not reflect "modern conditions," to many Southerners they are true both now and for the future.

The presence of large numbers of Negroes — especially in the tidewater regions of Virginia, the Carolinas, and Georgia, and the plantation country of Alabama and Louisiana, Mississippi and East Texas — means that the races necessarily live in intimate daily association. Why, then, should not the children of people who live in the same community — sometimes as close neighbors — attend the same schools?

Southerners believe they have valid reasons, aside from "prejudice" about the color of skin, for their insistence on sending white children to exclusively white schools. Without debating superiority of either race, they are keenly aware of cultural differences. In some ways the standards of white people are none too high. The same economic conditions that have held back Negroes have worked against the whites. The increasing prosperity of the South is removing some of these disadvantages for both races, though not necessarily in precisely the same way.

Whether all the differences will eventually be removed, or enough of them to make mixed education acceptable to a substantial number of white people, the differences are too great *at present* to encourage white parents to permit their children to mingle freely in school. This has nothing to do with the frequent practice of children of both races playing together when young, or with cordial relationships in many other contacts of ordinary life.

Volumes could be written on racial differences from many angles, including anthropology and sociology. I shall merely try to summarize five of the differences that most immediately come to the minds of white parents in the South. These are health; home environment; marital standards; crime; and a wide disparity in average intellectual development.

(1) **Health.** Negro parents as a whole—for reasons that white people may sympathetically deplore but which nevertheless exist—are not so careful on the average as their white neighbors in looking after the health and cleanliness of their children. The incidence of venereal disease for instance is much greater among Negroes than among whites.

Statistics to document this statement are difficult to come by, though the statement itself would be generally accepted in the South. The U. S. Public Health Service some years ago quietly stopped identifying statistics by races. South Carolina figures, available for 1952–53, give a clue to the situation in that state; it probably is much the same elsewhere in the South. Out of a population 60 per cent white and 40 per cent Negro, 6,315 cases of syphilis were reported, of which 89 per cent were among Negroes. Infection with gonorrhea was found in six Negroes to one white person, but some physicians report that many cases of gonorrhea among Negroes go unrecorded.

During the same period—1952–53—a campaign against venereal disease was carried on, county by county. A spot check of four representative counties in different parts of South Carolina showed that cases of syphilis were found among 1.3 per cent of the white persons examined. This was a fairly constant percentage. The percentage of infection among Negroes ranged in the same counties from 8.5 to 10.8 per cent, averaging more than 9 per cent.

Fastidious parents do not favor joint use of school washrooms when they would not permit it at home—and there's no use to tell them that it is unlikely that anyone will catch venereal disease from a toilet seat. They just don't want to take risks of any kind with their children.

(2) **Home environment.** For most colored children in the South

the cultural background is different in many ways from that of their white neighbors—and while these differences may have various explanations, they add up in the public's mind as racial. Slavery is so long in the past that nobody thinks about it any more, but the master and servant, or boss and laborer, relationship between whites and Negroes is still the rule rather than the exception. The emergence of a middle class among the Negroes has been extremely slow—again, the reasons count for less in the minds of white parents than the fact itself. Indeed, the professional and commercial class among Negroes is so small that its members are in perhaps the most unenviable position of all. They have progressed beyond the cultural level of the vast bulk of their own people, but are not accepted among the whites, who fear to let down any dikes lest they be engulfed in a black flood.

Someone may suggest that here is an opening wedge for integration in the schools, by admitting a few well scrubbed and polished colored children of cultivated parents. In reply, let me say that this would be no more acceptable to the colored people than to the whites. The solution, perhaps—as it is among upper-bracket white people who do not send their children to public schools—might be private schools for prosperous Negroes as for prosperous whites. In any case, white people feel that cultural gaps on other levels should be filled in before discussing integrated schools.

(3) **Marital habits.** Among many Southern Negroes they are, to state it mildly, casual—even more so, in fact, than among the often-divorced personalities of Northern café society. Many Negro couples—the statistics are not readily available, for obvious reasons—do not bother with divorce because there was no actual marriage in the first place. Statistics on the results of such casual unions, however, are available. On the average one Southern Negro child in five is illegitimate. It is possible the figure may be even higher, since illegitimate births are more likely to go unrecorded. Even among Negroes who observe marriage conventions, illegitimacy has little if any stigma.

Many white persons believe that morals among their own race are lax enough as it is, without exposing their children to an even more primitive view of sex habits. Moreover, while these parents do not believe there is any surge of desire among their offspring to mate with colored people, they abhor any steps that might encourage intermarriage. They believe that lifting the racial school

400

barriers would be such a step. Miscegenation has been on the wane of recent years. Whatever mixing of blood may have occurred — and admittedly that was due largely to lustful white men seeking out acquiescent Negro women — has been without benefit of either law or custom. On some levels of society, breaking the racial barriers might lead to mixed marriages. The mixture of races which white Southerners have observed in Latin American countries gives them a dim view of legalizing cohabitation with Negroes.

(4) **Crime.** For many years, crime in the South has been more prevalent among Negroes than among white people. Though the Northern press no longer identifies criminals by race, white Southerners have reason to believe that much of the outbreak of crime and juvenile delinquency in Northern cities is due to the influx of Negro population. They believe the North now is getting a taste of the same race troubles that the South fears would grow out of mixed schooling, on a much bigger scale. They want no "Blackboard Jungles" in the South.

Maintaining order is a first concern of Southerners. What they have heard about the fruits of integration in the North does not encourage them to adopt the Northern race pattern. In Chicago, three hundred policemen have been assigned for a year or more to guard a nonsegregated housing project, with no bigger population than a Southern village where a single constable keeps the peace. In the County of Charleston, South Carolina — with 190,000 population, nearly half Negro — the total law enforcement manpower of combined city and county forces is 175.

While the homicide rate in the South is high, it is due in large measure to knifings and shootings among the colored people. Interracial homicide is relatively rare. (One of the reasons why the ghastly killing of Emmett Till in Mississippi made hot news — and some of that news was superheated and garnished with prejudice for the Northern press — was the very fact that it *was* unusual. No lynching, as even most Northerners now realize, has occurred in years.)

With racial bars down and rowdies of both races daring one another to make something of the vast increase in daily contacts, opportunities for interracial strife are frightening. Conservative, law-abiding people — and believe it or not, they constitute the bulk of Southern whites — are deeply fearful that hatred and bloodshed would increase without separation of the races.

And they know that, in the long run, if there is riotous

bloodshed it will be for the most part Negroes' blood. The thin tolerance of the ruffian and lower elements of the white people could erupt into animosity and brutality if race pressure became unbearable. Schools would be a focal point for such disturbance, first among pupils themselves and later by enraged parents. Instead of learning out of books, the younger generation would be schooled in survival—as several Northern sources have told me already is happening in some areas of New York, Philadelphia, and Washington, D. C.

(5) **Intellectual development.** Again for whatever the reasons may be, Southern Negroes usually are below the intellectual level of their white counterparts. *U. S. News and World Report*—the fairest nationally circulated publication I am acquainted with in its treatment of the race issue—has reported that in Washington, colored children are about two grades behind the whites in attainment. This discrepancy, I believe, is about par for other communities. In Washington it was found that there were even language difficulties to surmount. The children used different terms for some things.

Some advocates of integration say the way to cure these differences is to let the children mingle so that the Negroes will learn from the whites. The trouble with this theory is that even if it works, a single generation of white children will bear the brunt of the load. While they are rubbing off white civilization onto the colored children, Negro culture will also rub off onto the whites.

Few Southern parents are willing to sacrifice their own offspring in order to level off intellectual differences in this fashion. They reason that their children will get along better in later life if they have, as youngsters, the best available cultural contacts. Such an attitude is not, I understand, altogether unknown in the North. Many parents in New York City, for example, make considerable financial sacrifices to send their children to private schools, to spare them the undesirable associations and the low-geared teaching standards of most public schools.

If this sounds snobbish to a Northern reader, let me ask you to examine your own conscience. Can you honestly say that you are eager to send your own child to a classroom where the majority of other pupils will be considerably more backward in their studies, and extremely different in social background and cultural attainment? Which would you *really* put first: your theory of racial justice, or justice to your own child?

THE NEGROES' CRUSADE

In reply to objections to integration by white Southerners, someone may ask: What about the Negroes? What do they think?

At the outset, let me say that as a person who has spent most of his life in the South, has known Negroes from earliest childhood, and as a newspaperman has been dealing with race matters every day for many years, I cannot say just what goes on in the minds of the Negroes. Nor do I believe that a white man can put himself in the place of a colored man any more than he can, by taking thought, add a cubit to his stature. Until the school question became agitated in recent years, however, race relations on the whole were good. Since the agitation, relations are not yet bad in a broad sense — but they are not improving by reason of the crusade for integration.

The leadership in that crusade comes from outside the South. It is sparked by the National Association for the Advancement of Colored People. Southerners have reason to believe that this organization has a very large measure of white influence among its leaders. They recognize that both major political parties are courting the Negro vote, which holds the balance of power in key cities of populous Northern states. They are bewildered by the array of power aligned on the side of the NAACP in press, pulpit, and politics. The NAACP and its allies seem well supplied with money. They have won legal victories and they are not disposed to compromise on any front. In fact, the NAACP seems — to white Southerners — more interested in forcing the Negro into the white man's company than in equipping the Negro to qualify fully for such association.

A small but pointed illustration occurred in Charleston when a white community theater group tried to produce "Porgy" (the original play, not the opera) with a Negro cast in the city where the story is laid. There was a grave question about how the community, in a time when racial agitation was so bitter, would accept a play performed almost exclusively by Negroes. Many difficulties had to be surmounted in casting and production. But the sponsoring group, in consultation with NAACP and other Negro spokesmen, decided to proceed, and spent a sizable amount of money getting the production under way.

One of the key questions was the seating of the audience. Under South Carolina law separate seating for the races is required. The chairman of the local NAACP chapter agreed in writing, I have been informed, to an arrangement for separate seating by means of a vertical line down the center aisle, whites on one side and Negroes on the other. At the last moment, with the play already in rehearsal, the NAACP repudiated the agreement.

The Negro cast pleaded with the white sponsors to go through with the production in spite of the NAACP. By this time, however, it became obvious that the delicate circumstances had become too explosive and the production was canceled. A possible good-will gesture, opening a new line of communication, thus was halted because the NAACP would accept nothing less than complete integration—regardless of both state law and local custom.

Whether the NAACP really speaks for the rank and file of Negroes is debatable. Public expressions of opinion from Negroes in the South, other than the NAACP, are relatively few. Some white people feel that a Negro is so accustomed to telling a white man what he thinks the white man wants to hear, that they put little stock in whatever the Negro says on race. It would not be hard to believe that, given a choice, a Negro would naturally prefer all restrictions to be removed. That does not mean, however, that all Negroes want to associate with white people. Far from it; many Negroes prefer their own churches and, it stands to reason, should be equally satisfied with their own schools, so long as an equal allotment of public money is given them.

While the allotment has not always been equal—Negroes pay only a small fraction of taxes—the sums of money spent on Negro schooling have increased by leaps and bounds. On the average the South spends a greater percentage of its per capita income on schools than other regions, and nowadays the Negroes are getting their share in most areas. One thing is certain: if the schools were integrated, many a Negro school teacher would lose his or her job. Even if the white people would accept mixed pupils—and few apparently would do so—they would insist on white teachers.

Whenever a Southern Negro does object to the drive for integration, he is subject to pressure from his own people. Two Negro clergymen—what are known as "local preachers"—recently wrote letters to newspapers in lower South Carolina opposing the mixing of schools. Both were disciplined by their church superiors. Many white people on friendly terms with Negroes are convinced that as a rule, the Negroes are not eager for mixed schools so long as the schools for Negroes are adequate.

BOOTLEG SEGREGATION?

This conviction leads them to hope that a voluntary approach eventually may help to solve the problem within the Supreme Court ruling. Judge John J. Parker of Charlotte, North Carolina, senior judge of the Fourth Circuit Court of Appeals, has said:

It is important that we point out exactly what the Supreme Court has decided and what it has not decided in this [the Clarendon County] case. . . . It has not decided that the states must mix persons of different races in the schools. . . . Nothing in the Constitution or in the decision of the Supreme Court takes away from the people freedom to choose the schools they attend. The Constitution, in other words, does not require integration. It does not forbid such segregation as occurs as the result of voluntary action. It merely forbids the use of governmental power to enforce segregation. The Fourteenth Amendment is a limitation upon the exercise of power by the state or state agencies, not a limitation upon the freedom of individuals.

The Alabama state legislature has set up a new basis for assignment of pupils which does not mention race, though its provisions might tend to keep white and Negro pupils apart. In South Carolina, a committee of fifty-two representative citizens is circulating a resolution—already signed by many thousands—asking the State Legislature to interpose its authority between the federal government and local school boards to maintain segregation. Such a move would be based on the Tenth Amendment to the U. S. Constitution, reserving to the states and the people all powers not specifically granted to the federal government.

These are only two of many tentative plans to get around the Supreme Court's decision by methods of law. Another proposal is revival of the principle of nullification, which states both in the North and South have used in years gone by. A recent example was the public disregard of Prohibition. Segregation, perhaps, may be bootlegged in some regions. How that can be done is not immediately apparent—but the resourcefulness of the rum-runners and speakeasies was not foreseen by sponsors of the Volstead Act.

As in Prohibition, there is danger that white hoodlums may enter the picture. Sporadic outbreaks of the Ku Klux Klan have been reported. To combat the lawless element, law-abiding white men—who are determined not to yield to pressures they still regard as contrary to the guarantees of the Constitution—have been forming protective organizations. These go under many names. In Mississippi, South Carolina, and some of the other states they are called Citizens Councils.

Much has been said about the adoption of "economic pressure" as a weapon by these white groups. In some instances Negroes have reported that their sharecropper contracts have not been renewed because they signed petitions to integrate schools. Other forms of pressure have been reported, and in some localities Negroes have retaliated with boycotts against white merchants who were active in the Councils. White leaders of the resistance movements repeatedly have said they were not organizing boycotts and pressures against the Negroes and that they are determined there shall be no reign of terror as predicted by some of the Negro spokesmen.

Hodding Carter—one of a handful of Southern writers granted access to the national magazines—has predicted that attempts to enforce integration in the public schools of Mississippi would be likely to create violence. White leaders are exploring many other avenues in hopes of preventing strong-arm methods from being tried. They fear also that the very existence of the public schools is in peril. Rather than accept mixed public schools, some white Southerners may seek other means of educating their children.

Even if the schools are not abandoned, it seems unlikely that the white people will submit to heavy taxation to operate schools that many of them refuse to patronize. If they are not throttled outright, the public school systems in some areas may be starved to death. The spread of resistance organizations, far from being the product of demagogues, is at the local level among ordinary people, without "big-name" leadership. School trustees and other officials are getting the message from the grass roots.

Acceptance of the Supreme Court's order in border states and lip service in some other quarters have encouraged some advocates to believe that many Southern communities soon will yield to integration. While the borders of the old Confederacy may narrow, the determination of white people in areas with heavy Negro population is not relaxing. Not only regions where Negroes predominate by ten to one are rejecting the prospect of mixed schools. Pickens County in Piedmont South Carolina has the smallest number of Negroes (about one in ten) of any county in the state; its grand jury — most fundamental of all bodies safeguarding the people's liberty — has gone on record against mixed schools. On Edisto Island, at the opposite side of the state, where a white face looks out of place, insistence on mingling would be almost academic. If any attempt were made to force white children into Negro schools, the white people would move off the island, or find other means of educating their children.

Talk about segregation may promote migration of Negroes from the South. Already thousands have left the cotton fields and villages to seek jobs in Northern cities. On the farms, machines have replaced them. With the minimum wage advancing to $1 an hour, Southern employers will demand production from their laborers that not all Negroes will be able or willing to supply. These employers also may seek ways to mechanize or to employ white labor. As industries move South, more attractive opportunities for white people are opening.

If the North continues to appeal to Negroes as a land of integration and the South continues to attract white settlers, the racial proportions may grow more nearly equal. Then the North may become more tolerant of the Southerners' view of race problems, and the South better able to handle its dwindling Negro problem. Southerners will gladly share the load.

Meanwhile, stripped of emotions, the race problem for both Southern whites and Negroes is a practical matter of daily living. The problem has been recognized by thoughtful Americans from the early days of the Republic. It would be foolish to deny that any Negro pupils ever will enter Southern white schools. (Some already have.) But it would be equally foolhardy to predict that their numbers will be significant at an early date.

73. The Moral Aspects of Segregation (1956)[1]

BENJAMIN E. MAYS

Whenever a strong dominant group possesses all the power, political, educational, economic, and wields all the power; makes all the laws, municipal, state and federal, and administers all the laws; writes all constitutions, municipal, state and federal, and interprets these constitutions; collects and holds all the money, municipal, state, and federal and distributes all the money; determines all policies — governmental, business, political and educational; when that group plans and places heavy burdens, grievous to be borne, upon the backs of the weak, that act is immoral. If the strong group is a Christian group or a follower of Judaism both of which contend that God is creator, judge, impartial, just, universal, love and that man was created in God's image, the act is against God and man — thus immoral. If the strong group is atheistic, the act is against humanity — still immoral.

No group is wise enough, good enough, strong enough, to assume an omnipotent and omniscient role; no group is good enough, wise enough to restrict the mind, circumscribe the soul, and to limit the physical movements of another group. To do that is blasphemy. It is a usurpation of the role of God.

If the strong handicaps the weak on the grounds of race or color, it is all the more immoral because we penalize the group for conditions over which it has no control, for being what nature or nature's God made it. And that is tantamount to saying to God, "You made a mistake, God, when you didn't make all races white." If there were a law which said that an illiterate group had to be segregated, the segregated group could go to school and

---

[1] *Three Views of the Segregation Decision* (Atlanta, Ga.: Southern Regional Council, 1956), pp. 13–18. Mays, William Faulkner, and Cecil Sims presented their ideas at a meeting of the Southern Historical Association in Memphis, Tenn., Nov. 10, 1955. Mays, born in South Carolina, received his Ph.D. from the University of Chicago. He has been President of Morehouse College in Atlanta since 1940.

become literate. If there were a law which said that all peoples with incomes below $5,000 a year had to be segregated, the people under $5,000 a year could strive to rise above the $5,000 bracket. If there were a law which said that men and women who did not bathe had to be segregated, they could develop the habit of daily baths and remove the stigma. If there were a law which said that all groups had to be Catholics, the Jews and Protestants could do something about it by joining the Catholic Church. But to segregate a man because his skin is brown or black, red or yellow, is to segregate a man for circumstances over which he had no control. And of all immoral acts, this is the most immoral.

So the May 17, 1954, Decision of the Supreme Court and all the decisions against segregation are attempts on the part of the judges involved to abolish a great wrong which the strong has deliberately placed upon the backs of the weak. It is an attempt on the part of federal and state judges to remove this stigma, this wrong through constitutional means, which is the democratic, American way.

I said a moment ago that if the strong deliberately picks out a weak racial group and places upon it heavy burdens that act is immoral. Let me try to analyze this burden, segregation, which has been imposed upon millions of Americans of color. There are at least three main reasons for legal segregation in the United States.

1. The first objective of segregation is to place a legal badge of inferiority upon the segregated, to brand him as unfit to move freely among other human beings. This badge says the segregated is mentally, morally, and socially unfit to move around as a free man.

2. The second objective of segregation is to set the segregated apart so that he can be treated as an inferior: in the courts, in recreation, in transportation, in politics, in government, in employment, in religion, in education, in hotels, in motels, restaurants and in every other area of American life. And all of this has been done without the consent of the segregated.

3. The third objective of legalized segregation follows from the first two. It is designed to make the segregated believe that he is inferior, that he is nobody and to make him accept willingly his inferior status in society. It is these conditions which the May 17, 1954, Decision of the Supreme Court and other federal

decisions against segregation are designed to correct—to remove this immoral stigma that has been
placed upon 16 million Negro Americans, and these
are the reasons every thinking Negro wants the legal
badge of segregation removed so that he might be
able to walk the earth with dignity, as a man, and not
cringe and kow-tow as a slave. He believes that this
is his God-given right on the earth.

Segregation is immoral because it has inflicted a wound upon
the soul of the segregated and so restricted his mind that millions
of Negroes now alive will never be cured of the disease of inferiority. Many of them have come to feel and believe that they are
inferior or that the cards are so stacked against them that it is
useless for them to strive for the highest and the best. Segregate a
race for ninety years, tell that race in books, in law, in courts, in
education, in church and school, in employment, in transportation,
in hotels and motels, in the government that it is inferior—it is
bound to leave its damaging mark upon the souls and minds of the
segregated. It is these conditions that the federal courts seek to
change.

Any country that restricts the full development of any segment
of society retards its own growth and development. The segregated produces less, and even the minds of the strong group are
circumscribed because they are often afraid to pursue the whole
truth and they spend too much time seeking ways and means of
how to keep the segregated group in "its place." Segregation is
immoral because it leads to injustice, brutality, and lynching on
the part of the group that segregates. The segregated is somebody
that can be pushed around as desired by the segregator. As a rule
equal justice in the courts is almost impossible for a member of
the segregated group if it involves a member of the group impos-
ing segregation. The segregated has no rights that the segregator is
bound to respect.

The chief sin of segregation is the distortion of human personality. It damages the soul of both the segregator and the segregated. It gives the segregated a feeling of inherent inferiority
which is not based on facts, and it gives the segregator a feeling of
superiority which is not based on facts. It is difficult to know who
is damaged more—the segregated or the segregator.

It is false accusation to say that Negroes hail the May 17, 1954,
Decision of the Supreme Court because they want to mingle

410

socially with white people. Negroes want segregation abolished because they want the legal stigma of inferiority removed and because they do not believe that equality of educational opportunities can be completely achieved in a society where the law brands a group inferior. When a Negro rides in a Pullman unsegregated he does it not because he wants to ride with white people. He may or may not engage in conversations with a white person. He wants good accommodations. When he eats in an unsegregated diner on the train, he goes in because he is hungry and not because he wants to eat with white people. He goes to the diner not even to mingle with Negroes but to get something to eat. But as he eats and rides he wants no badge of inferiority pinned on his back. He wants to eat and ride with dignity. No Negro clothed in his right mind believes that his social status will be enhanced just because he associates with white people.

It is also a false accusation to say that Negroes are insisting that segregated schools must be abolished today or tomorrow, simultaneously all over the place. As far as I know, no Negro leader has ever advocated that, and they have not even said when desegregation is to be a finished job. They do say that the Supreme Court is the highest law of the land and we should respect that law. Negro leaders do say that each local community should bring together the racial groups in that community, calmly sit down and plan ways and means not how they can circumvent the decision but how they can implement it and plan together when and where they will start. They will be able to start sooner in some places than in others and move faster in some places than in others but begin the process in good faith and with good intent. To deliberately scheme, to deliberately plan through nefarious methods, through violence, boycott and threats to nullify the Decision of the highest law in the land is not only immoral but it encourages a disregard for all laws which we do not like.

We meet the moral issue again. To write into our constitutions things that we do not intend to carry out is an immoral act. I think I am right when I say that most of our states, certainly some of them, say in their constitutions "separate but equal." But you know as well as I do that on the whole the gulf of inequality in education widened with the years. There was no serious attempt nor desire in this country to provide Negroes with educational opportunities equal to those for whites. The great surge to equalize educational opportunities for Negroes did not begin until after

1935 when Murray won his suit to enter the law school of the University of Maryland. It is also clear that the millions poured into Negro education in the last 20 years were appropriated not so much because it was right but in an endeavor to maintain segregation.

We brought this situation upon ourselves. We here in the South have said all along that we believe in segregation but equal segregation. In 1896 in the Louisiana case, Plessy versus Ferguson, the United States Supreme Court confirmed the doctrine "separate but equal." But from 1896 to 1935 there was practically nothing done to make the separate equal. When Murray won his case in 1935, we knew we had to move toward equalization. Since 1935 many suits have been won.

It would have been a mighty fine thing if we had obeyed the Supreme Court in 1896 and equalized educational opportunities for Negroes. If we had .done that the problem would have been solved because gradually the separate school system would have been abolished and we would have been saved from the agony and fear of this hour. We didn't obey the Supreme Court in 1896 and we do not want to obey it now.

Let me say again that the May 17, 1954, Decision of the Supreme Court is an effort to abolish a great evil through orderly processes. And we are morally obligated to implement the Decision or modify the federal constitution and say plainly that this constitution was meant for white people and not for Negroes and that the Declaration of Independence created mostly by the mind of the great southerner, Thomas Jefferson, was meant for white people and not Negroes. Tell the world honestly that we do not believe that part of the Declaration of Independence which says in essence that all men are created equal, that they are endowed by their creator with certain inalienable rights, that among these are life, liberty and the pursuit of happiness.

We are morally obligated to abolish legalized segregation in America or reinterpret the Christian Gospel, the Old and New Testaments, and make the Gospel say that the noble principles of Judaism and Christianity are not applicable to colored peoples and Negroes. Tell the world honestly and plainly that the Fatherhood of God and the Brotherhood of Man cannot work where the colored races are involved. We are morally obligated to move toward implementing the Decision in the deep south or lose our moral leadership in the world. If we do not do it, we must play the role of hypocrisy, preaching one thing and doing another. This is the dilemma which faces our democracy.

The eyes of the world are upon us. One billion or more colored people in Asia and Africa are judging our democracy solely on the basis of how we treat Negroes. White Europe is watching us too. I shall never forget the day in Lucknow, India, when nine reporters from all over India questioned me for 90 minutes about how Negroes are treated in the United States. I shall remember to my dying day the event in 1937 when the principal of an untouchable school introduced me to his boys as an untouchable from the United States. At first it angered me. But on second thought I knew that he was right. Though great progress has been made, for which I am grateful, I and my kind are still untouchables in many sections of the country. There are places where wealth, decency, culture, education, religion, and position will do no good if a Negro. None of these things can take away the mark of untouchability. And the world knows this.

Recently a group of colored students from Asia, Africa, the Middle East and South America were visiting an outstanding Southern town. All the colored people except those from Africa and Haiti could live in the downtown hotels. The Africans and the Haitians had to seek refuge on the campus of a Negro College. That incident was known to all the other colored students and it will be told many times in Europe, Asia, Africa—and it will not help us in our efforts to democratize the world.

Not long ago a Jew from South Africa and a man from India were guests of a Negro professor. He drove them for several days through the urban and rural sections of his state. The Negro, the host, a citizen of the United States, could not get food from the hotels and restaurants. His guests, one a Jew and the other an Indian, had to go in and buy food for him. The man who introduced me in India as an untouchable was right. The Negro is America's untouchable.

Two or three years ago a friend of mine was traveling in Germany. He met a German who had traveled widely in the United States. He told my friend that he hangs his head in shame every time he thinks of what his country did to the Jews—killing six millions of them. But he told my friend that after seeing what segregation has done to the soul of the Negro in the South, he has come to the conclusion that it is worse than what Hitler and his colleagues did to the Jews in Germany. He may be wrong but this is what he is telling the people in Germany.

Make no mistake—as this country could not exist half slave and half free, it cannot exist half segregated and half desegregated. The Supreme Court has given America an opportunity to achieve greatness in the area of moral and spiritual things just as it has already achieved greatness in military and industrial might and in material possessions. It is my belief that the South will accept the challenge of the Supreme Court and thus make America and the South safe for democracy.

If we lose this battle for freedom for 15 million Negroes we will lose it for 145 million whites and eventually we will lose it for the world. This is indeed a time for greatness.

417

Printed in U.S.A.